RICHARD SANTERRE

SAINT JEAN BAPTISTE PARISH
AND THE
FRANCO-AMERICANS
OF
LOWELL, MASSACHUSETTS

1868 – 1968

With an epilogue
"From the Centennial to the Present"

Translated by
Claire Quintal and Lucien Sawyer, O.M.I.

Saint Joseph Shrine
Lowell, Massachusetts
2013

Dedication

To my parents and to all the parishioners
living and deceased of Saint Jean Baptiste Parish

**Publication of this work by the Missionary Oblates of
Mary Immaculate was supported in part by:**

**Le Cercle Jeanne Mance
Le Club Richelieu de Lowell
Le Comité de la Semaine Franco-Américaine de Lowell
Le Comité de Vie Franco-Américaine
La Librairie Populaire
Section Domrémy, Royal Arcanum
Monique Blanchette
Ruby Duhamel Cook
Cécile Lamoureux
Gertrude Lamoureux
Claire Lemieux
Albert Marceau
Claire Quintal**

Translation of the original edition:
*La paroisse Saint Jean-Baptiste et les
Franco-Américains de Lowell, Massachusetts,1868-1968.*
Editions Lafayette, Manchester, N.H., 1993.

**Copies may be purchased at
The Shrine of Saint Joseph the Worker Gift Shop
37 Lee St., Lowell, MA 01852-1103
www.stjosephshrine.org
(1)978-459-9522
(1)800-287-9522
Email: Giftshop@stjosephshrine.org**

*Frontispiece: Pencil drawing of Fr. André Marie Garin, O.M.I., widely disseminated
among Lowell's population.*
Cover and book layout: Sarah E. Abbott
Printed by: Missionary Oblates of Mary Immaculate

Contents

Foreword iii

Preface to the French edition vii

Preface to the English edition viii

1. Lowell, the "Spindle City" 1
2. Establishing the Faith 6
3. The Arrival of the French-Canadians
   and the First Attempts at Starting a Parish 8
4. The Massive Immigration
   "He has sent me to evangelize the poor." 11
5. A Providential Encounter 15
6. Fathers Garin and Lagier and The First Mass 20
7. Consolidation and Outreach 33
8. The Curates and a First Bereavement 40
9. Father Garin's Right-Hand Man:
   Fr. Joseph Alexandre Fournier 45
10. "The most admirable of churches" 53
11. The First Franco-American School of the Archdiocese 61
12. Saint Joseph Residence — "Saint André Church" 75
13. Le Collège Saint Joseph — The Apotheosis of Father Garin 91
14. "Our Father is dead. He is gone." 104
15. "Do not forget me." 111
16. The Wise and Prudent Father Mangin 124
17. "The Father of the poor has passed away." 136
18. Two Apostles: Fathers Joseph Lefebvre and Joseph Campeau 140
19. The Apostle of the Sacred Heart 156
20. "Resurrexit" 176
21. "Saint Thérèse, protect us " 185
22. Saint Jean Baptiste Province 192
23. Saint Joseph Hospital 216
24. Beloved Father Emile Bolduc 241
25. "Prince of Peace, have pity on us" 270
26. Father Henri Bolduc — Saint Joseph Shrine 303

27. Urban Renewal 332

28. A Weighty Responsibility 349

29. The Centennial... 359

Epilogue: From the Centennial to the Present 364

Appendices:

1. Baptisms in 1868... 397

2. Marriages in 1868 401

3. Vocations to the Priesthood 402

4. Vocations to Religious Life: Brothers 403

5. Vocations to Religious Life: Sisters................................... 404

6. Curates at Saint Jean Baptiste parish 412

Index of Names... 416

LJCeML

SUPERIOR GENERALIS

MISSIONARIORUM OBLATORUM

B. M. V. IMMACULATÆ

Rome, le 18 Mars 1968

294-68
Rév. Père Anatole LESSARD, O.M.I.
Supérieur et curé
Eglise St-Jean-Baptiste
725 Merrimack St.
Lowell, Mass.
U.S.A.

Bien cher Père,

Vous avez bien fait de me signaler que du 21 au 28 avril
ont lieu, à St-Jean-Baptiste de Lowell, des cérémonies spéciales
pour souligner le centenaire de la fondation de cette admirable
paroisse. Je veux m'y unir par la pensée, par la prière, puisque
tout en vous remerciant de votre cordiale invitation, je sens bien
qu'il m'est impossible de me joindre à vous.

Je connais cette histoire de la paroisse St-Jean-Baptiste
pour l'avoir étudiée au temps de mon scolasticat et pour en avoir
suivi l'évolution depuis près de 50 ans. Le R.P. Carrière a écrit
là-dessus des pages très lourdes d'histoire où se résument toutes
les phases de l'apostolat intense d'une vie communautaire chrétienne
des plus fortes et des plus rayonnantes.

Et cette histoire est aussi écrite dans le coeur et dans
l'âme de tous vos paroissiens. Un grand nombre sans doute de vos
paroissiens appartiennent aux familles qui ont fondé la paroisse.
Ils peuvent trouver le nom de leurs parents, grands-parents, arrière
grands-parents dans les annales de la paroisse et ces chrétiens
ont participé intimement et intensément à la vie de cette petite
église particulière qu'était la paroisse St-Jean-Baptiste. S'il
y a une page admirable, c'est bien celle de la coopération du laïcat
à l'apostolat des Pères, des missionnaires, des religieux, des religieuses. Si tous ces chrétiens vaillants et convaincus n'avaient
pas assisté, appuyé, secondé le prêtre, le Frère enseignant, la religieuse enseignante, ou en charge des malades, des pages admirables
de la paroisse auraient-elles été écrites avec autant de relief et
exprimé autant de succès ?

Et puis les paroissiens de St-Jean-Baptiste de Lowell ont
tellement aimé leurs Pères. Savez-vous, en vous écrivant ceci, il
me revient un souvenir d'enfance à la mémoire. En ce petit coin de
Montréal où je vivais dans l'est de la ville il y avait quelques

familles apparentées à des familles de franco-canadiens émigrées quelque temps auparavant à Lowell ou dans les environs. Une chose me frappait c'était l'affection avec laquelle ces familles parlaient des prêtres de Lowell, des Pères comme ils les appelaient. Cela me surprenait parce que, à Montréal, dans ma paroisse, on n'appelait pas le curé le Père. On me mentionnait des noms que je retrouvais après en entrant chez les Oblats. Mais je reviens à ce qui me frappait, c'était l'affection, la vénération, la gratitude que l'on avait pour les Pères. Il n'y avait pas à Montréal, dans ma paroisse, ce sentiment d'union avec le curé ou les vicaires, mais ces personnes qui venaient de Lowell se sentaient tout près de leurs Pères et en parlaient avec ferveur. Pardonnez-moi ce souvenir de mon jeune temps. Est-ce parce que je vieillis que je parle ainsi ? En tout cas, le souvenir est tout frais comme si c'était hier, je pourrais même donner les noms des familles: l'une s'appelait Pageau, une autre Jetté.

Je reviens à vos fêtes centenaires pour les souhaiter très cordiales, très encourageantes, très pastorales. Certes, je le sais, la situation de la paroisse évolue. Il en est ainsi dans toutes les villes dont les quartiers se transforment. Il faut donc regarder vers un nouvel avenir. Il faut y discerner quels sont les signes de Dieu. Il faut le faire avec foi, avec confiance, avec espérance. Il faut surtout penser à cette petite église au sens très spirituel fondée à Lowell en ce site de la paroisse St-Jean-Baptiste qui restera toujours vivante et toujours forte quelles que soient ses transformations.

J'adresse mes félicitations à mes frères les Oblats, ceux qui travaillent actuellement à la paroisse et je dis ma reconnaissance aux anciens pour leur apostolat intense, leur service si complet de l'Eglise et des âmes.

Vous désireriez qu'au cours de mon séjour aux Etats-Unis, au moment des fêtes du Centenaire, au mois de septembre prochain, je me réserve un moment pour la paroisse St-Jean-Baptiste. Peut-être pourriez-vous organiser cela tout autour du séjour même où aura lieu la grande fête, je crois que c'est le 18 septembre ou quelque chose comme cela. Je ferai mon possible pour répondre à vos désirs. Ce sera quelque chose de bien familial; vous savez que je n'aime pas les grandes cérémonies triomphalistes. Que ce soit une cérémonie de prière, de souvenir, une cérémonie qui nous porte tous vers l'avenir que le Bon Dieu nous désignera.

Je vous bénis, cher Père Lessard, avec vos compagnons de travail et tous ceux qui s'associent à votre tâche: religieux, religieuses, laïcs, et je vous dis mes sentiments très fraternels en N.S. et M.I.

Léo Deschâtelets, O.M.I.
Supérieur Général

(TRANSLATION)

L.J.C. et M. I.

Superior Generalis
Missionariorum Oblatorum
B.M.V. Immaculatae
294—68
Rev. Father Anatole Lessard, O.M.I
Superior and Pastor
St. Jean Baptiste Church
725 Merrimack St.
Lowell, Mass.
U.S.A.

Rome, March 18, 1968

Very Dear Father:

You did the right thing in pointing out to me that from the 21st to the 28th of April, special ceremonies will be taking place at Lowell's St. Jean Baptiste to highlight the centennial of the founding of this admirable parish. I want to be united with it all in thought and prayer since, while thanking you for your cordial invitation, I am well aware that it will be impossible for me to be present.

I know this history of St. Jean Baptiste parish for having studied it at the time of my scholasticate and for having followed its evolution for nearly 50 years. Rev. Father Carrière has written weighty historical pages about it wherein are summarized all of the phases of the intense apostolate of a Christian community life at its strongest and most radiant.

And this history is also written in the hearts and souls of all your parishioners. A large number of them no doubt belong to the families who founded the parish. They can find the names of their parents, grandparents, and great-grandparents in the annals of the parish and these Catholics participated intimately and intensely in the life of this particular little church that was St. Jean Baptiste parish. If there is a page to be admired it is surely that of the cooperation of the laypeople with the apostolate of the Fathers, the missionaries, the religious men and women. If all these valiant and convinced Catholics had not assisted,supported, and helped the priest, the teaching Brother or the Sister, teaching or in charge of the sick, would admirable pages of the parish have been written with as much depth, and expressed with such success?

And also, the parishioners of St. Jean Baptiste of Lowell loved their Fathers so very much. Do you know that in writing this to you, a childhood memory comes to mind? In that small area of Montréal where I lived, in the eastern section of the city, there were a few families related to Franco-Canadian families which had emigrated to Lowell or the environs some time before. One thing struck me, it was the affection with which these families spoke of the priests of Lowell, of the Fathers, as they called them. That surprised me because in Montréal, in my parish, we did not call the pastor Father. Names would be mentioned that I later found when I entered the Oblates. But I come back to what struck me at the time, it was the affection, the veneration, the gratitude that they had for the Fathers. That feeling of union with the pastor or with the curates did not exist in my Montréal parish while the persons who came from Lowell felt very close to their Fathers and spoke of them with fervor. Pardon me this memory of my youth. Is it because I am growing old that I am speaking in this manner? In any case, the remembrance is just as fresh as though it were yesterday and I can even give you the names of the families: one was called Pageau, another Jetté.

Coming back to your centennial festivities, I hope that they will be very cordial, very encouraging, and very pastoral. Of course I know that the situation of the parish is evolving. That is the case in all the cities whose neighborhoods are being transformed. So, we must look towards a new future. We must try to discern God's signs in this. It must be done with faith, with confidence, with hope. One must especially think in a very spiritual way of this small church founded in Lowell on this site of St. Jean Baptiste parish which will always remain very much alive and always strong whatever its transformations may be.

I address my congratulations to my Oblate brothers, to those who are currently working in the parish, and I express my gratitude to those of the past for the intensity of their apostolate, and such total service to the Church and to souls.

You are desirous that during my stay in the United States at the time of the [Congregation's] centennial celebrations next September, I set aside a moment for St. Jean Baptiste parish. Perhaps you could organize that all around the stay itself when the great feast will take place, on September 18, I believe. I will do my utmost to respond to your wishes. It will be something very familial; you know that I do not like grand triumphalist ceremonies. Let it be a celebration of prayer, of memory, a ceremony which will carry us all towards the future that God will designate to us.

I bless you, dear Father Lessard, along with your working companions and all those who are associated with your work: religious men and women, laypeople, and to you I express my very fraternal best wishes in Our Lord and Mary Immaculate.

Léo Deschâtelets, O.M.I.,
Superior General

PREFACE TO THE FRENCH EDITION

When I undertook the writing of this book twenty-six years ago, who could have foreseen that it would appear in the very week that Saint Jean Baptiste parish was closed.

Shorty before his death, Father Maurice Savard was asked to read the manuscript. His commentary that I had not written a traditional parish history with its buildings and institutions, but rather a history of the people, is still very dear to me. I believe that it is God's will that we not forget the history of these people, that great family that was Saint Jean Bapiste parish.

I wish to thank all of those who in some way have helped me carry out this work, and especially I want to thank Attorney Louis Eno without whom this book would never have appeared.

*   *   *   *

Acknowledgement is also due to Marthe Biron Peloquin for her assistance in preparing this manuscript; to Madeleine Eno for the design of the cover and to Jeannine Tardiff for her sketch of the church that is reproduced on the cover.

PREFACE TO THE ENGLISH EDITION

When the French language edition of this history was published, I had the unspoken thought that perhaps, one day, it would be good for it to be made available in English. Little did I expect that some ten years later, Fr. Lucien Sawyer would come knocking at my door with the translation already begun.

Happy at the event, I gave my permission and the project began in earnest. Soon, given the complexity and the difficulty of the task, Prof. Claire Quintal, foundress of the French Institute of Assumption College and a noted expert in French-English translation joined in the endeavor.

The resulting translation is faithful to the original with some corrections and small additions. The main difference between the two books is the complete revision of the lists of baptisms and marriages for 1868 based on the original manuscript registers and the addition of an epilogue recounting the events following the centennial of 1968.

At the book signing in December 1993, Fr. Anatole Lessard, in the conclusion of his moving address said:

> *À ce livre, peut-être qu'un supplément pourrait y être ajouté: celui des vingt-cinq dernières années. Mais je crois qu'il y faudra quelque temps, pour que cette histoire soit narrée objectivement, comme l'abbé Santerre l'a si bien fait pour les premiers cent ans.*

> (Perhaps a supplement could be added to this book: for the last twenty-five years. But I believe that it will take some time, so that this history may be narrated with objectivity, as the abbé Santerre has so well done for the first hundred years.)

In response to his wish and to that of many others, I wrote the epilogue which I sincerely pray he would be pleased with.

There are no words to thank Claire Quintal and Fr. Lucien Sawyer for their devotion and uncounted hours of work. Without them, the book would not have been possible.

There are also a great many people to thank for all the information needed for the epilogue. I cannot mention them all by name but I want them to know that I am very grateful. To Albert and Barbara Côté and Albert and Thérèse Daigle my sincerest appreciation for all the documentation and encouragement.

1. Lowell, the "Spindle City"

A site that had once been home to a small Native American community and a few English colonials, at the confluence of the Merrimack and Concord Rivers in Massachusetts, evolved in the nineteenth century to become the largest concentration in the world of textile mills for the cotton industry. In this astounding expansion the Franco-Americans of Lowell played a significant role. Industrious and diligent, they became an essential and reliable part in the manufacturing process.

While their hard work contributed to the economic growth of the city, their customs and traditions, solidly grounded in the faith of their forefathers, enriched everything which constitutes the soul of a city: culture, politics, and a religious frame of mind. The history of Saint Jean-Baptiste parish is neither that of a working-class parish, nor of an ecclesiastical division, but rather the history of missionaries and their parishioners who, while laboring on behalf of souls for the glory of God, brought their share of culture and religious feeling to the soul of the "Spindle City."

Lowell, Massachusetts, because of its historic role as the first modern industrial city in the United States, has been called the "Spindle City" since the nineteenth century. This title, far from being a fanciful designation, aptly describes the source of what produced the wealth, not only of Lowell's inhabitants, but also of the American nation – the famous "mile of mills" along the Merrimack River.

Writing in 1886, Judge Josiah Abbott stated the following: "Lowell marks the beginning of an epoch in the history, not only of New England, but of the whole country. With the foundation of Lowell were laid the foundations of the manufacturing industry of the country."

Lowell owed its immediate wealth to its location, twenty-six miles north of Boston, on the banks of the Merrimack and Concord Rivers. There is a bend in the Merrimack – discovered by Samuel de Champlain in 1605 – as it passes through Lowell, where it drops suddenly forming rapids and waterfalls thirty-two feet high before reaching the mouth of the Concord River downstream. The terrain at the confluence of these two rivers forms a shallow depression thanks to which the location lends itself superbly to the utilization of the immense driving power created by the flow of the rapids.

In the seventeenth century, before the arrival of the first English colonists, this area between the two rivers was the major meeting ground for one of the most powerful Native American tribes in New England, the Pawtuckets. What is now Lowell was the great capital of this tribe, and the residence of its chief, Passaconaway. When the first colonials arrived, they found the Native

1

Americans decimated by disease, and grouped in a village called Wamesit.

In 1653, twenty-nine colonists from Woburn and Concord were granted this land at the juncture of the Merrimack and Concord Rivers by the Massachusetts General Court, except for the property of the indigenous people. Two years later, the colony was officially incorporated as the town of Chelmsford. In the meantime, the Native American population had already begun to decrease and many were killed or dispersed during the bloody King Philip's War of 1675. That is how, in 1686, chief Wannalancit, the last remaining son of the great Passaconaway, and the few other surviving chiefs, sold the village of Wamesit and all their other vast property holdings to the English colonists. The small band withdrew to Canada where they became part of the Saint François tribe.

Now firmly established and with a civil government in place, the Chelmsford pioneers lost no time in taking advantage of the riches and possibilities which the site offered. By the beginning of the eighteenth century, a sawmill and a gristmill were already in operation by the Pawtucket Falls of the Merrimack River. Around 1737, the first cloth-making mill in Lowell, a fulling mill, was built on one of the banks of the Concord River. This was only the beginning. On June 25, 1792, capitalists from Newburyport formed a corporation called "Proprietors of the Locks and Canals on the Merrimack" whose aim was to dig a transport canal that would bypass the falls. This was the first canal of its type on the North American continent.

Up to that point, Lowell's destiny closely resembled the development of the other industrial centers in New England. There were a few small cotton and woolen mills, as well as sawmills, etc. Only the excavation of the Pawtucket Canal, and soon afterward, the Middlesex Canal, presaged Lowell's future growth as the city of thousands of spindles. The creation of the first major American industrial city can be dated from the second and third decades of the nineteenth century.

In 1814, an inventor named Francis Cabot Lowell, assisted by Paul Moody, an engineer, set up in Waltham the first factory in the United States where thread could be woven into a finished product on the Lowell loom. Up to that time, the small mills of Lowell, Pawtucket, and Providence only prepared the thread which farmers' wives then wove themselves at home. The Waltham experience was immensely successful and the capitalist leaders of Boston began to consider expanding this business of theirs.

The factory in Waltham was small, and limited by the restricted supply of hydraulic power. A site was needed with an unlimited supply of waterpower to activate the looms where the capitalists could establish a manufacturing community. East Chelmsford, near the rapids of the

Merrimack and Concord Rivers, and linked to Boston by its canals, was eminently suited for the enterprise.

The shareholders: Kirk Boott, J.W. Boott, N. Appleton, P.T. Jackson, and Paul Moody bought out the old Locks and Canals Corporation and purchased vast tracts of land between the two rivers. In 1822 the Merrimack Manufacturing Company was incorporated with a capital of $600,000. A huge textile mill was built bearing this name. For the first time in the United States, except for Cabot Lowell's experiment in Waltham, raw cotton came into a large mill and emerged as finished cloth. Kirk Boott, selected as the company agent, was also appointed by the investors to look after their properties and interests, in addition to becoming the manager of the East Chelmsford village.

The first step had been taken. With success smiling from all sides, events rushed forward at a dizzying pace. In 1824, Boott and the stockholders founded St. Anne's, the first Protestant church in the city itself. That same year, the first school, named Bartlett, opened its doors, and the first newspaper, The Journal, appeared. Given such rapid progress, the need for new political positions became inevitable. So, on March 1, 1826, by an act of the Massachusetts Legislature, the industrial area called East Chelmsford became the town of Lowell. The new name was chosen in memory of the deceased Francis Cabot Lowell, the genius whose invention of the power loom made possible the American textile industry on a grand scale.

The accelerating, rapid pace of progress led to the establishment, one after the other, of additional cotton mills, as well as woolen and carpet factories. The Hamilton, Appleton, Lowell, Suffolk, Tremont, Lawrence, and other mills opened their doors in quick succession. Between 1822 and 1835, the year of the foundation of the Boott Cotton Mills, the eight largest mills in Lowell had begun to operate. Along with the mills, each company built for its employees, on its own land, a boarding house called a "corporation" for its exclusive use and subject to its control and regulations,

But, Boott and his associates did not stop there. They founded churches, built municipal buildings, banks, more canals and locks, one of the first railroads in the United States, and, in 1839, a hospital dispensing free care, in a word, all the best services that a paternalistic system could offer. The final political step was taken the following year, on April 1, 1836, with the incorporation of Lowell as an industrial city.

It wasn't long before Lowell joined the ranks of the largest manufacturing centers in the world. The "mile of mills" along the Merrimack River and the good behavior of the workers, thanks to the paternalistic system, had become the topic of conversation in many old capitals of Europe. Soon the seal of importance was placed upon the city by those unavoidable "noted" travelers who came to

The "Mile of Mills" along the Merrimack River.

visit. In June 1834, the French economist Michel Chevalier sent home his impressions in a series of letters to France from Lowell. This is how he described for his French readers what he saw from his hotel window:

The immense mills of five, six, or seven stories, each capped with a little white belfry which stands out against the red-brick masonry of the building, are clearly delineated against the dark hills which border the horizon. The small square wooden houses, painted white, with green shutters, are very neat, very snug, very well-furnished, with carpeting and with a few small trees around them, or brick houses in the English style, that is to say, pretty, simple on the outside and comfortable indoors; on one side are the shops, the stores, innumerable fashion boutiques, for

Merrimack Street around the time of Fr. Garin's arrival.

women constitute the majority in Lowell; and vast hotels in the American style, very much like barracks – the only barracks in Lowell – on the other side are the canals, waterwheels, the waterfalls, bridges, foundries, banks, schools, and bookstores, for people in Lowell read a lot – reading being the only distraction available – and there are no fewer than seven newspapers. All around are the churches and meetinghouses of every sect: Episcopalian, Anabaptist, Congregationalist, Methodist, Universalist, Unitarian, etc.; there is also a Catholic chapel.

It is the sound of hammers, of shuttles, of bells which call the hands to their work or allows them to leave, of six-horse stagecoaches leaving or arriving, the din of dynamite blasting the rocks to clear the way for a millrace or to level the land.

In his final letter, he declared: "In Europe, it happens frequently that hands are without work; here, by contrast, it is the occupation that is in search of men's hands." This lack of workmen for the job, which would last until the twentieth century, is what attracted the first immigrants who brought with them their faith and opened the first Catholic chapel.

2. Establishing the Faith

A considerable workforce was needed to erect the huge mill buildings, dig canals, and construct all the facilities required by a burgeoning city. The first immigrants to Lowell were mostly men employed at these undertakings. Later on, their ranks grew significantly with the arrival of a large number of textile-mill employees as the number of spindles and looms multiplied.

Except for the English and the Scots, the children of the Emerald Isle were the first immigrants to head for Lowell. In April 1822, the first thirty Irishmen proceeded on foot from Charlestown, near Boston, to Lowell where they were to be employed in the widening of the Pawtucket Canal and the excavation of its channels. As soon as they arrived, they pitched their tents and built their shacks in the center of the city that came to be known as "The Acre."

Prior to their arrival, Catholics were scarce in Lowell. However, these rugged Irish laborers, without education or refinement, ousted from their homeland by English oppression, had brought with them their only possession, the Catholic faith. In the summer of that same year, 1822, a missionary priest, Rev. Patrick Byrne, celebrated the first Catholic Mass in Lowell for the "Irish Camp" in a house on Tilden St. On August 20th this same priest baptized all the Catholic children of the region.

As time went on, a missionary priest passed through periodically, to look after the spiritual needs of the small colony. In 1827, at the request of a few influential Irishmen, Boston's Bishop Benedict Fenwick assigned Father John Mahoney of Salem as their regular priest. He reported to the bishop that the Lowell congregation then consisted of twenty-one families and thirty unmarried Catholics. In the presence of a large group of faithful, and some curious Protestants, he celebrated Mass on October 7, 1827, in the small school owned by the Merrimack Company. By 1830, the Catholic population had grown to 400. That July, Bishop Fenwick traveled to Lowell announcing to the faithful that the Merrimack Company, through the mediation of Kirk Boott, had donated land for the construction of a Catholic church.

It took an entire year to build the little wooden chapel which stood out in the cluster of the small group of huts and cabins that constituted The Acre, near the newly excavated Western Canal. The dedication by the bishop, of Lowell's first Catholic church, St. Patrick's, took place on July 3, 1831. The following year, the generous Agent Boott donated land for a Catholic cemetery.

However, the tiny chapel seen by Michel Chevalier in 1834 did not suffice to contain the crowd for very long, given the continuing increase in the population. So it was that in October 1842, another parish was founded and dedicated as the second Catholic church in the city – St. Peter's, situated at the corner of Appleton and Gorham Streets. But, since the mother parish continued to grow constantly, the pastor, Father McDermott, assumed responsibility for the purchase in his own name of a Methodist church at the corner of Lowell and Suffolk Streets. This church, named St. Mary's, opened its doors as a second church for St. Patrick's, in March of 1847.

In spite of all these foundations, the small wooden church, which had sheltered Lowell's Catholics since 1831, had become clearly inadequate. Hence, on July 4, 1853, the pastor, the justly famous Father John O'Brien, laid the cornerstone for the beautiful stone church that we still admire today.

The construction of the mills, with the concomitant growing need for unskilled workers, which had attracted the first immigrants, aroused intense interest in Canada, and set in motion the second major wave of immigration towards the Spindle City.

3. The Arrival of the French-Canadians and the First Attempts at Starting a Parish

At the end of 1835, there were 129,828 spindles rotating in the Lowell mills, occupying 6,793 workers in a population of 15,000. In fewer than thirty years, by 1860, the population had more than doubled to 36,827. It was during that period of intense activity that the first French-Canadian immigrants set foot in Lowell. Like the Irish before them, they too were at first employed in construction.

Although it is practically impossible to determine precisely who was the first *Canadien* to arrive in Lowell, it is nonetheless certain that the earliest pioneers came between 1840 and 1850, and that they were followed by many others from 1850 to 1860. The first one seems to have been Louis Bergeron who reached Lowell in 1841. Next was Alarie Mercier, in 1845. By 1852, Joseph Miller, Paul Lesieur, Edouard Courchêne, Pierre and Luc Viau, Joseph Dufresne, M. Gobeil and Narcisse Rémy could be found in the city. Some of these men lived in a rooming house located behind the old Richardson Hotel on Middlesex Street. Louis Bergeron was a blacksmith, but many others, like Joseph Miller, were carpenter-joiners. Little by little, their numbers increased so that in 1860 the small Canadian community now included Hilaire and Calixte Dozois, Samuel P. Marin, Jean Baptiste Laflamme, Jean and Anselme Lemire, Joseph S. Lapierre, Jean Baptiste Allard, Joseph Beaudreau, Joseph Lemay, Félix Provencher, Louis Leclair, Jean and Thomas Lachance, and Charles Bélanger. Included in this number was the first French-Canadian physician in the city, Dr. Déodat Mignault, who arrived in 1859. He was related to Father Mignault, the former pastor of Chambly, in Québec, who had become vicar-general of the Dioceses of Boston, Albany, and Burlington in 1828.

This first wave of Canadian immigration ended at the beginning of 1861, with the Civil War between the States. Lowell then fell into an economic depression since cotton from the South could no longer reach the mills. More and more men were needed for the conflict, and all of the economic power was concentrated on the war.

Within the small *Canadien* population, including some who came to Lowell in spite of the war, patriotic fervor ran as high as with Lowell's Yankees. The 5,000 soldiers and sailors who left Lowell to serve in battle included eleven French-Canadians: Pierre E. Lamontagne, David Bourbeau, Edouard Cormier, Thomas C. Giroux, Georges A., Henri A. and Jean A. Lamontagne, Olivier Plamondon, Jérémie Tétreault, Adolphe Tétreault, and Ovide Baril. Three of these combatants gave their lives for their newly adopted land: Georges A., Lamontagne, Olivier Plamondon and Jérémie Tétreault.

Once the war was over, in 1865, prosperity exploded at all levels. The South returned to the cultivation of cotton, which was shipped almost entirely up North, and Reconstruction set in motion New England's entire industrial base. In Lowell, the cotton mills, the carpet factories, and the machine shops rapidly began to buzz with renewed activity. But, the war having reduced the city's population to 31,000, its industrialists began to clamor for workers.

Agents from the mills and factories of New England began to roam throughout the Canadian countryside circulating enticing descriptions of good salaries to be earned, and the image of a land where everyone could get rich. In 1865, several of Lowell's manufacturing companies hired Samuel P. Marin to visit his native province of Québec in search of labor for their mills.

In 1896, Joseph L. Chalifoux recalled memories of that time when he spoke to a group of his elderly contemporaries:

> Let us allow our imaginations to wander back to the years from 1866 to 1870, at the start of the great emigration of Canadians to the United States. At that time the salaries in Canada were very low. Day laborers in the Canadian countryside were only earning 25 cents per day in good weather. On Sundays, after High Mass, at the church doors of many parishes, the discussion always centered on the great prosperity of the neighboring Republic, and the fortunes that could be made there. We were dazzled by the beautiful clothing worn by Canadian travelers who had made the trip to the United States. They were even better dressed than the sons of rich farmers. At that time, except for a few wealthy farmers, everyone's Sunday best was made of the rough gray local homespun.

The stream of people which, in the 1880s, would become the great exodus of French Canadians towards New England, was only beginning. The old rural counties of the Province of Québec could not absorb their manpower. The land could no longer sustain large families. Machinery was replacing man in agriculture. Canada's tariff policy limited the market for farmers, and industry in Canadian cities was developing in a very sporadic manner. All of this, combined with the ease of crossing at the Canadian-American border, resulted, especially but not only in the Eastern Townships, in infecting many with *"la fièvre des État-Unis"* (United States fever) or *"le mal des États-Unis"* (the American sickness).

The Canadian population of Lowell continuing to grow, it was inevitable that people would begin to dream of founding a distinct parish. Since the immigrants of that period were unfamiliar with either the language or the customs of the country, they had to follow, as best they could, religious services in the city's Irish churches. The Irish clergy, for their part, already overburdened with their own large congregations, did what they could to provide for the spiritual needs of that part of its flock which knew no English.

In Canada, the parish had played a unique role in the lives of these decent people. The homeland, language, and national identity revolved around the faith of their forefathers. Their hopes were based on this faith that had sustained and consoled them during the hard years of colonization and the dark period of the conquest. The parish, at least, belonged to them. It embodied all their ethnic aspirations for a better world, for a homeland all their own. A day's work in the mills was long and harsh. The factory bells called them out in the morning and sent them home at night after eleven hours of work in the choking cotton dust and the stifling heat of the large work spaces. The chiming of the bells in the old parish churches was now only a memory, but the recollection of the beautiful tones of the sung "Royal Mass" from France and the Divine Word spoken in French remained vivid.

Wanting to have a church of their own, Lowell's Canadians decided in 1866 to ask for a French-speaking priest and the establishment of a separate parish. Hilaire Dozois, who had to go to Montréal on business at the beginning of that year, was delegated to plead their cause before Bishop Bourget, of Montréal. The bishop, although encouraging, replied that he was powerless to act without an official request from the bishop of Boston, who had jurisdiction over Lowell. He gave Mr. Dozois a letter of introduction to Boston's Bishop John Williams. As soon as their spokesman returned to Lowell with the precious letter, a meeting of the most influential members of the community was convened to study the project. A committee comprised of Hilaire Dozois, Jean Baptiste Raymond and Joseph Courchêne, traveled to Boston to present the letter to Bishop Williams who received them with kindness, listened to their account of the religious situation of the Canadians in Lowell, and promised to help them. He immediately contacted Bishop Bourget, asking him for a priest to establish a French-language parish in Lowell and also to look after the other Canadians scattered throughout the diocese of Boston.

At the beginning of April 1866, Father Charles A. Boissonnault, from the diocese of Montréal, arrived in Lowell to preach a mission in anticipation of the foundation of a parish. This mission was held in the basement of St. Patrick's church. Unfortunately, the moment was not yet favorable for such a foundation. Father Boissonnault returned to Canada the following July.

However, in spite of the failure of this first attempt, Bishop Williams did not forget the French-language faithful of his diocese. Knowing that these immigrants needed a French-speaking priest to keep their ancestral faith alive, he did not delay in renewing his attempt to find one for them.

4. The Massive Immigration
"He has sent me to evangelize the poor"

When John Williams became bishop of Boston, in 1866, there wasn't a single Franco-American parish in his diocese which included the entire Commonwealth of Massachusetts. The great immigration had only begun in 1865, and the first attempt at founding a separate parish in Lowell had not been very encouraging. By 1867, however, the religious situation of the French Canadians in the diocese was becoming alarming. Lowell, Lawrence, Worcester, Holyoke, and Fall River all had French settlements that were increasing at a dizzying pace.

In Canada, the massive and permanent emigration to the "States" was making itself felt. Everywhere in the Province of Québec, families were selling their furniture at auction, closing their houses, and joining the exodus. Entire sections of the old historic parishes were being emptied of their inhabitants. Canadians were migrating by the trainload, and it had become a daily sight in the railroad stations of New England to see them arrive with their fur caps and carrying their possessions on their backs. In a single month, in 1868, 2,300 emigrants from Canada passed through the depot at St. Albans, Vermont, on their way to the industrial centers.

The situation was deteriorating. On all sides, the Canadians were clamoring for separate parishes. Bishop Williams, in his zeal, required his young clergy to study French, but this was only a stopgap measure, for he knew that French-speaking priests would have to be found. The great obstacle to ministry among the immigrants and the establishment of separate parishes for the French Catholics remained the lack of missionaries.

The first one to notice the true gravity of the situation and sound the alarm which finally mobilized the Canadian and American religious authorities, was the apostle of the French Canadians, Bishop Louis de Goësbriand, the first bishop of Burlington, Vermont. Soon after his elevation to the See of Burlington, in 1853, he faced the spiritual and material problems of the immigrants. He quickly realized that, left without leadership, organization, or parishes, and having no spiritual direction, they would soon be assimilated, losing thereby their Catholic and ethnic identity in the American Protestant society. Given the bond and solidarity between the French language and the Catholic faith among the immigrants, he realized that they needed not only priests who spoke French, but also missionaries who were familiar with their habits and state of mind, in a word, priests of their own kind. He was one of the first to see the truth of the adage that would soon be applied to Franco-Americans: "Whoever loses his native tongue loses his faith." (*Qui perd sa langue perd sa foi.*)

11

After the Civil War, the bishop of Vermont approached the bishops and colleges of Canada for missionaries. In the space of three years, from 1866 to 1868, the French-Canadian population of the dioceses of Burlington and Boston had doubled. He sounded the alarm in Montréal as well as in Québec stating: "If we do not fly to the rescue of these immigrants, even within the shadow of the cross, they will lose their faith and bring dishonor to their nation." Pursuing his search in France, he even went as far as Rome to obtain the backing of the Holy Father. Cardinal Barnabo, prefect of the Propaganda, aroused the concern of the bishops of the United States. The result was that in May of 1866, Pope Pius IX granted an indulgence of 100 days to all persons in the diocese of Burlington who would recite the following prayer: "Queen of the Apostles, conceived without the stain of original sin, pray the harvest Master to send laborers into His harvest."

Thanks to the efforts of the apostle of the Franco-Americans in making known the plight of the immigrants, Bishop Williams finally found his missionaries for Lowell through a providential encounter. The Queen of the Apostles answered the prayers of her faithful subjects by sending into the harvest the Missionary Oblates of Mary Immaculate, her devoted servants.

The Congregation had been founded in Aix-en-Provence, France, on January 25, 1816, by Charles Joseph Eugène de Mazenod, who would become bishop of Marseille in 1837. The holy founder, canonized in 1995, whose missionary zeal was worthy of the Apostles, gathered around him priests from the region of Provence to repair the spiritual havoc wreaked by the French Revolution. The aim of this small congregation, then called the Missionaries of Provence, was to evangelize the poor and the most abandoned souls of the countryside, the cities, and later of far-off missions. Morally strengthened by poverty and the devotions of community life, Father de Mazenod and his companions went about preaching wherever ministry beckoned them, whether in the rural villages or in the slums of the cities. Nothing was neglected which could provide spiritual assistance to the poor people of the countryside or the destitute population of the cities.

Ten years later, on February 17, 1826, Pope Leo XII approved the Rules submitted by Father de Mazenod for his community and established the Institute under the name of Congregation of the Missionary Oblates of Mary Immaculate. Since the field of their apostolate had now gone beyond the region of Provence, the founder had changed the name of his community, and as a result of a fortunate inspiration, he placed it under the protection of the heavenly Mother. For Father de Mazenod, the title "Oblate of Mary Immaculate" was "a mark of predestination . . . a passport to heaven!" It was indeed predestination, since the dogma of the Immaculate Conception had not

**Saint Eugène de Mazenod founder of
the Missionary Oblates of Mary Immaculate.**

yet been promulgated. As a motto, the congregation chose the Gospel text *"Evangelizare pauperibus misit me"* (He has sent me to evangelize the poor).

On December 2, 1841, in response to a request by Bishop Bourget of Montréal, six Oblates arrived there to establish the Congregation in Canada: Fathers Honorat, Telmon, Baudrand, Lucien Lagier, and Brothers Louis Roux and Basile. Bishop de Mazenod wrote to the Fathers: "Montréal is perhaps only the door which will introduce our family to the conquest of souls in many countries." These were prophetic words, for it was indeed the beginning of the great Canadian epic of the Oblates. These religious would be in the vanguard of ministry to the settlers in Western Canada, in Hudson Bay, among the Inuit, and down to Mexico and the United States.

As early as 1842, the zeal of the Oblates carried them beyond the limits of Canada to evangelize the many Canadian immigrants who were spilling over the border into the United States, especially in northern New York State. Father Lucien Lagier was the first Oblate to preach in the United States. He and his confreres spent month after month, day and night, laboring to bring the support of faith to these abandoned souls. In 1851, they settled in Buffalo. The following year, they accepted the vast and difficult missions of Texas and, in 1853,they agreed to serve the Canadian parish of Plattsburgh, New York, and to minister in the neighboring towns.

Providence then guided them toward the Spindle City, to this young industrial center which was incorporated as a city in the same year that the Oblate Rule had been approved by Rome. Another door was opening for the future of the Congregation in the United States.

5. A Providential Encounter

On December 8, 1867, Bishop Williams went to Burlington, Vermont, to attend the consecration of Bishop de Goësbriand's new cathedral. Father Florient Vandenberghe from Montréal, provincial of the Canadian Oblates, was present among the throng of priests and ecclesiastical dignitaries from the United States and Canada. This was to be expected, since the Oblates, who were already well known for their work among the French Canadians of New York State, had also been ministering for a few years in the diocese of Burlington.

Divine Providence being ever watchful, Bishop Williams met one of his former classmates from the Montréal seminary, with whom he had struck up a friendship. He was Father J.-B. Leclerc, pastor at Our Lady of the Angels in Stanbridge, in the diocese of Saint-Hyacinthe, Québec. The bishop explained the problem which had been preoccupying him for a long time, and asked his friend if he knew of some Canadian priests who would be willing to settle in his diocese. Father Leclerc suggested to the bishop that he approach the Oblates who were well-suited for this type of work. He then offered to introduce Bishop Williams to their provincial, Father Vandenberghe.

The bishop was pleased with this advice for he was already familiar with the commitment of these missionaries. In the fall of 1866, Fathers André-Marie Garin and Basile Dédebant, at the request of the Canadians in Springfield, Massachusetts, and with the consent of Bishop Williams, had come to the diocese of Boston to preach missions in Springfield and its environs. The results of these missions had exceeded everyone's hopes and the bishop had declared himself to be well-satisfied.

Once introduced to Father Vandenberghe, Bishop Williams recalled the fine work accomplished by the Oblate Fathers during the preceding year, and offered to give them a French parish in an industrial city. The provincial asked him, however, if the work of his religious would be confined to this parish alone. The bishop quickly added that the parish was to serve as a steady source of income to the community, and that the Oblates would be in charge of missions for the French-Canadians of his diocese. The provincial replied enthusiastically, stating that the General Administration of the order would most likely be in favor of such an arrangement, since the Oblate Congregation had been assiduously seeking a place to settle in the Eastern States to come to the help of the Canadians. Moreover, the growth of religion in the United States required an increase in the number of priests. Father Vandenberghe therefore willingly approved the bishop's proposal, on condition that he establish the Oblates in a large city, that his religious not be limited to that one parish, that they should be especially engaged in preaching missions, and be allowed to live as a community of at least four or five religious.

For the time being, it was agreed that Bishop Williams would write to Montréal to settle the matter. Father Vandenberghe was quite right in enthusiastically assenting to the wishes of the bishop of Boston. Ever since Fathers Garin and Dédebant had preached in Springfield and, given the appeals of Bishop de Goësbriand, the Oblates fervently aspired to come to the aid of the poor immigrants of New England. Father Garin would later write:

Ever since we became aware of the spiritual plight of the Canadians who had emigrated to the States, the provincial administration had resolved to try to make an attempt on behalf of these abandoned souls whose poverty was compelling to our dear Congregation. We tried many times to organize the ministry of missions in that area, but we only encountered indifference, and even some opposition. The English-speaking clergy as a whole was far from wishing to have these French missions.

That the bishop and the provincial were both desirous of establishing the Oblates augured well for the future.

Five days after the meeting in Burlington, Father Vandenberghe wrote to Father Fabre, the superior general of the Oblates, pronouncing himself in favor of the installation:

Two priests would be needed at once, and later, four. Therefore, without delaying any longer, Most Reverend Father, I am asking for your consent to this project, should the conditions be acceptable.

Because the Oblates were first and foremost a missionary congregation, governed by its own constitutions and rules, they could not accept the responsibility of a parish without an indult, i.e. permission, from Rome.

While waiting for the indult, the provincial communicated by letter to the assistant-general to the effect that he and his councilors were desirous of establishing the Congregation in the diocese of Boston because they considered it to be important and very advantageous for the Oblates. On December 30th, the provincial received both the news that the General Administration was in favor of this establishment in principle, and that he was now authorized to begin serious negotiations. The plan was put into action and, on January 9, 1868, the letter from Bishop Williams arrived.

If Father Vandenberghe was pushing the matter, Bishop Williams was far from dragging his feet. On January 9th, the bishop wrote to the Oblates in Montréal indicating that the foundation should be in Lowell, and that he had already taken the steps needed to purchase a church building. Thus, he wanted to know when the first religious could arrive there. The provincial hastened to answer, on January 14th, that although the indult from Rome had not yet come, there would probably be no difficulty from that quarter . . . . Although he could not set up a community before the end of summer, he, nevertheless, could, in the meantime, send two priests. . . .

Keeping the superior-general in France informed of the steps he was taking, the provincial wrote, on the 21st of the same month, that Lowell would have to be the site, but that he was withholding his final decision until he had had a chance to visit the city. He then added these prophetic words:

> If we believe that the foundation in Boston is very useful and opportune, it is not because the laborers are many, but because we believe that the future development of the Congregation belongs in the United States.

On January 20th, the indult having finally arrived, the superior-general let it be known that Bishop Williams's proposal was very acceptable. Accordingly, on January 27th, the provincial council officially approved the installation in the diocese of Boston, sending the document to the bishop. This was all that Bishop Williams needed. On March 2, 1868, he informed Father Vandenberghe that a church for the Canadians of Lowell had been purchased, and invited him to come to the city to examine it and make the necessary arrangements.

The provincial accepted. Seeking to have further details on Lowell, he wrote immediately to Sister Slocombe, superior of the General Hospital of the Grey Nuns in Montréal, whose community was managing a hospital in Salem, Massachusetts. On March 17th, Sister Marie answered from the Looby Asylum in Salem, that "the population of that city (Lowell) was about 32,000 of which 12,000 were Catholics. Of that number there could be 2,500 French Canadians." She disclosed that indeed the pastor of Saint Patrick's, Father John O'Brien, had just bought old Saint Mary's church from the heirs of his predecessor, Father McDermott. The building had been closed for several years, and it was intended for the French congregation. Already well-informed regarding the Oblate project, young Sister Marie exulted with optimism:

> I am convinced that the good Fathers will have no trouble finding enough to live on, for our Canadians are earning a lot of money, and the thought of having a church of their own will suffice to make them generous. So, tell the dear Fathers, I beg you, to come without fear, that they not bring provisions or money; they will find all that here.

On March 17th, Father Vandenberghe arrived in Boston. The bishop, who was known for his sincerity and frankness, explained his project. He wanted the Oblates to settle in Lowell to look after the Canadians; from there they could extend their preaching ministry to other Canadians in the diocese. It was agreed that the priests would not have to minister in English either in Lowell or elsewhere in the diocese.

The provincial found such a proposition inadmissible and he was on the point of abandoning everything. He made it clear to the bishop that it was impossible to begin ministry in a country without adopting its language. He argued that ministry to the Canadians would be too precarious, and especially too uncertain, if the immigrants returned to Canada. To establish themselves, the Oblate Fathers had to be able to become identified with the local clergy and even recruit in the country. He did not want the Oblates to be in the country as complete strangers in a diocese of 350,000 Catholics. Moreover, since community life forms the basis of the Oblate Rule, it was necessary to find work for a community of at least four religious.

To this, Bishop Williams replied: "Now that you are here, let's examine all the possibilities. Let's go to Lowell to see on the spot what we can do."

On the way, that very same day, the 17th, the bishop took the religious priest to Lowell, where they spent two days lodging with the pastor of St. Patrick's. After lunch, they went for a carriage ride to visit the city. As they passed before the newly built St. John's Hospital, founded in 1866, where a public chapel was being constructed, the bishop remarked: "I intend to form a third parish in Lowell. Perhaps an arrangement could be made by which one of your Fathers would officiate at this chapel for a time, while serving as the hospital chaplain. Then later, this chapel could possibly be the basis for an Irish parish. This service could be pursued alongside your ministry to the Canadians." They visited the hospital, which was served by seven Daughters of Charity, and the small wooden chapel that the sisters were having built.

Father O'Brien proved to be very favorable to the creation of a French parish, and offered to sell Saint Mary's church to the Oblates for $6,000. It was a brick building that could seat 800 to 1,000 people, right by and almost in the shadow, of Saint Patrick's. Having visited it, the provincial found it badly built and in an especially disadvantageous location . . . . However, in the middle of the city, very near Lowell's railroad station, a Protestant church was for sale for $11,500. It was smaller than Saint Mary's, seating only 600 or 700, but it was better constructed, and its location offered great advantages. During their two-day tête-à-tête, the plans were revised, and the provincial was pleased with the bishop's new suggestions. The Fathers would be responsible for the Canadian congregation and would service the hospital chapel for at least three years. After that time, the chapel would become an Irish parish to be administered by the Oblates.

Before returning to Boston, Bishop Williams, wanting to give Father Vandenberghe more time to study the situation and the sites, advised him to send two priests, around Easter, to preach a retreat to the Canadians who wished to fulfill their religious duties. Then, if it seemed opportune, they would group the people into a parish and offer them the opportunity to purchase one of the two churches. It was agreed that after this first attempt, the bishop would make known his final instructions and, at that time, a final decision could be arrived at concerning the establishment of the Oblates in Lowell. Everything now depended upon the results of the mission, and the frame of mind of Lowell's Canadian population.

6. Fathers Garin and Lagier and The First Mass

In Lowell, the news that the Oblates were coming to stay had preceded their arrival, and had been causing great excitement since February in the Franco-Canadian colony. News like that had not taken long to get around and everyone was talking about it with joyous approval.

Father Vandenberghe did not delay in putting the bishop's suggestion in motion. Since the fate of the Lowell foundation rested on the success of the preparatory mission, he selected his missionaries with care. He decided that, at the beginning of April, he would send Fathers Lucien Lagier and André-Marie Garin to Lowell.

Not only had these two religious men been trained under the founder, Bishop de Mazenod himself, but both had also to their credit, experienced long years of arduous work in the missions. They embodied the apostolic spirit which

Fr. Lucien Lagier, O.M.I.

emanated from the founder and energized the whole Congregation. Accustomed to living only for the salvation of souls, they were the very spirit of charity, and they had become inured to sufferings and obstacles. For them, the Holy Rules of the community were not only a set of exercises to be followed, but a whole way of life which opened the interior way to the grace of God.

Father Lucien Lagier was born on October 4, 1814, in Saint-André, France, near Embrum in the diocese of Gap. His parents were deeply devout Catholics. When his brother, Father Jean-Marie Lagier left his post as associate-pastor in Embrum, to enter the Congregation of the Missionary Oblates of Mary Immaculate, Lucien followed him to the novitiate. On August 14, 1834, the venerated founder invested him with the religious habit of the congregation at the novitiate in Saint-Just, near Marseille. Having finished his studies, he was ordained to the priesthood by Bishop de Mazenod on May 25, 1839. Shortly thereafter, in 1841, he received his obedience for North America and was part of the small band of Oblates who were the first to leave the shores of France to establish the Congregation in that vast and unknown land destined to add a glorious chapter to the history of the Church.

From the time of his arrival in Montréal, in 1841, until his death, Father Lagier was, of all the Oblates in Canada, the one most constantly employed at the task of missions and retreats. For thirty-two years, barring a few rare interruptions, he was entirely given over to his vocation as a missionary. He preached over one thousand missions or retreats, and was recognized as the pioneer of the Oblate missions. In 1842, he was the first Oblate to cross over the American border in order to come to the aid of the Canadian immigrants. Love of duty dominated everything else for him. He always understood poverty as it should be practiced by those who take this vow, and that is how he faithfully observed it in practice. In his travels, he always brought along bread and some fruit so that he wouldn't have to step off the train to eat at railroad stations. His practice, which never varied, was to rise at 4 o'clock in the morning during the summer, and at 4:30 in winter. Endowed with sound judgment based on observation, his prudence and dedication could always be relied upon. He was a true leader, who never shied away from difficult missions. Thus, in 1856, he undertook the difficult task of evangelizing the Canadians who had settled in Watertown, New York, and had not seen a priest for many long years.

During two full months of daily labor, he endured the fatigue of days and evenings packed with active and exhausting preaching. As soon as he arose, Father Lagier had to prepare the hall, hear confessions, preach, celebrate Mass, in a word tend to everything before seven in the morning when people had to leave for work in the mills. During the rest of the morning, he would gather the women and children for a catechism lesson. The afternoon was busy with visiting the sick and seeking out other Canadians, scattered throughout the distant countryside, in an effort to bring them back to the fold. At seven in the evening, the mission exercises began again. Hardly had he descended from the pulpit after the sermon, with perspiration streaming down his face, than he entered the confessional. At midnight he dropped onto a flimsy straw mattress, only to begin the whole process once again on the following morning at four o'clock.

Two years later, in 1858, a greater ordeal was inflicted upon him when his superiors sent him to Illinois with another Oblate to counter the spiritual outrages caused by the apostate priest Charles Chiniquy, who had created a schism in that State. Upon arriving, Father Lagier plunged right into the fray, mindful of the agitation that was roiling in Saint Anne, the very village where Chiniquy lived. During the mission, many of the schismatics came back to the Church in spite of the efforts and threats of their leader. Father Lagier even converted a few Protestants. When he returned to Canada, Chiniquy's departure from Illinois was only a matter of time.

In 1868, Father Lagier had been appointed as provincial councilor to Father Vandenberghe, all the while continuing his hunt for souls. Six years later, on February 27, 1874, Father Lagier, the dean of the Oblates in North America, died like a soldier, in full combat, struck down suddenly while out in the field of the Lord. He was preaching a Lenten novena in the parish of L'Ile Verte, voluntarily subjecting himself to his strict regime, when the pastor found him one morning in his bed, deep in the slumber of the just. Recounting the emotion of the people and the public manifestations of grief at the news of his death is not necessarily part of our story here, but it is important to note, however, that he was unanimously referred to as *le bon père Lagier*, (good Father Lagier), the same title that would later be given to his traveling companion, Father André-Marie Garin.

Born on May 9, 1822, at Côte-Saint-André, in the diocese of Grenoble, in France, André-Marie Garin spent his youth under the protection of the "good Lady of the Dauphiné" region Notre Dame de l'Osier (Our Lady of the Willow). His pious mother, who had a great devotion to the Blessed Virgin, had consecrated him to *Notre Dame de l'Osier* before he was born, because of a private vow she had made. Having kept the secret to herself, her heart leaped for joy when her son announced to her with tenderness that he wanted to become an Oblate priest. With tears in her eyes, she recounted the circumstances of his consecration, telling him: "I never spoke to you about it until this day, but today it is my duty to do so. Go, my son, and fulfill the promise your mother made to heaven!" This revelation removed from him all doubts concerning his vocation. After making a pilgrimage to *Notre Dame de l'Osier* for enlightenment and counsel, he entered the novitiate. From there he went on to the major seminary at Marseille to study theology and perfect himself in religious life under the watchful eye of Bishop de Mazenod.

In August 1843, he was ordained to the subdiaconate by the founder and pronounced his vows, thus becoming the 100th Oblate to be incorporated into the Society. At the time, plans were being made for a foundation in Ireland, and Brother Garin was designated to form part of the original group. But, since he was only 21, Bishop de Mazenod, to his great regret, could not ordain him to the priesthood, although the young man stood out for his deep piety and attachment to the Rule. However, by moving things along as much as they could, he was ordained a deacon by the founder in June of 1844. Fortunately for Franco-Americans, it was decided at the last minute to send him to Canada instead of Ireland. At the end of that month, he embarked for Montréal with two other Oblates. The founder wrote immediately that he was sending, along with the two priests, "Brother Garin, a charming Oblate who is still only a deacon, but who will provide many services to the mission." He was ordained to the priesthood on April 17, 1845, at Longueuil, by Bishop Ignace Bourget of Montréal, on whom he also made an impression, since the ordaining bishop made it known to Marseille to what extent he had been struck "by the modesty and seriousness" of this young religious.

Now that he was a priest, the young man could devote himself entirely to the apostolate. Divine Providence would find a way to test him. Only a few days after his ordination, he left with the celebrated Father Laverlochère for the Indian missions of Temiscamingue, in Abitibi, Québec, and great Victoria Lake. This first assignment among the Native Peoples would prove to be prophetic, for during the following twelve consecutive years, from 1844 to 1856, Father Garin would devote almost all his time and talents evangelizing the tribes of the Far North. With Fathers Laverlochère and Durocher, he became one of the trailblazers in these distant missions. From the Gulf of St. Lawrence to James Bay, to the Saguenay Basin, among the native *Montagnais* and Cree, Father Garin could be found, trudging on snowshoes, preaching and baptizing, with cross in hand. He had to face so many dangers and alarming obstacles that many pages of his life during this time read like an adventure novel.

His tact and simple, straightforward good manners, enhanced by his great knowledge of the indigenous languages, were very much appreciated and his teachings endeared him to everyone. He put a great deal of vim and vigor into his undertakings. Fatigue, long marches and the most arduous tasks were mere child's play for him. All those who came in contact with him could only experience profound respect and deep admiration. No sacrifice made him back away, and he mastered the language of the Cree Nation living in the James Bay region, to the point where he could write and publish a Way of the Cross, prayers, and hymns for their use. In the summer, when he was not busy preaching to the children of the woods, he ministered at St. Pierre parish in Montréal, and preached in several dioceses of Canada. Just like Father Lagier, a frequent companion on long treks through the Canadian forest in search of souls, Father Garin, through his deep piety, was a strict observer of the vow of poverty and the Rules of his Order. He always arose at five in the morning and never missed his daily religious exercises. Owing to his magnificent work in the missions, he had become one of the most esteemed members of the Congregation, and his zeal had earned him the confidence of his superiors.

Because he had mastered English, Father Garin, with his diplomacy and total lack of pride, was the perfect choice to be designated for another apostolate, just as difficult as that to the Canadian aborigines — the missions to the United States. In 1853, his superiors fittingly named him pastor in Plattsburgh, New York, where the church was still under construction and the parishioners in total dissent with the Oblate Fathers. When he left the parish in 1862 to become superior in Buffalo, harmony reigned in the parish, the church was finished, and a convent for a community of nuns had been constructed. In Buffalo, he was not only superior, he also had to assume the role of peacemaker in order to settle the grave difficulties that had arisen with the bishop of the diocese. He succeeded, not only in saving the parish, but he also managed to start a second one. Needless to say, during all this time, he was also preaching missions to the Canadian immigrants here, there, and everywhere in the area. The unbounded activity of Father Garin in the remote Indian missions and in New York State would have been sufficient to fill the life of another man, but in fact all of this constituted but a miniscule part of his long missionary life. He would give his full measure in Lowell.

*   *   *

The two Oblates alighted from the train at the Lowell railroad station on Saturday evening of April 18, 1868. During the celebration of his birthday in 1884, Father Garin remembered the arrival and the beginnings of the mission in these terms:

We arrived on a Saturday night, my old friend Father Lagier and I. Father O'Brien, the pastor of St. Patrick's church gave us the most cordial and sincere welcome possible. On the next day, Sunday, we offered the first Mass in the lower church. That evening, after prayers, we held a large gathering of the Canadians of this city, a meeting at which I myself presided. The first question that I asked was this: "My dear friends, do you wish to separate yourselves from the others and form your own parish?" They responded unanimously: "Yes, we want to do it." The second question was this one: "There are two churches for sale at this moment, one is near St. Patrick's church, and the other one is on Lee Street. Which of the two would you choose?" Again the response was unanimous: "The Protestant church on Lee Street." It was even decided that evening that on the next day I would discuss the matter with the owner who was an American. Indeed, the following day I went to his home

Photograph of Fr. André Marie Garin, O.M.I., taken about the time of his arrival in Lowell.

accompanied by good Mr. Bergeron and the devoted Mr. Miller, for whom we are still grieving, for at the time, he gave me much good advice that I followed and which always turned out well.

These two men, Louis Bergeron and Joseph Miller, who were well-known in the Canadian community because of their business experience and their many years in Lowell, quickly became Father Garin's reliable advisors. Louis Bergeron, who had arrived in Lowell in 1841, had since opened his own blacksmith shop on Cabot Street and was fairly well-off; Joseph Miller, born in Canada, had arrived prior to 1852, and while working as a carpenter and cabinet-maker, had become an entrepreneur in the construction business. Mr. Miller would die young, in 1876, and Mr. Bergeron followed him in death in 1890 at the age of sixty-three.

So, on the following Monday, April 20, the three men went to the residence of Gerrit Bradt, the administrator of the building on Lee Street. After Father Garin had asked his questions, the American requested a few days to consult with the other members of the committee before deciding on a method of payment. Three days later, on Thursday, April 23, he returned with his two advisors. Let's listen to Father Garin once again:

This American received us cordially. I asked him how much he wanted for his church. He answered: "$11,500 dollars with $3,000 as a down payment, and the remainder in five years, with interest." I said right away: "It's a deal!" He was greatly astonished by this. I gave him $50 to seal the agreement, and he gave me a receipt.

The Canadians in Lowell were now the owners of a church. The building had been constructed in 1850, at a cost of $20,000, by a group of Unitarians who had occupied it until 1861. It had been sold in 1864 to a society of Spiritualists who elected to dissolve in 1868 after selling the building. Capable of accommodating 600 people, the church was fifty feet wide, eighty feet long, and rose to a height of fifty-eight feet. It was a brick structure, with a façade of blue stone from Somerville. The window openings and frames were of gray granite from Dracut. Lee Street was a very advantageous site at the time because it was in the center of the city and handy to the Canadian population which was to be found especially at the very end of Broadway, near Dutton Street, and on Dutton, Worthen, and Tilden Streets. "Little Canada", that vast stretch of land west of the Lawrence Corporation, bound by Moody and Pawtucket Streets had not yet been developed at the time.

Father Garin himself then had only $2 left in his pocket, and the church having been purchased, he now had to find the means to pay for it. Father

26

O'Brien warned him that the Canadians donated very little to Saint Patrick's in the Sunday collections. Nevertheless:

We then began a small mission in the basement of St. Patrick's church and every night, after the service, our good Canadians brought me their offering. Each day I would gather $300, $400, even up to $500 this way and I was in the habit of counting my receipts every night. Let me tell you a little story about this. Father O'Brien always watched me counting my money and would say to me: "Dear Father Garin, I believe you must be counting the same $300 night after night."– "But no, no, Father," I replied, "and I'll prove it to you by counting the $2,000 that I have in this pouch at this moment." Father O'Brien could hardly believe his eyes: $2,000, practically all of it in one dollar bills. "This must be money that you borrowed from the bank?" – "No, Father, it is our poor Canadians who have given this, and they have proved to me that they would give more." "Well, Father Garin, you will certainly succeed in whatever you undertake, for I must admit that my own people could not do as much." Ah, how devoted my Canadians were. They were working for the glory of God.

As soon as Father Garin announced the purchase of the church and the opening of the subscription drive, the faithful got to work and enthusiastically began to anticipate taking possession of the church. On the spot, among the first to give were the Messrs. Miller and Bergeron who pledged a considerable sum. Even their spouses became involved, heart and soul. Mrs. Aurélie (Ritchie) Miller, who had arrived in 1845, and spoke English with ease, accompanied by Mrs. Célina (Dufresne) Bergeron, solicited money from non-Franco-American citizens. In addition, the two women also began sewing the first Mass vestments for their church.

At the end of their first week in Lowell, by Sunday, April 26, the missionaries had $2,000 in hand. In the meantime, on April 18, Father Garin had performed his first baptism at St. Patrick's: little Joseph Edmond Buisson, son of Edmond Buisson and Aristine Gill, and his first marriage, on April 26, between Jules Lavallée and Marie Lacouture. Eight days into the mission, it was time to evaluate the situation. The results were not yet decisive. In his letter to the provincial, dated April 26, Father Lagier gave the following report:

We are now at the eighth day of our mission, and we have given communion to merely 640 persons. The number of adults is not as great as we had at first believed. There are a fair number of people at the evening service. They are not in a hurry to receive the sacrament of penance. I cannot foresee what we will be able to do during the second week. We need all the time we have to complete the work that we have begun. The Protestant church, which you visited, has been bought for the sum of $11,500. The open subscription has already brought in almost $2,000. I do not think that we can go much above this amount. The people are poor, and not as numerous as we thought.

In fact, after taking a census during the first week, it seemed that the population was not as large as they had been told. There were only 1,200 Canadians, including "five or six hundred girls." So, Father Lagier concluded: "I do not think that we could satisfactorily establish ourselves as a community here. There would be enough to keep one priest busy, but not a community." This recommendation to the authorities was not made without sadness. "Our poor Canadians are much to be pitied . . . There is a tremendous amount of good to be accomplished here among these poor young people who find themselves thrown, without protection and without the help of religion, in the midst of infidels." On the next day, Monday the 27th, the two Fathers went to Boston to give an account of the situation to Bishop Williams. The bishop, with his usual concision and benevolence, did not speak of the future, and did not ask them to take an immediate decision. . .

Once again they returned to the task facing them. The people were, in fact, very poor, but the momentum favorable to the establishment of a parish became so pronounced that they generously imposed enormous sacrifices upon themselves to ensure that the Oblate Fathers would remain among them. The second week of the mission had barely begun when the zeal and generosity of the congregation surpassed all Father Lagier's hopes. By Thursday, April 30, the subscription amount had reached $3,000, so Father Garin went ahead with the transfer of titles and paid this entire amount in cash to the owners, James Carney and Franklin Coburn. The purchase of the church was now an accomplished fact, and Father Garin lost no time in convoking a general meeting of all the Canadians that same Thursday evening, to announce that the official taking possession of the church would be held on Saturday morning, and that Mass would be celebrated the following morning, Sunday.

The Canadians having proved their devotion and their eagerness to acquire a parish, Father Garin's judgment and strength of character came into play. During the mission, he had listened, questioned, and faced the facts. Father Lagier, now an enthusiast of the foundation, wrote to his provincial on that Thursday:

Father Garin, who at first had pronounced himself against this establishment, has, after careful consideration and also after a serious study of the project, and having closely examined all the circumstances – the present, the future, the various opinions, the present and future resources – is now leaning towards the affirmative.

Father Garin, as we have seen, had men he trusted among the older folk, but as he would be in the habit of doing in the days to come, for all his important undertakings, he also had his well-informed "American" advisors and knowledgeable men whose opinion he sought out:

A few capable men, God-fearing themselves, whom Father Garin has met, have strongly advised him to accept, even though conditions would not be brilliant at first. What is certain is that Lowell is surely a city with a future, unless some unforeseen reversal takes place. There will always be quite a fair-sized French congregation, especially when they learn that there are Oblate Fathers.

This opinion was accurate, and Father Garin showed how very clear-sighted he was. The mills were multiplying the number of spindles and immigrants were arriving on a continuing basis. Between January and June of 1868, the Merrimack Company alone added 10,500 spindles to its mills, and by the end of June the number of spindles in the city's mills had reached 483,864. These were run by 13,729 "operatives" as the workers were called. The industry had come a long way from the 7,000 workers of 1835. Father Garin must also certainly have noticed a series of articles in the local press explaining that in spite of prosperity, the mills and factories were not operating at full capacity.

Moreover, quite apart from the church for the Canadians, "there is a strong possibility that a beautiful parish may be established in the vicinity of St. John's Hospital." Therefore, with a good aide at his side, Father Garin was ready to attempt anything for the new foundation. Father Lagier ended his letter by adding that there would certainly be work for three priests, and that "in a few years we could have here quite a respectable, perhaps even a flourishing establishment."

That Saturday morning, the new owners entered their church for the first time and began immediately to prepare it for divine worship. They had very little time, but the workers, understandably, were numerous. A small crucifix was placed atop the Protestant minister's lectern which was placed against the wall to serve as a temporary altar. While the men built a provisional communion rail, and the women did the cleaning, Mrs. Miller and Mrs. Bergeron, brought in the vestments which they had sewn. After a few more alterations here and there, everything was set for the divine service.

The bright sun that shone over Lowell on that Sunday morning, May 3rd, was particularly comforting for the Canadians. After so many years, and so many sacrifices, and, yes, after so many prayers, the great day had come at last. The small church was packed with worshippers. Before Mass, Father Garin

**St. Joseph's Church on Lee Street as it appeared in 1868,
the year of its purchase by Fr. Garin**

asked for singers from among those present. Twenty men stepped forward and improvised a choir. In spite of being slightly indisposed, owing to all the work of the past week, Father Garin, nonetheless, played the organ while Father Lagier offered and sang the first *messe royale* for the Canadians of Lowell. The collective joy and gratitude became a touching scene, in spite of the discomfort of having to stand during the entire service, since those in attendance could not kneel on the old Protestant pews without turning their backs to the altar, although they managed to do so with some difficulty during the Elevation.

The beautiful sounds of the *Royal Mass* plain chant, little known in the United States, resonated beneath the vault of the building and deeply moved the worshippers. Some remembered their native parishes in Canada; others were reminded of their youth and their departed or distant parents. Sixteen years later, the founder would say with emotion: "Many tears flowed on that day from the eyes of Canadians who were saying to themselves: 'We are at home here, we have a church of our own.' All in all, we could almost believe that we were back in one of the old Canadian parishes." That first Sunday of May 1868 would not soon be forgotten. The Canadians of Lowell, just like those almost everywhere in New England, had had a dream – a very simple dream – that of founding a parish, and to have priests and beautiful religious ceremonies "just like in Canada." And what a pleasure it was for Canadians to meet one another on the church steps after Mass! Since that day was also the Feast of the Solemnity of Saint Joseph, Father Garin placed the church and the parish under the patronage of Saint Joseph.

The Mass was followed by the renting of pews. Mr. Miller was the first to come forward and many paid $30.00 for their pew. In a short time, half of them had been rented and Father Garin had raised $500. As agreed upon at the time of purchase, $3,000 had been paid when the title was transferred, and $500 had to be added six months later. Even though this last amount was not yet due, Father Garin paid the $500 immediately since he had that amount in hand.

On May 11, Father Lagier left Lowell, having accomplished the greater part of his task. He returned to Canada to give a live report to the provincial council regarding the foundation. Bishop Williams came to Lowell on Thursday May 20 to confer the Sacrament of Confirmation on the children of Saint Peter's parish. After the ceremony, Father Garin had dinner with the bishop who inquired whether any news had been received from the provincial. Father Garin assured him that he and Father Lagier had already sent in a favorable report, and that the official acceptance was almost certain. On hearing this, the bishop then went to the Registry of Deeds to have the titles to the church entered under his name. The Canadian parishioners and Father Garin had purchased Saint Joseph church, but, as was customary, the bishop held the title to the church buildings of the diocese. All other buildings, such as schools, orphanages, etc. belonged to the ones who built them. In this particular instance, that was doubly prudent, since the Oblates were not yet officially part of the diocese, and they had not been civilly incorporated.

The bishop came to Lowell again on Wednesday, June 3, to bless Saint Joseph church, and open it officially for worship. History has not recorded his words on that occasion, but his sentiments were undoubtedly the same as those he expressed at Lynn, Massachusetts, in 1887: "Now you are at home. Serve God, and be good Christians, as you were in the country from which you came, by retaining the beautiful traditions of your forefathers."

7. Consolidation and Outreach

Once Saint Joseph parish had been properly and actually constituted, Father Garin, the only one staying in the city that he would never leave again, began consolidating his parish. In the third week of May, the women and young ladies took up a special collection which brought in $206.00 to purchase church linens. On Pentecost Sunday, a collection was added to provide furniture for the future rectory, and, during the same month, an Irishman presented a chalice as a gift to Father Garin. During the week of June 28, the pastor prepared the children for their first confession prior to their first Communion as well as for Confirmation. The first Communion was held on Sunday July 5, in Saint Joseph church while Confirmation was administered the next day in Saint Patrick church, Monday, July 6.

The parishioners had purchased their church building by paying $3,500 towards the sum of $11,500. In 1869 the second installment of $1,845, including interest, was due. The parishioners provided $1,355.77, and the Oblates made up the difference. From May 1868 to December 1869, the expenses for the purchase of the church, for furniture and improvements amounted to $10,574.70, while the receipts for the same period came to $11,324.27. There thus remained a small balance of $749.57. They were not rich, but all was going well, and by the end of 1870, the debt had been reduced to $4,800. Gradually, from 1868 to 1870, up to the coming of the first assistant priest, everything was falling into place so that by 1872 the character of the parish had now become well-delineated.

Saint Joseph's very quickly took on the joyous appearance of a true parish church where everything was done just like in Canada. The Masses and Sunday Vespers, meticulously performed in plain chant, thrilled with delight the good people who told themselves, and could almost believe, that they were back in their land of origin. Add to all this a regular schedule for confession, visits to the sick at all hours in every nook and corner of the city, catechism before Vespers on Sundays, and during the week from eight to nine in the evening. It was through these religious practices that the parishioners also learned to know and love their pastor. The first curate, Father Tortel, has left us this beautiful description of it all:

> Grace seemed to flow in abundance during those first years of the foundation, and we could count on our fingers those who stayed away from the paschal feast. The word of God was listened to and served as a guide for behavior. Without any doubt there were excellent curates to understand and support the work of forming and developing the Canadian parish, but it is also undeniable that Father Garin was the soul of this

movement. His incomparable common sense, his patient prudence, his practical knowledge of persons and things, which derived from his keen sense of observation, the charming easy-going directness of his behavior toward everyone, especially with his people, the noble simplicity of his manners, a superb, very kindly tone of voice, all of these qualities taken together quickly established his indisputable authority over the minds and hearts of Saint Joseph parishioners.

The faithful especially loved to hear him speak from the pulpit where he was considered an expert. Blessed with a dignified and majestic bearing, yet relaxed in manner, he was the perfect gentleman. Gesturing with great facility, his beautiful rich voice conveyed the clarity of his doctrine and penetrated everyone's heart. His preaching never resorted to mouthing beautiful phrases empty of meaning since the sermon, in and of itself, was not his means of action. He himself said: "I have all my sermons in my billfold." As a matter of fact he had four sermons, one of which dealt with the four marks of the Church. According to Father Tortel:

A few sermons for the missions or for special occasions were his entire stock in trade. He had reached the point of leading the parish through his announcements, his advice, and his homilies, following the example of our old Fathers who drew the secret of the success of their missions from this same source. It was through this sort of preaching: simple, familiar, but devoid of triviality that he exercised his true authority and his fatherly direction which reached without discrimination both individuals and families, present or absent, since his words did not fall on deaf ears. They were repeated as the news of the day: "Did you hear Father Garin's announcement? Did you understand his advice?" Repeated often during the week, the people impatiently awaited the following Sunday to hear some follow-up advice or else some other new remark or a particular fact of interest. How many times did the curates, during their home visitations, hear Canadian mothers cry out to their children: "Mind you, my boy, my girl. Watch out! You know what Father Garin said! Watch out!"

His love of quips and anecdotes was not restricted to his homilies. The pastor, who spoke in a familiar tone with everyone, would often stop on the street to chat with his dear Canadians, and he always had the knack of embellishing his pleasant conversation with anecdotes or clever sayings that remained embedded in the memory. One day he stated, "If you don't have a brain, you need to have legs."

In the total magnanimity of his soul, the pastor had become the father, guardian, and counselor of his large parish family. Soon, whenever the people in the city spoke of Saint Joseph's church, they simply referred to it as Father Garin's church.

*   *   *

Now that everything was moving along well in the spiritual realm, Father Garin turned his attention towards the temporal aspect. He was well aware of how strongly the Canadians were attached to their traditions, and no doubt judging that a small celebration was in order, he did not allow the feast of Saint John the Baptist to pass unnoticed.

At his suggestion, the women and girls of the parish organized a small music festival in honor of Saint John the Baptist on Wednesday evening, June the 24th, 1868. The Canadian women displayed their good taste and skill in decorating the basement of the tiny St. Joseph church, where the musicale was held. The hall was festooned with blue, white, and red ribbons – the colors of the French flag – intertwined within large wreaths of green maple leaves. Maple leaves and flowers also decorated the tables, replete with fruit and sweets. At various times during the evening, the guests were entertained with songs and musical selections played by the women and men responsible for the musical program. They also had the pleasure of hearing the young Finn ladies, one of whom, Lizzie Finn, was the first organist for the parish. The evening was a perfect success on all counts, and it was with regret that the guests departed at midnight. To top it all, the evening brought in about $200 for the parish, after expenses. Father Garin noted in a letter: "Our little celebration of the feast of St. John the Baptist was quite fine. Everyone had a very good time. The whole event went very well without hard liquor and without quarrels. I am told that Lowell had never seen such soirées where decorum and order were so well maintained." From that date forward, planning for the patronal feast became an annual undertaking for Father Garin.

Having seen to the successful planning of this celebration, the tireless pastor turned his attention to the material well-being of his flock – he hoped to fill a gap by providing them with something that was grievously lacking. The working population of that time was in dire need of mutual support associations. Existing Saint Jean Baptiste Societies in New England for the Franco-Americans were sources of mutual aid as well as centers for rallying people to the cause of ethnic unity. At a time when there were no automobiles, movie theaters, television, or radio, nationalistic societies like these not only provided financial aid for their members and supported the work of the clergy, they were also meeting places for wholesome recreational activity. In 1868 there existed only two small groups in Lowell – one of which was quite unusual – and they were far from meeting this need for a mutual benefit society.

J. L. Loiselle in 1868 had founded the *Institut Canadien-français de Lowell* which declared itself to be "literary, political and mutual" in its aims, proclaiming: "Let us never be ashamed of our language and our religion; let us respect one another as brothers." This Institute had a reading room, and night classes were taught there by a man from France, H. Paignon. Courses in French Reading, Writing, Arithmetic, and English were provided at 7:00 P.M. on Monday, Wednesday and Thursday evenings. In addition, the members, under penalty of a fine, had to attend the general meetings held on the first Wednesday of every month. As far as can be ascertained, the Institute did not survive very long, for by the end of 1869, no trace of it can be found. This did not prevent Messrs. Loiselle and Paignon from being directors of another little society.

Médéric Lanctôt, a Canadian politician, and an opponent of Georges-Étienne Cartier, one of the founders of the Canadian Confederation, had come to the United States, where he had organized, in certain cities, societies dedicated to promoting the cause of independence for Canada by peaceful means. He came to Lowell in 1868 where he founded such a society, whose dignitaries were: J. L. Loiselle, L. T. Montferrand, H. Paignon, E. Fecteau, Maurice Racicot, Victor Ayotte, Charles Bélanger, and Alfred Courchêne.

But, in July of 1868, Father Garin had convened a meeting of his leading parishioners to launch the idea of forming a benevolent society. This resulted in the successful founding, on January 14, 1869, of the *Société Saint-Jean Baptiste de Bienfaisance de Lowell*. Among the founders can be seen the names of: Louis Bergeron, Samuel P. Marin – who in 1874 would be the first Franco-American elected to the Lowell Common Council – Côme C. Langelier, Luc Viau, Joseph-S. Lapierre, Honoré Constantineau, Moïse Lafaille, Joseph Patenaude, Edouard Courchesne, Camille Laurin, Fabien Roy, Joseph Raymond, Alex. Lavigne, François Ducharme, Godfroy Landry, Frank Viau, and Alarie Mercier.

It must be said here that, at first, all was not harmony and accolades. Father Garin's tact was put to the test, as he noted in the parish record:

> For a number of years, a progressive party had existed among them (the population) with exaggerated literary and nationalistic pretensions. They would have liked to control the actions of the priest; they wanted to establish too liberal a library and hold balls and meetings. Fortunately, Rev. Father Garin managed to control these leanings, and prevent the balls. As a result, this party was reduced to four members.

36

The archives discreetly conceal the names of these "progressives," but we do know about the methods used by the pastor to subdue the skeptics when he believed that his flock was in danger. According to Father Tortel:

> Ever the vigilant sentry, with open eyes as well as ears, he would mull over from Monday to Saturday, at his leisure, what he saw and what he heard, and then, at times a few minutes before mounting in the pulpit, he would discover a plot which could have proven dangerous for the souls of his flock. How many pleasure parties, wild and dangerous trips, dances, how many outings devoid of spiritual or worldly benefit. announced in large print by the newspapers, were brought to a halt faced with Father Garin's announcement! His lively mind lent itself to every tone of voice: soft or trenchant, solemn or familiar, grave or pleasant, with kindness as the dominant note. Whoever heard him, whether they liked it or not, could not forget him. It must be said that his early preaching risked taking the wrong turn because he made allusions which were transparent or too personal. He had the good sense to realize this, and correct it by returning to the right approach.

*   *   *

Quite apart from his work organizing the parish, Father Garin, by the month of May, as we have seen, had not yet received any news from his provincial regarding the definitive acceptance of the Lowell foundation. Saint Joseph parish was well-established, and as of June 28, 1868, St. John's chapel had become the parish church for the Irish who lived in the Belvidere section of the city. In addition, the Oblates were being sought out to preach retreats here, there, and everywhere. Bishop Williams was waiting only for this acceptance, and, in the meantime, at the beginning of July, he offered the Oblates another parish, the Billerica mission. Father Garin's position was becoming more complicated. As the intermediary between Montréal and Boston, on the one hand, he had to treat the bishop with consideration, while on the other he was dispatching letter after letter to the Oblate authorities, imploring and beseeching them to arrive at a favorable decision.

For his part, the provincial kept badgering the superior-general in Paris: "It has become urgent for us to arrive at a definite decision concerning the refusal or the acceptance of the Lowell mission; the more we examine the matter, the more advantages we find to establish ourselves in that country." But, neither the provincial nor the superior-general in France could do anything or arrive at a permanent decision as long as Bishop Williams had not issued the official documents accepting the Oblates in the diocese, and constituting them as a community with all canonical rights and privileges. Nevertheless, on June 18th, Father Vandenberghe conveyed to the bishop that the province was willing to accept the commitments in Lowell while asking him to put in writing the conditions for an arrangement. The worthy bishop, in all his sincerity and total absence of artifice, was a man of few words who was not very fond of ceremony or formalities. As far as he was concerned, he had asked the Oblate Fathers to come into his diocese, and he had given them everything they wanted. They worked very well, so there was no rush as to formalities. He was dealing directly with Father Garin, and it was to him that he responded orally to the provincial's letters. Finally, after much negotiation back and forth, the provincial proclaimed the canonical institution of a religious community in Lowell on November 1, 1868, while Bishop Williams did the same on June 19, 1869.

The outreach of the work of the Oblates had begun as soon as they arrived, for at the end of May 1868, Father Garin had preached a retreat to the Canadians in Haverhill, where he distributed communion to 182 persons, young shoe-factory workers, for the most part. Preaching retreats to Canadians was the main reason for the Oblate presence in New England. To that end, Father Garin, and later his companions and successors, worked unsparingly. Fortunately, Lowell was so situated as to enable them to reach out in all directions, thus facilitating their endeavors. Five railroads reached it; there were ten trains a day to Boston, and direct connections to New York and Montréal. During the first year, the zealous Father Garin visited, among other places, Lawrence, Haverhill, and Marlborough, Massachusetts. In a letter, he stated: "We shall regularly visit the Canadians in Lawrence, Nashua, Manchester, Haverhill, etc., etc., some once a month, others every third or fourth month." In 1869 we find him in Nashua, New Hampshire, Webster and Fitchburg, Massachusetts, and the following year, the Lowell Oblates went to Fall River, Massachusetts, Biddeford, Maine, and even Ogdensburg, New York. Today, many flourishing Franco-American parishes owe their existence to the direct intervention of Father Garin.

In November 1871, the bishops of the Province of Québec, meeting in Québec City, passed a resolution placing the Oblates in charge of all the missions to the Canadians in the United States. The archbishop of Québec, in the name of all the bishops of the province, then wrote to the various bishops in the United States, to interest them in missions for the French Canadians, adding that the Oblate Fathers were prepared to respond to all requests. Their work thus expanded rapidly. For many years, even after the foundation of the Franco-American Province, and the full-time assignment of priests as missionaries, the curates at Saint Joseph parish also invested their energies in the field of parish retreats. Father E. Hamon, S.J. paid a deserved and well-founded tribute to their missionary zeal when he wrote, in 1891:

The Oblate Fathers hastened to fly to the aid of their emigrated compatriots, multiplying missions, exhorting Canadians everywhere to organize themselves in parishes as rapidly as possible, and build churches and schools to preserve their religion and nationality.

The merit of the Oblate Fathers is all the greater because for many long years, they were the only missionaries dedicated to this patriotic and religious effort. They valiantly bore the weight and the heat of the day, and throughout all of New England, there are very few Canadian centers, if there is even a single one, where the voice of these zealous apostles has not been heard.

8. The Curates and a First Bereavement

After Father Lagier's departure, on May 11, Father Garin remained alone as the guest of Father O'Brien at Saint Patrick's rectory until Sunday evening, June 28, 1868. At ten o'clock on Saturday evening, Father J. Cosson arrived, and the following evening, the two moved to St. John's Hospital, administered by the Daughters of Charity. They had "two good rooms" in the former Livermore mansion, a wooden structure on the site of the present Saints Memorial Hospital. One of these two rooms, situated on the ground floor, measured eighteen square feet and served as the reception room and parlor for the Fathers. On the floor above, the nuns had a small chapel, where Father Garin offered Mass in his capacity as chaplain for these religious women, a post which he held for a great many years. A search for more spacious quarters led Father Garin to sign, during the week of September 5, 1868, a three-year lease for a little house located on the site of today's Immaculate Conception church. The rent was $250.00 per year for this residence on High Street Court, today known as Fayette Street. This small house, now a rectory, faced St. John's church, separated only by the width of the street. The two priests took up residence on November 17, and hired domestic help.

Since the work of ministry in Lowell was constantly increasing, the house soon became too small. By June of 1869, as we shall see later, the community had grown to four priests, and three others were expected in October. The tiny house had no chapel, making it difficult to observe the daily exercises of the Oblate Rule. It then became necessary for Father Garin to purchase a neighboring two-tenement house from a Mr. Leavitt. This residence was also located on the present site of Immaculate Conception church. In October of 1869, the Oblate Fathers moved into one of the tenements while Mr. Leavitt and his family, by prior understanding, continued to inhabit the other until the spring of 1870. Their new lodgings consisted of eight large rooms, three small ones, a spacious hall, a double wing, and below, a kitchen, dining room, and a cellar.

On the feast of the Immaculate Conception the Blessed Sacrament was brought into the chapel with the community which, from then on, began the regular observance of the exercises of the Oblate Rule. There being only a thin wall between the chapel and the Leavitt parlor, often, when the Fathers were gathered for their evening prayers, Mrs. Leavitt "entertained" them with all kinds of bizarre piano music, not at all conducive to meditation. All things considered, this could only be a temporary living arrangement, even after the departure of the Leavitts and their piano, for the land was soon needed for the construction of Immaculate Conception church. The house was sold and moved in 1870, and another neighboring three-tenement building, which already belonged to the Oblate Fathers, was moved to the end of Fayette Street, at the corner of Stackpole, the site of the present Immaculate Conception rectory. The eight Fathers entered their new community house in May or June of 1870. This building served as a rectory for the parishes of Saint Joseph and Immaculate Conception until 1887 when the priests separated into two communities.

Fr. Adolphe Tortel, O.M.I., the first curate.

*   *   *

Ever since his arrival, in June of 1868, Father Cosson had served mainly at the chapel of St. John's Hospital, leaving Father Garin to serve St. Joseph's parish. With the establishment of a residence in mind, the provincial sent two men to Lowell – Father Joseph Guillard on September 10, and Father L. Lebret on October 8. The provincial, not being able to delay any longer the canonical institution of an Oblate community in Lowell, arrived there at the end of October. The 31st was a retreat day for the Fathers, and on the following day, Sunday, November 1st, the feast of All Saints, he transmitted to Father Garin letters naming him superior of the Saint John the Evangelist Community of

41

Lowell. The new superior was made responsible for Saint Joseph parish; Father Guillard, who was named first assistant to the superior and his adviser, would look after the Irish of Saint John's parish, while Father Lebret, named second assistant to the superior and bursar for the community, would serve the new St. André's parish in Billerica, founded on November 15, and dedicated to Father Garin's patron saint. Father Cosson was not given a special assignment since he had to leave Lowell, November 15. The parish and community of Saint John the Evangelist, where all the Oblates of Lowell resided, would later become the parish and community of the Immaculate Conception after the construction of the new church of the same name.

During his stay, the provincial, while attending the Masses at St. Joseph's, noted that Father Garin was distributing between 300 and 400 Communions to the faithful. It was clear that the stalwart Father, what with his responsibilities as superior of the community, pastor of the Canadian parish, and overseer of the construction of Immaculate Conception church, would soon need a curate. The Canadian population increased considerably in 1869, and around January 6, 1870, the first curate of Saint Joseph's parish, Father Adolphe Tortel, stepped off the train.

Born in France, in 1826, in the diocese of Valence, Father Tortel had pronounced his vows in 1846, and been ordained to the priesthood by Bishop de Mazenod in 1849. One of the first Oblates to be sent to England, he later taught Dogma at the major seminary of Marseille. Sometime after 1856, his

Fr. Christophe Phaneuf, O.M.I.

The cross erected on Fr. Phaneuf's grave.

superiors had assigned him to the New World. Before coming to Lowell, he had ministered in Buffalo, New York, and had preached retreats as far away as Cleveland, Ohio. In Lowell he threw himself wholeheartedly into parochial ministry, and retained from this "good and truly appealing population" memories which would remain vivid for many years. Later in life, he wrote in 1896: "Whoever lived at that time in this milieu found there the best and most indelible memories of his life." He served as a curate in the parish until April 1873, before leaving for ten years of teaching in Canada where he also became superior. He would return in June of 1883 to his beloved Saint Joseph's parish as a curate and superior of the Community. On February 22, 1901, six years after the death of his friend Father Garin, Father Tortel left this world. At the time he was the oldest Oblate in Lowell.

A second curate, Father Christophe Phaneuf, gave support to his religious brothers from May to August 1871. Gifted with a likeable personality, this young religious, who was only twenty-seven at the time, was a perfect choice to look after the religious education of the children who attended catechism classes on Sundays at Saint Joseph church. According to Father Mangin, he managed to make himself "loved by everyone for his cheerful character, his piety and zeal, but especially for his dedication to the instruction of the children. He had a truly remarkable talent for leading the children. He loved them and was loved by them."

Early in April 1872, the young priest returned once again to Lowell. Unfortunately, he was not to remain for very long among the parishioners of Saint Joseph for he had contracted smallpox which flared up in a violent manner on Saturday morning, April 13. He was immediately transported, by order of the mayor, to the Pest House where, in spite of the truly solicitous care of Dr. St.Cyr, he died at noon, on Tuesday, April 16, after three days of illness. To avoid frightening the people and sowing the seeds of panic, since there had been a serious epidemic the year before, his body was carried directly from the Pest House to Saint Patrick's Cemetery, bypassing the church. He was secretly buried that same night, in the presence of his religious brothers.

The following year, Father Garin ordered the raising of an eight-foot-high gothic cross, in black granite, over Father Phaneuf's grave. Impressive in its simplicity, the monument bears only three letters: O.M.I. It was then proposed that it be blessed. Since the burial of the deceased had been secret and held in private, the Fathers determined to impart as much solemnity as possible to the event so as to provide the parish with an opportunity to pay a public tribute of its esteem and admiration for Father Phaneuf. Around four o'clock on Sunday afternoon, June 8, 1873, after Vespers, 300 Sunday School children and a few hundred parishioners formed ranks and began a procession on that beautiful summer day. The parade led to St. Patrick's Cemetery after passing along all the principal streets of the city. At the cemetery, where a large crowd had already gathered, a French-Canadian band played funeral music prepared by H. L. Desaulniers; Father Garin blessed the cross and delivered an appropriate sermon.

After songs and prayers by the children and the church choir, in addition to the playing of other musical passages, the young people came one after the other to place flowers on the grave of the good, beloved, and greatly missed religious. "Then everyone left, their hearts gladdened and gratified at having attended such a beautiful ceremony."

Fathers Phaneuf and Tortel would be followed by a phalanx of other devoted Oblates. Among the early workers were: Fathers Jean-Marie Royer, Michel Froc, Basile Dédebant, Aloïs Gladu, Louis V. Petit, Charles Bournigalle, and Georges Marion. There is one, however, whose memory stands out above all the others, and who was called "Father Garin's right-hand man." He was Father Joseph Fournier.

9. Father Garin's Right-Hand Man: Father Joseph Alexandre Fournier

Fr. Joseph Alexandre Fournier, O.M.I.

As the pastor and his curate labored together, parish life moved along peacefully. In 1870, Father Lagier came from Montréal to preach on the Jubilee Year of the First Vatican Council. On June 6, the Oblates formed a legal corporation in the Commonwealth of Massachusetts, under the title of "Society of Oblate Fathers for Missions Amongst the Poor." A celebration held for the feast of Saint John the Baptist, on June 24, at Huntington Hall brought in $300 for the parish. In that same year, on November 20, Bishop Williams confirmed 181 children in the first administration of this sacrament to he held in Saint Joseph church. For this first occasion, Fathers Garin and Tortel served as godfathers to the children. Two years later, on June 3, 1872, Mrs. Scholastique Lalumière, a widow, and Mr. Pierre Gaudet were the godparents for 219 children confirmed by Bishop de Goësbriand. The heart of the elderly apostle must have thrilled with joy at the sight of these 219 young Canadians who, strong in their faith, would bring honor to religion and country.

As we can see from the increase in the number of children confirmed, the small colony was constantly gaining in scope. The hustle and bustle of the Saint John the Baptist celebration, the musical and dramatic soirées – the first French play *Le Proscrit* (The Outlaw) was presented in 1870 – made Father Garin quickly aware of the need for another mutual aid society. So, on August 15, 1871, Samuel P. Marin, J. S. Lapierre, Luc Viau, Victor Ayotte, Louis N. Bergeron, and Stanislas Duff met at the home of Mr. Bergeron to found a new benevolent society – *L'Union Saint Joseph,* named after the patron saint of the parish. Father Garin was designated as the chaplain, and he remained in that position until his death.

Both mutual aid societies gathered as a body in Saint Patrick church, on November 4, 1874, along with a delegation from Saint Joseph parish, headed by their pastor, to attend the funeral of Father O'Brien, the first friend of the Canadians in Lowell.

In spite of all this splendid activity, the provincial, following a visit to Lowell, remarked in a letter to the superior-general that there was a total absence of parish societies at St. Joseph. Such a situation was easy enough to understand because the pastor, who was busy supervising major undertakings, including the construction of two churches, and occupied with parish ministry as well as mission service, had no time to direct religious societies. All this changed, however, on October 28, 1874, with the arrival of Father Joseph Alexandre Fournier to replace Father Basile Dédebant.

Born on September 19, 1843, at Sainte-Scholastique, Québec, the son of Alexandre Fournier, a merchant, and Julienne Major, Joseph Alexandre entered Sainte Thérèse classical college where he was soon noticed for his brilliant academic accomplishments. After graduation, he assiduously studied law for a year and a half, before his Oblate vocation directed him toward the order's novitiate at Lachine, in Québec. From there he advanced to the scholasticate in Ottawa, in November 1866, where he was ordained to the priesthood by Bishop Guigues on March 7, 1868. After a brief stay at St. Pierre parish in Montréal, he arrived in Lowell where, except for a few brief interruptions, his long and devoted apostolate would end only with his death.

As Father Garin's only assistant, to look after a population of over 4,000 souls, his zeal was a perfect complement to, indeed a mirror image of Father Garin's, so much so, that their names and the people's memory of them are inseparable in the annals of the parish. No sooner had he arrived than Father Fournier's abounding charity and goodness found an easy outlet among the unfortunate and the needy. The angel of charity seemed to hold him by the hand and lead him. Wherever there were tears to dry, consolation to be brought, or alms to be distributed, Father Fournier could be seen there as Father Garin's right-hand man. His dear poor people would in time call him "Father of Saint Joseph's poor" with gratitude and love. One day an elderly woman parishioner, remembering Christmas Day at Saint Joseph's, wrote: "I seem to hear Father Fournier inviting the children to come to the Midnight Mass – at six o'clock in the morning – and to bring a portion of their gifts to the baby Jesus. Each child would happily drop fruit and candy in large baskets placed in front of the crèche. These baskets would later be brought by this good Father, helped by

Fr. Joseph Alexandre Fournier, O.M.I. in his later years.

some members of the Guardian Angel Society, to the children at Saint Peter's orphanage. Oh, how happy this offering made us!"

Along with the titles of friend of the poor and that of missionary – for, as with all Oblates, he did not neglect the preaching of missions and even laid the foundation for the parish of *Notre-Dame-des-Victoires* (Our Lady of Victories) in Boston – he is also legitimately renowned as the great founder of the parish societies. Beyond any doubt, it is Father Fournier who put in place the underpinnings for the spiritual life of the parish.

Foremost in the heart of all Canadian women has always been Saint Anne, the great miracle-worker of Canada. And so, on August 15, 1875, Father Fournier convened a meeting in Saint Joseph's church of the married women and widows of the parish which resulted in the founding of the *Congrégation de Sante - Anne* or *Les Dames de Sainte-Anne,* (The Ladies of Saint Anne) as they where commonly called. Once they had been received as members, they elected their officers: Mrs. Olivier Leblanc, president, Mrs. Basilide Roy, secretary-treasurer and, of course, Father Fournier as spiritual director. The women observed the prescribed exercises of monthly communion, an annual novena, and involvement in works of charity.

In July 1877, given the society's expansion, Father Fournier divided the parish into four sections, each of which would have two councilors: the Sainte Marie Section, which covered that part of the city between Merrimack and Central Streets, up to the Pawtucket Canal; the Saint Joseph Section, which included both sides of Merrimack Street and the area between Merrimack Street and the Merrimack River up to Bridge Street; the Sainte Monique Section, which included Centralville and Belvidere, as well as Bridge and Central Streets up to the Concord River; and the Saint Joachim Section, covering Middlesex, Appleton, and Jackson Streets, as well as all the cross streets between Gorham and Appleton Streets. The following month, the administrative council chose a nurse for each section, to call on sick members, and two sacristans to look after the St. Anne chapel in the church to assist the councilors.

That took care of the married women, but the question of the young ladies remained. On August 15, 1875, the same day as the founding of the Ladies of Saint Anne, Father Fournier instituted, at a meeting of young ladies under sixteen, *La Congrégation des Enfants de Marie* (The Children of Mary) for the younger ones after their First Communion. For adolescent girls prior to marriage, the *Congrégation des Demoiselles de Notre-Dame-de-Lourdes* (Young Ladies of Notre Dame de Lourdes) was started as stated, "the aim of this Congregation is to preserve young persons living in the world from the dangers that surround them, and to form their hearts to virtue." The two societies also had their own chapels, where the members observed the religious exercises of each group, first wearing a blue veil and later, a white one. Their governing bodies were structured like the Ladies of St. Anne, except for the councilors.

At the same time, neither wanting nor willing to neglect the young men, Father Fournier, on May 7, 1876, after the first Vespers for the Feast of the Apparition of St. Michael the Archangel, held the first solemn installation of young men, from First Communion to age sixteen, into the *Société de l'Ange Gardien* (The Guardian Angel Society). The first directors were Henri Constantineau, president, Elzéar H. Choquette, first vice-president, Xiste Patenaude, second vice-president, and J. S. Côté, secretary. "The purpose of this society is to keep these young men faithful in the practice of their religious duties, and to bring them frequently to the sacraments. A special purpose is to militate against the bad habits of blasphemy and indecent conversations." The rules stipulated that the members would meet on the fourth Sunday of each month for Mass, hymns, and instruction.

The young society developed rapidly and produced remarkable results if we take into consideration the young age of its members. From May 7, 1876, to November 8, 1878, nearly 300 children between the ages of eleven and sixteen, were enrolled under the banner of the Holy Guardian Angels. The group even ventured into dramatics, presenting their first publicly staged play: *Les Jeunes Captifs* (The Young Captives), on July 27, 1876. From July 1876 to November 1878, they presented twelve soirées for the benefit of parish activities. Because many meetings were needed for the numerous rehearsals, the young men escaped the temptations of the street, while acquiring within the society, solid principles for the future, under the surveillance of Father Fournier.

However, towards the end of 1877, the continuing growth of the society, along with the advancing age of a great number of its members, brought the director to the realization that what had sufficed up to that time no longer met their needs. Young men have different aspirations from those of children. Hence, in 1878, Father Fournier selected twelve of the older members, and organized them into a two-tiered society. The first was named *L'Association Catholique des Jeunes Gens de l'Église Saint Joseph* (The Catholic Association of Young Men from St. Joseph Church), set up on February 7, 1878. The president was Henri Constantineau and the members: Elzéar H. Choquette, Pierre Fournier, Jean S. Côté, Jean Baptiste Miller, Xiste Patenaude, Arthur Racicot, Cyrille Constantineau, Xavier Hamelin, Arsène Paquette, Arthur Roy, Marcel Roussel. This society was essentially Catholic and social in its goals, its aims being to foster the intellectual and moral advancement of its members, and to provide them with decent forms of recreation. Their first meeting place was the basement of the church. The second level of the society, named *La*

REGLEMENT

— DE LA —

SOCIÉTÉ DES ENFANTS DE MARIE.

ARTICLE I.

BUT DE LA SOCIÉTÉ.

1. Le but de la Congrégation des Enfants de Marie est de préserver les jeunes filles qui vivent dans le monde des dangers nombreux qui les entourent et de conserver dans leur cœur la ferveur angélique qui les animait au beau jour de leur première communion.

2. Pour atteindre ce but, elles se placent sous la protection toute spéciale de la Ste. Vierge, leur bonne et tendre mère, qui les prémunira contre les séductions de tout genre auxquelles leur âge, leur inexpérience et leur faiblesse naturelle les exposent.

3. Par une consécration solennelle faite au pied de son autel, elles lui promettront de l'honorer, de la servir et de l'aimer toute leur vie, lui assurant de ne rien dire de ne rien faire qui puisse l'attrister, lui promettant de fuir les amusements dangereux où tant de vertus font naufrage, et d'éviter les mauvaises compagnies dont le démon se sert si souvent pour faire tomber dans le péché.

4. En entrant dans cette société, les Enfants de Marie trouvent tous les moyens que le zèle peut inventer pour nourrir et entretenir leur piété ; outre les instructions particulières et les pieuses lectures qu'elles y entendent et les conseils et avis qu'elles y reçoivent, elles trouveront encore un grand secours dans l'exercice public qui les réunira deux fois par mois aux pieds de la Vierge Marie. C'est là qu'elles viendront retremper leur cœur, renouveler leurs bonnes résolutions et se préparer dignement à la confession et à la communion mensuelle.

ARTICLE II.

CONDITIONS D'ADMISSION.

1. Pour être reçue Enfant de Marie, il faut être confirmée ou tout au moins avoir fait sa première communion et s'être faite remarquer par sa bonne conduite et son assiduité au catéchisme.

2. Toute postulante s'adressera au directeur ou à la sœur directrice pour lui donner son nom. Pour le jour de sa réception, elle doit se procurer : 1. Son ruban bleu et sa médaille d'Enfant de Marie ; 2. Un voile blanc, (la robe blanche n'est pas exigée, mais seulement conseillée) ; 3. Elle doit payer son entrée qui est de 25 cents.

3. En entrant dans la société on contracte l'obligation de donner le bon exemple, non seulement à l'Eglise, mais encore dans le monde : du moment où l'on cesserait d'édifier ses parents et ceux que l'on fréquente on se rendrait indigne de rester dans la société.

Vu et approuvé,

ARTICLE III.

REGLEMENT.

Toute congréganiste se fera un devoir d'observer le règlement suivant :

1. Chaque jour : Fidélité à faire ses prières et à réciter 10 *Ave Maria* pour les membres de la société.

2. Chaque mois : Réunions le 2ième et 4ième dimanche à 2½ P. M. Communion générale le 3ième dimanche à 8 A. M.

3. Chaque réunion : Revêtir son insigne dès le commencement. Récitation du chapelet. Chant d'un cantique. Instruction, avis et conseils. Cantique. Quête pour l'entretien de l'autel. Prières diverses.

4. Chaque communion : Se rendre dans le soubassement un quart d'heure avant la messe pour mettre son insigne, son voile et sa robe blanche (si on en a une) et se préparer à monter deux à deux dans l'Eglise.

5. Chaque année : 1. Pour avoir son nom inscrit sur le tableau et avoir droit à un service en cas de mort, il faut payer la contribution qui est de 40 cents pour les années qui suivent la réception, (le mois d'Août est le terme fixé pour payer sa contribution). 2. La fête patronale des Enfants de Marie est le 8 Septembre, fête de la Nativité. Triduum de prières. Communion générale. Consécration solennelle à la Ste. Vierge. Réception. Election des dignitaires, etc.

ARTICLE IV.

AVANTAGES DE LA SOCIÉTÉ.

1. Dès l'instant qu'on est Enfant de Marie on a droit à toutes les bonnes œuvres et à toutes les prières qui se font dans la société.

2. On a à sa disposition une bibliothèque dont l'abonnement n'est que d'un cent par livre et par semaine, (seules les enfants de Marie peuvent en user).

3. Quand une Congréganiste sera malade elle aura soin de le faire connaître, on priera pour elle et ses plus proches compagnes se feront un devoir de la visiter pour la consoler.

4. Si une Congréganiste vient à mourir toutes les Enfants de Marie qui le pourront assisteront au service, et quatre d'entre elles, vêtues de blanc, l'accompagneront au cimetière.

5. Quand une Congréganiste quittera la paroisse ou qu'arrivée à l'âge de 16 ans, elle voudra rentrer dans la Congrégation de N.-D. de Lourdes, le directeur lui donnera un diplôme d'Enfant de Marie qui sera comme un certificat de bonne conduite.

6. C'est avec le concours des RR. des. Sœurs et le zèle des dignitaires que le Rév. Père Directeur s'efforcera de faire observer ce Règlement et de rendre la société prospère.

REV. PERE A. GARIN, O. M. I., Curé de l'Eglise St. Joseph.

The rules of the *"Société des Enfants de Marie"* (Society of the Children of Mary). The rules, approved and signed by Fr. Garin, were framed and placed in their meeting room at St. Joseph Church.

Congrégation de Notre-Dame-du Sacré-Coeur (Our Lady of the Sacred Heart Society), made up of the same members, and founded December 8, 1878, was exclusively religious in nature.

A short time later, Father Fournier modified the societies once again. He limited *La Société de l'Ange-Gardien* to boys from fourteen to sixteen years of age, who met every Sunday at three o'clock in the church basement, and followed the same exercises as those of the fourth Sunday. The children from seven to fourteen were grouped into *L'Association des Saints-Anges* (The Holy Angels Association). These younger ones had to attend parish religious instruction faithfully, and give a contribution of 25 cents per year.

All of this resulted in having the *Dames de Sainte-Anne* for married women, the *Demoiselles de Notre-Dame-de-Lourdes* and the *Enfants de Marie* for young women, and for the boys, the *Saints Anges* for ages seven to fourteen, and the *Anges Gardiens* for those from fourteen to sixteen as well as the *Congrégation du Sacré-Coeur* or *Association Catholique* for young men. All of these societies were well-established and hummed with successful activities. Father Fournier used every means available, and neglected nothing

The officers of the *"Congrégation des Demoiselles de Notre-Dame-de-Lourdes"* (The Congregation of the Young Ladies of Our Lady of Lourdes) in 1916 with their chaplain Fr. Charles Dénizot, O.M.I.

to ensure their success. Novenas, sermons, and prayers complemented the public soirées and leisure activities organized for the amusement of the people and the benefit of parish activities. All of these meetings, religious exercises, and dramatic presentations were held in the little church on Lee Street. It deserves a closer look.

10. "The most admirable of churches"

From the time of its purchase, Saint Joseph church became the religious and social center of the Canadian population. The first and second celebrations of the Feast of Saint John the Baptist were held in the church basement; all the parish societies met in that same hall; soirées and plays took place there, and new arrivals from Canada, seeking employment, met with owners and employers on the church steps after the Sunday Masses. Father Garin even used the church as a post office:

> In the early days of his stay in this city, French was practically unknown. Not a single employee at the post office spoke our language. Consequently, many letters never arrived at their destination. What did the devoted priest do about it? He struck an arrangement with the post office whereby all letters to the Canadians would be delivered to him. He held mail call in the church, with a hint of mischievousness in his voice when some of them anglicized their name. Thus did he render outstanding services to his parishioners.

However, this bustling hive, which Saint Joseph church had become, proved to be too small from the start. In 1868 there were 1200 Canadians in Lowell, but the flock kept growing, so that by April 1869, Father Garin had a wall torn down which separated the vestibule from the church itself. This added about 100 extra places. But even at that, he foresaw that before long he would have to add balconies. Thus, at the end of October of the same year, galleries were added at a cost of $1800, which now allowed the church to accommodate 900 persons. The parishioners raised $648 for this addition; the Oblate Fathers provided the rest.

From 1870 on, the emigrants were rushing to get into *les États,* the States. In Lowell, industry continued its prodigious development. The huge Lowell Hosiery Company had opened its doors in 1869. The population of the city grew to 41,000 people in 1870, and by 1873 the mills had installed 500,000 spindles. The parish census of 1872 registered 2,400 communicants and a total Canadian population of 3,700. On Sunday mornings there was a first Mass at 7:00, a children's Mass at 8:00, and a High Mass with sermon at 10:00. In the afternoon catechism classes for the children were held at 1:30, followed by Vespers at 2:30. Since the church's capacity was woefully insufficient, the pastor saw the need to expand the building itself, and so he eyed two small neighboring houses which could suit his purpose.

On April 11, 1872, Mr. Alden Richardson bought the land and the two houses next to the church from Benjamin Weaver for $2,795. The following

May 18th, Mr. Richardson resold the same property to Father Garin for $2,820. Whenever there was a delicate or difficult purchase to be made, for the Saint Joseph or the Immaculate Conception churches, Father often resorted to the services of someone he trusted, to act as a third party. The total cost, with additional expenses, came to $2,955. Added to the fourth payment of $1,744 on the original purchase of the church, this brought the total outlay of funds to $4,699. For these expenses, the parishioners raised $2,906, and the Oblate Community, as usual, made up the difference of $1,793.

After acquiring the land, the pastor selected another trusted friend, the well-known architect P.C. Keely, for help in drawing up the plans, just as he had done for Immaculate Conception church. Father Garin had just recently finished overseeing the construction of the basement of this church, which he had opened for worship in July of 1872. For the extension to Saint Joseph's, the pastor told everyone that he had no "architectural" aims for it, he simply wanted space and accommodation for those who came to Mass.

Nevertheless, Mr. Keely's plans demonstrated a great deal of imagination and good taste. On Monday, June 16, 1873, the demolition of the houses took place and construction began.

And so we find the devoted priest overseeing the construction of two churches at the same time – Immaculate Conception for the Irish and Saint Joseph for the Canadians. His experience along these lines was based on solid judgment and a great deal of common sense, in addition to the experience he had acquired in Montréal during the construction of Saint Pierre church, which he had supervised for a certain length of time. Often, in his eventful life, he would recount his builder's creed:

> When we have to build, we must build well. We will always regret it if we build badly. Good construction costs more, but we always end up being able to pay it . . . . We must not pare down the architect's plans. If we do, we will regret it. We must, however, control his plans, examine them, and have them examined before they are finalized. It doesn't cost anything to have to change some lines on paper.

Towards the end of October, the roof was put in place, a step towards the official opening. On the evenings of November 10 and 11, a Monday and Tuesday, the women and the mutual aid societies, along with the clergy, organized a huge fair at Huntington Hall for the benefit of the church. The cost of admission was 25 cents. The Canadian band played, the men's church choir sang, there were amusements, sweets, and a raffle was held. One of the prizes was a ton of coal. The event brought in a nice profit of $1,400. The new construction cost $3,685.40, towards which the parishioners raised $2,861. By

November 10, 1873, all the construction work had been completed. All that remained was the decoration of the interior and the installation of the new altar, purchased in Montréal. This final work would be finished shortly thereafter.

Since the church could not be extended lengthwise, because of Lee Street in front and Kirk Avenue in back, it was extended along the side by adding thirty-three feet. The church now had a square shape measuring eighty-three by eighty-three feet, completely transforming the interior. The altar, which previously had faced the Lee Street entrance, was now facing a new portal on an exterior gallery along the side. The church could, as a result, accommodate a grand total of 1,500 persons. This made it quite suitable, as the pastor noted in the annals: "The enlargement of the church is a real success. The debt contracted to obtain this objective is insignificant." Built of black granite from Dracut, framed by bricks and gray granite, the overall appearance of the addition harmonized well with the style of the old church. The basement of the church became a special chapel for the parish societies, while that of the extension served as a large hall for meetings.

The construction had been carried out by two contractors who were faithful to Father Garin: Mr. Patrick Corcoran was responsible for the masonry, and Mr. Pascal Harnois, for the carpentry and cabinet work. Father Napoléon Pelletier wrote as follows about these men as well as about the building efforts of the great founder:

> He had the following built: Immaculate Conception church and school; the basement of Sacred Heart; Saint Jean Baptiste school and church; the Brothers' school known as the *collège*; the convents of the sisters at Immaculate Conception and at Saint Joseph on Moody Street. For all of these constructions, except Saint Jean Baptiste church, he relied on the same architect – Mr. Keely, a Catholic from Brooklyn. He also used the same contractors, or rather the same superintendents – two trusted men, a Canadian, Pascal Harnois of Fayette Street, Lowell, and Patrick Corcoran from Immaculate. Both were paid five dollars per day and were responsible for all the construction. Mr. Harnois, though he had little education – he could barely read or count – was the more capable of the two and better understood the plans.

Five dollars per day, or $2,861 raised by an entire parish do not seem like very much today. But, if we consider the economic situation of that time, we can easily appreciate the great sacrifices that such an amount implied. Around 1880, rent for a family apartment was $8.00 per month. Used furniture for an entire family could be purchased for $22.00. A pound of pork cost 11 cents. During the busy season, a day laborer could earn $1.75 per day, and a little ten-year-old girl could earn $3.25 per week in the mills. If the tickets for a soirée were sold at 25 cents, think of the number of admission and raffle tickets that had to be sold in order to reach $1,400! Truly, these good workers gave to the parish without counting the cost. By 1878, they had paid the final installment for the purchase of the church, with the result that Bishop Williams transferred the title of ownership to the Oblate Fathers for the sum of $1.00.

At that particular time, the immigration movement had stabilized. Since there were no laws prohibiting the exploitation of child labor, a great many children began working in the mills at the age of ten or eleven. Thus, entire families of ten children could find work and the sum total of all the salaries gave the appearance of great prosperity. Labor strikes were not as frequent in Lowell as they were in Fall River – the other great manufacturing center in Massachusetts – and the immigrants continued to pour through the gates of the Spindle City. The ready availability of work, the steady salaries, and the relatively comfortable life style, compared to life on the farm, or in the lumber camps, distanced them once and for all from the land of their birth. There was no longer any question of returning to Canada with their savings. As Félix Albert wrote in his autobiography: "During those years I was beginning to forget my birthplace because I enjoyed my new country more and more." People even began to apply for naturalization. The Canadian population of Lowell soared to 11,000 in 1881, and once again it became necessary to consider enlarging the church.

Fortunately, Father Garin had seen far ahead during the construction of the addition. By 1873 he had completed only the first part of Mr. Keely's plans. He had not yet begun the other section that called for a sacristy and a grand sanctuary. But, in order to carry this to a successful conclusion, it would be necessary to purchase the remainder of the abutting land, and four more houses next to the church. This was easier said than done. Complications arose regarding titles and proprietors, the project took on the appearance of a Chinese puzzle. Transactions began in March of 1880. On the 10th, $9,000 was paid to Robert Dawson for a lot on Lee Street; on March 12th, $1,800 to Michael, Bridget and Sabina Kelley, for two lots on Kirk Avenue – which became the small alley behind the church—on July 5th, $3,150 to Hugh Campbell, for a lot on Lee Street; on July 24th, $25 to George W. Bedlow, for a tiny plot of land on Kirk Avenue; on July 27th, $2,444.20 to the heirs of Fisher Hildreth, for land on Kirk Avenue; and at the end of July, $50 to John McAlvin for a plot of land on Kirk Avenue.

The land and the four houses, two on Lee Street and two on Kirk Avenue, had cost a total of $17,000. In August, demolition began and in May of 1881 the final addition was finished and the new Saint Joseph church was now complete. The decent, honest Canadians had every right to be proud of it. The church building on Lee Street had reached its final dimensions: 83 feet wide by 150 long, thus becoming the largest church in the city, since it could easily seat 2,200 people at a time. The richly decorated sanctuary and elegant interior were admired by all those who entered it.

The beautiful sanctuary was surrounded by a communion rail of cherry wood which enclosed, at the left of the main altar, a side chapel dedicated to Our Lady of Lourdes, and on the right, a chapel honoring Saint Joseph. The wooden main altar was temporarily the same one that had been bought in Montréal in 1873. In April of 1884, that altar was almost completely destroyed by a fire ignited by a candle. It was replaced by a marble main altar which was used until the 1960's. The side altars were of sculptured marble and onyx. The only stained-glass windows were in the apse above the main altar: in the center, Saint Joseph and the Child Jesus and, on either side, Our Lady of

The new St. Joseph Church on Lee Street. On the right is the facade of the original church and on the left, the new addition.

The vast interior and sanctuary of the new St. Joseph Church shown at the beginning of the twentieth century decorated for Christmas.

The vestibule and choir loft of St. Joseph Church with the organ donated in 1887, shown at the begining of the twentieth century, decorated for Christmas.

Lourdes, gift of the Notre Dame de Lourdes Congregation; Saint Anne, donated by the Ladies of Saint Anne; a Guardian Angel, given by the Guardian Angel Society; and Saint John the Baptist. The choir loft could accommodate eighty singers and a great organ, but that would have to wait. In the meantime the original organ remained in service. The woodwork and the furniture were of cherry wood and ash. The interior decorating and painting had been entrusted to Philias David & Sons. The basement of the original church – which would later accommodate the Baron bookstore – had been furnished as a chapel for the parish societies and could accommodate 300 people, and the large church in the basement of the addition, where the old pews from the upper church had been placed, could comfortably seat about 1000 persons. For many years this lower church was used for the very early morning Masses, for religion classes, and for confessions. Until 1883, it also doubled as a theater for shows, such as one put on by the young men, in November 1881, which attracted 1000 spectators. This double usage provoked amusing incidents at times. One elderly lady parishioner wrote one day:

I remember having attended a presentation of *Ste-Germaine Cousin* played by the young ladies of the parish in the church basement. The good people, accustomed to respecting a holy place, signed themselves devoutly with holy water and genuflected as they entered. This provoked a great deal of laughter among the children.

The parish, with its profusion of activities, and proud of its beautiful church, went forward with preparations for its first grand manifestation, namely, the solemn dedication of the edifice, which took place on Sunday, May 22, 1881. The church was jam-packed from early morning; chairs had to be placed in the middle aisle, and there was even a crowd of people standing in the rear. The procession began at 9:30, with Archbishop Williams in the lead, surrounded by a large number of clergy – among them Father Millette of Nashua and Father Boucher from Lawrence. Upon exiting the church, the venerated prelate sprinkled the walls with holy water, before blessing the interior walls. The archbishop of Boston then presided from the episcopal throne while Bishop Fabre, of Montréal, assisted by Father Antoine, provincial of the Oblates, celebrated the Pontifical High Mass. The sermon was given by the master of ceremonies, Bishop Duhamel, of Ottawa. His chosen text was: "Solomon then held a solemn feast, and all Israel rejoiced with him." Miss Lizzie Finn played the organ and the men's choir, under the direction of Mr. Casaubon, performed the sixth mode Mass in B Major. The grandiose display of liturgical pomp, the lights, the decorations, the singing, everything contributed to etching an imperishable memory in the hearts of the faithful, especially the older ones who remembered the early days of 1868. In the afternoon, Father Antoine presided at the Vespers, and Bishop Fabre gave an address.

As a first religious demonstration, it was totally dazzling. Bishop Duhamel, at the conclusion of his morning homily, underlined the success of the Oblate and Franco-American enterprise of Lowell in these terms:

I often imagined an ideal church, ornamented with the best parts of all the known churches. I can now say that what I imagined has become a reality, for a church that is governed by such a learned and saintly archbishop, ministered to by such pious and devoted clergymen, and attended by so Christian a people, is this not the most admirable of churches?

The church now being complete, another undertaking needed to be tackled, as noted by Father James McGrath:

The parish now needs to have a school annexed to it, like at Immaculate Conception. We hope to realize that project some day, and then the Canadian colony of Lowell will have nothing to envy of others.

11. The First Franco-American School of the Archdiocese

As we have seen, catechism was taught to children on Sundays from the start. And then, as the religious societies were founded, they were grouped under numerous banners to foster in them the development of a religious frame of mind. Since there were no schools, Father Fournier and the other two curates, Fathers Aloïs Gladu and Louis Petit, increased the number of evening programs, meetings, sermons, and counsels. By 1881, Father Fournier had added two extra meetings per week – on Fridays and Saturdays – to the weekly meeting of the *Anges Gardiens*. On those evenings, the young men gathered, under the supervision of their chaplain, "for instruction and recreation" in the new halls of the *Association des Jeunes Gens Catholiques* at 53 Market Street. This group had as its chaplain the learned and well-read Father Aloïs Gladu, who had been ordained in 1870. He was active and devoted, and his noble character and great personal sanctity, as well as his zeal for the Canadian missions, not only in Lowell but throughout the diocese, set him apart. As an accomplished man of letters, he would later start two periodicals in Canada: *La Bannière de Marie* and *L'Ami du Foyer* and would become editor of the *Annales de Notre-Dame-du-Cap* published at the important Marian shrine at Cap-de-la-Madeleine, Québec.

The directors of each society had also distributed books, each group having its own small library. That of the Anges Gardiens contained over 300 books, while that of the *Association Catholique* received twenty newspapers, along with the best Catholic magazines from France, Canada, and the United States. While grouping the children and instructing them, the societies began to assert the principle of Bishop Laflèche of Trois-Rivières: "Language is the guardian of the faith." Already, in 1875, Father Gladu was giving French lessons in the church basement. And there was good reason for this. Protestant door to door evangelists, colporteurs, were spreading their doctrine that the Canadians, had to become anglicized and join the American Protestant institutions in order to destroy the "noxious Roman faith." In 1877, the French Congregational Church of Lowell was founded for this purpose.

However, the school problem had not been overlooked by the vigilant pastor. Father Garin knew that societies, meetings, and Catholic libraries would not suffice for very long as substitutes for the solid formation that a French Catholic school could provide. He thought of this for a long time, and was on the lookout for a favorable occasion to do something about it. In the meantime, Father Gladu continued with his French classes during the year 1875, and, in 1876, Father Garin started a night school which was attended by 800 children, both boys and girls.

In September 1880, Immaculate Conception school, built by Father Garin, opened its doors with a staff of six Grey Nuns of the Cross of Ottawa, four of whom were English-speaking and two French-speaking. Father Garin continued to dream of his French school. Father James McGrath, the pastor of Immaculate, who was also the superior of all the Lowell Oblates, invited the French-Canadian parents to send their children there, hoping to be able to put off setting up a school at Saint Joseph for the French, because the Oblate community was financially strapped at the time. Regardless, Father Garin never lost sight of his hope for a school and was preparing his plans. At the beginning of 1881, the superior, hardly sympathetic to the idea, began to suspect that Father Garin was secretly mulling something over, and preparing arguments to plead his cause. So, Father McGrath wrote a letter to the provincial containing an advance warning against the project. Yet, for whatever reasons, after the extension of St. Joseph church, Father McGrath accepted the idea. He agreed also that "one day" a Canadian school would be needed, "for then the Canadian colony of Lowell will have nothing to envy of others." This conversion of the superior – a victory of some import – the words "nothing to envy of others," and the year 1881, provide an insight into the factors which might have weighed in his decision.

The nationalistic spirit and collective pride of the Lowell Canadians had begun to awaken in 1873 when, on the feast of Saint John the Baptist in June, their city hosted a Convention of the French Canadians of Massachusetts. The huge success of this gathering, with its parade of 1500 persons, its delegates from all over the state, and its distinguished orators, brought the Canadians closer together. The occasion, by making it possible for them to get to know one another as a group, gave them a sense of what could be accomplished by acting collectively. Following this, and until 1879, Father Garin and the parish societies worked diligently to organize entertainments and parades. However, since the feast of Saint John the Baptist was gaining in importance, on May 3, 1879, Father Garin had selected representatives of the commercial and industrial class from within the societies and from the general population, to form a National Committee that would be "a powerful and united body" whose purpose would be to organize each year the annual celebration of the patronal feast. J. H. Guillet, a former pontifical Zouave, became its president, and Fathers Garin and Fournier were members. The immigrants determined to remain in the United States were slowly beginning the process of naturalization, and were becoming more interested in their milieu, and in the special role they could play in the American nation, their land of adoption.

As Auguste Jean, one of the first Canadian overseers, said at the time: "We are all seeking the same goal, that is to say the happiness and prosperity of our adopted country, and we can all work together for this without obliging anyone to renounce his memories or his affections." Throughout New England, French Canadians were organizing at the political level, and for the purpose of founding churches, convents, societies, and newspapers. The élite of Lowell, in July 1880, formed a literary and cultural society called: *Le Cercle Canadien.* Everything was moving along peacefully when a thunderbolt struck from Boston, at the beginning of 1881.

Colonel Carroll D. Wright, head of the Massachusetts Bureau of Statistics of Labor maintained in his *Twelfth Annual Report* that the French Canadians were the "Chinese of the Eastern States" and "a horde of industrial invaders" who care nothing for American institutions, indeed, a sordid and low people. The insult was applicable to all Franco-Americans, but those in Lowell were the first to react loudly to this outrage and insult! Under the impetus given by J. Henri Guillet and through his articles published in *L'Abeille,* a Lowell newspaper, which he founded in 1880, the entire parish became involved. Both religious as well as mutual benefit societies organized an out-and-out protest. Everyone demanded that justice be done; meetings upon meetings were held and petitions signed. The Lowell immigrants, in spite of their poverty, lack of formal education, and many injustices to which they had been subjected had, nevertheless, succeeded in building and paying for a beautiful church, forming societies, publishing newspapers, becoming merchants, and electing some of their own to public service. Samuel Marin had been elected to the Lowell Common Council in 1874 and re-elected in 1881, the first Franco-American to hold an elective office.

In 1881, Canadians numbered 11,000 in Lowell, in a total population of 60,000 people. Of this number, 232 had become naturalized, in spite of the very difficult requirements they faced, 134 were running their own commercial establishments or businesses, seven held positions in the municipal government, and six had risen to the important post of overseer in the mills. Hence, when Saint Joseph church was dedicated in May of 1881, it was not only a religious celebration for the parishioners, but also a public demonstration of pride in the success of this endeavor. The large public rally took place in June, on the feast of St. John the Baptist, sponsored by the National Committee. Lowell had never seen such a splendid display of ethnic accomplishment: the parade included 2000 marchers, floats, 150 conveyances, representatives of every trade and each business class, all passing in review before the mayor and the City Council. That evening, in accordance with the spirit of the day, the Oblate Fathers organized a grand celebration at Huntington Hall with patriotic living tableaux. The desired effect was produced. The American press lavished its praise upon these "industrious, religious and well-behaved" people from whom

One of the work rooms of the Lawrence Hosiery Company in 1870. By 1881, the "fancy work" section was staffed almost entirely by Franco-American women.

"come very fine citizens." If the celebration of 1873 had united the people more closely by making them aware of themselves as an ethnic group, the commemoration of 1881, and the results that followed, brought them into the spotlight of American public opinion. Now, as others began to appreciate them, they could take their rightful place in American society.

Colonel Wright, as a result of a storm of protests, in October 1881, met in Boston with a Franco-American delegation from the New England States and New York State. After hearing their testimonies, he agreed that he had been misinformed and promised to say so in his next report.

*   *   *

The "Chinese of the Eastern States" Affair had called attention to the numerical importance of the Canadians in Lowell. Furthermore, Father McGrath, seated in the sanctuary during Father Gladu's sermon at the dedication of the renovated Saint Joseph church, must certainly have taken to heart the speaker's eloquent account of "the providential Catholic mission" of the Canadian people on American soil. Father Gladu extolled the French Catholic pioneers, whose zeal "served to make us what we are, imprinting upon the national character a distinctive tendency, typical of the race to which we belong, elevating the character of the nation and fostering among us the great dedication which nourishes true patriotism. Having been faithful to this providential Catholic mission, which is a blessing for religion and honors the Canadian name, is what constitutes the greatness of our people." And "if we wish, on this alien soil, to draw the blessings of Heaven upon us, we will remain faithful to the traditions of our fathers."

After arriving for the celebration at the Fair Grounds by carriage with Father Garin, Father McGrath heard the editor of *L'Abeille,* L. E. Carufel affirm:

> What have educational institutions not done for the glory and greatness of the Canadian people? . . . Let us not forget that if we wish to preserve the precious heritage entrusted to us of traditions and our language, we must have educational institutions. With education we will maintain our language for, according to one of the great men of Canada, "language is, after religion, what unites the heart to the native land . . ." Yes, let us preserve our language and improve our knowledge of English. To attain this dual goal, which must constitute our strength and be a rallying point for us in the future, let us not neglect to give our children an education that is in accordance in every way with our religious and social principles . . . Let us always remain above all else French and Catholic: let us be that in ourselves and in our children . . .

The thinking of the day was clear. The providential Catholic mission, the traditions, the religion, and the language must be passed on to the children by the parents and by an institution – the French Catholic school – for, as was added that day, it must not be forgotten that "it is our priests who have our nationality under their protection, and who guide it always along the path of duty and virtue."

Father McGrath was now of the opinion that if the parishioners of Saint Joseph, so numerous and so devoted to their parish, wanted a school, they must have it—"one day." That day was not long in coming. In June of 1881, Father Garin made an official request to his superior for such a school to open immediately. He had already selected a site and he could see only advantages in the project. A property was available, and if it were purchased right away, a few classrooms could be ready as early as September. Father Garin was quick to act, but his superior, believing that he could see things other than advantages, objected to the idea. In his view, the plan seemed unachievable, for the mother general of the Grey Nuns herself had acknowledged that she did not have the nuns required. Father McGrath had won his case for the moment, but Father Garin did not give up for long. On November 23, 1881, he bought the former residence of Luther Sawyer at 189 Moody Street for $12,000. The sale included 15,000 feet of land surrounding a beautiful large house that he planned to remodel, for the time being, into classrooms that would be ready by September of 1882.

In the meantime, he announced in church on Sunday, December 4, that the following day, the city would be opening night classes in French at the

Common Street school for Canadian children. The director of these classes was Mr. Guillet who deserves the honor of having persuaded the city to establish these free and separate schools. His assistants were the Misses Catherine Gill and Emma Miller, daughter of Joseph Miller – who, shortly before, had become the first Canadian teacher in the Lowell school system – and Mrs. Desilets. They were expecting only about eighty children on the first night and they were astounded to welcome around 400. These night classes were an immense success, and later, after the opening of the parochial school, they directed their efforts also to adolescents and adults. So successful were they that in a year they employed as many as thirty French speaking instructors, and provided a much-needed service for a great many years.

On December 13, 1881, the council of the Oblate Fathers reconsidered all the aspects of the school question, including housing for the Grey Nuns. It was proposed to lodge all the sisters in one residence, Immaculate Conception convent. Father Garin found this proposal unworkable since this would force the nuns to travel from the convent in Belvidere to the school on Moody Street, morning and afternoon, in all kinds of weather. Besides, since there was no kitchen or refectory in the French school, the sisters would not be able to have a decent meal at noon. Why not provide these nuns with their own convent having a small garden? As for the school itself, all were agreed on the site, and the council was unanimously in favor of a partial opening in September 1882, reaching full capacity by September 1883. However, faced with the cost of such an undertaking, Father McGrath took fright. The school itself would come to about $35,000 which meant that, with the convent, the total sum of at least $40,000 would be needed. The Lowell community was still $45,000 in debt, hence their total commitment would amount to $85,000! To make matters worse, the parishioners had only donated $1,710 for the school, up to that time. The members of the council had reason to hesitate. The superior thus concluded, why not have a wooden school instead of a brick structure? Such a building would cost only $20,000 and would last from twenty-five to thirty years. Furthermore, didn't the city of Lowell, richer than the Oblates, already have several such schools?

Father McGrath's proposal was financially realistic, but it had one major flaw. Besides the fact that Father Garin did not like badly built buildings, a temporary wooden school would give the impression of wanting to maintain the Canadian population in a condition of inferiority, compared to the Immaculate Conception community. Making them seem to be second-class citizens would be an ill-considered mistake, for ethnic pride was no longer separate from parish life. At the Convention of the French Canadians of Massachusetts and Rhode Island, held in Lowell in October 1882, under the presidency of J. H. Guillet, all the talk was about schools and the clergy as being "the instruments of religious and ethnic salvation." *L'Abeille*, which on Thursday, December 1, 1881, became the first Franco-American daily newspaper in the United States, echoed these feelings and kept the population on the alert. According to Father Garin, the Oblates had come to Lowell first and foremost for the Canadian population, and with his intrepid courage and confidence in God, he did not budge an inch.

Indeed, the matter of inferiority was not merely an impression. At the end of 1881, the Massachusetts State Board of Health released its annual report which caused a sensation. Commenting on the deplorable living conditions in "Little Canada," and the inferiority of its schools compared to those in the better sections of the city, the report noted that in Lowell, ". . . there seems to be a difference in the school accommodations furnished poor children and those of better parentage. . . The prevailing idea seems to be that better accommodations would scarcely be appreciated." The report concluded:

> The reason given, that better school accommodations would be unappreciated, hardly seems to be a good and sufficient one; for it is certainly fair and reasonable to suppose, other things being equal, that children prefer to be cleanly, and out of the region of constant smells, and that where such can be obtained without trouble to themselves they would be apt to appreciate the luxury far more than those whose daily life is passed in better quarters. At all events, give them a chance.

Father Garin had finally won his case, and he began to raise funds using all his customary approaches. In April 1882, the priests organized a great bazaar, and launched a friendly competition between the two mutual aid societies – St. John the Baptist and St. Joseph – for a funeral banner made in France. The St. Joseph Union emerged victorious and presented the pastor with the sum of $545.00. On June 24th, an evening concert was held.

Father Garin also came up with an unusual idea. Bishop de Goësbriand of Burlington had made a trip to the Holy Land in 1879 and 1880. At Father Garin's request the bishop wrote up a brief account of his visits to Bethlehem and Nazareth, commenting on the life of Christ in these two places. He chose as the theme of his account, "Jesus Christ, the Incarnate Word, the Friend of Children." Father Garin had it printed and sold copies for the benefit of his school. What an admirable way of raising money, for, as the author stated at the end of his concluding paragraph: "Our Lord rewards in eternity the benefactors of youth, but will also punish in eternity those who have neglected to work for the sanctification of children."

In the meantime, the ground-breaking took place and construction began. Having obtained the bishop's authorization, Father Garin went to Ottawa in search of a religious community of women. He called on the mother general of the Grey Nuns of Ottawa. Their foundress, Mother Bruyère, had often had reason to be pleased with the kindness and tact of Father Garin toward her sisters in Plattsburgh as well as in Buffalo. For his part, he was profuse in his praise of the sisters at Immaculate Conception, who saw to the decoration of the altars of St. Joseph church on festive occasions, and how they had helped in preparing the religious pageants for the feast of St. John the Baptist in 1881. As a result, the discussions were so successful that, in 1882, an agreement was signed between the Oblates of St. Joseph parish in Lowell and the Grey Nuns of Ottawa. It was understood that: ". . . the schools would be parochial, and under the direction of the Reverend Father Superior or his delegate, and that the sisters would provide eight teachers capable of teaching English and French, that they would teach girls and boys, that the sisters would help out at Mass on Sundays and Holy Days, and that they would do their part in teaching catechism on Sundays to the public school children, and that it would be desirable for the students to learn sewing and singing." For their part, the Oblates would provide and maintain the school and an "appropriately furnished" convent, would look after the spiritual needs of the sisters, pay a salary of $200.00 per year for each teaching nun and $100.00 dollars for the lay sister, and finally that they would not allow boys over twelve years of age to attend the school.

In 1883, a large and beautiful four story granite and brick building, measuring 85 feet by 70, had already risen from the ground. The first three

St. Joseph Elementary School, *"Le Couvent St.-Joseph"* on Moody Street. In front is the convent of the Sisters and behind, the new granite and brick school.

Sister Plante, S.G.C., the first superior of the school.

floors were divided into four classrooms each, thus providing twelve spacious classrooms, well-furnished for that time. The fourth floor included a stage for theatrical productions, served as a parish hall, and contained storage space for all necessary accessories. The basement of the church would no longer have to do double duty. The total cost of the school and convent came to $50,000.

On May 3, 1883, the general administration of the nuns appointed Sister Plante, who was at the time the bursar at Ottawa General Hospital, as superior of the new foundation in Lowell. Once the Oblates alerted the sisters that all was ready to receive them, Sisters Plante and Marie-du-Saint-Sacrement left Ottawa by train for Lowell at nine o'clock on Saturday morning, October 27, to prepare the way for their companions. At nine o'clock in the evening, they arrived at the Lowell station and were taken to Immaculate Conception convent, where they were received with open arms. It is interesting to read what happened on the day following their arrival, as recorded by the chronicler of Saint Joseph convent. After a Sunday morning visit to the rectory:

> Our sisters then went to Saint Joseph church for High Mass. Reverend Father Garin announced their arrival to his parishioners, and told them how happy he was to know that their children would soon be under the care of the nuns. He also announced that the opening of classes would take place on November 12, and that the event would be preceded by a

solemn procession. "We will not take the small side streets, but walk along Merrimack, the main street. We are not ashamed to show ourselves to the Protestants, for we are not about to cause mischief. On the contrary, it will be the best thing we've ever done." And he added, ". . . if you don't see Father Garin on that day, you may pray to God for him, for it will be a sign that he is gravely ill."

That afternoon, Madame Doctor Vincelette and several young ladies went to Immaculate Conception convent to see "our Sisters" as all the Canadians call us. Their visit was most interesting. They made it clear how happy they were and we even recognized, in some of the young ladies, a strong attraction for religious life.

On October 29 (Monday) our good Sisters Plante and Marie-du-Saint-Sacrement came to St. Joseph convent, where they found the builders at work. They thought they should ask them to hurry, for it would be impossible to bring in the other sisters until all the work they had started was completed. They kept an eye on them while providing the building with the furniture and other articles necessary for the opening of the house . . .

On Thursday November 1 (All Saints Day) Reverend Father Garin asked from the pulpit for ladies to help us with the linen that we absolutely needed for the opening day of the house, that was approaching at a rapid pace. A great number of women showed up on the following Tuesday. Among them were Madame Dr. Vincelette, Mmes Duprez, (from Little Canada), Parent, Constantineau, Alexander, David, and many other ladies and young women whose names we do not know. These kind ladies came with several sewing machines, so that a great deal of work could be accomplished in a single half-day. Several of them offered sheets and pillow cases while categorically recommending not to wash them before returning them.

On November 7, Sisters Colombe-du-Précieux-Sang, St. Dosithée, St. Félix, and St. André arrived at one o'clock to take possession of their convent. It was the large three-story wooden house, located right in front of the school, and which had been purchased along with the land. On the next day, Mother Phelan arrived in Lowell to see herself to the installation of her daughters, and to offer them two other nuns: Sisters St. Pierre and Ryan, who was a postulant. During the week Sister Ste. Clothilde from Immaculate Conception convent joined the ranks at the new residence, bringing the personnel to nine sisters. The house chronicle provides us with the details of the happenings on Sunday, November 11:

Our dear Sisters Marie-du-St-Sacrement, St. Dosithée and St. Félix went to Saint Joseph church for High Mass, during which Reverend Father

Garin repeated his announcement regarding the procession he had been planning for so long. This good Father encouraged all his parishioners to bless the Lord for the favor they were receiving. "Ah yes, let us thank the Lord," he said, "for giving our Canadian children all the advantages that had heretofore been lacking to them: the good fortune of having Catholic schools and, even better, of having nuns who will teach them to practice their Christian virtues. And, as a proof of our gratitude to such a good God, we will sing a High Mass at eight o'clock tomorrow morning with as much solemnity as possible. Come, all of you, my brothers, with your dear children, come to witness the procession which will be organized as we shall indicate tomorrow morning."

Needless to say, all eyes were turned towards the sisters who were in attendance during these announcements. From early morning, these good people followed us, albeit with some difficulty because of the crowd along our way when we returned from the 7 o'clock Mass. The children, especially, encircled us, each with a personal word about the sisters. In the afternoon, as we returned from Vespers, we were once again surrounded by a large crowd of people when suddenly we heard the voice of a small child saying: "Look, the sister laughed." Many people had rushed to be near the convent in advance and had formed a row on each side in order to get a better look at us. Others followed us up to the door of our residence. We were barely inside the house when most of them came in with us. Each one expressed his or her joy and happiness, and then left. And that's how the day ended.

The great day having arrived, on Monday, November 12, the parish population made its way toward the church for the High Mass of the Holy Spirit. Father Candidus Lagier, nephew of Father Lucien Lagier, who had arrived in March, was the celebrant while the indefatigable Lizzie Finn played the organ and H. A. Racicot directed a choir of fifty singers. Following the Mass, a procession was formed which proceeded down Kirk, Merrimack, and Spaulding Streets. Let's listen once again to the chronicler:

As Reverend Father Garin had announced, there was a solemn celebration this morning at St. Joseph church. The singing at the High Mass was superb, and all the decorations in the church demonstrated that all the Canadians of Lowell were jubilant. After Mass, which we all attended, except for Sister Colombe-du-Précieux-Sang, the procession was organized in the following manner: Sisters Marie-du-St-Sacrement and St. Dosithée, 200 little girls, Srs. Clothilde and Ryan, 190 girls, Sisters Superior, St. Félix and St. Pierre, 400 boys followed by the young men's society, after whom

71

came the Reverend Fathers themselves. (Fathers McGrath, Garin, Napoléon Pelletier, C. Lagier, and Georges Marion).

The children were hardly out of the church when we heard shouts and unbelievable howls. The Protestants, who were on one side of the street, were insulting our Canadians who were answering insults with insults. We tried to appease them, but it was impossible to quiet those who were at some distance from us. When they arrived at Spaulding Street, the boys began bunching together and reached Moody Street throwing themselves one upon the other. Our very dear Reverend Mother and good Sister Thérèse-de-Jésus, who had come there during the Mass and were eagerly awaiting the procession, were astonished to see the children behaving in such a manner.

Having entered to the schoolhouse, it was only with difficulty that we were able to quiet them down, but as long as they saw the sisters, the poor children didn't dare say a word. We did not leave them alone for a single instant, for it would have been impossible to keep them silent during the blessing of the house. Once the parents and the children became a little more orderly, Reverend Father Garin spoke a few words to his people who were all very happy. We saw many tears flow from their eyes while this good Father was speaking to them.

The blessing of the house having taken place, parents began recommending their children, each one wanting to show us his or her boy or girl, which would have been very tiring for us if the good Fathers had not been there to exhort them over and over again to leave, in order to allow us to call a halt to all the shouting and jumping of the children. It was late morning before we were free, but we nevertheless had had time to re-establish order and encourage everyone to come back that afternoon.

Then, each teacher having given the signal for departure, the children rushed for the stairs, pushing and fighting one another, just as when they arrived. It goes without saying how gripped with fear we are at the sight of the very difficult task that we have to accomplish. However, we do not despair for, with God's help, we may perhaps succeed in disciplining them.

In truth, the sisters had a tough row to hoe, but mother general and her assistant, before their departure on November 17, offered their sympathy and promised to recommend them to the prayers of the community!

According to Father Mangin, the "American" population was greatly astonished by the procession and "were asking themselves if there were really that many Canadian children in the city of Lowell." From its perspective, the *Lowell Courier*, commenting upon these 400 boys and 390 girls taken out of the public schools, foresaw the closing of six elementary schools, three on Cabot Street, two on Race, and one in the attic of the Common Street school.

In fact, these schools now had very few students, but since the parochial school did not admit children under seven years of age, it was only necessary to close the one on Race Street, which was converted into a fire station.

Understandably, the sisters soon had the upper hand over the children, since it was imperative that they do so. The same sister chronicler added:

> This afternoon (Monday, November 19) we went to St. Joseph church with all our students so as to assign them the places they would occupy for Sunday Mass. All the people, who were standing on their doorsteps to see us go by, noticed the great change in the children. As a matter of fact, they were walking in line without shouting as they had on the first day.

The boys and the girls attended the same school, but were not in the same classes. One side of the school was reserved for the girls and the other for the boys. As to the courses, an attempt was made to follow, as much as possible, the same program as in the public schools, with Catechism and French added. Most of the classes were taught in French. The financial support of the school fell upon the parish. The children paid nothing.

By the month of November 1883, Father Georges Marion had been named chaplain of the nuns as well as director of the school. The sisters had begun religion classes on Sundays and the little boys made their musical debut by singing at the six o'clock Mass on Christmas morning. Everything became organized: novenas, retreats, the Month of Mary, processions on the Feast of the Immaculate Conception, singing in church and grand celebrations at Christmas. The sisters prepared their pupils for their First Communion as a true and unforgettable triumph of faith while enthusiastically seeing to it that the students entrusted to them became members of the Children of Mary and other parish societies. They also looked after the poor and visited the sick. The parishioners, in return, whose joy knew no bounds, established the custom of treating the sisters to a car ride and a picnic on September 1st each year.

Father Garin was legitimately proud of his school and his children, as he liked to call them. After the visit from the School Department in 1884, he expressed himself as follows that same year, at the great celebration in his honor:

> In conclusion, however, allow me to make a minor confession: I'm feeling very proud. You will say to me: "Why, Father Garin, and how come are you experiencing so much pride?" It is in seeing the total success of our Canadian schools. Not very long ago, I went to see the mayor of the city, the Honorable Mr. Donovan, to invite him, along with the School Committee,

to come visit our parochial school. He received me very well and promised to accede to my request. Thirteen days later, he showed up at the school, accompanied by those other gentlemen, who were received by the sisters with the customary urbanity for which they are known. They visited the whole building, from the basement to the beautiful and magnificent hall we have on the top floor and marveled at everything they saw. As they were leaving, one of the members of this committee couldn't help saying: "You are asking me, Sir, for my impressions? Very well then, I'll tell you: We have nothing better here ourselves." That is why, my good friends, I am proud of your magnificent parochial school.

12. Saint Joseph Residence "Saint André Church"

Following these events, the parish and its religious societies seemed imbued with renewed enthusiasm. The *Dames de Sainte-Anne* were receiving thirty and forty members at a time into their ranks, and when their chaplain, Father Gladu, left for Canada in March 1885, they numbered 800 women. Father Légaré, vicar-general for the diocese of Québec, presented a relic of Saint Anne to the parish, in September 1881 and, from that date, each year during the annual retreat to *la bonne Sainte-Anne* (good St. Anne), held in July, could be seen the touching spectacle of mothers approaching the communion rail with their sick children to venerate the relic. Several times the pastor and his faithful were able to intone hymns of thanksgiving for a healing obtained. In 1884, the society became affiliated with the Archconfraternity of Saint Anne in Rome and Father Pelletier, who had provided the *Enfants de Marie* (Children of Mary) with a 300-volume library, affiliated that society with the Roman Congregation of the *Prima Primaria* with all its indulgences. Father Fournier having done away with the societies of the Saints-Anges and the Sacré-Coeur, the young men passed directly from the society of the Anges-Gardiens to *L'Association des Jeunes Gens Catholiques*.

The charitable and social aspects of the *Dames de Sainte-Anne* found concrete means of expression. For example, in 1885, when the priest-director announced that a Mr. Touchette, of Middlesex Street wished to give his five children, aged 2 to 12, to whomever wanted them, within two days, five women and their families had adopted them while the society paid all the legal fees for the adoption. It was the great bazaars and recreational evenings prepared by the *Dames de Sainte-Anne* which paid the costs of the school while their generosity also contributed to the continuing embellishment of the church with statues, chandeliers, etc.

Since all the religious societies held an annual retreat and, in some years, the parish held a two-week retreat, Father Garin was not in favor, nor did he see the need for holding lengthy four-week missions as a preparation for Easter. According to him, these retreats did not amount to much and distressed the consciences of the faithful. As a result, none were held for many years, but in 1883 the opinion of the curates prevailed. Two religious came from Montréal to preach for four weeks during Lent, with each week devoted to a different category of persons: married women, single ladies, young men, and married men. It was an immense spiritual success, for the church could hardly hold all the attendees. Upon seeing this, the pastor said, "Missions are a good thing, so we shall now have one every year during Lent." He immediately wrote to Montréal to secure preachers for the following year. During the mission of 1885, five thousand communions were distributed. The financial success was as astonishing as the spiritual one. A supply of religious objects had been ordered which were sold after the religious services and, since there was not a single store in the city where these objects could be obtained, the sales were considerable, amounting to nearly $4,000 in all, bringing in a net profit of $1,800. This encouraged the *Dames de Sainte-Anne* to install a small shop in the basement of the church, which was open from time to time.

Because of this fine spirit, it is not surprising that when a defrocked French monk, the former Father Hyacinth – now the Reverend Charles Loyson – came to Lowell in November 1883, to preach in favor of his "National Catholic Church," not a single Canadian attended his lecture. In spite of Charles Chiniquy, who had returned to Lowell for a second time in October 1881, and who had declared that the ground of Lowell had shaken under his feet, so permeated was it with

Attorney Joseph Henri Guillet

the weight of Catholic error, there were very few defections among the French Canadians to the French Protestant Church. The large Catholic parochial family was prospering.

On Saturday, September 20, 1884, the fourteenth anniversary of the capture of Rome and the fall of the Pontifical States, the parish hosted a very unusual gathering. J. Henri Guillet, a former pontifical Zouave, had convened a convention in Lowell, to which had been invited all the former Zouaves living in the United States for the purpose of forming an association. Besides Mr. Guillet and Charles Bigonesse of Lowell, twelve veterans replied. On that Saturday afternoon, they founded *L'Union de Charette* in honor of General Baron de Charette, their former commander. On the next day, Sunday, at the High Mass an impressive procession took place, preceding a reception organized by the *Jeunes Gens Catholiques* in the school hall. A beautifully moving ceremony was held in the church where Father Garin, surrounded by the Zouaves in uniform, consecrated these men to the Sacred Heart while extolling the courage of these brave defenders of the Holy See. The same ceremony was repeated with even greater pomp and splendor in 1886 when General de Charette himself came to Lowell.

Up to that time, the parish had organized no ceremony to honor its dear pastor. The school children had celebrated him in November 1883, on the feast of Saint André, but the following year, on November 30, 1884, when the feast occurred on a Sunday, the entire parish insisted upon honoring Father Garin. This man, who hated compliments, had to endure a great many of them on that occasion. During this *family fête*, the parish societies, in their addresses, highlighted, with great delicacy of feeling, using a felicitous choice of words, all the good that Father Garin had accomplished. The evening celebration, at Huntington Hall, organized by a committee of twenty-five of the most distinguished men among the residents: names like Guillet, Parthenais, Bergeron, Dozois, Choquette, Jean, Gauthier, etc., was a veritable triumph. Célestin Lavigueur, a famous Québec composer who had settled in Lowell in 1881, and died there on December 11, 1885, composed, in Father Garin's honor, a grand cantata for orchestra and mixed voices. After the cantata, while the orchestra and the large choir of singers were still on stage, the pastor stood in front where he received more compliments, and then accepted for his church a gilded bronze sanctuary lamp, as well as a set of Stations of the Cross. The hall resounded at every moment with applause and cheers, but suddenly fell silent when it became Father Garin's turn to speak. As he would do each year for close to twenty years at least, on the third Sunday after Easter, the anniversary of the opening of the church, he recounted how the parish had been founded. It was an unforgettable chapter in his life. Then, with his words of appreciation, in which his sense of humor often broke through, his voice resonated as he made the following remarks:

I also accept, in my name and in the name of the Reverend Fathers, this magnificent cantata composed by good Mr. Lavigueur. Although we are not yet longtime acquaintances, he is, nonetheless, one of my friends, for our hearts have understood each other. But, if I accept the music, I do not in every case accept the words, which are too laudatory, and contain a few white lies. If I knew Mr. Lavigueur's confessor, I would enjoin him to inflict a good stiff penance on him. . .

After thanking everyone, he added:

My dear friends, it is now time to really set the record straight, or, as the Canadians put it, *"bien tirer nos comptes."* You state in your speeches that it is I who have created and founded everything in this parish. Well, when everything has been made clear, you will find that poor Father GARIN, after all, played but a very small part in all of this. The true founders of this parish are first of all you, my dear friends. Then there was my old friend Father LAGIER, who has now gone to heaven to receive the reward that he earned so well. There was also the superior, Father TORTEL, who left such good memories in this city, as he does everywhere he goes, and Father DÉDEBANT, who died recently after ten years of illness and who has also gone to heaven to claim the reward he well deserved. Lately, once again, some good Catholics of this city asked to have a Mass celebrated for the repose of his soul, and I thank them with all my heart. There is also Father GLADU, against whom I bear a slight grudge, because I suspect that he was the secret organizer of this celebration. He knows so easily how to convince everybody with his persuasive words. And Father PETIT who, in spite of his feeble health, was always so dedicated to the good of souls, and has left such good memories among us. There is Father LAGIER, a zealous missionary and the nephew of my old friend Father LAGIER who, like his uncle, is a devoted soldier in defense of religion and Holy Mother Church. There is good Father MARION, so gentle and affectionate, always ready, night and day, to fulfill his religious duties for the salvation of souls. There's Father FOURNIER who, though I name him last, is not the last one in my heart for you all know the dedication and affection he bears for your children, and how the young respond in kind. It is he who is the founder of that beautiful society the *Jeunes Gens Catholiques*, a model for the youth of this city, as well as of the *Société de l'Ange-Gardien* that is inculcating in the children principles of honor and religion. There is the Society of Notre-Dame-de-Lourdes, for our sweet young ladies. And, finally, there are all of you, Catholics of Lowell. And so, my dear friends, when we give each one his or her due, you can see that poor Father Garin's share is very small.

I also accept with joy, particularly these beautiful Stations of the Cross, which, as was stated in the address by the parish, will probably be arriving soon. I accept them, my dear friends, for many reasons. First of all, because they will be a magnificent ornament for our church, and will help to maintain the faith in our congregation. And secondly because, if in four years, two years, six months, two months, or only a few days, the Good Lord calls me to Himself, then the sight of these Stations, given in memory of my feast day, will inspire some good and pious *dame de Sainte-Anne*, some good and gentle child in the Society of Notre-Dame-de-Lourdes, some young men of *L'Association Catholique*, or some good Catholic of the parish to say perhaps: "That poor Father GARIN, who baptized us, married us, spoke to us very often in his sermons about the sufferings endured by the souls in purgatory, may be there now. Let's pray the Stations of the Cross for him." Some clever persons might say perhaps that these Stations were offered to me as symbols of the sufferings that I may have endured in this congregation. Ah, but no! The road to Calvary is strewn with brambles and thorns, while the road that I have followed here has been strewn only with roses and flowers. I can say from the bottom of my heart that the seventeen years that I have spent among you are the most beautiful of my life.

He ended his discourse by saying how proud he was of the parochial school. The echoes of these magnificent festivities traveled far. Ferdinand Gagnon, of Worcester, founder of the Franco-American press and the great defender of ethnic survival, praised the parishioners and their pastor in these terms:

The zeal of these good Oblate Fathers, among whom the venerable Father Garin is the trail-blazing guide, has been rewarded, since your example, dear compatriots of Lowell, has been the cornerstone for a great many Canadian Catholic houses of worship throughout all of New England.

But he also addressed somewhat of a reproach to the Lowell organizing committee:

But, must I tell you that in the midst of the elation I felt in reading your speeches, and the modest but so eloquent response of the good old priest, my heart felt a touch of bitterness. I was saddened to realize that the celebration committee had not invited representatives of all our other communities in New England to join with you on this occasion. They had a right to be there to profess to the old Oblate of Mary and to all his colleagues, the gratitude of all the immigrated Canadians, for all the numerous and so precious services rendered by the children of Bishop de Mazenod to our Canadian parishes.

Every year until Father Garin's death, the feast of St. André was the occasion for a grand celebration in the parochial schools with gifts, performances, speeches, and plays in honor of the venerable pastor. All of the curates, as well as the Oblates from Immaculate Conception parish and some Franco-American pastors from the region, were happy to attend these annual commemorations.

In spite of his efforts to muffle their praises, good Father Garin's parishioners knew what they owed him, and would not, for a long time to come, cease to thank him, for his foundations had not yet come to an end!

In 1868 the parish numbered 1,200 faithful, but by 1887, the numbers had reached 12,000. Along with the constant ongoing immigration, the population center was moving closer to the mills where, because of available land, the workers could settle and have easy accessibility to their workplace. In 1868, the vast tract of land on the other side of the Northern Canal, west of the Lawrence Mill, had been only a field, but the Locks and Canals Company quickly decided to divide this area into lots for prospective construction. When the Canadian school opened, the area including Salem, Merrimack, Moody, and James Streets, up to Ford was almost exclusively "American" – no Canadians lived there. The school children came mostly from Little Canada which had grown little by little on the other side of the Northern Canal, on Cheever, Aiken, Tucker, and Ward Streets.

In 1875, Samuel Marin had built the first "block" of tenements in Little Canada, on Aiken Street. Later E. H. Duprez followed his example, and in 1884, Félix Albert erected the first building between Ward and Perkins Streets, behind the little school on Cheever Street. The time for speculation had arrived, and with a vengeance. Everyone was building "blocks" of buildings in Little Canada, often without regard for the quality of the work or the health of the tenants. In 1881, it was found that only about half a dozen of the houses in Little Canada belonged to Canadians, while the rest, that is about four fifths of the houses and "blocks" were the property of American speculators. In an area of fewer than two acres, 1076 people were living in twenty-four buildings. However, the situation began to improve, for as soon as better times began to smile on them, the Canadians moved across the canal and purchased properties on the "American" side, where the houses were better built. By 1887, they were invading Austin, Cabot, Race, lower Merrimack and Moody Streets. Two-thirds of the parish lived in the eastern part of town, in this ever-expanding Little Canada.

The Oblate Fathers, who lived at Immaculate Conception rectory, suddenly found themselves a good mile away from their flock, a situation which was making their ministry increasingly difficult. As they had neither an automobile nor a buggy, they had to walk or take the tramway at all hours of the day. They began to speak of the need for a residence, and later a church, near Little Canada. However, Father Garin, who had founded and built Immaculate Conception, was hesitant; he favored large religious communities where the Rule could be observed to its fullest extent. But, on the other hand, he was aware of the communication problem becoming more acute between the French, the Canadian, and the Irish religious, who were not all bilingual. Moreover, it had also become imperative to separate the finances of the two parishes. Therefore, in the summer of 1887, the question of separating the religious of Saint Joseph from those of Immaculate Conception was submitted to the General Administration in Paris which pronounced itself against the idea. It was only after a great deal of insistence and much negotiation that Father Garin was able to obtain the required permission. In September, when Father McGrath, the first provincial of the American province since its inception in July of 1883, suggested that the time had come for the separation of the two groups, Father Garin immediately began to look for a residence.

He found a princely one at the corner of Austin and Merrimack Streets belonging to the lawyer and banker A. P. Bonney. It was surrounded by 20,000 feet of land, extending to Moody Street. Since the Congregational church had its eye on the property, Father Garin hastily resorted to a trusted friend. On September 30, William Anderson bought the Bonney property for $26,000, and on the same day transferred the title to the Oblates. In October, the priests who served Saint Joseph parish left the Immaculate Conception rectory to live in a provisional residence. On November 1st, Mr. Bonney left his home, and, after a few minor but necessary modifications to make it more suitable, the house was ready to receive a community. During the evening of November 17, 1887, the date of the official separation, the Oblate Fathers assigned to St. Joseph came to live at their rectory. Following the recitation of the Divine Office in the chapel for the first time, a private celebration was held. The parishioners wanted to express their joy at having their priests close to them, so the women provided the food for the meal, and the nuns contributed all their talents in preparing it. The atmosphere of rejoicing and relaxation, accompanied by a great many songs and witticisms, lasted until almost midnight.

Saint Joseph rectory at the time included the front of the present-day rectory with a two-story wooden extension at the rear for servants, the kitchen, and storage. The addition to the side, where the chapel is today, was smaller than it is now, and served as a library. That same week, the pastor went across Austin Street to hire Mrs. Marie Paquette as a housekeeper. The great-grandmother of Father Armand Morissette, she ran a boarding house there.

The new community was made up of Father Garin, as superior and pastor, and Fathers Fournier, C. Lagier, J. Pelletier, S. Lancelon, B. Gény, A. Gladu, and A. Marion. Saint Joseph parish, with its eight priests at the service of 12,000 faithful, was the largest in the city – Immaculate Conception parish had only five priests for 5,000 parishioners – and was continuing to grow. The vast church had now become cramped for space. Yet, with its superb marble altar topped by a statue of Saint Joseph; with its beautiful painting of the Sacred Heart appearing to Saint Margaret Mary which, in November 1884, had been placed on a panel above the side altar to the right, and the magnificent painting of the marriage of Saint Joseph, copied from Raphaël's masterpiece, placed soon after over the left side altar; with the beautiful statue of Notre-Dame-de-Lourdes, purchased at Lourdes by the provincial, Father McGrath, and installed later, after it had washed ashore on the coast of Nova Scotia following a shipwreck; with its chandeliers and decorations, this church inspired piety and devotion in ever-growing numbers of people. In November 1887, the *Dames de Sainte-Anne*, as a result of hosting evening gatherings and organizing lotteries, were able to install on a marble altar a monumental statue of Our Lady of Pity, the Pietà which, to this day, still attracts many faithful.

The installation of the great organ was to be the last improvement to the church for many years. The older organ was no longer sufficient for a church that could contain 3,000 people on religious holidays. On September 26, 1887, the older instrument was transported to the school hall, and set up there under the direction of Professor A. Mirault. The great organ with its 1900 pipes and 33 stops had been purchased at the cost of $6,500. The solemn blessing took place on November 6. Dr. Arthur Vincelette, who had become the organist in 1884, was at the organ, accompanied by an orchestra and a choir of seventy-five voices, directed by H. A. Racicot. The old temple resounded to the accents of Fauconnier's Mass of the Assumption. The provincial from Montréal, Father Célestin Augier and Father McGrath, the Lowell provincial, presided at this Concert-Mass and Father Augier, in his homily, spoke for everyone when he drew attention to this marvelous concert in which the angels, the human soul, and material nature blended into such a well-orchestrated and varied harmony.

Since the church could barely accommodate the throngs of worshipers, the large hall in the school was transformed into a chapel for 500 people, as a temporary measure. It served for parish devotions and, on Sundays, two Masses were said there. Its opening was held on Sunday, October 23, 1887, at a 10 o'clock solemn High Mass, celebrated by Father Stanislas Lancelon, newly arrived from France. A choir of students sang for the occasion.

Fathers Fournier and Pelletier provided services regularly, until the basement of St. Jean-Baptiste church was ready.

The opening of Saint Joseph rectory was the prelude to the eventual construction of another church, but before any serious thought could be given to this, the financial system then in use would have to be modified. Until 1887, the specific revenues of Saint Joseph's had not been very considerable. The income came mainly from the renting of church pews and nothing was collected for the pews at low Masses. The cost of the various constructions had been met through drives, special collections, bazaars, and funds collected by the societies. To all of this, were added the revenues of the religious, an effective and important element in this financial system. From the start of the foundation, the Oblate Fathers had taken no regular salary from the parish income, keeping only what was necessary for their personal expenses, which were quite minimal. The revenues that should have gone to them: salary, fees, Mass stipends, even the money earned by preaching retreats all over the area, were all left to the parish. The system was based upon the principle that since the churches belonged to the Oblate Fathers, it was up to them to provide for their upkeep. Father Garin loved to vaunt this system since it proved that the religious were very good to their people. Besides, Father Garin, who placed all his confidence in Divine Providence, did not worry about money matters. One day he said to Father Pelletier:

We must take the time, take the people as they are, and take the money when there is some. He added, however, we must especially never refuse money. I refused money once, and I have regretted it all my life. How? A man came to me to pay for his pew rental; since I was busy I said to him: "I know you well, come to see me at another time." He never came back. Little Father, never refuse money. When one has no head on his shoulders, he needs to have legs.

At the time of the separation of the Lowell Oblate community in two, the floating debt of both churches was $16,091. The Oblate Community had no debt since they had no revenue, a system which was to continue until 1898, when they began to retain a fixed salary. As a result, each of the two houses assumed one half of the debt. To this $8,045.50 was added the amount due for the purchase of the residence, along with the loans and obligations specific to the parish. Thus, the new foundation began with a debt of $33,390.07. Over and above this amount, the money required to maintain the school, the need to build another church, to buy the land, and expand the school, quickly brought everyone to the realization that pew rentals would have to be increased, and the entire financial support system would have to be modified.

Parents who sent their children to the school paid nothing, and a mere $10 was the honorarium for funerals. The priests succeeded in convincing the pastor that he risked not being able to pay his bills if he did not raise parish fees. Henceforth, a fee of 50 cents per month for each child would be charged for attending the school, insofar as the family could afford it. The pastor was finally persuaded to request $25 for a funeral with deacon and subdeacon, and later even $100 for a solemn service with catafalque, black draping of the church, etc. There were four such solemn funerals during the first year that this rule was established. As had been done at Immaculate Conception, stylish marriages continued to be held in the private chapel of the rectory. Lavish weddings, enhanced by a white silk carpet extending from the sanctuary to the sidewalk, etc., were held in the church. Then, in 1889, the annual tithe was established and paid around Christmas time. There was usually only one collection at Mass, and the Fathers themselves took it up. Pew rent was paid once a year. The income for 1887 was $25,769.89 and the expenses totaled $24,582.28. In 1888 the income increased to $34,227.70 while expenses added up to $62,855.61. The difference had to be made up by borrowing.

The chapel in the school did not suffice for very long because immigration was growing at a frenetic pace. In 1888, the population grew from 12,000 to 13,000 and Little Canada was overflowing with people. In sections of the city, the Canadians had become strong enough to present candidates for municipal elections. A Naturalization Club had been constituted in September of 1885. From the pulpit, Father Garin, in 1887, encouraged the parishioners to become American citizens. By way of example, Father Pelletier took the first steps toward citizenship. Father Gény admitted 315 young women into the *Enfants de Marie* society in 1888, and the *Dames de Sainte-Anne*, having over 1,100 members, saw the need to add a new administrative section, called *le quartier Sainte-Anne* for Little Canada.

Father Garin decided that the time had come to build his church. Hardly had he taken possession of the new rectory that he got down to work with the help of his curates. Realizing that there was not enough land behind the rectory to build a church that would face Moody Street, as he had proposed to do when the residence was purchased, he looked next door. On March 31, 1888, he bought the neighboring house and property from the Tremont and Suffolk Mills for $25,000, and in the spring of 1889 the land was cleared and, regretfully, the magnificent brick residence of Agent Shaw had to be torn down so that construction could begin as soon as possible. For his plans, the pastor turned to the excellent, but very slow architect, Mr. Keely, who delayed so much in presenting them that the pastor turned to the Boston architect, Patrick Ford. Nothing would be too beautiful or too grand for Father Garin. According to the architect's plans, the parishioners would have no cause to be envious of others, with their vast church in cut stone of pink and gray granite from Fletcher's Quarry in North Chelmsford.

Father Garin had the children sell stones, and they were scrupulous about carefully registering the name of each buyer. For their part, the *Dames de Sainte-Anne* and all the parish societies launched into the organization of bazaars. The great one of 1888, which lasted for five days, brought in $7,264 while the 1889 one brought in $12,200. Beyond their tangible lucrative value these bazaars provided a wonderful opportunity for recreation and amusement. For the parishioners, driven by a remarkable esprit de corps, these bazaars, requiring months of preparation, were always a high point in their daily lives. At the bazaar of 1889, people flocked to the kiosks where pictures of the Oblate Fathers, taken by the Loupret Studio, were being sold. Everyone wanted to acquire a portrait, either of Father Garin with his curates, or the picture of a particular priest. There were even some Yankees who paid a visit especially to purchase a picture of Father Garin or to taste some of the pastries for which the "French ladies" were now well-known.

The original intention was to name the new church in honor of Saint Jean Baptiste, patron of the French Canadians, but, little by little, some began to

Souvenir of the "Grand Bazaar" of 1889. At the top, center, Fr. Garin, surrounded by his curates.

ask themselves whether it should not be named St. André's church, in honor of the founder. The idea caught fire, and *L'Étoile*, a French newspaper founded in September of 1886 by the *Cercle Canadien*, promulgated this designation in its columns. However, even though this idea was appropriate, and enjoyed public approval, it did not receive the endorsement of religious authority, since Father McGrath, the provincial, wrote in 1889:

> The Provincial, in a semi-official way, had already given a name to the new church. Persons who are not members of the order, and who have nothing to say in the matter, have changed this name. We cannot accept that laypersons should determine our affairs, and that is why the new church will be dedicated to Saint Jean Baptiste.

The discussion was ended.

To the joy of having a church, was added at this time that of seeing one of their own sons ascend to the altar. On Sunday, June 24, 1888, the feast of Saint Jean Baptiste, Father Henri Constantineau sang his first Mass at Saint Joseph church as an ordained Oblate. This young man, son of Honoré Constantineau and Emilie Roy, born at Saint-Jean-d'Iberville in Québec, on April 29, 1861, had come to live in Lowell with his parents in 1865. He had been the founding president of both the *Anges Gardiens* Society and *L'Association des Jeunes Gens*. The benevolent influence of Father Fournier in these societies had taken root, and soon the young man had felt an increasingly compelling call to the religious life. He entered the Oblate novitiate in Lachine, near Montréal, and was ordained to the priesthood on May 26, 1888, at Archville, near Ottawa. On Sunday, July 5, Father Fournier and the *Jeunes Gens* organized a reception at the Association's hall on Middle Street, in honor of the first child from the parish to become an Oblate. On that occasion, Father Fournier spoke in moving terms of the young Oblate and the beginnings of the society.

Father Constantineau would bring honor to his origins as the first Franco-American Oblate, and the first Oblate from Saint Joseph parish, by his exemplary life and extraordinary talents. Lowell did not have the joy of keeping him as a curate in the parish, for the Congregation, recognizing his worth, had marked him out for its great undertakings. He was quite a remarkable man, endowed with exceptional intelligence and ability, especially for business matters, yet his simplicity and humility were exemplary. He was an excellent religious, who never missed either daily prayer or neglected the requirements of the Rule – an ideal which he maintained, in spite of his numerous occupations, throughout his entire life of seventy-nine years! He was a born orator, and bilingual, being

Fr. Henri Constantineau, O.M.I.

equally at ease in French as in English. Starting in 1888, he was in succession a professor, and later the secretary of the University of Ottawa whose rector he became in 1898. Sent to Texas to recover his health, he became the instrument of Divine Providence by founding there a new Oblate province in 1904. He became its founding provincial, a post which he held until 1912, when he was named bursar. He was not only an eminent educator, he was also responsible for the founding of many institutions, in addition to churches, rectories and convents: colleges, schools and houses of formation. At his death, in 1940, the Texas Province, which had hardly been able to provide for its own existence in 1904, had become one of the most prosperous and best organized in the entire Congregation.

On that same auspicious day of the reception for Father Constantineau, July 5, 1888, Father Garin had presented to Attorney Guillet – who that same year had become the first Franco-American lawyer in Lowell – a certificate from His Holiness Pope Leo XIII, granting him the rank of Commander in t he Order of St. Sylvester. This was in recognition of the services he had rendered to the Holy See as a Zouave, and for his unfailing support of Catholic education. At the ceremony which took place that afternoon in St. Patrick's church, Bishop Williams and Monsignor Keane, rector of Catholic University in Washington, invested him with the insignia of the order.

In the meantime, the construction of the crypt of Saint Jean Baptiste church was moving along so that by November 1889, the plastering of the interior could begin. With a joyful heart, the pastor announced that it would be dedicated on Sunday, February 2, 1890. On that day, amid a huge gathering of faithful and priests, Bishop Isidore Clut, an Oblate bishop in the Canadian Arctic, conducted the ceremonial of dedication and celebrated a Pontifical Mass. In the presence of the bishop, seated on his throne, the homilist, Father Célestin Augier, the Canadian provincial from Montréal, extolled the virtues of the indefatigable pastor. The next day, Bishop Clut consecrated the altar with the sacred chrism of the new alliance. Then Father Joseph Lavoie offered the first Mass on the new altar. From then on, Mass would be offered daily on that same altar until 1968. On the evening of the first Mass, the parishioners held a reception in honor of the missionary bishop. The basement of the new church, built at a cost of $32,000, was considered to be the most beautiful in the city. Measuring 170 by 70 feet, with its red ash paneling, twenty-six stained glass windows, rich ornaments, and sacred vessels – a gift of the Assistant General, Father Joseph Antoine – it excited everyone's admiration. But it was the white marble altar, fourteen feet long by five feet wide and which rose to a height of eighteen feet, that dominated the sanctuary. It was a masterpiece sculpted of white marble and onyx from Mexico.

Once the basement had been completed, the roof was placed over it until more money could be raised for the upper church. From then on, all baptisms, weddings, and funerals were held at Saint Jean Baptiste church, since it was so close to the rectory, but the two churches shared the religious societies, which continued to expand at a rapid pace.

In the fall of 1887, Father Charles Bournigalle had established the Third Order of St. Francis, for the men and women of the parish. Its "purpose is to communicate to all the faithful, without discrimination, the advantages of religious life and to spread the spirit of St. Francis everywhere." The celebrated French Curé of Ars, St. Jean Vianney maintained that, according to the counsels of Divine Wisdom the spreading of the Third Order of St. Francis was destined to bring about the salvation of civil and religious society. Its members, from the age of fourteen, after being examined by a Board of Discreets, and completing a novitiate, received a scapular, a waist cord, and a tunic. They were afterward expected to live according to the exercises of their Rule. In 1891 there were 330 Tertiaries in the parish, the majority of them women.

On December 14, 1890, Father Alphonse Dazé founded *L'Association de la Tempérance*. The members promised never to take strong drink, beer, or wine in the "saloons," and to abstain from all inebriating beverages except for a pressing health need, and then only within the confines of the family according to the strictest observance of Christian sobriety. If a member lapsed by getting drunk once, he had to spend six months of probation, observing total abstention from drink. In 1890, the society counted over 300 members, aged from fifteen to seventy. The Oblate Fathers had been waging war against alcoholic beverages for many years by distributing the black crosses of temperance. It seems that there had been a small temperance society around 1875, and, in November of 1881, Father Gladu, while preaching on total abstinence during a retreat, did not mince his words when he fulminated against the three kinds of liquor: that of the enraged, that of monkeys, and that of pigs! Father Garin, who rarely became involved in politics, intervened at City Hall on this matter to successfully prevent the granting of liquor licenses in Little Canada. As for other social needs, a group of men founded a mutual aid society on February 28, 1889, to protect its members in case of sickness or death. It was called the Saint André Corporation, in honor of Father Garin who was its chaplain.

At that time there also existed a Sewing Circle, organized by Father Fournier around 1892. It was composed of devoted married and single women who made clothes for poor children. This work increased in volume with the opening of the orphanage later on.

The parish now had two French churches in Lowell, and the pastor wrote to Father Antoine, in June of 1890, that Saint Jean-Baptiste church was well-attended. Nine hundred of the twelve hundred pew places were rented and, in spite of this, no change was seen in the numbers who attended Saint Joseph's which was always filled to capacity. Saint Jean-Baptiste rectory and church had, nonetheless, become the center of the Canadian population, and the immigrants, expanding into the neighboring districts, were displacing the Anglo-Saxons. By 1890, the population had increased again by another thousand, and the *Dames de Sainte-Anne* had to reorganize their sections once more. There were now eight sub-divisions: two for Little Canada, on each side of the Northern Canal up to Fletcher Street, and one each for Belvidere, Centralville, Pawtucketville, and the neighborhoods of Middlessex St., Saint Joseph's church, and Fletcher St. up to the Pawtucket Canal.

The eight priests who were serving the parish began to be overburdened and, foreseeing the need for more curates, in 1890, the pastor added to the rectory a brick annex three-stories high, at a cost of $18,000. The new community house, with a common room, a library, and a refectory, was able to accommodate twelve religious. Father Garin now realized that he had to limit his activities. He no longer presided at High Mass or took any sick calls during the night. He wrote: "I am no longer a young man." Nevertheless, he never missed singing a psalm and especially the Salve Regina with his magnificent voice at the Sunday afternoon Vesper service in Saint Joseph's. Though at seventy-one he was no longer young physically, Father Garin's heart and spirit had remained youthful. He always insisted on doing 100 times more than the others. Each year he had his personal contingent of converts from Protestantism. His zeal brought him into contact with all sorts of people and his heart burned with the desire to bring back to God all the lost sheep who had wandered from the fold. His confessional was always besieged by penitents, and every year he had his large share of baptisms and weddings. But Father Garin was not yet ready to lay down his trowel. He kept meditating on a major project that was close to his heart: a separate school for the boys of the parish – what was called in France a *petit collège*. It was not a college in the American sense, but a grammar school for boys.

13. Le Collège Saint-Joseph
The Apotheosis of Father Garin

From the very day of its opening, it was apparent that Saint Joseph school would quickly outgrow its space limitations. In September of 1884, despite the pleas of parents, all children under seven years of age had to be sent home by the nuns, since there was room for no more than 800 students. As a consequence of the influx of children in such numbers, two years later, the Oblate Fathers requested two additional nuns. In September 1887, the residents of Merrimack Street, who came out to watch the annual procession of the children marching to church for the Mass of the Holy Spirit, could count 1,300 children all walking in perfectly straight rows. One spectator was heard to remark: "I guess these children were made to order."

To resolve the situation, on August 13, 1887, Father Garin purchased a small house facing the convent, at the corner of Spaulding and Moody Streets, from John Callahan for $5,000 to make room for two more classes. The "little white school" housed about 250 of the smallest boys.

Saint Joseph school, due to the number of its students and its organization, had become one of the most important Catholic schools in the archdiocese. After the third plenary Council of Baltimore, held in 1884, which obliged Catholics to open parochial schools, insofar as this was possible, the question of Catholic schools became one of major importance, and visitors flocked to visit Saint Joseph's. When Bishop Williams visited it in 1885, he declared himself to be very pleased with the large number of students enrolled there. The same sentiments were echoed by the Xaverian Brothers of Lowell, the Sisters of the Good Shepherd from Lawrence, the Franco-American pastors of Lawrence and Haverhill, Massachusetts, and Nashua, New Hampshire, as well as Bishop de Goësbriand in 1889. When Bishop Vital Grandin, O.M.I. of Saint Albert, Alberta, in Canada, visited in April 1886, and Bishop Louis Laflèche of Trois-Rivières, in May, both bishops were entertained in the school hall with a grandiose reception which included plays and addresses presented by the nuns and students, in honor of their distinguished visitors.

However, although the parents were eager to have their children attend the parochial school, they would often pull them out at eleven or twelve years of age, sending them to work in the mills, or keeping them at home to help with the younger children not yet of school age. The Massachusetts Labor Laws stipulated that it was illegal to hire children between the ages of ten and fourteen for work in the mills if they had not attended school for at least twenty weeks during the year prior to their hiring, or if they could neither read nor write. Many of these children, who began working in the mills, had to attend night school after a ten-hour workday if they wanted eventually to earn their diploma.

Such a situation made it difficult for the sisters to organize the curriculum, and the majority of the students never went to high school. In order to counteract this situation and emphasize the importance of education, graduation exercises and school promotions were greatly enhanced. At such convocations, with the pastor presiding, and in the presence of all the parish priests and the parents, dozens of silver medals, certificates, and other prizes were distributed to the students, after the pastor had praised the value of a good education.

There were 1,300 students in 1887, but the following year, when the parents learned that they were expected to pay tuition for the first time, the number diminished by almost 300. Nevertheless, the nuns found themselves in need of hiring a lay teacher to help them, Miss Alma Alexander. In September 1890, enrollment rose to 1,092 children and in 1891 to 1,200. Once again, children had to be turned away for lack of space.

Mulling over this problem, Father Garin came to the realization that he would need to resort to a major overhaul in order to provide room for all the children. He liked to say that the children in the schools were the consolation of his old age, and so, in spite of attacks in the Protestant press, and the ill will of the civil authorities, he was ready to sacrifice everything for his schools.

It so happened that in March 1889, an organization of fanatic Protestants "The Committee of One Hundred" brought a bill before the Massachusetts Legislature aimed at bringing about the disappearance of parochial schools by transferring them to the complete control of municipal school committees. Father Garin urged Mr. Guillet, as a lawyer, to become a spokesperson in Boston for Lowell's Franco-American population, and defend their interests. Representative Hugo Dubuque of Fall River, along with Attorney Guillet, succeeded in blocking passage of the bill.

The pastor had finally concluded that another school was needed, serving the boys only. It would be a *petit collège*, an elementary school, under the direction of an order of teaching brothers. While visiting at St. Pierre church in Montréal in 1889, he heard the local superior, Father Drouet, praise the work of the Marist Brothers, also known as the Little Brothers of Mary, a community founded in France in 1817. He recommended them highly for Lowell. Since their arrival in Canada in 1885, the work of these brothers had begun its remarkable expansion. Father Garin immediately wrote to the Brother "Visitor," i.e. supervisor of studies, at St. Athanase, who responded that it was the right moment to present his request to their superior-general in France.

Upon his return to Lowell, Father Garin sent a dispatch to the superior-general of the Marist Brothers, outlining his plans. He had begun to negotiate with the owners of the Lawrence Mills to purchase the magnificent property located near Saint Jean- Baptiste church, whose brick buildings could easily be converted into schools. If the brothers accepted, classes could begin by September 1890. However, negotiations concerning the property dragged on, and when the assistant-general, Brother Stratonique, arrived in Lowell, in 1890, nothing had yet been decided. Finally, in February 1891, the entire property was offered for the then exorbitant sum of $60,000. Father Garin was willing to pay $40,000, but not one cent more. The only remaining choice was to build elsewhere. Later on, he was able to say that he was glad that the transaction had fallen through, since the buildings and property later became Aiken Street.

Brother Théophane, superior-general, accepted the new Lowell Foundation on January 11, 1890, and in April 1891, Father Garin purchased two lots and their houses on Merrimack St., almost facing the church. One was purchased from Daniel Gage for $11,000, and the other from a parishioner, Thalles P. Hall, for $9,000. The Gage residence was moved elsewhere and in September 1891 the laying of the stone foundation for the *collège* began. The other twenty-six-room wooden house – later the site of the parish hall – was converted to serve as a residence for the brothers. The construction work advanced according to plan, and in May 1892, Father Garin and Brother Théophane signed a first five-year contract between the parish and the Marist Brothers. This agreement, which was to be renewed every five years, was similar to the one with the sisters, but with a few interesting differences:

> The brothers may follow their own methods and rules in their teaching. They must care for the house furnishings, which will become theirs at the rate of one tenth each year. An annual salary of $250 per brother shall be paid each trimester and in advance. The brothers will not make any collection or money drive without authorization from the pastor.

The pastor wanted to have twelve brothers, but was only able to obtain eight for the opening in September 1892. He sent $80 per brother to France to pay for their passage from Lyons to Lowell, and he pushed the construction forward as quickly as he could.

For the time in which it was built, the *collège canadien*, as it was called, was a splendid edifice. It cost over $60,000, but everything was new and modern. It consisted of four stories, 104 feet by 54. The outside of the first floor was built of granite, and the other three had a brick exterior – Father Garin liked things that were solid. The ground floor contained the library and rooms for recreation, music, and art. The second and third floors contained six classrooms each, while the top floor housed two small classrooms and a large reunion hall

Brother Chryseuil, F.M.S., the first director of the *Collège St-Joseph*, the grammar school for boys.

with a stage for plays and parish get-togethers. This meant that there were now two parish halls, but in August 1897, when the hall in the sisters' school was divided into classrooms, the one in the *collège* became the parish hall.

On September 3rd, the superior of the brothers arrived from Iberville, in Québec. The first director was Brother Chryseuil, F.M.S. Born in the town of Belmont, in the French diocese of Lyons, in 1855, he had arrived in Iberville in 1886. He was to remain as principal until 1906. With the arrival of the seven founding brothers from France: Brothers Priscillianus, Paul-Marie, Pierre-Vincent, Joseph-Athanasius, Patrice, Jean-Honoré, and Primien, the community was complete for the time being. On September 12, although only six classrooms were ready, St. Joseph *collège* opened its doors. On the first day, 500 boys came to enroll. In October, another brother arrived to open one more class, and on March 15, 1893, Brother Théophane sent four more brothers from France who opened their classes on the 20th of that same month. Finally, in September 1893, three more brothers arrived and the *collège* reached its full complement with a community of sixteen Marist Brothers.

In 1892, 1,332 children were enrolled in the parochial schools, and 1,043 others from the parish were in the public schools. The new construction was intended to make room for them all. At the beginning of the school year, in September 1892, fourteen sisters and three lay teachers accepted more than

The new *Collège St-Joseph* grammar school for boys. Photograph taken after the brothers' residence was changed to Moody Street, and the area of the former residence turned into a school yard.

1,200 students, divided into seventeen classes, all girls except for two classes of small boys which they kept. At the collège fifteen brothers taught 1,000 boys divided into fourteen classes. It is worth noting that each class in both schools contained an average of seventy students! The parishioners had succeeded in accomplishing a herculean task – 2,200 students in their parochial schools – at the cost of enormous sacrifices. In 1894, the maintenance of both schools cost $10,129!

The curriculum at the *collège* left nothing to be desired. Brother Chryseuil based the program on the one taught in the public elementary schools. In the upper grades, however, he taught the same subject matter as at the public high school: advanced mathematics, chemistry, electricity, bookkeeping, etc. All the science courses were taught in English, but everything else was in French. After the regular classes, special courses in Latin and Greek were offered for those who were interested. Of course the French brothers brought with them many customs from their homeland. Discipline and conduct were modeled after the religious schools in France. Classical literature was emphasized, along with elocution and translation. There was daily homework, a lesson to be recited each day with the results kept in a grades book, and one composition per week. Everything was organized according to a timetable and a very meticulous system, accompanied by much bell-ringing, and it remained in use for more than thirty-five years.

In order to counteract the attraction of the mills, the brothers, like the sisters, did all they could to encourage education: they organized a small fund to reward the most deserving, they sent weekly reports to the parents, they held monthly sessions at which the names of the best students were called out and then placed on an honor roll, rewards were offered, etc., and an occasional holiday was awarded to the outstanding students. In June of 1894, the Lowell School Committee was quick to give full approval to this excellent institution, and in June 1897, Brother Théophane, visiting the United States, upon seeing the beautiful structure of the *collège* Saint Joseph, which had now become one of the largest Marist schools in North America, congratulated himself on having accepted Father Garin's offer. He may perhaps have remembered the letter of request from the pastor: "Reverend and dear Brother, it is a first-class establishment that I am offering you."

*   *   *

Seeing these well-built structures and magnificent schools rise from the ground, one after the other, products of an industrious but poor population and a devoted clergy, Americans considered Father Garin as something of a prodigy and a financial genius. One day, one of the greatest American financiers in the city, speaking to one of the leading parishioners, remarked:

"Do tell me, Sir, where does Father Garin find the money to have so many and such beautiful structures built?"

– "Well, Sir, this is most embarrassing! Father Garin is not in the habit of sharing the secret of financial affairs with his friends, but I do know that he makes quite a bit of money with pew rents, baptisms, funerals, and weddings."

– "Bah! Bah!" answered the financier, "I know what pew rents can bring in; and it would take quite a few baptisms and funerals to make half of the money that Father Garin has spent on property purchases and construction! Believe me, there is something else, and since you are his friend, ask him, will you, if he has stock on California."

The message having been duly transmitted, Father Garin answered with this quip:

Tell him I'm a Freemason (in French *FRANC-Maçon*) and that masonry sees to it that I have everything I need. Father Garin is a freemason of churches, schools and convents. With the Blessing of God it is that masonry which supports him and his brothers, and which especially supports a Canadian and Irish population of twenty-five to thirty thousand souls in leading a Christian life.

Along with all his activities, Father Garin was ever humble and smiling. He was always happy, nothing seemed to preoccupy him, always seeing the bright side of things, no matter what happened. He was loved by everyone, the esteem with which he was surrounded only grew, and the Americans who loved his broadmindedness often came to consult him regarding their dealings with the Canadians. The figure of Father Garin, with his old round hat, trudging through his parish had become dear to all. For instance, his religious concept of poverty had brought him to a kind of holy indifference. Not concerned for himself, he accepted whatever garments were handed down to him, and he wore them until they were threadbare, even beyond what was considered basically suitable. For many years, he had kept a light winter coat, which had been turned inside out, again and again, and dyed according to need. At the beginning of each winter, Americans who lived along Merrimack Street never missed a chance to watch from their windows to enjoy seeing the famous coat appear once again, and good-naturedly comment on the wearer.

For almost twenty-five years he had shepherded the Franco-Americans of Lowell. At the time of his arrival, they were a mere 1,200 poor immigrants, unorganized and without influence, but in 1892, they numbered over 18,000 and had two churches, two schools, newspapers, and societies. More than 225 of them were merchants, 200 others owned property, and three were members of the Municipal Government. Father Garin was truly the father of his people, devoted to their advancement and their well-being. For a quarter of a century, he had baptized and married them, had shared their joys and sorrows, and had led many of them to their eternal rest. With the approach of his 50th jubilee of religious life, in 1892, his Oblate colleagues and the parish population decided unanimously to offer him a spectacular testimonial of their affection and gratitude.

On an August evening in 1892, in a somewhat secluded room of the rectory, seven priests of the Saint Joseph community sat in a circle to discuss the celebration and draw up the first plans. All agreed that nothing should be overlooked to make the 50th jubilee celebration as grandiose as possible. The homilist was chosen. It was also decided that there should be a theatrical production, to be directed by Father Joseph Emard. Father Dioscoride Forget would see to the decoration of the church and the liturgy. Father Alphonse

Photograph of Fr. André Marie Garin, O.M.I. taken in 1889.

Dazé would be the coordinator of the celebration and Father Léon Lamothe would be in charge of writing the souvenir program. The parish societies were then encouraged to move forward. Upon hearing from their directors and chaplains, the societies became enthusiastic and the entire population was set in motion. Mr. Avila Bourbonnière, assistant assessor for the city, oversaw with his committee the organization of the civic aspects of the celebration.

After two months of preparation, the happy day was approaching. On Tuesday, November 1st, a contingent of Canadian and American Oblates entered the rectory for a private celebration. The provincial, Father McGrath, the pastors of Immaculate Conception and Sacred Heart in Lowell, the rector of the University of Ottawa, Father Tortel, and many other of Father Garin's old confreres gathered for the celebration. In all, some twenty Oblates, acting in unison, had come to show their high regard for this worthy old man. At that dinner, the provincial announced to his old friend that he had obtained an Apostolic Blessing from the Holy See for the jubilarian, a blessing which also extended a plenary indulgence to the parish. During that week, other Oblate Fathers continued to arrive: Father Lefebvre, provincial of Montréal, Fathers Petit and Fournier from Plattsburgh – the latter had been superior in Plattsburgh since September 1888 – Father Constantineau from Ottawa, Oblates from Buffalo and Québec, and some elderly white-bearded missionaries had come out of the woods from some of the most distant places in Canada.

When the great day arrived, on Sunday, November 6th, there was a great crush at the doors of old Saint Joseph's church. The church itself was resplendent in all its best finery, including greenery, flowers, and streamers. After the proclamation of the Gospel of the Mass, with a full orchestra providing the music, the venerable missionary, Father Moïse Lecomte from Montréal, ascended into the pulpit. He was an accomplished orator and he began his homily with a text from the Acts of the Apostles: *Pertransiit benefaciendo* – "He went about doing good." For one solid hour, the homilist, adding all the emotion and gestures of classical sacred oratory, described in great detail the life and accomplishments of the jubilarian. In summing up, he concluded:

Add new accomplishments to the first ones already so numerous! Complete those you have begun! Embellish with even more sparkling diamonds the rich crown that the Angels have already begun to fashion for you, so that we may one day write in letters of gold these words of Holy Writ: *Pertransiit benefaciendo* – Reverend Father André-Marie Garin, Oblate of Mary Immaculate, went about doing good. Amen.

The eloquence of the preacher, the music and singing, directed by Edouard Vincelette, editor of the Lowell *National*, the solemnity of the Mass, celebrated by four priests, etc., all of this produced a profound effect on the aithful, and handkerchiefs were often used. At the end of the Mass, the parishioners witnessed a ceremony that was new to them, and all the more impressive because of this. In the center of the sanctuary, before the altar, Father Garin, kneeling at the feet of his provincial, solemnly renewed, in a strong and vibrant voice, his vows as an Oblate, the same vows that he had pronounced fifty years before, those of poverty, chastity, obedience, and fidelity to the Congregation which his whole life had exemplified. Then his confreres advanced to kiss his Oblate cross, that cross which, in the words of Father McGrath, he had carried with him everywhere, and which in the past had been his consolation and his strength, and was today his crown and his glory. Just as on the day of his perpetual Oblation, this cross shone in its purest splendor.

The religious ceremony was all that could have been wished for, and it was now the people's turn to rejoice. While the Oblate Fathers were celebrating in the rectory, horses were harnessed, carriages were prepared and the procession with its cavalcades was assembling on the North Common. Crowds had already swarmed into Merrimack, Cabot, Salem, and Common Streets. Onlookers were at their doors, their windows, on porches and rooftops. At the appointed time, the lead contingent, made up of fifty riders in gold-braided uniforms, began the cortege, as their commander, Charles Laflamme, gave the signal to get under way by raising his sword. The grand procession included bands, horse-drawn carriages – the one in which the jubilarian rode was surrounded by an honor guard – and delegations from all of the Franco-American socictics. As they arrived at the collège where 200 boys awaited the hero of the day, they halted to hear them sing: *Que sur nos fronts, Enfants, la gaîté brille* (Children, may gaiety shine upon our brows), followed by *L'ami de la jeunesse* (The Friend of Youth). After a beautiful address, read by Wilfred Caisse, the procession resumed its march. As they paraded down Moody Street, they stopped at the girls' school, which was decorated with flowers and banners. At the sight of the jubilarian, all the little school girls lined up in neat rows two or three deep on both sides of the street and, waving small star-spangled flags began to sing the beautiful *Vivat pastor bonus*. After addresses read by Girardine Larochelle and Délia Cornellier, and the singing of *Chantons ce bon pasteur* (Let us Sing of this Good Pastor) the parade went on to Saint Joseph's church.

At 3:30, the church was filled to overflowing with 3,000 members of the parish societies for their reception. Accompanied by music from the orchestra, the delegates of every society read their addresses and presented their gifts, each in turn: *La Société Saint Jean Baptiste, L'Union Saint-Joseph, Les Dames de Sainte- Anne, Les Demoiselles de Notre Dame de Lourdes, Les Enfants de Marie, Les Anges Gardiens, Le Tiers-Ordre, La Corporation Saint André, L'Association Catholique, La Société de la Tempérance*, and a new one – *La Société du Règne de Jésus* (The Reign of Jesus Society), an association of prayer for little children. Father came forward and thanked each society individually, emphasizing its importance and the beneficial role played by each of the religious and mutual benefit societies in the parish. He did his best not to "monopolize" for himself alone all the praises contained in the addresses by turning back all the honors to the parishioners themselves. The afternoon concluded with Solemn Vespers accompanied by an orchestra and the choir in its entirety.

The last refrain in the songs of praise, which had soared since morning, took place in the evening at Huntington Hall. The entire city, through its elected officials, joined the Franco-Americans in publicly paying an homage of veneration and love to the happy jubilarian. The famous soirée that was the talk of the city for so many years had taken place before an audience of Franco-Americans, Yankees and Irish who had come from all corners of the city. After a dramatic presentation of *La Hache Ensanglantée!* (The Bloody Hatchet!), more tributes were read to the jubilarian, a message from the governor was presented, formal recitations were given, as well as a poem composed by Charles Daoust. The venerable pastor was deeply touched. He thanked his parishioners and friends for their kindness, all the while asserting that he did not deserve any praise. His triumph and the honors being bestowed upon him were rather, as he saw it, a manifestation to the glory of God:

As I said to you this morning, you have praised me a great deal and you have forgotten yourselves in the process.

For what could I have done without your generous participation? You have understood and you still understand that God needs churches and your dear children need schools. The glory that you attribute to me for the construction of these edifices, that are a tribute to your nationality, I give back to God, first of all, and then to you. I have been but a feeble instrument; and anyone could have done like me, and perhaps better.

Since this morning, brilliant manifestations have been given. You have engaged in an act of faith, religion, and patriotism. Other nationalities saw the lines of your unsurpassable procession file past and they said: "Now here are a people who remember their homeland and honor their forefathers." Protestants saw you go by and they said: "Here are persons who love their priests!" Let us hope that God for His part said, as He saw you crowding into his blessed temple: "Here are children who love Me, their Father, Who watches over them."

He was able to rest from all the testimonials during the night, but on Monday morning they all started afresh, for the nuns also wanted to do their part in honoring him. At 10 o'clock Father Garin and his retinue of Oblates entered the school hall where 1,200 children were waiting. The sisters had employed all their expertise in the preparation of this celebration and the children artistically and skillfully performed cantatas, delivered declamations and allegorical dialogues, and staged an operetta. As a tangible memento, they gave the pastor a handsome well-padded coat and an otter-skin cap. The good Father, who was so fond of "his schools, his children and his nuns," was deeply touched.

Delighted with this entertainment, the priests then went to the Provincial House, at Immaculate Conception rectory, where the local superior, Father Joyce, received them with open arms for a family celebration. Then, the new parish of Sacred Heart, wanting to do its share, the pastor, Father Guillard extended an invitation to everyone for Tuesday morning, where the jubilee festivities were brought to a close.

The religious and nationalistic societies had spared no sacrifice and had even zealously competed with one another to give this commemoration as much splendor as possible. As a concrete sign of their esteem they had presented a gift of $6,025 to Father Garin. In turn, this man, totally devoted, body and soul, to the service of God and His flock, deposited this sum in the construction fund, and in the spring of 1893, he returned to the task by beginning the building of the upper church of Saint Jean Baptiste. However, he had to lay down his trowel once more for, in the month of April, he was again honored by being named as a delegate, along with Father McGrath, to the General Chapter of the Congregation in France. This trip, his last, gave him the opportunity to visit his surviving relatives, and granted him the gentle joy of celebrating his golden jubilee in the parish of his birth.

No sooner had he left for overseas, than the parishioners began to plan for his return reception. Informed that he was due to arrive in New York on Monday, June 19, they delegated Father Joseph Emard – brother of Bishop Emard, the first bishop of Valleyfield, in Québec – Messrs. Hilaire Dozois, Philias David and Attorney Guillet to meet his steamship in New York. A squad of policemen accompanied them to form an honor guard at the dock. The good Father arrived at the Middlesex Street Depot at 8:10 in the evening. Thousands of people had swarmed into the station and adjacent grounds, and as soon as he appeared, three loud hurrahs resounded, as well as many acclamations. He mounted into a carriage with Father Antoine Amyot, who had directed the parish during his absence, and Attorney Guillet.

Hundreds of men carrying torches led the procession to the music of marching bands. Everywhere, the streets were packed with thousands of people who were waiting for a chance to greet their Father. All along the way, the houses and shops had been decorated with Chinese lanterns, hangings, flags, and portraits of the pastor, all of it together composing a fairy-tale sight. The *collège*, the brothers' residence, the girls' school, and the rectory were illuminated with Chinese lanterns, and, for the entire length of the route, Bengal lights lit up the scene as fireworks crackled in the sky. Everyone was happy to see *le bon père* once again, and the parishioners remarked to one another with an affectionate smile: "Our Father is still wearing his old hat."

Having arrived at Saint Joseph's church for the *Te Deum*, Attorney Guillet read an address of welcome and Father Garin recounted his voyage. After the ceremony, his friend, Dr. A. St. John Chambré, pastor of St. Anne's Episcopal church, who had attended the service of thanksgiving with his wife, approached, along with citizens of every nationality, to bid him welcome home.

When the procession finally arrived at the rectory, at ten in the evening, the approaches to it were overrun with well-wishers. The pastor stopped on the steps of the entrance and, removing his hat, he greeted his people before entering as everyone sang "Home Sweet Home."

This triumphant reception bestowed upon a humble Franco-American pastor in Lowell had impressed the Americans who could not praise him enough. The sister who was the chronicler at the convent expressed the feelings of the population when she wrote:

All of these demonstrations, I tell you, are evident proof of the respect and gratitude that the Canadians feel towards their worthy pastor, Reverend Father Garin. The newspapers tell us that Lowell has never witnessed such a grand, such a magnificent reception, even for men mentioned in history books . . . All of it was proof once again that the venerated pastor is not working for ungrateful hearts.

14. "Our Father is dead. He is gone."

The pleasant feelings experienced by the *curé* upon his return from France were tinged with sadness. Father McGrath had received a letter from the superior-general naming Father Avite Amyot as the superior of the Saint Joseph community, replacing Father Garin. So as not to dampen the triumph of his return, the provincial had withheld the letter until all the celebrations had come to an end. The old Oblate accepted his superior's decision in the finest spirit of religious submission. He wrote the following to his superior:

I kissed your letter with respect, and I went to see Father Amyot who was overwhelmed by his humility. I told him that he could count on my good will to assist him everywhere and at all times. That afternoon the new Provincial—Father Joseph Guillard, elected in June 1893 – came to install Father Amyot as superior of the Saint Joseph residence. We then had supper in an atmosphere of unconstrained conviviality.

This change in responsibilities, an indication that Father Garin's career was approaching its end, did not prevent him from putting all his energy into the pursuit of his favorite project, the completion of Saint Jean Baptiste church. Father Amyot was the superior of the community, but Father Garin remained the pastor and the two of them worked together as one.

Born on a farm, Father Antoine Avite Amyot, who was blessed with great goodness of heart, and whose biography will be detailed later in these pages, came from a large family. He had known Father Garin for many long years and the parishioners were accustomed to seeing Father Garin, architect's plans in hand, surveying the progress of his church while Father Amyot, having scaled the scaffolding, could be observed helping the workmen lift and put into place the heavy cut-granite blocks. As a matter of fact, Father Amyot was extraordinarily strong physically. People would remember for many years to come the time he climbed up onto the platform to defeat the famous strong man Louis Cyr during one of the latter's visits to Lowell.

The elderly pastor now began to depend more and more on the young parish bursar, Father Dioscoride Forget, for the supervision of the construction and the dealings with the contractors, etc. The younger priest had assisted him in directing the construction of the *collège* and the basement of Saint Jean Baptiste church. By the beginning of 1894, the walls of the upper church had risen to a height of twenty-six feet at a cost of $28,000.

During this time, at the beginning of 1894, the pastor of St. Patrick's parish announced that the only Catholic cemetery in the city was so full that henceforth only St. Patrick's parishioners would be buried there. Father Garin had long wanted to provide the parish with its own cemetery. He used this situation in March 1894, to purchase, on April 6, thirty-three and a half acres of a large farm in East Chelmsford from Mr. John Kennedy for $5,500. He entrusted the drawing up of the plans for the cemetery to the firm of Brooks, Jordan & Graves of Lowell. Mr. Pierre Tremblay was hired as the first caretake – a position which he would hold until his death in 1936 – and, on March 22, 1894, the first person was buried there, Mr. Alphonse Desormeau. The administration of Saint Joseph Cemetery was given to Fr. Forget.

During the summer, the church walls were completed and the roof of the upper church was put in place, all of this costing $50,000. The exterior alone of the church came to $110,000. By the end of September 1894, the work was finished in time for the visit of the superior-general of the Oblates, Very Reverend Father Louis Soullier. Since this was the first visit of an Oblate superior-general to Lowell, the parishioners displayed all the pomp they could muster for a welcome worthy of the "Father of the Fathers."

Following a reception at each of the two schools, on Sunday, December 23, a parade of bands, men on horseback, honor guards, and delegates from the societies escorted Father General to St. Joseph church. Charles Belanger, president of the Saint André Corporation, greeted the august visitor in the name of the parish. He praised the Congregation of "the Fathers who are the guardians of our faith and our nationality," and Father Garin "who for the past twenty-six years has been working for our happiness and the preservation of our faith." He then thanked the superior-general, without whom none of this would have been possible: "Yes, thank you, thank you for your fond concern! Thank you for your ministrations on our behalf! Thank you for the generation that is now emerging . . . thank you in the name of our dear children!" Father Soullier was deeply moved, thanked his "dear Canadians" from the bottom of his heart, and brought back to France incomparable memories of Lowell.

Father Garin, beginning to feel the inroads of ill health, pressed forward with the completion of his church. He concentrated all his activity and all his know-how on this project. Saint Jean Baptiste church was the costliest of his constructions; the work had required and still necessitated vast sums of money. In general, the parishioners, though devoid of wealth, were very proud of their beautiful church and were thus willing to impose heavy sacrifices on themselves, not only to finish the church, but also to maintain their clergy, their schools, and their societies. Men and women workers who toiled painfully in the mills, too often victims of epidemics, strikes, commercial recessions, nevertheless vied with one another to open their humble purses, with little regard for their own future. Everyone's mind was set on funding undertakings that depended on their generosity. Those who could not provide as much money as their hearts desired were unstinting in approaching others to do so, besides helping to organize bazaars and fairs. Following the example of their pastor, they made sacrifices for the new church and the parish.

Unfortunately, since 1893, the country had been going through a deep economic depression which, by 1894, was being harshly felt in the factories and mills of Lowell. Thousands of workers were out of work, many thousands of parishioners returned to Canada, and that June, even the public celebration of the feast of Saint Jean Baptiste was cancelled. The income from the pew rents of both Saint Joseph and Saint Jean Baptiste churches diminished by $4,000 from 1893 to 1894. Even so, Father Garin still hoped to finish his church and raise at least one of the two steeples. The stone for the steeples had been bought when the bank let it be known that it could no longer advance him the money, for the parish now had a total debt of nearly $200,000. Father was thunderstruck, but he placed all his confidence in God, and when asked about the future, he merely replied, "God will see to it."

However, the decrees of God are impenetrable and, almost immediately, the sickness that had been undermining his health for quite some time, laid him low. Shortly before the end of the year, he felt worn out by an overall weakness and the doctor forced him to rest. Since there was no immediate danger, a few friends came to visit him. Dr. Chambré, the Episcopalian minister from Saint Anne's, having come to see him, Father Garin, in his habitual humorous tone asked: "Well, Doctor, have you come to hear my confession?" "Very willingly, if that is necessary." "Not for the moment, I don't believe I'm in any danger yet, but if my condition worsens, I'll have you notified." But the moment had arrived when pleasantries were no longer in order, and on Saturday, December 29, 1894, Father Garin was taken to Saint John's Hospital. The Daughters of Saint Vincent de Paul had not forgotten the man who had offered Mass for them every morning for twenty or so years while he was living at Immaculate Conception rectory. These nuns provided, with unsparing delicacy, all the care at their disposal.

As soon as the news got around that the *bon père* was hospitalized, crowds came daily to inquire about his condition, leave small gifts, or try to see him. His physician, Dr. William Carolin, had given orders that allowed only visits from his old friends.

The patient, who had always been gentle and thoughtful of others, never complained, and maintained his smiling spirit. When Dr. Chambré came to see him in the hospital, Father Garin remarked with his light-hearted smile: "Aha, Doctor, you have come to hear my confession, eh?" During his sickness, his only hope was to live long enough to see the completion of his Saint Jean Baptiste church. In the end, this wish turned to regret, while day after day he waited patiently to rejoin his Master. Peace and joy reigned in his soul and many times he said to his confessor, Father Tortel: "I am happy. I'm going home."

On Thursday, February 14, he received the holy Viaticum and bade goodbye to his Oblate confreres. Friday, while the bells rang the Angelus, he whispered his last words to the nuns: "I'm going home." Seeing his weakness increase, yet without too much pain, Fathers Tortel and L. A Nolin sat at his bedside until Saturday morning. The provincial, Father Guillard, arrived early in the morning on that Saturday, February 16, and all three of them knelt, along with the nuns, around his bed. At 7:35, as the bells chimed for morning prayer, the very gentle Oblate kissed his cross and fell asleep peacefully in the arms of the Lord.

> *Il rêve doucement et son âme ravie*
> *En un hymne d'amour s'élève jusqu'aux cieux,*
> *Près du trône où l'attend le repos glorieux.*
>
> – Dr J.-H. Roy

> (He dreams softly and his delighted soul
> Rises up to heaven in a hymn of love,
> Near the throne where glorious rest awaits him.)

*　　　*　　　*

Even though the grievous news was not unexpected, the blow was no less sharp. On Saturday morning, at the funeral of Evariste Pagé, who had been president of the Saint Jean Baptiste Society, Father Amyot gave the first public announcement of Father Garin's death from the pulpit, before the members of the oldest Franco-American society in Lowell. The superior, shaken by his tears and in a voice trembling with emotion, eulogized the venerated founder. Immediately, all the newspapers in the city, Protestant as well as Catholic, dedicated long pages to the biography of the humble Oblate, singing the praises of this grand "gentleman," and as with one voice deemed his death an irreparable loss.

No one felt this loss, this pain, more deeply than the parishioners of Saint Joseph. The sad news threw the parish into an emotional turmoil, as on all sides people cried out: "Our Father is dead." *L'Etoile* expressed the feelings of everyone in this way:

> It is difficult for us to get used to the thought that this good Father is no longer with us, that we will never again see his face, illuminated by the goodness and serenity of a pure and noble soul. But, we have to face the fact: he is gone! It is a harsh blow which has befallen all the Canadians of

this city who loved and venerated him so much. Mourning will envelop us all just as if we had lost our own father.

At one o'clock in the afternoon on Saturday, the undertaker Joseph Albert, and his manager Amédée Archambault, brought the body to the rectory where the Oblates, the clergy, the men and women religious came to pray by the mortal remains. At the Sunday Masses, the saddened Fathers announced the details of the funeral to the parishioners, and special prayers were recited in all the churches of the city.

In the evening at seven o'clock, 700 parishioners, along with delegates from the various societies, gathered in the hall of the *collège*, to prepare the details of the funeral. The assembly, presided over by J. L. Chalifoux, decided on the order of the cortège, named police inspector Charles Laflamme as the grand marshal, and sent a delegation to ask the mill agents for permission to allow the Franco-Americans to attend the funeral. All the Franco-American businessmen were asked to close their shops out of respect.

The walls, windows, and columns of the lower Saint Jean Baptiste church were draped in black and on Sunday afternoon, the Fathers brought the mortal remains to the church and placed the casket on a catafalque before the altar. A huge gathering, assembled on Merrimack Street, was pressing to enter the church. The large flow of people continued unremittingly for as long as the body was there to be viewed. Police officers Breault and Provencher maintained order while fifteen to twenty thousand mourners, some say thirty thousand, filed past the casket, some leaving a flower, others shedding tears. The *Dames de Sainte-Anne* placed at the catafalque a spiritual bouquet of twenty-five High Masses, attendance at 2,300 Masses, 2,000 Communions, 2,000 Stations of the Cross, 3,000 Rosaries of the Blessed Mother, and 5,000 Rosaries of the Sacred Heart.

Since all who wanted to do so could not get into the church at the same time to attend the funeral, the provincial, Father Guillard, sang a Requiem Mass on Monday morning for women only at Saint Jean Baptiste church. Then, later in the forenoon, so that the children would also be able to pray for Father Garin who had loved them so much, Father Charles Paquette sang another Mass just for them. Early on Tuesday morning a throng assembled around Saint Jean Baptiste church in Moody, Pawtucket, and Merrimack Streets along the length of the funeral cortège while the French and American flags flew at half-staff at the girls' school. The mill agents allowed their employees to go, and entire departments of the Tremont and Suffolk Mills closed completely so that their workers could attend the funeral.

The whole population of the city was up and about to pay homage to the memory of the one who had served them for so long. A special train pulled into the station that very morning from Québec. Aboard it were many priests and friends of Father Garin. The provincial from Montréal, Father Joseph Lefebvre, who had known Father Garin for forty years, and had been his assistant at Immaculate Conception church for two years, had been invited to deliver the eulogy. He later described the difficulties he had encountered that morning upon reaching the station: "So, I came to this city. Having arrived at the Middlesex Station, I was unable to find a carriage to take me to the residence of our Fathers. When I inquired as to the reason, I was told: 'There is a very large funeral this morning, all the hacks are engaged'."

At nine-thirty the open casket was placed in the hearse, and, preceded by fifty cavalrymen and a band of thirty musicians, the long procession headed towards Saint Joseph church.

The nuns and women had worked all night to prepare the old church and when the column arrived, the open casket was placed on the catafalque in front of the sanctuary. Seeing the old pastor's features once again, in the middle of his church and his people, deepened the parishioners' sorrow at the thought that he would no longer be there among them. The packed church was reserved for the delegates of the societies, the nuns, religious brothers, and members of the municipal government. Mayor Courtney, his aldermen, the city councilors and many of the most eminent citizens were seated in the main aisle, along with a large delegation from Immaculate Conception. Archbishop Williams and his coadjutor, Bishop Brady, officiated before an assembled clergy of one hundred priests. The American provincial, Father Guillard, celebrated the Mass, with Father Amyot as the deacon, and diocesan priest, W. Alexander, as subdeacon.

A choir of one hundred voices, directed by A. N. Duval, with Edouard Vincelette as organist, performed the Perrault Mass. In his homily, given in French, the Canadian provincial, Father Lefebvre, underlined the fact that Father Garin would always live on in his works. Father O'Riordan, rector of the University of Ottawa, stressed the charitable and benevolent aspect of Father Garin's nature by declaring: "Father Garin was one of the best friends the Irish people had." He then asked his people never to forget him, and to pray for him.

At twelve-thirty, the cortège constituted itself once again, and the procession of thirteen hundred people and some forty carriages advanced down Merrimack, Central and Gorham Streets towards Saint Joseph's Cemetery. The crowds that lined the streets, swelled by thousands of people during the noon hour, were able to witness the love and the respect that this humble priest had inspired. For example, Edouard Courchesne, a founding member of the parish and of several societies, aged seventy-one and crippled, walked all the way from the church to the cemetery in East Chelmsford and back again, with the delegation of *L'Union Saint Joseph.*

According to the local press, the city of Lowell had rarely seen such a funeral. The *Lowell Morning Star* commented: "It is certainly encouraging, in these days especially, that for once, respect for a consecrated life, so fruitful in results, is stronger, broader, deeper than any feeling of sectarianism."

The pastor of Immaculate Conception church had sung a Solemn High Mass and a delegation of men had attended the funeral, but the parish wanted to do more. On their own initiative, they undertook to organize a memorial service encompassing everyone, regardless of nationality or religious belief. So, on Sunday, March 10, at three in the afternoon, hundreds of people jostled against each other at the doors of Huntington Hall, hoping to find a seat. Irishmen, Canadians, Americans, Catholics and Protestants, mill workers and bank president, all attended this unprecedented memorial service. The Immaculate Conception choir, along with the Rossini choir, sang a sacred cantata with orchestral accompaniment in the presence of the municipal government and representatives of the governor. A letter from the governor was read, and then Father Dacey, along with Philip Farley, a distinguished lawyer, pronounced masterful eulogies.

If all of Lowell was in deep mourning, other localities also felt deeply bereft. For example, in Billerica, the pastor of St. André, Father Pierre Gagnon, sang a special Mass. In Plattsburgh, New York, the parishioners of St. Pierre's met in a large assembly with their pastor, Father Fournier, to formulate expressions of condolences and organize a solemn service, and the elderly Franco-Americans of Nashua, New Hampshire, although they had their beautiful church of St. Louis de Gonzague, gathered in the same Protestant church where Father Garin had brought them together for the first time in 1869.

Praise for the gentle and good Oblate came from all sides, sometimes for his accomplishments, sometimes for his charity, but the finest eulogy came from the most unexpected quarter, the *Lookout*, a journal published in the interests of the Congregational Church:

> Whatever may be your thoughts regarding the religious beliefs of Reverend Father Garin, we cannot help but admire a life that engendered so much love and deep respect. This life, which has served as an example to so many people and has been a subject of admiration, must have been as sincere as the regret caused by his death. Fear was not the motive for such a striking display of friendship. Love alone can inspire such sorrow, just as only love could move an entire population to celebrate as it did his golden jubilee of religious life, and his return from Europe. And even the staunchest Protestant, without compromising his principles, can attest to his respect for a man who was so loved.

110

15. "Do not forget me."

The reason parishioners loved their *bon père* was that he had given himself over entirely, and without reservation, to the love of God and his neighbor. In return, he had asked but one thing for himself: "Do not forget me. Pray for me, my children, pray for your elderly Father."

Father Garin had nothing to fear. He would not be forgotten, for his people retained a special affection for him in their hearts and prayers. They all said to one another: "He is no longer here, but let us never forget him." After his death, memorial cards were distributed with the last photograph of Father Garin, taken in Paris, during his last trip there. As a more tangible souvenir, Father Forget had engaged the services of J. Fontaine, an artistic photographer, to make hundreds of photographs to be sold at the rectory. The large downtown shop, G. C. Prince, advertised the sale of portraits of all sizes, in the local papers. Nevertheless, the people of Lowell wanted something more substantial to perpetuate his memory. The idea of erecting a bronze statue to immortalize the "good father" arose almost spontaneously. Father Lefebvre had said at the funeral:

A LA MÉMOIRE
DU
REV. PÈRE

ANDRE MARIE GARIN,
O. M. I.,

Né à Vienne, France, le 7 Mai, 1822.

Ordonné à Montréal, le 27 Avril, 1845.

Décédé à Lowell, Mass.,
le 16 Février, 1895.

TO THE MEMORY

of Father André Marie Garin, O. M. I., who died February 16, 1895, at the age of 73; founder of the French Canadian parish of Lowell, whose first Pastor he was during 27 years.

"The just shall be in everlasting remembrance." Ps. cxi, 7.

"He hath raised for himself an indestructible monument in the hearts of his parishioners."
--From Fr. Garin's Funeral Oration.

PRAYER FOR THE SOULS DEPARTED.

Eternal Father, unto thee I offer the blood, the passion and the death of our Lord Jesus Christ, the sorrows of the Blessed Virgin, and those of St. Joseph, for the remission of my sins, the deliverance of the souls in purgatory, for the prosperity of Holy Mother Church, and the conversion of sinners. (100 days' indulgence).

In holiness, O Lord, he hath spent his life and finished his course; grant now unto him the heavenly joys and eternal rest.

R. I. P.

Memorial cards for Fr. Garin. On the left, with his last photograph, taken in Paris, is the card in French, and on the right, the card in English with an earlier photograph.

Fr. Dioscoride Forget, O.M.I.

His great works would deserve a monument in his honor. True, he already has a monument, the most precious of all monuments, in the affection and admiration of his fellow citizens of all religious persuasions, and all national origins, as well as the gratitude of all who were the object of his zeal and his uncommon dedication. He will also have this monument in the pages of history that will show him to coming generations as having been a man of genius, forgetful of himself, who lived in poverty so as to occupy himself fully with the well-being of his fellow men and women. Today, let us erect another monument to him, a monument of stones whose summit will pierce through the clouds carrying a voice of supplication to the feet of the Eternal One.

On the following day, the *Lowell Morning Star* commented:

The Star ventures to express the hope that measures will be taken immediately to start a popular subscription for the erection of a statue to be placed near St. Jean Baptiste church and which may forever preserve the lineaments of the features which have become so dear to many thousands of people . . . . Such a monument should receive the sympathy and the substantial support of every citizen whose soul is broad enough to comprehend the elements of true greatness.

On Wednesday, February 20, at a meeting of *L'Union Saint Joseph* all the talk was about a monument, a bronze statue. On April 1, at the suggestion of the *Société Saint Jean Baptiste* a large assembly of parishioners gathered at the collège for the purpose of organizing and selecting a committee to look into the best way of going about elevating such a monument. A general committee, made up of delegates of the various societies, undertook the direction of this campaign, and on Sunday, May 5, a grand musical evening was presented at Huntington Hall as a fund-raiser for the monument.

However, in spite of these auspicious beginnings, fund-raising activities for the monument slowed because the parish had other priorities. The pastor explained that before thinking of erecting a monument, other matters had to be considered: improving parish finances and finishing Saint Jean Baptiste church, which was Father Garin's final undertaking.

The pastor's mantle had passed to the shoulders of the bursar, Father Dioscoride Napoléon Forget. He was the natural choice for pastor, since he was well-known by the parishioners for his charity, and for having been Father Garin's right-hand man during the constructions. According to the nuns:

> His great heart, his charity towards the poor, and his warm response to all who turned to him for help made everyone consider him as a friend, a protector, and a brother. He had only to express a wish for everyone to rush to meet it because his zeal was well-known and everyone was happy to respond.

As an example of this zeal, Father Forget had noticed that in spite of the multiplicity of parish societies and mutual support associations, no such benefit association existed for women. So, on June 19, 1895, he founded *L'Association de Notre Dame de Bon Secours* for them. After only five months, the society had enrolled 258 members and had $1,200 in the bank.

Dioscoride Forget was born at St. Janvier, Terrebonne County, Québec, on November 24, 1855, the son of Jean-Marie Forget and Tarsile Nadon. They were good, honorable farmers and the parents of seventeen children. At thirteen years of age, Dioscoride entered Sainte Thérèse Classical College where he soon discovered his vocation to become an Oblate. He entered the Congregation's novitiate and was ordained to the priesthood at the University of Ottawa on June 11, 1881. He taught French for ten years at the university, after which, in August of 1891, his superiors had sent him to Saint Joseph church in Lowell.

The pastor, Father Forget, the superior, Father Amyot, as well as the curates, Fathers Athanase Marion, Pierre Féat, Léon Lamothe, Charles A. Paquette, Louis A. Nolin and Joseph Sirois redoubled their efforts and worked as one to finish Father Garin's final endeavor. They all knew how much the construction of Saint Jean Baptiste had been on the mind of the old patriarch during his final days, and the special place it had held in his heart. The parish

Oblates were deeply attached to the memory of their beloved spiritual father. No religious could ever have wanted a superior who was more gentle or more just than he. In community, Father Garin had been goodness personified, and the comfort of the others. Though he was no longer present, his spirit and his example were still very much alive, and they wanted to remain faithful to these at all costs.

Immigration was then on the increase, Canadians were arriving by the trainload. The pastor and his assistants organized contests, raffles, soirées, and plays so that they managed to raise enough money to resume construction on the church. In July, the exterior was completed and work could now begin on the interior.

A partial census in August revealed that the parish was made up of at least 18,043 persons, of which 13,717 lived in Little Canada. Thus the church had to be finished as soon as possible.

In August also, Father Forget began planning a three-day bazaar which included a "huge oyster party," to take place at the beginning of November. The high point of the bazaar was to be a great fund-raising contest offering as a prize the gold-knobbed cane that had been presented to Father Garin at his golden jubilee. The affair opened on Wednesday, November 13, 1895, in Huntington Hall. It was an immense success. The crowds flocked to the flower, candy, and fruit booths; others admired the tableaux vivants shows, and young Canadian ladies had no trouble selling their tickets. On Friday evening, after an operetta and a play, the contest winners were announced. Charles H. Boisvert, who raised $1,210 for the event, won the cane. This same Charles Boisvert and his brother Moïse had served as altar boys for the first Mass in Saint Joseph church. So much money was raised by this fête for the construction fund that part of it was set aside for the poor.

In September, plastering had begun on the interior of the church, and thereafter a contract had been signed for the gas system. With the church nearing completion, Father Forget announced on November 24th that contributions should be solicited immediately if the monument to Father Garin was to be completed in time for the benediction of the cemetery by the bishop on May 30, 1896, since it was proposed to place the monument on his tomb.

That same week at a meeting of the general committee, composed of delegates from all the parishes of the city, all the Franco-American societies, as well as citizens of American and Irish descent, it was decided to place the whole matter in the hands of an executive group of five, who were given total power. Atty. J. H. Guillet was named president of this executive committee, Atty. Philip Farley, secretary, Mr. Hilaire Dozois, treasurer, while Charles L. Knapp and Father Forget completed the group.

The executive committee went to work without delay. On December 29, at a meeting that was open to all of Lowell's population, subscription lists were distributed. Father Forget announced that $7,000 to $8,000 would be needed. Immediately, contributions began arriving from everywhere. Father Joyce, the pastor of Immaculate Conception, sent in the proceeds of a special collection in his church; on the lists of contributors could be found the names of some of the most important American men in the city along with their substantial contributions: the Pratts, Pollards, Hoods, Churches, etc. Alongside them were the names of the humblest Franco-American, and Irish millhands, with their modest donations, the result of so much fatiguing labor. At first, the provincial, Father Guillard, was opposed to the idea of a monument, thinking that it was not appropriate for a religious, but when he became aware that the citizens of all nationalities were vigorously desirous of such a memorial, he accepted the idea and entered into the spirit of the campaign.

At the end of one month and a half, enough money had been raised to begin asking artists for estimates. A meeting was arranged at the rectory for February 21, 1896 to allow them to present their projects. Louis Philippe Hébert, a celebrated sculptor from Québec, who proposed creating a bronze statue of heroic proportions, was selected. He had sculpted many works for the Oblates in Canada. A former Pontifical Zouave, he had been the comrade in arms of Attorney Guillet.

Meanwhile, money continued to flow in, and the question of where to place the monument had to be settled. Many wanted it to be installed on the tomb of Father Garin at the cemetery, but others, especially the Americans, thought the statue should be located where it could be seen by the general public. After all, they argued, a bronze statue intended to immortalize the figure of this remarkable man, who had done so much for Lowell and its citizens, shouldn't be hidden at the back of a cemetery. Such a monument belonged in a public place, among the people that he loved so much. It had to be where everyone could see it, on Merrimack Street, close to his church and near his faithful parishioners and religious confreres. That settled the question.

On Sunday May 10, Father Forget, Atty. Guillet, and Mr. Knapp, were called to Montréal by sculptor Hébert, to see his final model. They were so moved by its resemblance to their deceased friend that the three of them accepted it on the spot. Hébert sent the plaster model to the Henry-Bonnard Bronze Co. of New York for the casting. On their return to Lowell the committee of three spread the good news that the sculpture had been accepted. On June 10, a plaster reproduction, prepared in natural colors by Mr. Hébert arrived. It was two and a half feet in height and would be available for sale to families. Now the anticipation had reached its zenith. On September 21, the entire committee accepted the bronze from the foundry and, at the beginning of October, the statue arrived in Lowell.

This ultimate triumph of Father Garin, an apotheosis of love and gratitude, had been very carefully prepared in advance. At 7:30 in the evening, of Thursday, October 22, 1896, twenty thousand persons crowded against one another on Merrimack Street, to the point of preventing the trolleys from passing through. The façade of Saint Jean Baptiste church, embellished with hundreds of blue, white, and red incandescent lamps and by a white electric cross, glowed in all its pristine beauty. The statue, covered with an American flag, was illuminated by multicolored lights. A podium for invited guests extended from the rectory to the church steps.

Suddenly, a murmur energized the crowd. Horsemen escorted the invited guests to the podium: first came the members of the committee, then former Mayor Palmer, Archbishop Duhamel from Ottawa, Bishop Bradley of Manchester, Father McGrath, Father Lefebvre, the provincial from Montréal, the Honorable L. O. Taillon, former prime minister of Québec, the mayor and the city council, delegates from the Catholic churches of Lowell, Reverend A. St. John Chambré, former Mayor Stott, Sheriff Cushing, Dr. Carolin, Judge S. P. Hadley, former Mayor Pickman, J. Chalifoux, as well as other important persons and delegates from numerous societies. After the speeches, Bishop Duhamel came forward, and to the strains of "America" sung by one hundred schoolboys from the *collège*, released the American flag covering the statue. Father Garin, who appeared holding the plans of Saint Jean Baptiste church in his left hand, close to his heart, and pointing towards the church with his right, seemed to be talking to his people. At the sight of this resurrection of their *curé*, a tremor passed through the throng and, in the silence that followed, one could have heard the words of Saint Paul: "Although passed on to another life, he still speaks."

The inscription on the base of the statue is eloquent in its simplicity:

REV. A. M. GARIN, O.M.I.
Born in France, May 7, 1822
Died in Lowell, Feb. 16, 1895
HE WENT ABOUT DOING GOOD
ERECTED BY THE PEOPLE OF LOWELL

After the unveiling, those who were fortunate enough to have a ticket headed for the vast upper church which had been prepared and decorated for a sumptuous banquet. On the menu were chicken, game and fish, everything washed down with the most select wines. Two hundred ladies of the parish served 953 guests with efficient skill. The bishops and dignitaries were seated at the table of honor. The Franco-American clergy from all parts of New England

The bronze statue of Rev. A.M. Garin, O.M.I., sculpted by Louis Philippe Hébert.

and New York State, as well as the rector of the University of Ottawa, were seated in the sanctuary, while a large number of Oblates mingled with guests of all nationalities to join the concert of praise to the great founder.

Atty. Farley presented the monument to the Oblates on behalf of the city of Lowell. The bishops and the mayor added their words of tribute, but when Father Forget rose to speak, thunderous applause arose from all sides, for according to *L'Étoile*: "Everyone knew that the brilliant success of this manifestation was due in great part to him since he had worked like a giant for months, sparing no sacrifice and no effort so that this apotheosis of Father Garin would be complete." The pastor emphasized with fiery eloquence all the good accomplished by Father Garin for his dear Franco-Americans, and added that this monument would not only perpetuate his physical traits, but would serve as an example and a lesson for the future when parents would point out the statue to their children saying, "Here is the man to whose goodness and many works we owe so much for the preservation of our language and our religion." To close the festivities, Father Lefebvre and the Honorable Mr. Taillon reviewed the life and accomplishments of the deceased.

Once the ceremonies were over, it didn't take long for the legend of Father Garin's life to take hold. Each family had its own special memory, or a favorite story, and old men would boast with pride: "I was baptized by Father Garin," or "I can still see him in his old coat walking down Merrimack Street." Each parlor contained a statue or a picture of Father Garin in a place of honor. Songs and poems were composed in his memory, and even in the 1940s, an elderly gentleman, who died in a boarding house, left all his money to have the monument cleaned and repaired. Inevitably, many miraculous healings were attributed to his intercession as attested to by the number of Masses of thanksgiving listed in the parish bulletin, even to our day.

*   *   *

After all this grand rejoicing, the parishioners were saddened to learn, on November 16th, that Father Forget had been assigned to Montréal. The news was received with great sorrow and deep regret. In all humility, and to avoid demonstrations of the esteem in which he was held by parishioners, he left quietly the following evening, from the Nashua, New Hampshire, railroad station.

In October, his cousin, Father Joïada Forget dit Despatis, having become the superior of the community, Father Antoine Avite Amyot succeeded Father Dioscoride Forget as pastor the following month. Born at Saint-Paul-de-Joliette on February 9, 1844, to Antoine Amyot, a carpenter, and Marie Ratel, Father Amyot had studied at Assumption College in Québec before entering the

Fr. Antoine Amyot, O.M.I.

Oblates in 1870. Ordained in Montréal on October 26, 1873, by Bishop Fabre, he was first assigned as a curate in Hull, Québec, then in Montréal, before becoming director of the minor seminary at Lachine, near Montréal. Later, he was named pastor of St. Pierre parish in Plattsburgh, and in 1888, he was assigned to Saint Joseph's parish in Lowell, where he would remain for the rest of his life. The best portrait we have of Father Amyot comes from the pen of his confrere, Father Armand Baron.

By temperament he was frank, sincere, strong in his ideas and opinions, a traditionalist and not the least bit capricious, He would have been inclined by nature to be stubborn and in conflict with others, were it not for having at the same time a very affectionate heart and a supernatural charity that cast a veil of gentleness and affability over the rough edges of his character. We have lived with him for over twenty years, and we always found him eager to be kind, always considerate and welcoming towards everyone and extremely sensitive and grateful for all the attentions he received from others. Thus, everyone liked him, and without the presence of good Father Amyot, something would have been lacking in the joys of our community.

The first duty of the new pastor was to undertake the preparation for the solemn blessing of Saint Jean Baptiste church. Father Garin was now

Print published in 1896 showing the institutions of St. Joseph's parish. The newly built St. Jean Baptiste church with the proposed bell towers that were never constructed and clockwise, St. Joseph's church on Lee Street. St. Joseph's grammar school for girls on Moody Street and St. Joseph's grammer school for boys, the "collège St-Joseph" on Merrimack Street. In 1896, St. Josph's with almost 19,000 parishioners was the largest Franco-American parish in the archdiocese of Boston.

immortalized, his church was completed, and it had been brilliantly presented to the public at the unveiling of the monument. All that remained was to bless it and open it for worship. However, before the dedication took place, the church was the scene of a special religious ceremony. On November the 11th, before an immense gathering of friends and spectators, the mayor, William F. Courtney, married Miss Alice Brouillette. The congregation, as well as the newspapers, admired the newlyweds as much as the new church.

In fact, the church, which had cost $203,000, is a masterpiece of Romanesque architecture in grey and pink granite. The monumental façade is ornamented by a beautiful rose window and a wide vestibule which dominates the street. The richly majestic interior consists of a single vast nave, without transepts, and elegant columns, surmounted by sculptured capitals, rising first to the galleries and then to the vault. Designs and moldings running along the walls give the church a grand air, and bring honor to those who worked for its realization. Unfortunately, the high bell towers were never erected.

On Sunday morning, December 13, 1896, everyone was in joyful anticipation of the solemn blessing and the inauguration of the church. The mayor, the City Council, the élite of the American and Irish populations, and a large number of Lowell's most notable citizens insisted on joining the parishioners for this imposing ceremony. The details were reported by *L'Étoile*:

At precisely ten o'clock, His Excellency Archbishop Williams of Boston pronounced the words of blessing at the threshold of the large main portal, thus consecrating the new edifice to the Lord's worship. Then the procession, preceded by a cross-bearer, advanced down the main aisle towards the high altar where His Excellency blessed the sanctuary and the altar.

Bishop Pascal of Prince Albert, in the Canadian Northwest, officiated at the Mass, with Father Lauzon, O.M.I., from Montréal as deacon, and Father Campeau, O.M.I., from Tewksbury as subdeacon. The bishop was assisted at his throne by Father Guillard, O.M.I., provincial of the United States, and the diocesan priests Father Chevalier from Manchester, New Hampshire, and Father Boucher, from Westfield, New Hampshire.

The entire celebration was under the direction of Father Emard, who gave himself infinite trouble and deserves our warmest congratulations for its magnificent success. A ninety-voice choir under the direction of E. J. Pinault rendered Gounod's Mass of Saint Cecilia with admirable taste and precision. They were accompanied by Miss A. Alexandre at the organ and the Columbian Orchestra of Lawrence.

The interior of St. Jean Baptiste church.

Father Camille Caisse, pastor of Sainte Marie's church in Marlborough, Massachusetts, gave a fitting homily, inspired by the words from the Book of Kings: "I dream of raising a temple in the name of the Lord." At the six-thirty evening service, Bishop Williams officiated, assisted by Father Amyot as deacon and Father Morin as subdeacon. After Vespers, Bishop Pascal preached on the missions in Canada's Northwest.

The blessing of Saint Jean Baptiste church, on December 13, 1896, marked the end of an era in the parish chronicles, and in Franco-American life in Lowell. The work of the great founder had borne fruit. From a humble colony of 1,200 souls, unorganized, but firm in their faith and their pride, the Franco-Americans of Lowell, through their beliefs and their institutions, had earned the respect and admiration of the entire population of the city. The monument to Father Garin immortalized his features and the love that he had inspired, but the eloquent numbers of the assessor, A. Bourbonnière, in his census of 1896, added another jewel to the crown of the priest who had been the father of his people for twenty-seven years. At the end of 1896, Mr. Bourbonnière observed that out of a population of 84,407 people in Lowell:

> I have found through meticulous research that we are now 19,545 Canadians here, grouped in 3,622 families . . . . We have two churches, but only one parish, a commercial school run by the Marist Brothers,

and a convent (girls' day school) under the auspices of the Grey Nuns of Ottawa: about 2,600 children attend these schools, and quite a large number of others are taking courses in the public schools. There are four mutual help societies of men with 1,935 members; a society of young men with 389 members, another of 350 young boys, and another of a great many children; a religious society of 500 women and two societies of young ladies numbering 1,600; two mutual help societies for women and young ladies have 423 members; a literary circle, a choir, and *L'Union Franco-Américaine*; a French newspaper, *L'Étoile*; six persons employed by the city; 367 persons in private businesses of which 188 are assessed at more than $200,000; 250 property owners whose assets are evaluated at $925,000; a population that pays at least $25,000 per year to the city in taxes.

He went about doing good

Wednesday, October 21, 1896.

Souvenir.

Printed silk souvenir ribbon of the
erection of Fr. Garin's Monument.

16. The Wise and Prudent Father Mangin

Father Amyot remained as pastor until June of 1898 when Father Pierre Gagnon replaced him. Father Gagnon, who was born in L'Assomption, Québec, in 1860, was the first novice from the United States Province when he pronounced his vows in 1884. Ordained in Ottawa by Bishop Duhamel in 1890, he had been the bursar in Buffalo, and pastor of St. André's in North Billerica before becoming a curate at Saint Joseph in October 1896.

He was an upright man, with an open and likeable character. The parishioners called him "the Providence of the poor and the help of the needy." At his death, Louis P. Turcotte wrote:

> He had no enemies and had never made any, even though he always expressed his way of thinking in plain language and at times very bluntly. And even if we disagreed with his opinion, he could always win everyone over by his friendliness. He was big-hearted and his generosity was proverbial. He never refused anything to anyone.

However, Father Gagnon barely had time to accustom himself to his position as pastor. The superior, Father Joïada Forget-Despatis had been in failing health for many months, and had to go to Montréal for a fairly long rest. The provincial, Father Guillard, was aging and approaching the end of his term. Father Joseph Lefebvre was therefore named provincial of the United States, and, at his express request, Father Joseph Mangin, one of the most renowned Oblates of the period, was appointed superior of the community as well as pastor

Fr. Pierre Gagnon, O.M.I.

Fr. Joseph Mangin, O.M.I.

of Saint Joseph. Since the parish was in a precarious financial situation and difficult to administer, given its over 18,000 souls, it was decided to combine the functions of superior and pastor, and to place each church under the care of a director.

Father Mangin was a former confrere of Father Garin on missions, and had held very important positions in the Congregation. Born at Neuvillers-lès-Badonviller, France, in 1830, he had studied at the Nancy seminary and entered the Oblates in July 1853. In October 1853 Bishop de Mazenod ordained him to the priesthood at Marseille. After a year, he was sent to minister in England and Scotland where he had the pleasant duty of serving as chaplain for the family of Sir Walter Scott at Abbotsford Manor. He then became moderator of the Irish scholasticate, and afterwards professor at the scholasticate of Autun, France, before being sent to Canada as a missionary in 1865. The young priest conducted missions throughout Canada and New England until 1871 when he was named to Immaculate Conception in Lowell with Father Garin as his superior. In 1876, he became superior of the Lowell Oblates and presided at the blessing of Immaculate Conception church. After returning to Canada in 1878, he was successively director of the Archeville scholasticate, founder of the Ottawa scholasticate, professor at the University of Ottawa, and director of the Ottawa seminary. When the religious authorities decided to assign him to one of the largest Oblate parishes in the United States, Saint Joseph's, the parishioners were receiving a priest endowed with pre-eminent spiritual and administrative qualities.

In addition to his solid judgment and his talents as a first-rate administrator, Father Mangin was blessed with apostolic simplicity and humility. He detested any sort of publicity or personal notoriety. He spoke very little, but thought a great deal. He was known as "the wise, the prudent Father Mangin." However, just like his relative, General Charles Mangin, hero of World War I, his character seemed to have some military aspects. Very punctual and remarkably cool-headed, his seminarians had nicknamed him "the Iceberg." Everyone knew, however, that this was only a cover, hiding his boundless zeal and great heart. The insightful chronicler at the convent noted: "He's a venerable old man whose manner is cold, but whose expression reveals much goodness and affability."

At his arrival in October 1898, Father Lefebvre had established all the responsibilities in the Community as follows: Father Mangin was installed as the superior and pastor, Father Amyot, as first assistant, Father Gagnon, as second assistant, and Father Fournier, as bursar. Father Fournier became responsible for Saint Joseph's church with Fathers G. Marion, J. Forget-Despatis, L. Lamothe, and C. Daveluy as his associates. St. Jean Baptiste church was placed under Father Gagnon with Fathers A. Amyot, A. Marion, L. Nolin, J. Sirois, and W. Perron as curates.

The parishioners now had many reasons to rejoice. They were receiving a new pastor and a new American provincial, Father Lefebvre, who had been a great friend of Father Garin. Father Lefebvre was the first native of Québec to hold this office. On Sunday, October 9, the parishioners gathered at Saint Joseph's as a welcoming party. Before a church filled to capacity, including the members of all the religious and national societies, J. S. Lapierre, president of *L'Union Saint Joseph* read a magnificent welcoming address which stated in part:

Religion – Language – Morals, these are the three words that we would like to emblazon in the sky-blue of our crest. We are poor, but we want to preserve intact the prestige of our nationality; we are poor, but we want to maintain the Catholic, Apostolic, and Roman Church; we are poor, but we want to keep our churches and our schools, French-Canadian schools where our children learn, along with religion, the principles which must guide every person along the way of life and truth. Undoubtedly, it is to encourage us to follow this route that you have come, Very Reverend Father Provincial, to establish your residence in our midst. The regretted Father Garin has been replaced. You are very welcome and we salute you.

In his response, speaking of "Canadian schools" and the proper education for Franco-American children, Father Lefebvre affirmed that he shared the same patriotic and nationalist sentiments as his flock:

> I say, *education that is suitable for them.* Here, my dear friends, we find ourselves in the presence of a very important question. It would not be sufficient to give our children just any sort of education. It would not be sufficient for them to be able to read, write, count, speak English, and be accepted for work in a store or an office. Without a doubt, all this is necessary, but for us Canadians, something more is needed, namely an education that is both French and Catholic. We must learn our language and our religion.

After this family celebration, *L'Association Catholique* organized, on Thursday night, October 13, a large public banquet at Associate Hall in honor of the two priests. The mayor, politicians, and numerous clergy from within and without the city, along with the presidents of the parish societies, joined in the celebration. During the meal, attended by 500 persons, 300 children in a combined choir from the boys' and girls' schools sang religious and patriotic songs from the balconies, alternating with the orchestra placed on the stage.

The parish was proud of its achievements, but especially of its schools, and rightly so. In September of 1896, the pastor, Father Amyot, had decided to call the girls' school *le couvent* (the convent) since no boys were admitted there. The brothers' school had become le *collège.* Since the nuns and the brothers refused no one, the children flocked to these schools. When there wasn't enough room in the classes, more seats were installed — in the lower classes for the little ones, the children sat three and even four to a bench. In 1897, three more classrooms were added to the convent and two to the *collège.* That same year, considering the importance of these schools, the archdiocese sent Father Walsh for a first official visit.

Although the parish wanted to enlarge the schools, nothing could be done because of the critical financial problem. Since 1887, it had borrowed $186,973.06 and in 1899, it still owed $175,750.47. Father Lefebvre decreed that the debt had to be reduced. The word was passed on among the pastor and his associates. The provincial wrote:

> Certainly the needs are great, the circumstances are difficult, and the financial situation needs to be promptly improved. But there is nothing we cannot do with such a large community that does not spare itself when it comes to work or dedication.

Father Mangin reorganized the parish's financial system and for the first time the priests received a salary instead of leaving the Community's resources in the parish account. However, this salary was only pro forma, for the sake of good book-keeping. In reality, the Oblate Fathers never drew their salaries, but deposited the money as donations in the parish receipts. For the future, where the schools were concerned, the children who attended the first two upper classes would pay 15 cents a week, then the next ten classes, 10 cents a week, and the five lower classes, 5 cents a week. The directors and chaplains of the societies for their part made strenuous efforts to organize entertainments and raffles for the benefit of the parish and its good works.

However, we must not imagine that the Fathers spent their time counting the receipts. It was a time of great fervor and at the rectory the Community rules established by Bishop de Mazenod were followed to the letter.

The annual parish visitation to the families furnished an opportunity for a collective examination of conscience:

> In the first days that follow the Easter celebrations, our Fathers will divide the city into districts and each one of them will visit his own, take the census, keep tabs on the changes, take note of the needs, visit the poor, crack down on scandals, and motivate those who are slow to come.

When Father Nolin, accompanied by Father Dozois from Montréal, preached a four-week retreat in 1899, 13,679 men, women, girls and young men received communion. Twelve hundred children participated in a gigantic r etreat at Saint Joseph church in preparation for the ceremonies of Holy Week. Saint Joseph's was the parish church with Saint Jean Baptiste as its auxiliary. The confessionals in the lower church of Saint Joseph's and the basement at Saint Jean Baptiste were always full. On Easter Sunday, Bishop Grouard, of Arthabaska-Mackenzie, in Canada's Northwest Territories, officiated at the High Mass amidst the greatest possible pomp. That same year there were 364 Confirmations and 400 First Communions.

The nineteenth century ended on a quiet note. The old Saint Joseph temple, which had received hardly any repairs since its opening, was now given a face-lift. Workers, at the cost of $4,000, labored from May to July 1899 repairing and painting the interior, and replacing the gas fixtures with electricity. On Sunday July 16th, the refurbished church was reopened with a celebration which included music at a High Mass and electric illumination at Vespers. It was at this time that a marble plaque was affixed to the vestibule wall honoring Fathers Phaneuf and Fournier as well as the outstanding benefactors to the restoration fund.

The blessing of Saint Joseph Cemetery had been scheduled for 1896, but it had been constantly put off due to Bishop Williams's advanced age. However, on Sunday, October 8, 1899, Father Lefebvre, delegated by the archbishop, and assisted by a large number of clergy and a throng of the faithful, officiated at the ceremony.

The twentieth century opened with a parish population of 21,142 souls ministered to by twelve Oblate priests and two lay brothers, aided by the provincial and his assistant, who also lived in the rectory. There were 1,200 children in the brothers' school, 1,350 with the nuns, and 800 in the public schools. The prodigious activity that had marked the beginning of the new pastor's mandate was to last until his replacement was named, in 1904.

From the very beginning of the century, the pastor had to confront two thorny issues that had troubled him for some time – housekeeping at the rectory and lack of space in the schools. As the size of the rectory community increased and the services to be rendered became more pressing, the upkeep of the residence grew more and more difficult and complicated for the lay women who were taking care of it. Such a large community required the stable influence of women religious who could not only take charge of the proper functioning of the house on a day-to-day basis, but also support the ministry of the priests by their prayers.

In 1896, Father Lefebvre had requested from his relative, Father Camille Lefebvre C.S.C., founder of the Little Sisters of the Holy Family, the services of his nuns for the Sacred Heart Juniorate in Ottawa. These sisters had been founded by Father Camille and Mother Marie Léonie in October 1874. The aim of the Congregation of the Little Sisters of the Holy Family was and is "the spiritual and temporal service of the clergy through prayer and manual labor." The provincial, who had seen these excellent sisters at work in Canada, did not hesitate to recommend them to his pastor. So, Father Mangin put in a request to the mother general, and in July 1900, the negotiations reached a successful conclusion. On the morning of August 31, 1900, Fathers Mangin and Fournier went to the railroad station to welcome Sister Marie du St. Sacrement, superior, Sisters Sainte-Bernadette and St. Sébastien for the kitchen, Sister St. Patrice for the dining room, and Sister St. Denis for the laundry. Mother Marie Léonie, who was beatified in 1984, accompanied them and remained for ten days to look after the Community's installation.

The school question proved to be a difficult one to resolve. Every year, two to three hundred children had to be turned away for lack of space. Major expenditures were out of the question, given the financial situation. Father Mangin decided to take short-term measures. In April 1900, he informed the members of *L'Association Catholique*, the CMAC, that they would have to vacate their quarters in the small brick building near the church which was parish property.

Blessed Mother Marie Léonie, Foundress of the Congregation of the Little Sisters of the Holy Family.

This association of young men, founded in 1878 by Father Fournier, had prospered so much that in 1889 it had become a mutual benefit society issuing insurance policies and guarantees of indemnity in times of sickness. It was now made up of married men as well as young men, and had obtained its charter of incorporation in 1891, as *La Corporation des Membres de l'Association Catholique*, the C.M.A..C., By 1900, it had become the most powerful Franco-American society in the city, and it took advantage of the need to relocate by constructing its own two-story building on Pawtucket Street, facing Merrimack. This spacious edifice, with its large auditorium, its library, its gym, and its function rooms became the center of Franco-American life in Lowell. The inauguration of its premises took place from September 30 to October 6, 1900, with a series of religious and social ceremonies.

Once the brick house had been vacated, the structure was converted into two classrooms for little boys. In October 1900, Sister Sainte-Léontine and her companion moved their 211 little boys into the new school, which became known as *le petit collège*. In that year 1900, the parochial schools served 2,700 children under the direction of twenty nuns, nineteen religious brothers and one lay person.

The busy pastor also had to look after housing the nuns who lived in crowded conditions in the convent facing the school. Some of the nuns even had to sleep in the attic and under the sloping ceilings of the garret. The property near the convent, at the corner of Moody and James Streets, was for sale. It had to be purchased since it was the only possible available site in the neighborhood for the construction of a future convent. But, given the enormous size of the parish debt, those in authority were strongly opposed and discussions extended throughout the summer. Finally, on September 6, 1900, the parish bought this house from Lillie M. Spencer for $5,900. The home was transformed into a dormitory for the nuns, while the former convent became the Community house.

The parochial schools continued to be admired by everyone. In 1900, Mr. Whitcomb, superintendent of the public schools, visited the classes and paid particular attention to the English and translation courses. He declared publicly in the newspapers that the children in the "Canadian" schools read and pronounced English well, "proving that this language was not being neglected." Moreover, to the astonishment of their parents, six-year-old children could read French and English fluently, and could then translate from either language the passages they had just read. At the end of the school year, in June 1901, the French consul in New York sent a silver medal and another one in bronze as prizes in French composition. The curriculum also included all the subjects of a basic elementary education: spelling, reading aloud, dictations, literary compositions, study of the English language, penmanship, history, geography, arithmetic, algebra, geometry, bookkeeping, typing, shorthand, vocal and instrumental music, linear and decorative drawing.

On Monday morning, August 12, 1901, the parishioners learned of the sudden and unexpected death of their former pastor and at the time director of St. Jean Baptiste church, Father Pierre Gagnon, at the age of forty-one. Mourning for him was profound and solemn. Father Joseph Campeau succeeded the deceased as director of St. Jean Baptiste Church.

During this period of immense activity, pride in nationality and parochial life were at their most intense and closely linked. The assistant priests and the directors of the societies multiplied entertainments, plays, and festivals for the benefit of the works of the parish. Father Perron organized Franciscan banquets with the tertiaries. The nuns put on play after play. The brothers presented sacred concerts, operettas, and even whist parties. In May of 1901, the Oblate Fathers sponsored a mammoth fair that lasted three days. One event or another took place each month. Although the primary purpose of these activities was to entertain the population and support parish undertakings – in June 1901, the plays added $2,186.50 to the general revenue – it was evident that the intention of the organizers was also to maintain a spirit of ethnic cohesion among the people.

In January 1902, a committee, set up by Father Nolin, invited the commanding Québec orator, Henri Bourassa, to Lowell, housing him at the rectory. It was the first time Bourassa had come to the city to speak, which he did in Huntington Hall before 1,600 people. His powerful and very nationalistic lecture caused repercussions in the Boston and Montréal press, and stirred up a great deal of emotion among the people of Lowell. The following year, in January, the C.M.A.C. presented in a gala soirée the Honorable Israël Tarte, the former minister of public works for Canada, at a formal gathering. In November of 1902, the Oblates, with the support of the *Club des Citoyens Américains*, launched a campaign for naturalization with Father Campeau as the principal speaker. Father Lewis gave a series of lectures at the C.M.A.C. on political economics and the role of trade unions in society. His treatment of the subject reflected the Christian and conservative morality of the parishioners for, according to the *Courier-Citizen*:

> Perhaps we owe more to the French Canadians of our city than to any other race for the status of labor here . . . . These people are industrious, sober, happy and contented, and it is a matter of comment that in a city where members of one race number one-fourth of the population, so few of that race figure in the police court records.

It is noteworthy that the first general strike affecting all the textile mills in the city took place only in 1903, and that it failed. There were no other general strikes up to the year 1912, after which complete statistics have been hard to find.

Franco-American awareness of their own nationality, so positive and so Christian though it might be, did not blind the parishioners to the needs of others. On the contrary, it made them more sensitive and sympathetic to the woes and difficulties of more recent immigrants.

As a result of persecutions in Poland, Poles were arriving in Lowell in growing numbers. They had no church where they could hear Mass in their own language and no place to gather among themselves. Following a retreat preached by two Polish Jesuit Fathers, in December 1901, they began to hold religious services in the basement of Saint Joseph church. They would remain there until September 18, 1904, the day their own church of Holy Trinity, located on High Street, was dedicated. At that time also, the basement of St. Joseph served as a church for Lithuanian immigrants.

132

Religious zeal did not diminish for all this activity. As proof of this, one can look at the important retreat of March 1903, during which 15,000 persons took part in the religious services. It is difficult for us today to imagine the sacrifices imposed by a retreat of this kind. Four thousand married men, after a long and tedious day of labor in the mills, had to go directly to church, only to arrive home quite late, at the end of the church exercises. The next morning, they had to leave before sunrise in order to attend Mass and receive Communion.

Father Mangin, in his simplicity and his usual pure-hearted, well-intentioned manner, continued to do his work without drumbeat or fanfare. In October of 1903, the parishioners and assistant priests conspired to mark the golden anniversary of their pastor's ordination. At first the old missionary objected strongly, but the young priests insisted so much that he finally agreed, but only on condition that everything be kept as simple as possible, without too much fuss or praise for himself. He had always believed that publicity about religious matters, including sermons, or photos of priests, had no place in the newspapers.

The poor priest's humility must have been severely tested because praises poured forth from all sides. The parish had not seen such festivities since Father Garin's golden jubilee. He was harassed by reporters who wanted pictures and an interview. In response to this, the pastor kept saying: "I want none of this. Let the priest do good without publishing it to the four corners of the world." The celebrations began on October 14, with a solemn Mass at which the children sang, followed by plays in the boys' and girls' schools with a great many speeches and gifts. On Sunday the 18th, the entire parish gathered at Saint Joseph church to celebrate his golden anniversary with a High Mass accompanied by an orchestra. Father Edouard Emery, rector of the University of Ottawa, pronounced an unusual homily on this occasion. It seems that when Father Mangin saw Father Emery, renowned for his eloquence, arrive at the rectory, he energetically forbade his colleague to say anything about him in his sermon. Father Emery respected this injunction, to the great astonishment of the whole assembly, which had expected a flight of oratory extolling the life and exploits of their illustrious pastor. The jubilee ended on the 19th with a sumptuous banquet in the *collège* hall which was attended by many lay and religious dignitaries.

This warmhearted celebration displayed once again the attachment of the parishioners for their "Fathers" and the family spirit and harmony which reigned at the heart of the parish. Unfortunately, the same spirit did not prevail in France. The passage of anticlerical laws by the French Legislative Assembly, in 1902 and 1903, whose aim was to disband religious communities, sorely tried the Oblates. They ceased to exist in France as a religious Congregation;

the superior-general was expelled from the motherhouse in Paris, and a great many French Fathers had to go into exile. As a result, in 1903, Saint Joseph parish received three new curates: Fathers Charles Audibert, Pierre Brullard, and Victor Viaud.

Father Mangin had now reached the age of seventy-three, and his health, weakened by his advanced years, should have allowed him to rest a little on his laurels. But such indulgence was not to be, for a very thorny problem had arisen. On January 26, 1903, a delegation composed of John H. Beaulieu, Jacques Boisvert, J. A. Filion, J. A. Foisy, Georges E. Langières, Charles Boisvert, Joseph Champagne, Siméon Lagassé, Thaddée Ducharme, J. A. Maillé, Alphonse Dalphond and Albert Cadorette arrived at the rectory. These parishioners, representing the Centralville section of the city, explained to the provincial and the pastor that they wanted a church and a chapel for their part of the city. Up to that time, Saint Joseph parish with its two churches and two schools had served the Franco-American population of the entire city. However, the outlying area known as Centralville, on the northern bank of the Merrimack River, had continued to expand. In the parish census, taken in the autumn of 1903, there were in Centralville and the territory extending "towards Lawrence and Nashua, 696 families, that is to say, 3,478 souls." *L'Étoile* at that time regularly announced lots for sale or houses under construction in the western part of Centralville.

Ever since the founding of the parish, the faithful who lived on the river's north shore had to cross the Bridge St. bridge in order to attend services. This was a fairly long and arduous trek, especially for the school children. The construction of the Aiken Street bridge in 1882 did not do much to help the situation, for the western part of Centralville was underdeveloped and the streetcar line only passed by Bridge Street. With the division into lots of large plots of land in West Centralville, it was anticipated that a great many people would move to that section of the city, with the resulting crucial need for a new parish. The problem was, however, that most of these parishioners worshiped at Saint Joseph. If the provincial and the pastor decided to respond to the needs of Centralville, by the same token they would also have to consider the request of the Middlesex area that was also beginning to agitate in favor of a separation. And then, what could be done with Saint Joseph church? Father Mangin wrote:

This request, which seems quite simple, nevertheless threatens to raise a very serious question, namely, the division of the parish. For there are other neighborhoods which are in a similar situation, especially the Middlesex area. These are precisely the two sections, Centralville and Middlesex, whose people attend Saint Joseph church. If the division occurs, what will become of Saint Joseph's?

Nonetheless, for the sake of justice, they promised to consider the petition and to consult with the bishop. In the meantime, the Centralville committee went into action. On May 1st, Jacques Boisvert, a contractor and well-known financier, brought Fathers Lefebvre, Campeau, and Fournier to see a large plot of land measuring 380,782 square feet, bordered by Ennell, West Sixth, and Victor Streets that he had just purchased from the Lawrence Manufacturing Company. He intended to divide this area into lots, to open streets, and build cottages to be sold to mill workers who wanted to become home owners. He offered to donate 20,000 square feet of this land for a future church. The Oblate Fathers found the proposition quite acceptable, and the land more than suitable. On November 15, it was announced from the pulpit that money could be contributed for the construction of a chapel in Centralville.

On December 29, Father Provincial consulted with Archbishop Williams in Boston. The meeting was short, with the prelate announcing straight away that he had found a priest for Centralville, and that he was about to send him there immediately to take over the parish. The question had been settled by the archdiocesan decision that Centralville would no longer belong to the Oblates. Father Lefebvre, as well as Father Mangin, had always thought that the new parish would be under the Oblates, at least for a certain length of time. A disappointed Father Mangin noted: "We did not ask for this separation; it was imposed upon us and we have accepted it. It was impossible to do otherwise given the circumstances." Father J. N. Jacques, pastor of St. Zephirin's church in Cochituate, became the founding pastor of Saint Louis de France parish in Centralville. On January 26, 1904, the Oblates announced the official division from the pulpit, adding: "It is not without regret that we are separating ourselves from this worthy population. This sacrifice was asked of us and we have accepted it, but not without sorrow." The parishioners had a hard time parting from their "Fathers" and a good many of them continued their habit of going to confession at St. Joseph's for a long while to come.

The separation of the parish was the last official act of the old pastor. On November 12, the provincial transferred him to Immaculate Conception parish, where he died quietly on August 22, 1909.

17. "The Father of the poor has passed away."

On Wednesday morning, February 17, 1904, Father Mangin announced at all the Masses that Saint Joseph parish's "Father of the Poor" had passed away. After a short-lived agony, Father Joseph Alexandre Fournier had died peacefully on Tuesday. This priest, who had been Father Garin's right-hand man, died on the same date and from the same illness as his venerated superior – cancer of the liver. Worn out by his sickness and his labors, he had felt his end approaching, but the old missionary had absolutely refused to respond to the entreaties of his brother, Dr. Joseph Fournier, of St. Jerôme, in Québec, that he retire and return to his family.

We have seen how, as a young priest, during the first years of the parish, he gave alms to the poor, organized religious societies, taught French to the children and directed plays with the *Association des Jeunes Gens*. Thus, when he left Lowell in 1888 to become pastor in Plattsburgh, New York, there was considerable sadness among the people, and this had touched his missionary heart. So, in 1896, he begged the authorities to send him back to Lowell. Upon his return, his assignment as director of St. Joseph church had been a great consolation to him, for the elderly priests and the faithful had always retained a sentimental attachment to the old house of worship on Lee Street. This was their church, the church of Father Garin.

The new director, supported by Father Lamothe, who was in charge of the altar boys, concentrated his efforts, first and foremost, on the correct execution of religious ceremonics. The services were most impressive. The electrical illumination, the rich vestments, the altar boys vested in red or purple cassocks, the great choir, everything concurred to enhance the splendor of the sacred ritual. The altar boys, chosen from the best voices in Brother Chryseuil's celebrated choir, alternated from the sanctuary with the main choir, equally famous for its Masses by Rossini, Perrault and Mozart. The mystical nature of the Mass, thus glorified and exalted, made it possible for the parishioners to share with their clergy in a sublime vision of beauty and peace which removed them from their daily fatigue and toil and gave them the strength and inspiration to overcome the difficult aspects of their lives.

Strongly united in a common bond of shared religious and ethnic interests, the people were living a parish experience at once intense and sincere. The parish, faith, and a feeling of community formed a counterweight to a life which contained more misery and suffering than current nostalgia allows us to imagine. Only the parish provided hope and consolation against the uncertainties of daily living, the imperious decisions of industrial management, and the constant threat of strikes and starvation. The priest was truly the consoler of the afflicted and the father of his people. The love which inspired it shone in every home of the parish family.

Realizing that there was as yet no religious society in the parish for married men or young men who had left school – *Les Anges Gardiens* being restricted to schoolboys – Father Fournier founded *L'Association de la Sainte-Famille* for them in 1896. This new religious society expected charity and setting a "good example" of its members. It required: "perfect obedience to laws and authority, fleeing from bad company, saloons, and entertainments contrary to decency; relief for the poor and visits to the sick." The success of this foundation was such that by 1903, 800 members were enrolled.

In everything he initiated, Father Fournier preached charity and help for the poor. The specter of poverty was ever-present in the parish. Even a temporary strike was sufficient to plunge an entire family into dire straits. Whenever the father of a family died, the widow and the orphans became victims of hunger and sickness. Father Fournier dedicated himself body and soul to works of charity. He went up and down the most miserable streets in the parish. He visited the most dilapidated and unhealthy tenements. His projects to benefit the poor knew no bounds. He published contribution lists, organized plays, and mobilized the *Dames de Sainte Anne*, the *Cercle de Couture* and the boys of *Les Anges Gardiens*.

In 1898, his work received a considerable boost. His father, Alexandre Fournier, a rich merchant in St. Jérôme, died leaving a fortune of $75,000. The will named Father Fournier as the executor and divided the inheritance evenly between him and his brother, Dr. Joseph-Emmanuel Fournier of St. Jérôme. Part of the inheritance was in the form of mortgages. When the school on Moody Street was built, Alexandre Fournier had accepted mortgages of $19,000 on the school. Father Fournier placed these loans under his own name and on January 26, 1904, transferred them to Father Lefebvre, who paid them off for the sum of $1.00 on February 15 of that year. Another part of his inheritance was given to the general administration of the Oblates which, in turn, offered it as a loan to the parish.

What was left of his fortune was used mostly to foster education and vocations. Ever since he had founded the *Association des Jeunes Gens* and had himself given French lessons to its members, Father Fournier had been watching over the formation of the young men of the parish. At noon, during recess time, he could be found in the yard of the *collège* surrounded by a crowd of children. If a young man from a poor family wanted to pursue his studies or become a priest, the good father would take him under his wing and pay for everything. How many priests, businessmen, and professionals owed their training to his generosity! All of this was accomplished without fanfare and he sought no other reward than the happiness of the poor.

To encourage vocations, especially Franco-American vocations, he established a $3,000 scholarship to attend the Oblate juniorate in Buffalo. Yet, he kept the dream alive of founding a Franco-American Oblate juniorate. At that time, quite serious difficulties had already arisen in the formation of bilingual Franco-American Oblates in the seminaries of the American province. Often, the students did not acquire a sufficient knowledge of the ecclesiastical sciences in French that they would have needed for parish ministry. Many young Oblates, who had been sent to complete their studies in Ottawa, or in the institutions of Québec, were often assigned to bilingual parishes in Canada by the Canadian provincials, rather than being returned to New England. Since this problematic question was nowhere near a solution, and the existence of a Franco-American province was not yet even a dream, Father Fournier made other arrangements. When the Texas province was founded, in 1904, his former protégé, Father Henri Constantineau, became its first provincial. Father Fournier made a gift of $20,000 to that province to help in the construction of a juniorate in San Antonio – St. Anthony's Apostolic School. Such was his generosity that at the time of his death he had only $872.51 to his name in the bank.

Folding celluloid souvenir of the convention of the former members of the Society of the Guardian Angel in 1902. On the left, Fr. Fournier, the founder, and on the right, Fr. Constantineau, the first president.

Just as the parish experienced such great joy in celebrating anniversaries, so they felt deep sorrow in the face of death. All the zeal expended for celebrations was put to use in preparing a funeral worthy of the esteem which the celebrations harbored for their clergy. On Friday morning, February 19, a first service was sung in the basement of Saint Jean Baptiste church. This was followed by a funeral cortège made up of delegates from all the church societies and conveyances bearing dignitaries which proceeded towards Saint Joseph church for the grand solemn service, at 10 o'clock. The choirs of both churches and the Rossini Choir, as well as a large number of clergy and faithful joined together in prayer to honor the memory of this Oblate who died poor having sought only to alleviate poverty and glorify the Creator by his life of love and renunciation. He was laid to rest near Father Garin in Saint Joseph Cemetery.

18. Two Apostles: Fathers Joseph Lefebvre and Joseph Campeau

Fr. Joseph Lefebvre, O.M.I.

In 1904, when the United States Oblate Province was divided into two autonomous provinces, one in the North, with Father Michael Fallon as provincial, and one in the Southwest, with Father Henri Constantineau as provincial, Father Joseph Lefebvre became the pastor and superior of the Saint Joseph community.

Joseph Lefebvre was born at St. Constant, in Québec, on April 13, 1835, the son of a farmer, Joseph Médard Lefebvre and Marie Tremblay. The future Oblate received his elementary education in the village school and completed his classical studies at the *Petit Séminaire* of Montréal in 1854. He then immediately entered the Oblate novitiate and was ordained to the priesthood on August 28, 1858, at the University of Ottawa where he taught theology until 1864. From there, he was sent to the parish of Saint-Sauveur in the city of Québec to help in the reconstruction of the church which had been totally destroyed by fire in 1866. He later spent two years in Lowell, arriving in 1871, where he served as a curate at Immaculate Conception church, before being sent to Saint Pierre in Montréal in 1873. He spent the next twenty-five years at St. Pierre where he served in succession as provincial bursar, superior, and provincial. On numerous occasions, he had been sent as a delegate to Europe, and was accustomed to dealing with the most complex and irksome of problems. His arrival in Lowell in 1898, as the American provincial, marked the beginning of an important period in the growth of the Congregation in the United States. Indeed, it was under his administration that the Texas province and the Mexican missions were established.

He was a skilled and prudent administrator, very active and dedicated who, nevertheless, maintained a fatherly and apostolic goodness of soul and fine sensitivity, in spite of his pressing duties. Having heard and appreciated his masterful homilies at Father Garin's funeral and at the unveiling of his monument, the parishioners at St. Joseph recognized in him the qualities that they had prized so highly in Father Garin. Accustomed to having as their pastors men who were outstanding for their sanctity, the parishioners were correct once again in according him their high esteem. Moreover, had Father Lefebvre himself not said, in speaking of Father Garin: "If I do not have his talents, I do have his same love for you."

On November 12, 1904, Father Lefebvre assumed his post as pastor, assisted by Father Joseph Campeau as director of Saint Jean Baptiste church, and Father Léon Lamothe as director of Saint Joseph. As was to be expected in this immense parish, a great many difficult problems awaited the new pastor.

Ever since the foundation of Saint Louis de France parish, it had become urgent to settle the question of setting up combination chapels-schools in other areas of the city at some distance from the parish, such as in South Lowell, Middlesex, and Pawtucketville. The provincial, Father Fallon, as well as Bishop Williams, had grave reservations on the subject, considering the large parish debt, the unstable condition of the textile industry, and the danger of adversely affecting the two churches of Saint Joseph and Saint Jean Baptiste. But, in the final analysis, they all admitted that sooner or later a decision would have to be taken.

On February 23, 1905, four parishioners, Messrs. Parthenais, Lorrain, Renaud, and Racicot, who lived in the Middlesex area of the city, came to the rectory. This was the part of Lowell along Middlesex Street in the Southwest section of the city which included the Highlands, Ayer City, and Middlesex Village. Acting on promises made by Father Garin in the past, they requested a church-school for their neighborhood which would be built with their aid and served by the Oblates. For the time being, there was no question of a new parish, only a parish extension.

The situation was difficult for those who lived that far from the church, and who had to walk a long distance or take the streetcar to attend religious services, but it was intolerable for the children who had to walk in all kinds of weather to attend schools located at the other end of the city. The pastor conceded that there was indeed a need for a school, but advised prudence and secrecy for the moment on their appeal since the Church authorities would have to be consulted.

At the end of November 1905, Herménégilde Brun, Sévère Dumont, and Napoléon Goyette presented the pastor with a petition, signed by the Franco American families of South Lowell, asking for the opening of a French-Catholic school and a chapel if possible. On December 3, Father Lefebvre, aided by Fr. Augustin Graton, called a meeting of all the signers to hear the reasons justifying this request, and to propose the means that would have to be taken to achieve the desired end.

Since the area in question was virtually a suburb on the extreme southeast side of Lowell, at the end of Lawrence Street, and at least three miles from Saint Jean Baptiste, a church and, especially a school, were clearly needed in South Lowell. What would happen otherwise to the faith and the French heritage, of children left to the care of the public schools? More and more workers had moved there since William Wiggin, in 1895, had developed lots in this vast quarter near Woburn Street, which he named Wigginsville. Nearby, the section called Riverside Park, near the Concord River, had been developed about 1902. And the U.S. Cartridge Factory in South Lowell was expanding its production. The city of Lowell had built a small school in Wigginsville and the Riverside school, to accommodate the children living in the surrounding district. For the parish, therefore, the problem was clear and the solution evident.

Pawtucketville, for the moment, was quiet. No formal request had been made by the parishioners, and it was felt that the project could still wait a few more years. The provincial and Father Lefebvre went to consult with the archbishop. Archbishop Williams, while counseling prudence, gave the Oblates permission to solve the questions of South Lowell and Middlesex. On January 15, 1906, Father Fallon, accompanied by Fathers Lefebvre and Campeau, visited the two areas and authorized the purchase of land in South Lowell, and the rental of a hall in the Highlands.

Saint Joseph parish began by borrowing $3,000. On February 16, 1906, a plot of land measuring 40,604 square feet on Woburn Street, the main road in South Lowell, was bought from Andrew Wheelock. Young Father Campeau, the old pastor's right-hand man, directed the operation. Since they did not have the funds to construct a new building, the public school in Wigginsville, which had been closed, was purchased from the city and moved by the parishioners themselves approximately 2000 yards to the new plot. Brother Demers, O.M.I., helped with the remodeling of the interior. The small chapel-school of Sainte Marie in South Lowell, a mission extension of Saint Joseph parish, cost $4,275.90 in all. The income and gifts to it totaled $4,375.70, which left a balance of $99.80 on hand. The solemn blessing by Fathers Lefebvre, Campeau, and Amyot took place on September 2, 1906, in the midst of a jubilant congregation. The 334 parishioners, composed of sixty-four families, finally had their desired chapel-school.

The chapel-school of Sainte Marie in South Lowell.

The new director of the Sainte Marie mission, Father Avite Amyot, announced that the school would open its doors on the next day in the hall on the second floor. It would be under the direction of Miss Emma Crépeau. At sunrise, sixty-five children showed up to enroll. Sainte Marie remained a mission of Saint Joseph's until November 25, 1931, at which time it was established as a distinct parish.

For all that the South Lowell question had been settled to everyone's satisfaction, this was not the case for Middlesex which presented problems difficult to solve. First of all, there was the predicament of finding a hall to be rented, or a convenient site. Then, funds were low and the families were expecting something to begin before making any sacrifice of a monetary nature. Although many parishioners wanted the chapel, a certain number of others had fallen into religious indifference and did not want to commit themselves. With the population thus divided, no solution could be found. The pastor consulted with the provincial councilors to help solve this dilemma.

At the beginning of 1907, the provincial council reached a crucial decision. Since the principal work of the Congregation was preaching parish missions, and since it seemed more useful to encourage the new foundations in other States rather than become immobilized in only one city, it was decided to entrust this district to the archbishop so that he could appoint a diocesan priest. Father Lefebvre and many of the older priests considered that the Oblates were first and foremost missionaries and that they should, therefore, not attach themselves too exclusively to parish ministry. Furthermore, a precedent had been set with the unforeseen separation of Saint Louis. It would perhaps be wiser, they concluded, to follow this example, and relinquish this neighborhood to the diocesan clergy, as well as the Sainte Marie mission later. It was hoped that a diocesan priest could shake the Highlands population out of its indifference and start the work on a solid footing.

Archbishop Williams gave a provisional approval to the project, but reserved the right to delay its execution until a detailed study had been completed. The archbishop also advised Father Lefebvre as follows: "Do not give away too much of your parish; make sure that you keep what you need. The separation of Middlesex must not impoverish you." The pastor, touched by these remarks, replied: "It is certain that this division will make us lose many fine families, but the new pastor also will need a few good families if he is to carry out his undertaking successfully. But what we are asking of you, Your Excellency, is that you allow us to keep what remains of Saint Joseph parish, that is St. Joseph church and St. Jean Baptiste church as well as Pawtucketville. This is necessary for us if we are to pay our debts and maintain our schools which lodge 2,200 children." That was how matters remained for the time being.

In 1905, there were nineteen Marist Brothers at the *Collège* Saint Joseph. These brothers were housed near the school in a wooden structure where they lived under cramped and uncomfortable conditions, especially in the summer. On September 27, 1906, the parish bought a property at the corner of Moody and Pawtucket Streets from the Bigelow Carpet Co., which had been the residence of their agent. In addition to the spacious house, which was easily converted into a religious residence, the purchase included a lot of 20,964 square feet, which the brothers were quick to convert into both a flower and a vegetable garden. Their former residence was demolished to make room for a schoolyard.

By the same token, the Little Sisters of the Holy Family had not left their "temporary quarters" since their arrival in the parish in 1900. They had been living in the open attic of the rectory. Therefore, the pastor obtained the required permissions, borrowed the necessary funds, and began the work of building a convent. On May 13, 1907, a contractor, Joseph Roy, broke ground, and on September 30, the Sisters of the Holy Family moved into their brick convent, contiguous to the rectory.

The success of these thriving activities was a sign for the clergy and the faithful, that God's favor rested not only on what had been accomplished to date, but also on the continuing efforts of the Franco Americans to remain Catholic and French in the heart of an American Protestant republic. Since triumphalism was in vogue at the time, the feast of Saint Jean Baptiste, in June of 1906, provided the perfect occasion for a popular display of French ethnic vitality in Lowell.

Scenes from the Saint Jean Baptiste day celebration of June 25, 1906. The top photograph is of the triumphant arch erected at the corner of Moody and Aiken Streets. The bottom picture shows the parade on Merrimack Street with one of the thirteen floats in the foreground.

Lowell had never seen such a grandiose celebration of the Saint Jean Baptiste feast day. Most of the stores and mills gave their employees a holiday for the occasion. City Hall was decorated with flags and banners, the shops were decked in blue, white, and red. Patriotic slogans could be seen on all sides. The general committee had erected triumphal arches on the principal streets along the route of the grand parade. The thirteen floats, the numerous bands and invited dignitaries awed the crowd of astounded spectators.

The parade passed a reviewing stand of the municipal government, on its four-mile route as far as Pawtucketville and Centralville before ending at the

Fair Grounds at the end of Gorham Street. Here an open air Mass was held, followed by speeches and games. The following maxim was displayed at the front of the altar: *"Soyons de bons citoyens américains tout en restant fidèles à notre foi, nos moeurs et nos traditions."* (Let us be good American citizens, while remaining true to our faith, our customs and our traditions.) Father Campeau was the author of this inspired adage, which sounded the right note in the enthusiastic chorus of the day. Young and old joined their voices to sing the glories of the land they had left behind, and the immense hopes they had placed in their adopted land. The sermon at the Mass was given by Father Louis Lalande, S.J., an orator much appreciated in Québec and New England. The day ended with a gala banquet in the halls of the C.M.A.C.

Priests and parishioners worked together for the preservation and development of the French-Catholic ideal. In the pulpit, Fathers Campeau and Lamothe fulminated against alcoholic beverages and societies indifferent to religion. In 1906, all the local religious societies were encouraged to federate under the banner of the *Ralliement Franco Américain*. Father Armand Baron, from France, who had arrived at Saint Joseph's in October 1905, reorganized the old parish library which had been founded by Father Gény in 1893, adding a bookstore displaying "good books" in French. On November 19, 1905, Louis Fréchette, the poet laureate of Québec, gave a lecture at the C.M.A.C. in support of the Crémazie Monument in Montréal, and that same year, Alfred Lambert, general president of the *Artisans Canadiens-Français* of Montréal, came to Lowell to preach ethnic loyalty.

These efforts to perpetuate the culture did not stem from blind or intemperate "nationalism." They arose from an evident need and the collective vision of a very sound ideal. Protestant Anglo-Saxon society was constantly exerting pressure – and not always in a subtle manner – for assimilation. Even the bishops and the Irish-Catholic clergy did not always understand or accept the Franco-American ideology. They too were trying to suppress the use of the French language and hence, even the "national" parishes themselves.

As a parish served by members of a religious community, St. Joseph's was able to elude many of these aggravations. Moreover, Archbishop Williams had always shown himself to be most favorably disposed towards the Franco-Americans. On the other hand, some members of his entourage were uncompromising and at times caused problems.

Father Campeau, as director of the parish schools, often had to come to the defense of "his children." The superintendent of diocesan schools, Father Louis Walsh, constantly complained that there was not enough English taught in these parish schools. This was in spite of the praises from the Lowell school superintendent regarding the high quality of bilingualism at Saint Joseph's.

146

Father Walsh, at his annual visit, tried to examine the students privately, in order to intimidate them. But Father Campeau refused to leave the classroom during these examinations, with the result that Father Walsh, angered by his firmness, left the parish and did not return for two years. The incident reverberated throughout the Franco American press. In 1906, Father Walsh was consecrated as bishop of Portland, Maine, where his fanatic anti-French bias pushed the diocese to the point of a revolt, resulting in the need for Rome to intervene in order to restore peace. The new diocesan director, Father John Graham, a serious and polite man, suggested to Father Campeau that there should be more English in the schools. The Oblate was quick to reply: "Our French schools are supported by the money of our Canadians, and we will continue to teach French in them as in the past." The diocesan authorities were not the only ones to be admonished on this subject.

Brother Chryseuil, in keeping with the new constitution of the Marist Brothers, left the *Collège* Saint Joseph in September of 1906, after fourteen years in Lowell. Brother Stratonique, the assistant-general, came to Lowell in May 1907, to negotiate a new contract. The pastor and Father Campeau took advantage of the occasion to point out that although the parish was satisfied with the quality of the lessons in elocution, declamation, dramatic presentations, singing, and English taught to the students, they were less so with regard to French reading which left much to be desired. They expected that in the future the Marist Brothers would be even more committed to the school.

On November 21, 1906, another event occurred, but of a quite different kind of importance. The famous dwarf, Count Philippe Nicol, who had frequently toured with the Barnum and Bailey Circus, and was now living in Manchester, New Hampshire, married Rose Dufresne, a Lilliputian from Lowell. This union of midgets, who would one day open the *Palais des Nains* (Palace of the Dwarfs) in Montréal, was celebrated with great pomp in Saint Joseph's church. Father Amyot officiated at the wedding in the presence of a very large assembly which had arrived from near and far.

During this time of such great activity, Father Lefebvre was nurturing a project that was very dear to him. In April 1897, the parish had inherited property and the buildings at 484 and 486 Moody Street from the estate of Aurélie Paquette, with the stipulation that these houses be converted into an orphanage for the Franco American children of Lowell. The wishes of this generous parishioner could not be fulfilled at that time, due to the lack of resources and personnel. The dream was kept alive however, until such time as the pastor could find the means to bring it to fruition, for it was very evident that there was a crying need for such an institution.

Fr. Joseph Campeau, O.M.I.

Besides the Ayer Home for Protestant children, Lowell in 1906 had one Catholic orphanage, Saint Peter's for young girls, to serve a population of 94,889. Franco American families, notable for having many children, often found themselves reduced to extreme poverty by the death of one or both of the parents. Generally, in these cases, the children were given up for adoption to relatives or neighbors who were willing to take them in. To open a Catholic orphanage where a solid religious and academic formation could be dispensed by devoted women religious became the overriding aspiration of both the curé and the people.

Father Lefebvre consulted with the Archbishop, and on August 28, 1906, Archbishop Williams wholeheartedly approved the project. Once the permission had been received, the pastor lost no time in searching for a religious community. On January 21, 1907, he went to Québec to offer the orphanage to the mother general of the Sisters of Charity of Québec who were experts in this type of apostolate. Archbishop Williams quickly accepted these nuns to be in charge of this work, and even promised a personal donation. In July 1907, Father Lefebvre, who had been searching for a site for the institution, proposed to his council the purchase of a magnificent plot of land in Pawtucketville, belonging to a lawyer, John McEvoy. Measuring 52,800 square feet, it was bounded by Mt. Hope, Avon, White Streets and Fourth Avenue. But at this stage, the elderly pastor, at seventy-two, burdened by age and infirmity, placed all his projects in younger hands during the month of August 1907. On the 18th of the month, Father Joseph Campeau, who had been his right-hand man all along, became pastor and superior of Saint Joseph's.

Father Campeau was young, affable and well-experienced in religious life, having received an outstanding formation. Born at Vaudreuil, Québec, on November 1, 1865, the son of Basile Campeau and Adéline Monpellier-Beaulieu, he had studied at Sainte Thérèse Seminary and entered the Oblates at Lachine, in 1884. After ordination in Ottawa by Bishop Duhamel in 1890, his superiors had sent him immediately to Winnipeg, in Manitoba, to minister in the missions of Portage-du-Rat. In 1893, Father Campeau was assigned to the Tewksbury novitiate, where he was first the bursar, and later the master of novices. In the aftermath of the fire of 1895 at the novitiate, he had been put in charge of the reconstruction of the building.

When Father Gagnon died in 1901, Father Campeau became responsible for the direction of Saint Jean Baptiste church. His great zeal and good judgment quickly gained the confidence and affection of his confreres and superiors. No one, except himself, was surprised when he was named pastor of Saint Joseph's. He tried to protest, alleging his unworthiness and lack of talent for managing such a considerable enterprise, but he got nowhere. His superiors had spoken and he bowed his head and obeyed.

The parishioners were jubilant. They perceived their new pastor to be a

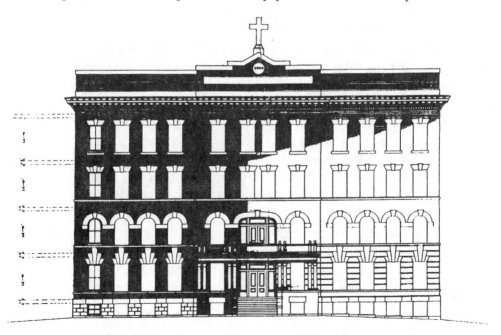

Architect's drawing of the proposed orphanage to be built in Pawtucketville.

good priest, humble and entirely devoted. He was the one who had defended the schools and he had never been too busy to visit the sick, to give advice, or to settle a family quarrel. Acclaimed by a chorus of enthusiasm, the pastor had only to say a word for the parish to fall into step and be of one mind.

Father Campeau set himself immediately to the task of carrying out the projects of his predecessor, the orphanage first and foremost among them. Archbishop Williams was gravely ill and his coadjutor, Bishop William O'Connell, granted the necessary permission, on October 22, 1907, for the Oblates to purchase the Pawtucketville property for $1,700. The venerable archbishop, who had called Father Garin to Lowell, breathed his last on August 30, 1907, at the age of eighty-five. Bishop O'Connell, his successor, a great apostle of Catholic social causes, wholeheartedly urged the Oblates to open their orphanage. Plans were drawn up for a magnificent four-story structure of stone and brick. Until funds could be raised for the new construction in Pawtucketville, it was decided to move forward, in the fall of 1908, with the previous plan of utilizing the Paquette residence. On March 7, 1908, Sister Sainte Christine, the assistant-general, and Sister St.Théodore, the general bursar, came to Lowell to examine the Paquette house. They found it totally inadequate and recommended that the Oblate Fathers build a new edifice. It was then decided to open the doors of the new orphanage in September, but the project nearly failed for lack of the necessary funds which were proving impossible to find. Everything came to a halt.

Fortunately, Providence was keeping a watchful eye and an ideal solution presented itself. Frederick Ayer, a lawyer and the philanthropic son of one of the oldest Yankee families in Lowell and New England, wanted to sell the imposing Ayer mansion, at the corner of Pawtucket and School Streets, a fifteen-minute walk from Saint Jean Baptiste church. Built around 1880, the château alone, without counting its outbuildings, contained a large number of rooms, and the gardens extended over a 110,000 square feet area. The conditions of the sale were extremely favorable. Attorney Ayer himself took on the mortgage and the $45,000 purchase price was to be spread out over a period of ten years. The Oblates seized the occasion, and waited only for the date of transfer of the property.

In the meantime, the energetic pastor, who was heading several other projects, found a solution to the question of a chapel for the Middlesex section of the city. During Archbishop Williams's illness, the difficulty had remained dormant. When Bishop O'Connell succeeded him, he refused to take any decision before coming to Lowell. There were good reasons to be hopeful that a favorable solution was at hand, for had not the new bishop said to the Oblates ". . . that he earnestly desired to see our Canadian centers served by Canadian priests, that this was much better in every respect. In addition, he exhorted us many times over to prepare young Canadian men for the diocesan clergy, and that, if need be, he would help them."

The archbishop settled the problem quickly. The Oblate ministries in Lowell were flourishing. Harmony reigned among the population; the good being accomplished due to the devotion of the Fathers was immense; Franco-American diocesan priests were few in number in the diocese; for all these reasons, Archbishop O'Connell declared formally, in a visit to Lowell on November 29, 1907, that the Oblates would keep the chapel in South Lowell, and that, as soon as possible, a chapel-school in the Middlessex area would be opened, under their care. He wanted no one other than the Oblates for these ministries. The minor scruples of the rule were of no interest to him, and, to put an end to all discussion on the matter, he even declared that the Oblates would have to wait at least ten years before he would reconsider the possibility of replacing them in these posts.

That ended the debate, but where were they to find the necessary money and personnel? Father Campeau and the provincial council were weighing the various possibilities when another delegation of Middlesex parishioners came to the rectory in March 1908, to reiterate their wish for a chapel and affirm their attachment to the Oblates. A few days later a person named Alfred Gervais, who called himself an organizer for the *Union St. Jean Baptiste* and a free lance journalist, convened three public meetings in the Middlesex Social Club hall where he stirred up the people on the subject of a new parish.

In May, the pastor found the long-awaited solution. He began negotiations with the owners of the Branch Street Baptist church, also known as the Branch Street Tabernacle, located at the junction of Branch and Middlesex Streets.

Father Campeau and his associates were so absorbed in these important transactions that they were taken by surprise upon being told that Father Lefebvre's golden jubilee of ordination was approaching. The former pastor, whose moral fiber was like that of his predecessor, Father Mangin, had hidden the fact so well from his confreres that it had taken a note from the general administration to reveal the secret to the St. Joseph community. Once the people were alerted, the parish organized an elaborate celebration that shook the modesty of the jubilarian.

Telegrams and congratulatory letters arrived from everywhere. The old missionary, visibly embarrassed, had to suffer through four days of celebrations. On June 21, 1908, plays open to the public were presented at both schools. On the following days, there was a High Mass at Saint Joseph's, a triumphal procession through the streets of Lowell, a banquet for the clergy, and a concert of sacred music to inaugurate the new great organ at St. Jean Baptiste, a gift of the parishioners in honor of Father Lefebvre. The festivities concluded in

The Ayer mansion at the corner of Pawtucket and School Streets.

the boys' school hall on Wednesday evening, June 24, with the granting of diplomas and the celebration of the feast of St. Jean Baptiste.

Deeply moved, the old jubilarian, while evoking the memory of Father Garin, once again declared his love for the Canadians of Lowell and his gratitude for the joyful years he had spent among them. To close the celebration, Father Campeau then rose and motioned for silence. In a clear and vibrant voice he announced that on that very day the parish had purchased the Ayer Castle which, in the fall, would be opened as the *Orphelinat Franco-Américain*; that soon a new parish for the Highlands would become a reality; and that in September, Saint Joseph boys school would begin a high school. The hall burst into thunderous applause. At that moment it would have been possible for all to murmur the words of Canon LePailleur who had come from Montréal to be the orator for the jubilee: "Honor to the Franco American people, honor especially to the devoted clergy who, following the example of Reverend Father Lefebvre, dedicate their lives to the cause of 'nationality' and religion."

On July 15, Father Campeau, in the presence of a lawyer, signed the papers for the purchase of the future orphanage, and on September 1, 1908, Sisters Sainte Ursule, superior, Marie de l'Incarnation, St. Luc and St. Alain arrived from Québec. The nuns were lodged at the rectory until the 15th of the month while work continued on the transformation of the mansion into a haven for orphans. On October 7, the other founding sisters: Ste. Zoé, St. Zoël, Marie-du-Bon-Conseil and Saint Alphine arrived. Each of these nuns received a salary of $50.00 per year, that is to say, $4.17 per month. Father Campeau blessed the chapel and named Father Lefebvre as the first chaplain of the orphanage, a post he would occupy until his death, on March 4, 1914, happy to spend his remaining years among "his" orphans.

Finally, on Sunday, October 11, it was announced at all the Masses in the Franco-American churches of Lowell that by two o'clock that afternoon, the orphanage would begin receiving children. On the following Sunday, the day of the formal opening, forty-one children were already housed there, and their number was constantly growing. The foundation attracted the support of everyone. A group of devoted ladies began a sewing circle to work voluntarily one afternoon each week. Medical Doctors Caisse and Payette, as well as Dentist Langis, donated their services. The women's societies took care of decorations and meals on important holidays.

On March 26, 1909, the *Corporation de l'Orphelinat Franco-Américain* was constituted to manage the enterprise and give it a solid legal base. It was made up of Oblate Fathers Lefebvre, Campeau, Lamothe, and Dubreuil, diocesan priest Father J. N. Jacques, and laymen Paul Vigeant, Elzéar Choquette, J. H. Guillet and Charles M. Williams. The title to the Paquette property was transferred to this new corporation, but the financial debt was left to the parish.

Activity in the Middlesex area quickened as well. The Baptists sold their temple to the Oblates for $26,000 on June 26, and vacated the building on

The Sisters of Charity of Québec, foundresses of the Franco-American orphanage.

July 19. The church, situated in the geographic center of the new parish, was spacious and the annex could easily be divided into four classrooms. On September 6, Father Campeau, surrounded by a jubilant throng of people, blessed the church in the name of the archbishop and placed it under the patronage of Notre Dame de Lourdes. A few days later, the inexhaustible pastor was searching for a rectory without having the funds to buy one. He approached Joseph Marin, a wealthy parishioner, asking him to buy the two small houses next to each other and near the church with the understanding that the Fathers would repurchase them from him in two years time at the price he would be paying for them. The new pastor, Father Michel Dubreuil, and his curate Father Victor Viaud, took up their posts. Two nuns from Saint Joseph, assisted by two lay teachers, opened the school with an enrollment of 249 children. The 500 Franco American families in the Highlands could finally say: "We have our parish."

The church was placed under the protection of Notre Dame de Lourdes as an act of reparation for the outrages previously committed in this Baptist temple by the apostate Chiniquy when he had preached there a few years earlier. In the same spirit of reparation, permission was obtained to have Benediction of the Blessed Sacrament every Saturday evening.

It should be noted also that the son of the Baptist minister who was in charge at the time of the sale, converted to Catholicism, and became a Benedictine priest, Father Hyacinth Dilts. He celebrated his first Mass at Notre Dame de Lourdes in the same temple where his father had been the minister.

By the end of 1908, Saint Joseph parish, in spite of having been dismembered, numbered 13,954 souls belonging to 2,857 families. The girls'school had 1,008 students and the *collège* had 1,127 boys plus eight in the new high school which had to be closed in 1910 for lack of money and personnel. The parish was flourishing and prosperous although its finances were still somewhat of a problem, but Fathers Campeau and Lefebvre had nevertheless managed to reduce the debt by $17,000, which meant that $88,139.75 still remained to be paid, besides the $45,000 for the orphanage and $27,000 for Notre Dame de Lourdes.

Harmony reigned in the Oblate community which consisted of Fathers Campeau, Lefebvre, Lamothe, Amyot, Brullard, Ehrhard, Baron, Barette, Graton, and Ouellette, along with Brothers Levasseur and Bedell. During his canonical visit of January 30, 1909, Father Fallon, the provincial, felt compelled to say:

This visit has been a pleasure and a consolation. I congratulate the Superior and all the members of the community on the excellent spirit that exists in the house. Everyone admits that union, harmony, charity, zeal, and regularity prevail more markedly than perhaps ever before.

Notre Dame de Lourdes church, the former Branch Street Tabernacle.

During his visit in July, the superior-general, Bishop Augustin Dontenwill, also praised the marvelous spirit which reigned at Saint Joseph's. It was on this occasion that Father Campeau, overjoyed, declared: "I have identified myself so completely with this parish that it truly seems to me that I could not live anywhere but in Lowell, among my Franco-Americans."

Divine Providence is often inscrutable. Three months later, on October 24, 1909, death claimed this likeable pastor. A hidden malignancy had been eating away at him, and when it was suddenly discovered, it was too late. The parish and the city were overwhelmed with sorrow at the death of the young missionary who was only forty-four years old. Archbishop O'Connell presided at the impressive funeral and as the cortège came out of the church, the bells of the firehouses in the city tolled forty-four times at half minute intervals. As the body was placed near that of Father Garin, everyone remembered the words of Archbishop O'Connell: "Reverend Father Campeau was the very model of a religious and a pastor."

19. The Apostle of the Sacred Heart

On December 8, 1909, the provincial, Father Fallon, presented the parish with a new leader, Father Henri Camille Watelle, who had been director of the juniorate in Buffalo. The news was received with some degree of astonishment.

Fr. Henri Watelle, O.M.I.

The new pastor, born at Malincourt, in the diocese of Cambrai, France, in 1877, was the son of Adolphe Watelle, a weaver, and Camille Roye. As a child he had acquired solid Christian principles from his family. As a young man, he led quite a free-wheeling life, having allowed himself to be seduced by the world. However, the virtues practiced at home came to the fore and began to trouble him regarding his lifestyle. During a trip to Lourdes, while listening to a homily being preached to the sick in which the priest exhorted them, saying: "If you want to be healed, stand up." He was deeply moved when many of the sick rose to their feet completely cured. After these manifestations of healing, and other visible proofs of faith, he too arose and was converted. From that moment he understood the goodness and fidelity of the Heavenly Mother and vowed eternal gratitude to her. In 1906, he would write, in a poem entitled: "O Lourdes!"

> *Lourdes! comme ce nom dans mon être remue*
> *Des instants vécus là, dans l'extase et l'amour,*
> *Le flot des souvenirs! Là, dans mon âme émue*
> *Quelque chose a passé du céleste séjour!*

> (Lourdes! How this name stirs in my being
> A flood of memories! Of the moments lived there
> In ecstasy and love. There, in my emotion-filled soul
> Something passed through of the eternal sojourn!)

Some time later, having returned to his home in the country, he was pursued by some bandits who wanted to do him harm. He hid in a stone grotto, invoking his heavenly protectress. According to his account, something resembling a cobweb or veil appeared at the entrance, and the bandits passed by without seeing anything. After that, the young man promised to become a priest.

Shortly after this episode, and undoubtedly upon the advice of his oldest brother Adolphe, himself an Oblate seminarian, Henri entered the Oblate scholasticate at Liège, in Belgium, where he pronounced his perpetual vows in 1901. After his ordination in 1904, he received an obedience for the Buffalo juniorate as a teacher of French and Theology. In 1908 he became the director of the juniorate where his great devotion caught the attention of the provincial.

Upon learning of his appointment as pastor of the important Lowell parish, the young priest strongly protested that he had little experience and that he lacked the talents for such a responsibility. At thirty two, and having been a priest for only five years, he had done very little ministry outside of Buffalo, and felt himself to be very inadequate for the task. But Father Fallon knew his man and was aware that the heart of Father Watelle burned with a zeal and dedication that were capable of the greatest accomplishments. In fact, even to this day, his eloquence and the ardor of his speech have remained legendary in Lowell. The provincial made him accept the nomination.

Having arrived in Lowell, the young pastor, frightened by the heavy responsibility that had been placed upon him, fell to his knees before the tabernacle in the chapel on his first night in the rectory. Remembering the words of the Lord to Saint Margaret Mary: "I will bless the ministry of priests who spread the devotion to my Sacred Heart," Father Watelle decided to consecrate the parish and his priests to the Sacred Heart of Jesus.

Devotion to the Sacred Heart was already one of the main pillars of Oblate spirituality. At the General Chapter of 1873, the congregation and all its members had been consecrated to the Sacred Heart. The *Sacré-Coeur* Basilica at Montmartre in Paris was the privileged work of the Oblate community. In Canada, the fiery oratory of Father Victor Lelièvre, at *Saint-Sauveur* of Québec, constantly proclaimed the love of the Sacred Heart of Jesus and consecrated parishes, homes, and institutions to this devotion. In Lowell, Father Garin had installed a magnificent painting of the Sacred Heart in Saint Joseph church, and had instituted the worshipful practice of the nine First Fridays of the month.

The pastor now launched a veritable crusade in the parish. His zeal increased that of the other priests and they all gave themselves over to evangelization through the Heart of Christ. In the pulpit, the confessional, in the societies and at reunions, everywhere, they spoke of the Sacred Heart.

Father Watelle proposed that the first Friday of the month become a day of adoration and prayer to the Sacred Heart a day during which the entire parish would kneel in the presence of the Blessed Sacrament, to present its accumulated sorrows and troubles. In addition, the evenings would be reserved exclusively for men, "the men of the Sacred Heart."

Many said to the pastor: "It can't be done. You'll never have more than three hundred men. Having the men of the parish come to consecrate themselves to the Sacred Heart, and then expect them to return for the following nine First Fridays is impossible. The men come to Mass on Sundays and receive communion on Holy Days, but special devotions . . . . ?"

The pastor had already foreseen the difficulties. His plan was to form an army of prayer, made up of children who would make a novena leading up to the feast. Had not the Lord said: "Let the little children come unto me"? The children are thus the great friends of the Sacred Heart. The orphans would be placed at the center of this army.

In the schools, the pastor and the Fathers asked the children: "Do you want to be friends and apostles of the Sacred Heart?" They answered "Yes," from the bottom of their hearts. Then on small pieces of paper, printed for this purpose, they indicated their little mortifications: observing silence, prompt obedience to their parents, rosaries, nine days of visits to the church. At the orphanage, the pastor gave every child a special assignment – each orphan would become an apostle. Each child had to convert one sinner through his or her prayers and sacrifices. This is how the army of two thousand children began to pray.

Father Watelle wanted to reach to the very heart of the parish in order to open it to the love from the Heart of Jesus. The Fathers visited families, the sick, those who lived alone, the abandoned, to prepare them for the great day and to gather prayer intentions. The *Dames de Sainte Anne*, the *Demoiselles de Notre Dame de Lourdes*, the *Ange Gardiens*, and the *Tertiaires* prayed and passed the word. Little by little, everyone felt carried along by grace – the pastor, the priests, the children, the adults, all felt pulled toward the merciful Heart of the First Friday.

On Wednesday and Thursday before the feast, the Fathers heard confessions all day long. On the first Friday of April 1910, the church was filled as early as 5 o'clock in the morning, for the first Mass. That morning there were 3,000 communions, a number that had never been reached up to that time. At eight o'clock the children sang at the High Mass. The pastor exhorted them to redouble their prayers and sacrifices. The *Garde Frontenac* under the leadership of Albert Bergeron, mounted an honor guard around the altar, and, during the morning, the faithful and the societies followed one another before the Blessed Sacrament. A succession of hymns, rosaries, acclamations, and supplications punctuated each hour.

At noon, a time when the church was usually nearly deserted, in came the procession of orphans. Contrary to the other parishioners, they marched straight into the sanctuary, the boys being placed on the steps of altar. There, with arms extended as on a cross, while looking at the monstrance, they implored their Father in heaven: "Sacred Heart of Jesus, have pity on us and convert the sinners in the parish. Sacred Heart of Jesus, have pity on us and cure the sick of the parish." The parishioners present in church could not contain their tears at this touching spectacle. In the afternoon the children, the young girls, and the women, continued the hour of adoration.

That evening, Father Watelle was getting ready in his room when someone knocked on his door. "Father, you must come, the church is already filled with men. There are even some on the stairs of the altar!" Three thousand men had crowded into the church. The vestibule, the stairs, the galleries, and the aisles were full. The pastor, overwhelmed with emotion, could not refrain from saying: "This is the most beautiful day of my life."

Father Graton began with the rosary. Between each decade, he read a few of the over 800 intentions that had been placed in a basket near the communion rail. Before the fifth decade, the men began to enumerate the graces they had obtained. Physical cures, spiritual healings, and conversions were proclaimed throughout the church. It was felt that the mercy of Jesus was answering all needs.

The pastor mounted in the pulpit and allowed the fire and eloquence burning in his heart to spill forth. His words electrified the assembled congregation. He painted a picture of the daily, and often sad, reality of the worker. Without rest or pause, the breadwinner must give himself over to labor and fatigue. Sweat runs down his brow, but he must accomplish his grueling task with courage. Happiness and prosperity do not always reign in the home.

Poverty, mutual wrongs, sickness, sin, all cause their ravages. In the face of this suffering and inexorable evil, where can one turn to find love and rest? The church of Jesus, the church of the Sacred Heart, is here. The One Who understands, the One Who heals, the One Who consoles is here.

Everyone began to sing in unison *Nous voulons Dieu* (We want God). The pastor prepared for the crowning glory of the celebration with supplications and exhortations. After the *Tantum ergo* Father Watelle prayed the Act of Consecration to the Sacred Heart:

O! workers, O! laborers, O! heads of families, O! you for whom worrying about daily bread makes you forget Sunday prayer, you who suffer, rejoice! On the first Friday of April, you have called out to the Sacred Heart of Jesus. You are sure of Him, you can count on His love, and the more you love Him, the more strength and consolation will you have to accomplish the great work of your salvation.

Cheers rang out from all sides as he concluded; then the men brought the ceremony to a close by singing the Montmartre hymn: *Pitié, mon Dieu* (Pity, my God)

Never had the parish seen such a first Friday. The parishioners promised to return every month and, for weeks, stories of healings and favors granted continued to be told or were published. One such story was that of a young woman at the school who, upon seeing the conversion of her father and the healing of her mother, promised to become a nun; another told of a husband who stopped his drinking; then there was the mother of a family cured of paralysis, etc.

The pastor had touched the spiritual heart of the parish, and his program was now clear – to strengthen the spirit of the parish by deepening its spiritual life. To accomplish this, he would use all the means available to him, and find new ones if need be.

To promote relationships among the parishioners, he founded *Le Bulletin Paroissial Franco-Américain* a monthly magazine of about fifty pages. The first issue appeared in May 1910. Under the able pen of its editor, Father Armand Baron, the Bulletin disseminated sound teaching to the families, and kept the population abreast of the many activities organized by the parishioners, spiritual as well as social.

It soon became apparent that the *Bulletin* was not appearing frequently enough to expedite the diffusion of news. Therefore, on Sunday, May 7, 1911, the parish announced a new publication *Le Supplément du Bulletin Paroissial.* This weekly newspaper, which first appeared in a small format, but was later changed to a large one, published all the news and activities of the parish, while the monthly Bulletin concentrated on feature articles, literary competitions, and columns of greater interest. These two publications became models of the genre. In Paris, at the annual general congress of La Bonne Presse in October of 1911, the *Bulletin Paroissial Franco-Américain* of Lowell was proposed as the model for parish bulletins throughout France. Subscribers from outside Lowell increased and *L'Action Catholique* of Québec, for its part, also proposed it as a model. The *Supplément* continued to be published under the auspices of the parish until May 2, 1913, when the Fathers sold it to its printer, Joseph Lambert, who turned it into a daily paper, until it ceased to appear in 1916.

The observance of the First Fridays not only held steady, it intensified. In 1910 the most celebrated missionaries of the time were brought in to preach the preparatory novenas: Father Lelièvre from Saint Sauveur in Québec, and Father Joseph Lemius, the former superior of Montmartre and by then the procurator to the Holy See for the Oblates.

In the history of the Church, the twentieth century was marked by the coming of a spirituality of the Eucharist that was more open and more sensitive to the graces of the Real Presence on a daily basis. In 1905, Saint Pius X published his famous liberating decree on frequent Communion and five years later, in August 1910, the Sacred Congregation for the Sacraments lowered to seven years, the age of admission to the Eucharist. The International Eucharistic Congress, announced for September 1910 in Montréal, proclaimed the triumph of the Eucharist in the twentieth century.

Father Watelle had noticed that in Lowell, on the Sunday of the Solemnity of the Blessed Sacrament, *Corpus Christi*, the Lord had never been taken outside the church. So he proposed a grand procession of the Blessed Sacrament throughout the streets of Little Canada, with solemn benediction at a public repository. The idea seemed daring, especially in a Protestant country, but the pastor did not hesitate in the least.

The procession with the Blessed Sacrament took place on May 29, 1910. The monstrance, carried by the pastor under a canopy embroidered in gold, was surrounded by the *Garde des Saints Anges*, preceded by the delegations of religious and "national" societies. They marched down Aiken, Cheever, Moody, and Austin Streets. The houses along the way were decked out with flags and   pictures of the Sacred Heart, while others had placed altars in their doors or windows. Twenty thousand people knelt in the streets of Little Canada on that day, as the Lord passed by. One mother who gave birth to a boy at the moment that the procession was passing, had the child raised to the window so as to consecrate him to God. The child, Armand Morissette, would become an Oblate priest.

At the end of Cheever Street, the procession stopped at a public altar, erected as a repository, for solemn benediction. Throughout Little Canada, silence and contemplation reigned as in a church, interrupted only by the praying of the rosary and the singing of Eucharistic hymns. The entire city of Lowell was moved by this public demonstration of such piety.

In September, the pastor, many priests, and a great number of parishioners, traveled to Montréal to attend the International Eucharistic Congress, accompanied by the *Garde Frontenac*, the only Franco American marching unit from the United States to take part in the opening procession of the congress. It brought back to Lowell the banner which had adorned the triumphal arch erected on St. Hubert Street, by the Franco-American societies of the United States. On their return, the priests and the faithful vowed to make the observance of the Feast of the Blessed Sacrament in 1911 even more memorable than that of 1910.

At the request of the archbishop, a Confraternity of the Blessed Sacrament was constituted in the parish on April 18, 1911. On every Tuesday night, the members gathered in St. Jean Baptiste church for an hour of adoration before the Blessed Sacrament in reparation for the sins of the parish. Generally, the church was packed, and to them the pastor added the organization of men and women mill workers who promised together to offer, in groups of ten to fifteen, one hour of their work in reparation for sins.

The "Young Ladies of Notre Dame de Lourdes" in procession.

The spirit of faith and penance, combined with great confidence in the sacraments as instruments of personal and collective sanctification, created a religious atmosphere and a very deep sense of the spiritual in the parish of that time. Young women read the *Bulletin Paroissial* at the mills in their leisure moments. The men, still fasting, rose at dawn to be able to attend the five o'clock Mass before going to work. The school children sang at the Masses and contributed regularly to the collections for the missions. In 1910, the parish gave $1,940 to the Society for the Propagation of the Faith. This was the highest amount contributed in the archdiocese. The Sewing Circle and the other women's societies collected contributions from each other for the upkeep of the orphans.

The religious societies competed with one another in numbers of activities and recruitment. In 1911, the two fraternities of the Third Order together numbered nearly 900 members, including the novices. The *Congréganistes*, namely the Young Ladies of Notre Dame de Lourdes, grouped 700 young women. The *Enfants de Marie* for their part had 850 members and, under the direction of the beloved Father Graton, an annual contingent of them left for the convent and religious communities. The *Dames de Sainte Anne*, a very powerful society of more than 1,100 members, had counselors and nurses in each section of the parish. All the societies were flourishing. In 1906, Father Viaud had added a military guard to the *Societé de l'Ange Gardien* and, shortly thereafter, a drum and bugle corps under the direction of Father Dénizot, an accomplished musician.

The activity of the priests also reached within the families. Each society had its major annual retreat, and a spiritual director who provided orientation on the direction to follow on the most diverse and specific questions. As an example, consider some of the "dangers" discussed in 1909 during meetings of the *Dames de Sainte Anne*: "birth control, French Protestant newspapers and bibles, public schools, children who sleep in their parents' bedroom or who sleep together, Jewish ragmen, theaters and movies, onanism, and drunkenness."

During that period, the Fathers waged a battle against the abuse of alcohol, and those who, without a license, sold liquor even on Sundays in Little Canada. From the pulpit, the pastor denounced in fiery, energetic accents the plague of alcoholism, and the horrors it brought to the heart of families. In encouraging his people to save money or to donate to a worthy cause, he often repeated: "Don't tell me there's no more money. I'll believe it when the doors of the saloons close for lack of drinkers."

Poverty was constantly lurking in the parish, and the Fathers did not like to see their charges succumb to the necessity of borrowing money from usurers, at a rate that often surpassed 100%. In 1909, Pierre Jay, the Massachusetts

Banking Commissioner, the descendant of an old Huguenot family, wrote, with the help of Alphonse Desjardins of Québec, the first law in the United States regulating the establishment of Credit Unions. This system of cooperatively based savings and loan associations, developed and finalized by Desjardins, answered a real need, and soon became implanted in the United States.

In July 1911, the Massachusetts government invited Desjardins to come to the Commonwealth in order to explain his system of Credit Unions. Immediately, Frank Ricard, a jeweler, invited him to come to Lowell, and put him up as his guest during his stay. When Father Watelle heard of this, he suggested that Desjardins speak at the great outdoor festival held on July 2 on the grounds of the orphanage. A thousand people heard the lecture and, on the spot, 200 people committed themselves to start a Credit Union in Lowell. The pastor and a group of influential men signed the official petition papers which were presented in Boston on July 19. The authorization having been granted, nothing was done until December 27, when Father Watelle convened a meeting in the halls of the C.M.A.C. At this meeting, presided over by Joseph Lambert and Attorney Guillet, the new *Caisse Populaire Jeanne d'Arc* received its first officers: Ephrem Pelletier was selected as president, Joseph Lambert was named secretary, Léonce Fortin, vice president, Albert Jean, treasurer,

Offices of the *Caisse Populaire Jeanne d'Arc* - the Jeanne d'Arc Credit Union - at the corner of Decatur and Merrimack streets.

164

Atty. Guillet, N. M. Lozeau, L. N. Milot, Thomas Caron, and Aimée Gionet, directors. The constitution was adopted on December 29, and on January 5, 1912, Joseph Routhier, Albéric Ducharme, and Ovide Ledoux were elected to the supervisory committee. For the moment, the *Caisse* limited itself to receiving the deposits of the school children and for this reason, Father Audibert was named collector. As of January 12, the good Father, after doing the rounds of the classes in the *collège* St. Joseph had in hand a total deposit of $2.91, provided by twenty-nine children. The most generous of them had donated 38 cents!

At a meeting on February 12, held at the Saint Joseph rectory, it was decided to begin accepting contributions for shares and deposits. At the May 17 meeting, the directors voted to begin making loans on promissory notes and issue mortgages, the former at 6% and the latter at 5% interest. As a result, by the end of the year 1912, the "Franco American bank" showed assets of $6,063.37 of which the amount of $1,536.50 was in shares, and $4,469.26 in deposits. The shares sold for $5.00 and Father Audibert, the chaplain-collector of the bank regularly deposited in the savings department, $150 to $160 received each month from the savings of the school children. In 1967, the credit union held $7,400,000 in assets and it continues to perform notable services for the economic viability of the Franco American community of Lowell.

Alphonse Desjardins also spoke on July 3, 1911, at another great outdoor festival, this one held at Washington Park, facing Notre Dame de Lourdes church. Forty-four parishioners immediately committed themselves to becoming incorporators of the Notre Dame de Lourdes Credit Union which was founded in October of that same year. Unfortunately, after having been prosperous for a time, this credit union foundered a few years after the disastrous economic Crash of 1929.

The question of Catholic schools was still a hotly debated issue. Archbishop O'Connell had ordered his clergy to refuse absolution in confession to parents who sent their children to public schools. Father Watelle, with his usual ardor, joined in the campaign. In their homilies from the pulpit, and in the confessional, he and his associates railed against the public schools and the indifference that these schools inculcated. Studying the parochial schools, he changed nothing in the regulations Father Campeau had established. The children in the upper grades, called the "academic classes," paid 15 cents per week; the others 10 cents. The little ones in the "baby room" paid 5 cents. If many brothers or sisters attended the same school, the oldest paid 10 or 15 cents according to the class, and all the others 5 cents. Even though the schools were flourishing, the pastor could not help but noticing the number of students in the public schools, especially in Pawtucketville.

There were 2,067 children in the parochial schools in 1910, and 405 parish children in the public schools. Of the latter, the largest number were from Pawtucketville. In 1909, there were 2,593 Franco Americans in Pawtucketville – 365 children attended the parochial schools and 250 went to the public schools. For the youngest of the children, the trek to Saint Joseph's schools was quite long, especially in the winter and on rainy days. As a result, the parents either kept the children at home or sent them to the public school which was closer for, in 1898, the city had constructed an eight-classroom school building on Moody Street – University Avenue, today.

To remedy the situation, the Misses Ernestine Alexander and Anisie Sawyer taught a few classes in the rooms of the Pawtucketville Social Club for the school year 1909-1910. During the summer, the pastor had some plans drawn up, and hired the contractor J. B. Morin to begin the construction of a small three-classroom school. Built at the cost of $6,579.57 on the Mt. Hope Street lot, which had previously been bought for the orphanage, the small school, called *Notre-Dame-du-Sacré-Coeur*, opened its doors on October 5, 1910, to 130 children: 50 boys and 80 girls. Sister Marie Arthur, Sister Sainte Solange, and Miss Alexander divided the three classes among themselves.

This encouraged the Pawtucketville parishioners to speak more vigorously about a separate parish or relief chapel. But the Oblates succeeded in postponing the project.

It was hoped that with the opening of the Pawtucketville school, more room would be available in the school on Moody Street. As early as 1909, the nuns had complained that there were too many children, and that more classrooms were needed. In January 1910, the pastor asked for four more religious, and had the auditorium in the girls' school divided into four classrooms.

On October 13, 1911, the parish rented from the city a small closed public school building, at the end of Cheever Street, for $1.00 per month, and had the needed repairs made to accommodate one classroom and a kindergarten for children under seven years of age. Four classes of small boys were eventually placed there and the building became known as Saint Rémi school. In June 1916, the city sold the property to Elie Délisle who rented it to the parish until 1919 when it was demolished. The classes were then transferred to the basement of the *collège*.

The nuns, more numerous now, held multiple novenas to Saint Joseph, so that the Fathers would find them new quarters. The old convent and the dormitory house, at the corner of James Street, had become clearly harmful to their health. These religious women slept in two old houses, without benefit of sunlight, which they called *les bas fonds* (the slums), abutting tenements housing twelve to sixteen families. Construction was deemed necessary, but

On the left, the new brick convent built in 1911, at the corner of Moody and James Street. On the right, the trellised fence and the white statue of the Sacred Heart.

where? After a great deal of discussion, projects which went nowhere, and innumerable difficulties, the exasperated sister superior finally said simply to the Fathers: "Do what seems fitting to you, but please find us larger and more convenient accommodations. The sisters work, are devoted, and they deserve some consideration."

Finally a plan and a site were agreed upon. Construction of a large three-story brick convent, on the corner of Moody and James Streets, began in May and ended on November 12, 1911, with the blessing of the building by Father Watelle, in the presence of Mother Duhamel, the superior-general. The old convent and the dormitory building were moved to the other side of the street, at the corner of Spaulding and Moody Streets, near the little white school. The parish rented out the two buildings for a few years before selling them.

A trellised fence separated the school yard from Moody Street and the sisters were hoping to erect a large statue of the Sacred Heart of Montmartre behind the fence, on the site of the former convent, facing Spaulding Street. The lack of money for this reverential project prevented its realization, to the sisters' great sorrow. But one day, it was noticed that a thick clump of clover had grown on the site and that each leaf bore the imprint of a blood-red heart. The pastor immediately promised the statue, and donated $50.00 towards its purchase. Sister MacMillan, the superior of the convent, donated the other

167

The Grotto of Our Lady of Lourdes on the grounds of the Franco-American Orphanage shortly after its installation. It is an exact replica of the original in France.

$50.00. On March 18, 1912, the statue arrived from France, and it was blessed on June 21st. This imposing statue of the Sacred Heart dominated the school yard and greeted passers by until September 21, 1938, when it was crushed by a falling elm tree during the devastating hurricane of that year.

Ever since his arrival in Lowell, Father Watelle had cherished a dream dear to his heart. His conversion at Lourdes had affected him deeply, and his great desire was to make the devotion to Our Lady of Lourdes more accessible to those who could not travel to that place of miracles in France. As an Oblate, consecrated by his vows to a special love for the Mother of God, he wanted his parishioners to have a more intimate union of prayer with the one who was the perfect image of prayer. He dreamed of erecting a shrine and, in the *Bulletin Paroissial* of October 1910, he wrote an article entitled *"Est il réalisable ce rêve?"* (Is this dream realizable?) In it, he announced his desire to build a replica of the Lourdes grotto on the grounds of the orphanage. "Now, I would like to place a statue of the Blessed Virgin on the orphanage property, which is as immense as a park, and give that statue a suitable setting, a beautiful grotto, a grotto which would be an exact copy of the one at Lourdes."

To this end, if the parishioners accepted the idea, he was willing to receive voluntary contributions. Not only did the parishioners accept "the dream" with enthusiasm, a veritable avalanche of gifts and donations ensued. Two generous sisters, who have remained anonymous to this day, gave $150.00

Float carrying the statue of Notre Dame de Lourdes, in front of St. Jean Baptiste Chruch, in the procession to the grotto September 4, 1911.

for the life-size statue. Some school children donated their five-cent Saturday movie money for the work of the grotto. Others organized whist parties, bean suppers, and raffles for this purpose. What the pastor believed possible only in four or five-years-time was accomplished in fewer than six months.

At the end of May 1911, Lourdes sent water to be distributed by the sisters at the orphanage, along with two stones taken from the Grotto there. One of those stones, the smaller one, came from next to the wild-rose bush on which the Blessed Mother had placed her foot. On May 13, a contract was signed with J. B. Morin, and construction began. This Lourdes grotto, the first in New England, reproduced in iron and cement the exact dimensions of the one in France. In the month of June, it was decided to make of the inauguration a public homage to the Blessed Virgin. On September 4, 1911, a long procession, made up of military guard units, bands, delegations of Franco-American societies from all over New England, and a great many floats, set forth to the sound of bells from City Hall. After passing in review before the mayor and the City Council, the parade led the way to the grotto followed by the float carrying the statue of Notre Dame de Lourdes. On the grounds of the grotto, 1,500 young girls intoned the glories of Mary while the statue was placed on the pedestal which it still occupies to this day. That night, it was Lourdes in Lowell when thousands of faithful gathered from eight to eleven, for the torchlight procession, and recited the same devotions as those of the pilgrimages to Lourdes itself.

Once again the pastor had judged correctly, and the heart of the people had responded with love and joy. On the blessed grounds of the orphanage, Lowell had its own sanctuary, its own small island of grace. In time its reputation spread, and even now, the faithful can be found there at all hours of the day. The following year, Stations of the Cross, imported from France, were added to the grotto, as well as a Calvary dominated by the crucified Christ. Pilgrimages to the site began immediately. First came the parish societies, then the other parishes, and finally cities from outside Lowell. The Oblate novices and scholastics from Tewksbury came on foot, and the grand procession for the Feast of Corpus Christi on June 9, 1912, the last of this kind, marched to the grotto for the benediction of the Blessed Sacrament. For nearly twenty-five years the *Enfants de Marie*, under the direction of Father Graton, made their annual pilgrimage there during the month of May.

In his address of September 4, Father Watelle emphasized one of the main reasons which had led him to propose this project.

O! how many times has my heart grieved with sorrow at the foot of the bed of a dying mother! I have never been able to overcome my emotion when, at the approach of death, the hands growing cold, the eyes filling with their last tears, the lips already pale, these mothers would say to me: "O, Father, for me, dying is nothing. But what will become of my poor children when they no longer have a mother?" I have wanted to give the orphans, who are here before us, the image of their Heavenly Mother. It seemed to me that they would be less sad when they could come every day to see the image of their Heavenly Mother. And that is why, encouraged by your generosity, I have built this Grotto.

The orphans and the work related to the orphanage occupied a large part of his apostolic heart. From his arrival at Saint Joseph's, he gave evidence of a special love for these children. This was no surprise since he himself had lost his father. His mother had become a widow shortly after the birth of her son, Henri, and he clearly recalled the long hours of fatigue and sorrow imposed upon this saintly woman who had prayed so much for her sons. He also remembered the absence of a beloved father, of the heart of this father, reputed to be as courageous as he was kind. Father Watelle's devotion to the Sacred Heart of Jesus and to Our Lady of Lourdes needs no further explanation.

From the time it opened, the orphanage was the object of everyone's prayers and affection. The work, supported by voluntary offerings, was in need of continual financial assistance. The monthly contribution of six dollars by the children who had relatives hardly sufficed. The offerings for food were called *l'oeuvre du pain* (project bread). So, the parishioners undertook the usual means of raising funds. Miss Clorilda Héroux, for example, the great organizer of whist parties, raised $375 for *l'oeuvre du pain* at one of these in July 1910, at the *Collège Saint Joseph*. On July 3 and 4, 1910, a large outdoor festival was held on the grounds of the orphanage, with booths and amusements, for the benefit of this cause. The need for funds constantly stimulated everyone's imagination.

The Fathers, having noticed how their parishioners were attracted to amusement parks in the summer, decided to take advantage of this situation. Instead of taking the electric streetcar to Lakeview or Willow Dale, why not utilize the vast grounds of the orphanage? So, it was announced that in 1911, from June 24 to September 3, there would be an outdoor fair every Sunday, with booths, races, amusements, and shows on the orphanage grounds. Some wealthy parishioners: Joseph Marin, J. B. Pelneault and others, lent their automobiles for a twenty-five-cent tour. One raffle offered a St. Bernard dog as the prize, another, the pastor's watch. On July 22, there were 2,500 people on the grounds, including the volunteers. On the closing day, September 3, 1,800 admission tickets were sold. The summer brought in a total profit of $4,042.59. The great summer celebration of 1912 would be the last for, with the erection of the shrine, fairs were no longer appropriate on these grounds.

The pastor kept watch over his favorite project, and as usual faced all obstacles without hesitation. In October 1911, he reorganized *l'oeuvre du pain* as a religious confraternity, with the usual privileges – the benefit of the orphans' prayers, a solemn funeral Mass at death, commemorative Masses. The members promised to give five cents a week for the food. The pastor even composed a hymn *Cantique de l'Oeuvre du Pain* to be sung by the children. In November 1911, Father Watelle announced from the pulpit that he wished to complete the work of Father Campeau. The orphanage could only house eighty-six children at its opening and, even when giving preference to the children who had lost both their parents, and crowding them in to accommodate 125 in 1911, space was still lacking for all those who were seeking shelter.

So, he proposed to add a very modern brick and granite extension, four stories high, which could accommodate 300 children. It would also include a spacious chapel and an auditorium. The parishioners were flabbergasted, but they accepted immediately, and in April 1912, a fund drive was launched among the people. Those who donated five dollars would have their names placed in the main altar. Others, especially the societies, funded beds at $100 dollars apiece.

On December 9, 1911, construction of the new orphanage began under the direction of J. B. Morin. The expenses were extensive, and in October 1912, the

St. Jean Baptiste Church in flames, November 21, 1912.

parish had to borrow $35,000 in order to continue work on the building. The orphans prayed, the pastor increased his multiple activities, and the parishioners organized bazaars and fairs. Everyone worked together, and the future seemed to have no surprise in reserve.

On Thursday morning, November 21, 1912, Father Guillaume Ouellette was saying the 7 o'clock Mass in the basement of Saint Jean Baptiste church when the altar boy, Arthur Labrecque, came out of the sacristy shouting: "The sacristy is on fire!" An explosion in the gas meter had spread the fire in the walls of the church and in short order the magnificent temple fell prey to the flames. The news circulated quickly throughout the mills: "Saint Jean Baptiste church is burning." Father Ouellette was able to save the Eucharistic Species and the sacred vessels, while Father Baron, aided by a host of parishioners who had rushed in from everywhere, was able to empty the bookstore and library. Once his task was accomplished, he collapsed in the arms of the firemen. The young Fathers carried old Father Lefebvre, in his bed, to the residence of Dr. Lamoureux, directly across from the rectory. Others, with the help of parishioners, did their best to empty the rectory while the firemen were bringing out the statues and the vestments from the church. Mr. Goodwin, who made the organ, found his way to the choir loft to close the openings of the organ pipes in the hope of avoiding too much damage. The heat was so intense that in less than three hours the roof and the vaults were in ashes. All that remained were the walls and the basement.

In the midst of the disaster, the parishioners rallied. As a young working woman wrote to the *Bulletin*: "No, nothing can bring hearts together as much as a disaster experienced in common. Not only at the mill, but in our rooming house, in the midst of families, everywhere, I have noticed that the loss of our church has revived a new spirit of charity and love of neighbor." The grief was deep and everyone felt the loss of this common home, so beloved and filled with consolation. Father Nolin, an amateur poet, expressed everyone's desire when

View of the façade during the fire.

he wrote:

Oui, l'amour, la pitié de là-haut vont descendre
Pour ouvrir le tombeau,
Et notre temple aimé renaîtra de sa cendre,
Et plus jeune et plus beau.

(Yes, love and pity from on high will descend
To open the tomb,
And our beloved temple will be reborn from its ashes,
Both younger and more beautiful.)

The pastor, in his first message, expressed himself thus:

Saint Jean Baptiste church. It is now but a heap of ruins—three hours of fire were enough to plunge to the ground this church in which we dared to pride ourselves, and to bury in the disaster the long years of savings and sacrifices. Our heart is bleeding too heavily for us to be able to talk very much. God has his designs in allowing this catastrophe. May His Holy Will be blessed. Saint Jean Baptiste church has fallen to the ground. We shall rebuild it.

The day after the fire, Father Watelle placed little Albina Moreau on a box in front of the church selling tickets, two for a quarter, to view the ruins. Without neglecting the orphanage, people began to raise funds for the reconstruction of the church. Donations arrived from everywhere, from Protestants as well as Catholics. At the end of one week nearly $1,000 had been collected.

Religious services for the moment took place at Saint Joseph's and, during the first week, at the C.M.A.C. In December a provisional roof was placed over the basement which, temporarily, became an auxiliary chapel. Saint Joseph's became once again the principal parish church, as in Father Garin's day.

Before the fire, the church had been assessed at $115,000, and the insurance paid $107,000.47. However, an extra $50,000 would be needed because of a proposal to modify the interior of the church. From the time of the opening of Saint Jean Baptiste church it was found that the balconies were so high that the people could see neither the altar nor the preacher. In February 1902, Napoléon Bourassa, a noted architect from Montréal, visited the church and gave his verdict that nothing could be done. It was thus decided to rebuild without galleries or internal columns. To accomplish this, the church would be covered with a roof of steel and reinforced concrete resting on steel columns in the walls. Using the least amount of wood possible, and brick firewalls to prevent fire from ever spreading within the walls, the church would be made absolutely fireproof. Mr. William Drapeau, a parishioner, was given the contract for the work. In April 1913, the workers began to clear the interior and the pastor signed the first contracts. By June the steel for the roof was already in place, while at the same time the construction of a new granite extension to house the sacristy and the library was progressing.

While all of this was going on, the orphans took possession of their new building on February 19, 1913. Father Watelle blessed the house, which had cost almost $60,000, and within a few days all 300 places were filled. The four-story building measured 146 x 60 feet, and the three-story extension for the chapel and auditorium, 36 x 78 feet. The Franco-American Orphanage of Lowell, with its personnel of twenty-two nuns and twelve lay persons became one of the most modern Catholic institutions in the State, and was the object of legitimate pride for the parishioners of Saint Joseph.

In August 1913, yet more news ran through Little Canada – Father Watelle was gone! It was true. The pastor, exhausted from his constant labors, having been sent by his superiors to a new field of apostolate, had judged best, to avoid all demonstrations, to leave Lowell quietly on the evening of August 15, for Campbell, Nebraska, where he replaced Father Arthur Bernèche. He died on October 8, 1931, as pastor of the small St. Patrick parish, in Manley, Nebraska.

An era in the life of the parish came to an end with Father Watelle's departure. For four years, souls had experienced an intense ardor and an almost unparalleled period of activity. The passage of the Apostle of the Sacred Heart in Lowell left, in the hearts of everyone, its mark of piety and fervor that are still visible in our day.

20. "Resurrexit"

Father Watelle's departure marked the end of an era in the life of the parish which had stabilized and was perceived less and less as mission territory. There was little change in the population. New immigrants were arriving in smaller numbers. Vocations to the priesthood were increasing constantly, and its chief endeavors functioned smoothly in the context of a rich and well-nurtured spirituality.

Starting in 1913, almost all the pastors of Saint Joseph's would be American-born, and the majority of them natives of Lowell itself. During these years, the pastors were mainly concerned with consolidating Franco-American life both within the parish as well as in civic institutions, adding new projects, as required by the evolution of society, and integrating the different perspectives of the twentieth century into a spirituality that was already firmly established.

On August 16, 1913, to everyone's joy, a child of the parish became the pastor of Saint Joseph's. Born in Lowell on November 22, 1881, Father Joseph Hervé Racette was the son of Jules Racette and Louise Beaupré. After attending the parochial schools, he entered the Oblate juniorate in Buffalo, completing his studies at the University of Ottawa before being ordained to the priesthood on June 17, 1905, one year after the ordination of his brother, Father Julien Racette. He was the assistant-superior at the novitiate in Tewksbury when he

Fr. Hervé Racette, O.M.I.

176

was assigned to Saint Joseph's.

Father Hervé was a peaceful and gentle man who was immediately liked by his parishioners. A very patient person and well-adapted to the mentality of his people, he was able to appease those few who had been somewhat troubled by Father Watelle's sometimes curt manner. Father Racette's goodness, joined to a subtle sense of humor, made him the ideal man to watch over the development of the parish and the reconstruction of the church.

The parish finances precluded any further borrowing. In 1913, the debt amounted to over $60,000 while the orphanage owed $105,402.99! Cardinal O'Connell had ordered that the reconstruction of the church be carried out without loans of any kind, stipulating that all decorations of the church itself – stained-glass windows, Stations of the Cross, frescoes – be paid for in cash with money received from voluntary donations. Raffles, special collections, plays, and concerts brought in the $50,000 needed for the reconstruction, but the Fathers and the parishioners themselves wanted Saint Jean Baptiste church to be a sumptuous and opulent temple, the most beautiful in the city.

Father Racette signed a contract with Kinkelin, an artist from New York, for the major frescoes covering the vaults and the apse, as well as the medallions over the nave of the church, two of which would remain unpainted, due to the sudden death of the artist in the course of doing this work. In the fall of 1914, the pastor announced a fund drive for the windows – thirty-four single ones at $100 apiece, nine triple ones at $200, and five in the sanctuary at $500 each. Saint Jean Baptiste church, like Saint Joseph's, had always had windows that were simply painted white. The prospect of stained-glass windows portraying saints and the life of Christ, appealed to everyone. Within less than a month the windows were paid for and ordered. The small single windows, each depicting a saint, were particularly prized by the donors, for each person wanted to see in them his or her favorite saint. The Stations of the Cross, imported from France, were also made possible through individual donations.

At long last, the laborers and workmen laid down their tools and pronounced the reconstruction complete. On Sunday, February 28, 1915, Saint Jean Baptiste church reopened for services. The people, overwhelmed by the grandeur and beauty of the temple, could not restrain their admiration and jubilation. The vast church, which could hold 1,800 people, had no columns, and its walls, interspersed with numerous stained-glass windows, bestowed upon the whole an appearance of simplicity and openness, but also one of great dignity, with its frescoes, rich alabaster lamps and marble communion rail enhanced with cast brass moldings. This magnificence, combined with the sober architectural lines of the interior, made the church one of the most beautiful in the city, as well as within the Oblate congregation. Its fireproof construction, and its nave, free of columns, were both considered to be marvels of the era. The solemn High Mass was celebrated by the provincial, Father Wade Smith, assisted by Father J. B. Labossière, pastor of St. Louis, and Father Graton. The 150-member choir, under the direction of the organist, Professor Louis Napoléon Guilbault, sang Gounod's Mass of Saint Cecilia.

The pastor, in his homily, was expressing what everyone was thinking when he stated:

> At last, the time of great trials and exile, so to speak, has come to an end. Your religious gatherings will henceforth be garbed with brilliantly imposing splendor. The grandiose ceremonies of the Catholic Church can now be displayed before your eyes without obstruction. And this happiness is being savored by you today. When you feel moved to the very depth of your soul by what you are seeing and hearing, can you, for a single instant, regret past sacrifices? When you feel overcome with admiration, what feelings of joy and gratitude must rise up in your hearts, what feelings of legitimate pride must take hold of you! Yes, here is your house, as it is that of your God. Yes, here is your monument, your glory lies here. May God be blessed for it. But it is useless to remind you, my dear brothers, that if your monument is here, this is especially a house of prayer, here is the temple of your God, here is the door to heaven. We do not come here out of shallow curiosity, we come here to pray. These paintings, these stained-glass windows, these statues tell you loudly and clearly that you are in a sacred temple where each thought that does not rise toward the Creator is profane and outlawed.

The reopening of the church served as a prelude to the grand celebrations of its blessing and solemn dedication by Cardinal O'Connell, on Sunday, May 16. The festivities of February 28 had the characteristics of a family celebration while those held on May 16 became the occasion for an official and public manifestation, first of all, of the Franco American parish, and then, of the universal Church. Cardinal O'Connell, a Prince of the Church since 1911, presided at the sung Mass and solemn Benediction, with an outdoor procession. This first visit of a cardinal to Saint Jean Baptiste would not be the last. That evening, His Eminence spoke to the Catholic men of Lowell at Associate Hall.

He exhorted the men to come together in an organization promoting Catholic Action and the lay apostolate. To this end, he proposed that they become members of the American Federation of Catholic Societies. This federation, backed by the hierarchy, saw itself as being the channel for Catholic social action and the voice of American Catholics. The group sought especially at that time to counteract the anti-Catholic propaganda that was rampant in the

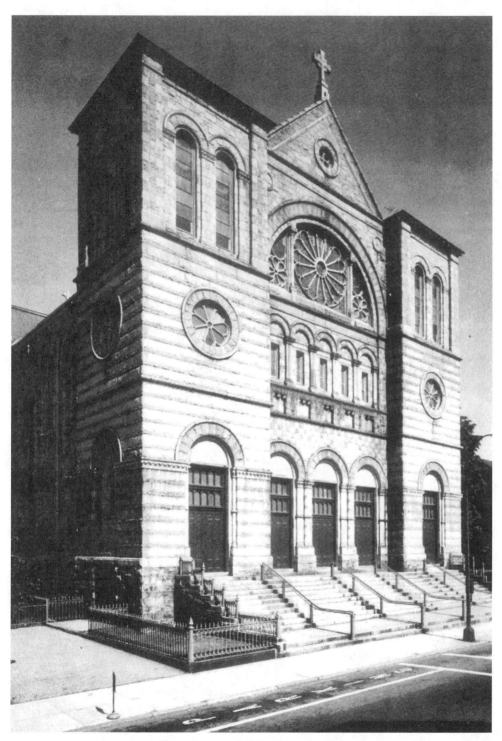

Façade of the reconstructed St. Jean Baptiste Church.

The new interior of St. Jean Baptiste Church.

country since the outbreak of war in Europe. The patriotism of Catholics and, even more so, that of ethnic groups, came under suspicion everywhere.

In 1914, Protestant legislators in Boston proposed a bill attempting to abolish parochial schools in Massachusetts. Using the pretext that the schools were not well-administered, they wanted to exercise strict control over the curriculum and eliminate the teaching of foreign languages. The Franco-American legislators, among whom was Henri Achin from Lowell, along with other Catholic legislators and the Cardinal's attorney, managed to defeat the proposed bill. In 1914 and 1915, Henri Achin presented his bill to make New Year's Day a legal holiday in Massachusetts. It was defeated each time for fear of creating a Catholic holiday. The bill passed only the third time it was presented, in 1916.

The cardinal, who was an energetic defender of Catholic rights, enjoyed a national reputation for his masterful discourses and his backing of the Federation of Catholic Societies. Therefore, when, on June 23, 1915, through the intermediary of Father Mullen, pastor of Saint Michael's, he convoked the Franco-American societies of Lowell at Associate Hall for the purpose of affiliating them to the Catholic Federation, the Franco-Americans, both lay and clergy attended, but not without certain misgivings for, to achieve its ends, this federation, and often the hierarchy itself, were sacrificing the linguistic aspirations of the various Catholic ethnic groups in the country. Their intention was to project the image of an American Catholicism united by allegiance to the American flag and the English language.

The meeting concluded without having decided anything at all. Father Racette and the other priests spoke in favor of the work already accomplished by the federation, but left it up to the societies to decide whether or not they would join. Finally, when, in September 1916, the major fraternal societies of New England founded *La Fédération Catholique Franco-Américaine* for the purpose of uniting the Franco-Americans in defense of their religious and ethnic rights, the Lowell societies, their chaplains at the head, wasted no time in becoming affiliated.

On August 27, 1915, Father Augustin Hickey, the archdiocesan superintendent of schools, "invited" the nuns and brothers to attend a conference held at Boston College to promote the development and expansion of the English language in the parochial schools. The following September 22, Father Hickey called to Boston the superiors and directors of parochial schools in the archdiocese. He announced that from that date forward, all these schools had to adopt a uniform program, and that, to ensure the application of this program, tests would be given in June of each year for Grades 3 through 8. These exams would be corrected by an inspector from within the respective religious teaching communities, and then sent to the superintendent. It would also be required that each class schedule, established by this imposed program of studies, be posted and followed punctually. Obviously the curriculum and the exams were entirely in English, with no time allocated for French or any of the other foreign languages. On October 6, the order was sent out to add the teaching of Hygiene and Physiology to the program. On December 13, a letter arrived from Boston expressing Father Hickey's desire that the schools adopt a hymnal composed by Cardinal O'Connell.

Faced with all these requirements, the Fathers and the teaching personnel organized accordingly. The nuns and brothers, with the help of their respective directors of studies, translated part of the program into French, and added to it the customary courses taught in that language. Father Racette refused to adopt the cardinal's hymnal, and he reaffirmed the Franco-American character of his schools. At the opening of classes in September 1916, he published this declaration in the *Bulletin*:

Our parochial schools opened for the year on Tuesday, September 5, and we are happy to note that the parents understand better

181

each year the serious obligation that is incumbent upon them to send their children to Catholic schools. And why should it not be so? It is acknowledged that our children learn enough English in our schools, with the result that a child who completes the course of studies either in the collège or the nuns' school writes better English and speaks it as well as a child who attends the public schools. Is it then an insignificant advantage for French-Canadian Catholics to have their children learn the French language and receive a good religious formation? Should this not, on the contrary, come before anything else? Why then would one send his children to public schools? Is it a question of money? Is someone truly sincere when that pretext is brought up? The school is free for the truly poor. As for the books, the brothers and the sisters make things as easy as they possibly can. Old textbooks that are no longer used are bought back. When a child needs new books, used ones can be bought at a modest price. Whether new books or used ones are bought, the possibility exists to pay for them by the week, even if it takes all year to do so. Finally, if a child is so poor that he can pay for absolutely nothing, either for tuition or school supplies, the parish provides everything free of charge.

The parishioners received high-level support in their struggles to maintain French bilingual schools. On Thursday evening, October 26, 1916, His Eminence Cardinal Bégin of Québec, primate of the Canadian Church, stopped in Lowell, coming from Fall River where he had blessed the Franco-American orphanage. At the convent, he spoke as follows to the nuns assembled in their community room:

Teach French well, teach it in depth so as to make the language loved and spoken well. I regard it as being the rampart of our nationality, and especially of our religion. Make every effort to reach this goal by all means possible, and with perseverance. There are too many examples which show that wherever the French language is lost, the faith soon disappears from among our people. Be sure to teach your students to be very faithful to attendance at Mass, and to frequenting the sacraments. Warn them against worldly outings, the theaters, the movies, and all other dangers. Do not tire of repeating this often. God will bless your work and you will do a great deal of good.

On the following November 10, the sisters received from the *Comité du Ralliement Catholique et Français de Québec* two thousand leaflets containing an image of Saint Jean Baptiste with a prayer to him "for the [French-Canadian] race." This prayer, written by Cardinal Bégin, carried an indulgence of 200 days and it was accompanied by a prayer to Sainte Jeanne d'Arc, composed by Bishop Latulippe and approved by Pope Benedict XV.

The brothers and the sisters accepted these instructions. Recitations, songs, dramatic plays for all occasions, and the celebration of Québec's old customs, such as the traditional observance of St. Catherine's feast day were faithfully continued in the classes.

On January 27, 1917, Father Hickey came to visit the classes in order to judge the competence of the students in English. He declared himself to be satisfied with the exemplary behavior of the students, the correct grading being applied, and the obvious progress of the schools. English was not neglected. Of note, in March 1916, Miss Yvonne Marchand, a student at the girls' school, won the third prize in an English essay contest conducted by the Chamber of Commerce in all the Lowell schools. When, in February 1917, two members of the Lowell school board, gripped by the prejudice of the times, sent a letter to the pastor berating the English being taught in the parochial schools, he rejected their criticism by sending them a copy of the school program and Father Hickey's comments. With 2,339 children enrolled in 1916, the parochial schools of Saint Joseph were the largest in the city and the archdiocese. They were maintained at an annual cost of $19,000 and hence were the object of unremitting care and sacrifices. No parent, priest, or teacher intended to allow the elimination or perversion of the French and Catholic character of this work, so dear to everyone's heart. The specter of the religious war being waged in Ontario at that time, over the question of French-Catholic schools, was proof that they had to remain continually on guard.

The hundredth anniversary of the founding of the Little Brothers of Mary in 1817 by Marcellin Champagnat, who was canonized in 1999, provided the parish with the opportunity to manifest all the love they felt and the gratitude that they owed the brothers. They did so by organizing grand festivities which lasted two days, Monday and Tuesday, May 21 and 22, 1917, ending with a brilliantly staged drama. On Monday evening, Father Louis A. Nolin gave a magnificent homily in the presence of the alumni: "Memor esto congregationis tuas" (Remember your congregation). In it he recounted the quite remarkable and tempestuous history of the Community. In 1917 Saint Joseph school, with its 900 boys and a faculty of eighteen brothers, was the most important school in the American province of the Marist Brothers. The Alumni Association, the *Association des Anciens Élèves du Collège Saint-Joseph*, founded on February 12, 1912, had hundreds of members and was a precious source of support for the brothers.

On August 9, at the sixth annual convention of the alumni, the parish celebrated the 25th anniversary of the school's founding. The celebration, enhanced by the presence of Brother Chryseuil, was splendid and enthusiasm reigned. Once again, everyone affirmed their pride and collective will to support the school and see it flourish. The celebration also became the occasion for the parishioners to get to know their new pastor. Father Hervé Racette had asked to be relieved of the position he had held for four years. He had arrived quietly, without fanfare, and he left just as quietly, but not without having earned everyone's respect and love. He died in Plattsburgh, New York, on May 29, 1948, having reached the end of a very active apostolic life.

Founding members of the "Association of the Former Students of the Saint Joseph *Collège*," the Alumni Association of the Boys Grammar School. Photograph taken in 1917 with Brother Chryseuil, F.M.S. in the center.

21. "Saint Thérèse, protect us"

Fr. Eugène Turcotte, O.M.I.

Father Joseph Eugène Turcotte was born on April 4, 1876, at L'Assomption in Québec, the son of Nazaire Turcotte and Rose Jolicoeur. Shortly after his birth, he accompanied his parents when they chose the route of migration. In Lowell, where they settled, he attended the *Collège Saint Joseph* before entering the Oblate juniorate in Buffalo. After his scholasticate studies, he was ordained to the priesthood at the University of Ottawa, on June 19, 1914. He remained there as a professor until 1917. That year he was sent as a curate to Saint Joseph's in Lowell. Known for his kindness and unbounded optimism, he assumed the direction of the parish when World War I was raging in Europe.

On April 6, 1917, the United States had declared war on Germany, but well before the official American declaration, the parishioners had felt the bereavement and sorrow inflicted by that hideous war. When it had broken out in Europe, in 1914, the French were called to arms, and Brothers Henri Désiré, Julien Émile and Gonzalvus, who were French by birth, had left the *collège* to enlist in the French army. Later, other Brothers would also leave and be wounded on the battlefield. In June 1917, Brother Julien Émile was killed in Belgium.

While the brothers sent letters from the front for publication in *L'Étoile,* Father Baron filled the parish Bulletin with accounts of French heroism and events of the war culled directly from the French Catholic press. Stories of

185

divine intervention and heavenly protection through the intercession of Saint Thérèse of Lisieux were highlighted. Like the French soldiers, Father Baron himself had a special devotion to little Thérèse. Although she would be canonized only in 1925, she had quickly become the patron saint not only of the French soldiers, but also, through the *Bulletin,* of all the young women of the parish.

While reports of healings and religious loyalty on the battlefield contributed to making the local population sensitive to the emotions and sorrows of war, the parish bookstore kept them informed of the facts and the larger picture by making available the works published by the *Comité Catholique de Propagande Française à l'Étranger* (The Catholic Committee for Propagating French News Outside of France). A constant flow of books and pamphlets arrived in Lowell from France — spirituality, religious history, war news — even music, for was not E. L. Turcot, the music publisher, selling the latest French ballads and patriotic songs in his store on Merrimack Street?

The small colony of people from France, Belgium, and Alsace in the parish also contributed their share of information and emotions to the general awareness of the situation.

Gripped by the suffering and horror of war, the parish population was united in heartfelt feeling to the cause of the French people, fighting for their homeland. In January 1917, the *Cercle Dramatique Français* (French Drama Club), under the direction of Father Denizot, presented a play for the benefit of the French Red Cross. The receipts of $220.00 were sent to Cardinal Amette of Paris who managed to have this fact reported in all the Parisian newspapers.

When the United States entered the war, the parishioners became committed to the Allied cause, not only emotionally as before, but also physically, by enlisting. It should be noted also that many had not waited for the American declaration, but had entered the armed services in Canada, at war since 1914. Father Turcotte, an ardent patriot, spoke often of the American patriotism of his people, and searched for ways to publicize this fact to the public. He announced on Sunday February 3, 1918, that the parish would unfurl a service flag. He then had a huge red flag, with a blue ground made up especially, on which were placed 405 stars, the number of men from the parish who were serving in the armed forces. On that Sunday, before a large crowd assembled in front of Saint Jean Baptiste church, an impressive ceremony was held. After a speech by the mayor, the large flag was placed on the church façade to the singing of the national anthem and "America." This flag proclaimed to everyone the patriotism of this Franco-American parish. A few spiteful persons complained to the pastor: "These 405 stars represent the soldiers from all three Canadian parishes in Lowell, and not just Saint Joseph's." Father

Turcotte responded by publishing the names and addresses of each of the 405 young men, noting that two thirds of them had volunteered to sign up. Before the war came to an end, the parish had 892 of its sons under arms, besides Léontine Lamoureux and Miss Racicot who served as telephone operators. Twenty-two of them gave their lives.

On Tuesday, March 26, the C.M.A.C. hall could barely contain the crowd that had come to hear Captain Duthoit and Sergeant Dobelle, of the French Army, who were on a lecture tour in Canada and the United States. Eight days later, Canon Cabanel, chaplain of the *Chasseurs Alpins* (Mountain Infantrymen), mounted the pulpit of Saint Jean Baptiste and, before a packed church, spoke of the French soldiers, describing features of their piety and the edifying deaths that he had witnessed. The parishioners, who were greatly moved, continued to pray, offer Masses, and follow the advice of their pastor: "While our soldiers are fighting courageously, our own duty is to pray without tiring, so that God may make peace reign once again among the nations."

The prayerful spirit of the parishioners made itself felt in Europe as well. Even to this day, people tell the story of a contingent of American troops, a good many of whom were Franco-Americans from Lowell, who were passing through a village in France. On Sunday morning, a group of these men came to attend Mass in the small, rather poor parish church. One of the soldiers brought with him a violin to serve as a musical accompaniment, while the others constituted themselves as a choir. At Communion time they knelt as a body to receive the Eucharist. The priest was so deeply moved by it all that he dissolved into tears. Turning to his parishioners, he commented that it took soldiers from overseas, the sons of young America, to come over to give old France, so often religiously indifferent, such an example of fervor and Christian faith. Seeing so many men, indeed soldiers, who were believers, openly practicing their faith, he was overwhelmed with joy, and praised God.

The social upheavals and disruptions in the economy caused by the war also affected parish life. Poverty was ever-present, even in the midst of a sporadic prosperity. So, in the month of June, at the request of the cardinal, the pastor established a Saint Vincent de Paul Society composed of men who were dedicated to getting to know the poor of the parish, and helping them, either by raising money or by distributing gifts of clothing, food, etc. Parishioners, known for their charitable spirit and their generosity on behalf of the parish, were selected as founding members of the Society: Ephrem Pelletier, Georges E. Mongeau, Frédéric Rocheville, John B. Richard, Joseph Morin, Amédée Lebrun, Joseph Rousseau, Camille Roussin, Paul Cossette, Gédéon Rochette, Alfred Bibeault, and Abraham Langlais.

Then, in September 1918, Father Turcotte found himself obliged to launch a major fund drive for the orphanage. Since its opening, the institution had received 1,600 orphans. In 1918, it was housing 280 children, of whom ten were war orphans. By 1917, its expenses could not be met and, as a result, the quality of the food and the provision of other material needs had deteriorated. Besides, until the war ended, another rise in the cost of living had to be expected and, even more seriously, an increase in the number of war orphans. In addition to this, there remained a mortgage of $35,000 on the orphanage which also owed $67,553.32 to the parish. The parish itself carried a large debt burden of $66,434.07 and was finding no way of improving the situation. For the moment, the most pressing need was to wipe out the mortgage on the orphanage because it required large interest payments. This mortgage had been taken out in 1912, and all attempts at reducing it had proved to be unsuccessful. The debt to the parish could wait, for it posed few inconveniences. With time, in fact, the parish was able to erase large portions of it.

Father Turcotte proposed to undertake a campaign drive lasting one week in order to raise $50,000 — $35,000 to wipe out the mortgage, and the remainder to constitute an endowment fund for the future and to cover the additional obligations for the war orphans. The drive was intended to be public and city-wide, for the orphanage was an institution that aided the whole population and saved the social services of the city a great deal of money. The pastor began by organizing teams of men and women from each of the three Franco-American parishes, and two executive teams, one composed of industrialists and businessmen, and the other for the members of the C.M.A.C. Congressman John Jacob Rogers was named as honorary chairman of the executive committee, along with State Representative Henri Achin as vice president, Ephrem Pelletier as secretary, and Attorney J. H. Guillet as treasurer. Other members included the mayor and the most prominent Yankee and Irish industrialists in the city. Matthew Lally, a professional organizer brought in from Maryland, supervised the entire operation and saw to it that the campaign functioned smoothly with the assistance of his secretary Germaine Lemire. He saw to it that ads were placed in the streetcars of the Bay State Street Railway Car Company, and that theater owners be asked to project an appeal on their screens.

The fundraising drive was launched on Monday evening, September 21, at a banquet held in flag-decorated Grafton Hall. The C.M.A.C. gave the first contribution of $500, and by the end of the evening, $4,000 had already been collected. Mill agents, merchants, and public officials all gave generously. Two Irish ladies made the rounds of the Boston and Maine Railroad car shop. Women parishioners obtained permission to go through the mills or collect at the entrance gates. At night, after a day's work, teams of men and women visited 4,500 families, sometimes in spite of heavy rain. By the end of the week, two-thirds of the total amount had been donated by workers, most of them parishioners of Saint Joseph, Saint Louis, and Notre Dame de Lourdes. On September 30, when the campaign ended, $40,094.60 had been raised. The debt was eliminated and the orphanage was now out of danger.

Henri Bourassa, who had come to Lowell on May 8, 1919, to give a lecture at the invitation of the Lafayette Club, could not contain his admiration when he visited the orphanage. Tears came to his eyes as he witnessed the eloquence and good manners of the orphans during a carefully prepared reception. The orphanage would always be the preferred commitment of the parish.

During the war, the faithful prayed at the foot of the victory altar. An American flag had been hung over the altar of the Sacred Heart, in the basement of Saint Jean Baptiste church, and, in front of the altar, an honor roll had been placed on which were inscribed the names of all the parishioners who were in the armed forces. When the Armistice was announced by the ringing of the city's bells at 5 o'clock on the morning of November 11, 1918, there was general jubilation. Spontaneously, during the day workers came out of the mills and shops, children came out of school, ran about, and everyone paraded through the streets to the sounds of bells and automobile horns from all sides. The war was over, and it seemed that all wars had come to an end. The allies were victorious. At four o'clock, the pastor sang a Te Deum of thanksgiving in the church and the following day, the parish gathered for a solemn High Mass.

The people of the parish sought out the altar of the Sacred Heart; they turned to the author of the victory. Since the days of Father Watelle, devotions to the Sacred Heart on a grand scale had diminished somewhat, but Father Charles Dénizot had taken over the legacy of the apostle of the Sacred Heart, spreading the custom of the Enthronement of the Sacred Heart of Jesus in family homes. This devotion, encouraged and blessed by Pope Benedict XV, was the indispensable complement to the First Friday observance. In each family, all the members being present, the Sacred Heart was enthroned as head and protector of the family. All of the family members would consecrate themselves to Him and commit to being faithful by praying together as a family, observing the First Friday devotion as well as attending the Holy Hour, and promising to receive communion frequently. Everyone signed the certificate of commitment while a blessed statue or portrait of the Sacred Heart was installed in a place of honor in the heart of the home. The Lord had promised Saint Margaret Mary that wherever the image of his Heart was exposed to be loved and honored, He would shower His graces upon that place, reunite divided families, and protect those who found themselves in some sort of need. Within a short period of time, this devotion became widespread throughout the parish. Each home had its image or even its "altar" of the Sacred Heart in the living room; this was in addition to an image or statue of Notre Dame de Lourdes.

The war and its devastation had brought forth a concert of prayers from the Catholic world in reparation to the Sacred Heart. Convents, cities, parishes, hospitals, and religious communities consecrated themselves to the Sacred Heart of Jesus. The king of Spain consecrated his entire country while Cardinal Mercier and the king of Belgium promised to build a national basilica dedicated to the Sacred Heart. Once the war was over, Father Turcotte called the whole parish together on June 27, 1919, at St. Jean Baptiste church. All the religious, social, and fraternal societies sent delegations: *Tiers-Ordre, Sainte-Famille, Ligue du Sacré-Coeur, Anges Gardiens, Saint-Vincent-de-Paul, Artisans Canadiens-Français, Association Catholique, Conseil Carillon, Conseil Rochambeau, Cour Saint-Antoine, Cour Saint-Paul, Cour Samuel de Champlain, Union Garin Nationale, Union Saint-Joseph, Anciens Élèves du Collège St.-Joseph, Caisse Populaire Jeanne-d'Arc, Club des Citoyens Américains, Club Lafayette, Club Passe-Temps, Club Social de Pawtucketville, Dames de Sainte-Anne, Demoiselles de Notre-Dame-de-Lourdes, Enfants de Marie, Cercle de Couture, Société de Bon-Secours, Conseil Sainte-Éveline, Conseil Sainte-Thérèse, Cour Blanche de Castille, Cercle d' Youville.* The church was filled to capacity. After a vibrant talk by Father Dénizot, the pastor read, in everyone's name, the act of consecration of Saint Joseph parish to the Sacred Heart of Jesus: "O Jesus, truly present in the Blessed Host, we, the parishioners of Saint Joseph parish, are kneeling at Your feet to consecrate ourselves entirely to Your Divine Heart." Children, parents, the sick, sinners, men and women religious, societies and clubs, all were lifted up to the Divine Master. The prayers, the hymns, and the consecration itself, were more than an echo from the past, they were the extension of a collective spiritual life that had always been alive and present. This day, as will be seen later, remained engraved for a long time in the parish memory.

In the fall, the parish experienced a very different kind of ceremony — the return of the soldiers. The celebration had been prepared with care, so that on Labor Day, September 1, 1919, the city of Lowell stood ready to honor its veterans. The Franco-Americans had every reason to be proud, for 1,537 of them had borne arms. In addition, 225 of them had enlisted in the Canadian army before the American declaration of war. On that day, more than 5,000 people gathered in the morning on the grounds of the grotto for a solemn High Mass, celebrated by the three Franco-American pastors. The grand triumphal march took place in the afternoon. Governor Coolidge, Congressman Rogers, Mayor Thompson, and a throng of dignitaries were in the reviewing stand, as the parade of almost one thousand soldiers, delegates of the societies, twenty floats, nine bands, garlanded automobiles, etc., followed a six-mile course through the main streets of the three Franco-American parishes. In all, 6,000 persons marched along the route filled with bystanders, who watched from the sidewalks, the windows of houses, balconies, and even a few rooftops. Upon arriving at the North Common, where the parade ended, the soldiers and sailors, preceded by a marching band, went to the property of Mrs. Anna de Lamothe, on Salem Street, where a banquet was served to one thousand people. The celebration ended in the evening with a concert of patriotic music at the North Common, interspersed with speeches by the governor, the congressman, and the other dignitaries.

The committee formed for the "Welcome Home" festival then proposed to erect a public monument in memory of the Franco-American combatants in this war, and to that end, contributions were solicited. The project developed very slowly, however, and finally in 1925, with $1,600 in hand, it was decided to place the memorial monument on the grounds of Saint Joseph Cemetery, where it can be seen to this day.

The city itself created public memorials of its own for the soldiers of Saint Joseph parish who had died on the field of battle when the city council decided to name city "squares" and intersections in their honor. Near Saint Jean Baptiste church, a first group of seven was designated: the corner of Clark and Common Streets became Armand Alix Square; that of Merrimack and Cabot Streets—Ralph Lashua Square; that of Tremont and Moody Streets—Joseph Mercier Square; that of Aiken and Moody Streets—William Clouâtre Square; that of Hall and Perkins Streets—Aldéric Veillette Square; that of Moody and Riverside Streets—Philippe Chalifoux Square; that of Merrimack and Pawtucket Streets—Henri Cognac Square. At the dedication ceremony, on Labor Day, September 4, 1922, Father Aurélien Mercil, accompanied by a large number of veterans in uniform, recited a prayer and gave a talk at each of these "squares." Later on, other names were added to that first list.

Once the war, with all its austerities and worries, was over, the parish entered wholeheartedly into the twenties, which were to be so prosperous and so full of activity.

22. Saint Jean Baptiste Province

The 1920s were a decade of intense Franco-American "national" sentiment. The feeling of solidarity with the group and ethnic affirmation were at their peak. They were now Franco-Americans, rather than French Canadians, and everyone felt proud and happy to be living in the American Republic. Their massive participation in World War I had demonstrated for all to see the patriotic pride of the group. In January 1922, the old, but still active *Comité Permanent de la Naturalisation* (Standing Committee for Naturalization) opened a special section for women, now that they had received the right to vote. If the Franco-American population had found its own American identity, it also felt more than ever a deep sense of its French heritage and of its duty to preserve the cultural patrimony entrusted to it as an innate richness. The motto: *"Qui parle deux langues vaut deux personnes"* (One who speaks two languages is worth two persons) expressed the popular ideology. The 25,000 Franco-Americans of Lowell, bolstered by their religious and social institutions, which were the most prosperous in the city, could not help but congratulate themselves on the vitality of their ideal of *survivance,* namely, of maintaining their French language and their Catholic faith. At the same time, they could not forget that constant vigilance would be necessary to highlight this ideal and perpetuate it.

Questions of religious, cultural and linguistic survival were a constant preoccupation for the parish and its pastors. As a result, in preparation for the 1920 General Chapter of the Congregation of the Missionary Oblates of Mary Immaculate, Father Turcotte and his confreres had to arrive at a rather grave decision. Since 1898, and the start of the century, an ongoing discussion had been taking place within the administration of the American province: how to confront the problem of the formation in French of the Franco-American Oblate seminarians. Some councilors had suggested the founding of a Franco-American juniorate, others had proposed a bilingual program for the juniorate in Buffalo, while still others wanted to send the Franco-American candidates to Ottawa. This last choice won out finally and was adopted as a definitive solution. However, with time it became apparent that the problem of recruitment was as complex as that of formation. The number of Franco-American seminarians was diminishing, and the province, under an administration where the majority was Irish, tended to recruit mostly among English-speaking candidates, leaving the recruitment of Franco-American candidates to the priests in their parishes. But the priests in these Franco-American parishes, especially Saint Joseph and Notre Dame de Lourdes, preaching missions throughout New England, and keeping up with a broad array of parish duties, plus trying to recruit candidates proved increasingly difficult.

The Franco-American Oblates feared that without a French formation for the seminarians, without more vocations, and without more support from the provincial council, there would be little hope for the future of the French-speaking parishes. This would also affect the well-being of souls entrusted to them in Lowell as well as elsewhere in New England. In 1919, the personnel of the Saint Joseph community consisted of Fathers E. Turcotte, pastor, A. Nolin, A. Baron, A. Mercil, A. Graton, A. Amyot, A. Marion, C. Dénizot, J. Bolduc, R. Jalbert, and L. Bachand. The average age of these men was 46. Added to this was the fact that, as we have seen earlier, the Irish clergy in the United States were pursuing an ideal of Americanization and assimilation that ran contrary to the collective aspirations of the other ethnic groups in the United States. Taking all this into account, the Franco-American members of the first American province decided to ask for official separation. Father Léon Lamothe, pastor of Notre Dame de Lourdes, was chosen to be their spokesman. He left for the General Chapter of 1920 armed with an official request: *A petition from the Franco-American Oblates of Mary Immaculate of the First Province of the United States, to the Most Reverend Bishop Auguste Dontenwill, Superior-General.* It was signed by Fathers Eugène Turcotte, superior of Saint Joseph's, Léon Lamothe, pastor of Notre Dame de Lourdes, Julien Racette, superior and pastor of Saint Pierre in Plattsburgh, New York, Edouard Duhamel, J.-B. Barette, Joseph Denis, Charles Dénizot, L.-G. Bachand, A. Amyot, L.-A. Nolin, A. Marion, A. Baron, J.-A. Bolduc, G.-E. Ouellette, A.-E. Mercil, J.-A. Graton, J.-R. Jalbert, Victor Viaud, C.-A. Paquette, Jos.-Charles Ehrhard, and Brothers Alphonse Marion, Isaïe Marion, A. Bedell, A. Jutras, O. Levasseur. The petition reads in part:

Given that at various times, and for many years, the question of separating the French element from the Irish element of this province in the North of the United States has been of concern to us, and considering,

That the reasons put forward up to now to obtain this separation are more urgent than ever;

That the Irish in the United States are pursuing a goal and aspirations which are in direct opposition to the most vital interests of the Franco-American population;

That under an administration whose mentality is different from our own it has become nearly impossible to recruit French-speaking candidates, and that the work of recruitment has collapsed to such an extent that in the last three years, there has not been a single student speaking our language at the Buffalo juniorate;

That since the number of our parishioners and our institutions is increasing constantly, thus requiring more personnel;

That the Franco-American diocesan clergy, especially that of New England, criticize us constantly for not being able to provide missionaries for them;

That should the separation come to pass, we would be better able to give rise to vocations among our own and ensure the future of our undertakings while providing more efficient ministry to our parishioners;

That without an energetic, effective, and immediate intervention of the General Administration to this end, the French-speaking Oblates will soon be forced, as a result of a constant reduction in numbers, and a shortage of subjects, to abandon the *oeuvres* which they have founded in this country at the cost of enormous sacrifices.

The Fathers also felt neglected by the Irish-American administration for, among other things, the provincial had not made a canonical visit of the Saint Joseph residence since 1909, and the provincial councilor from Saint Joseph's was rarely consulted. They, therefore, added in their petition:

That this separation being an act of simple justice should not create a division between the two nationalities. On the contrary, by removing the causes of friction and discontent, it would serve to achieve more amicable relationships, as experience has shown elsewhere.

In conclusion, the Fathers were making a formal request for "a complete separation from the Irish group. . . for the sake of the general good that would result for the Church, as well as for the preservation of the language and faith of our compatriots who have become so numerous in the United States."

At the chapter, Father Lamothe clearly presented the reasons for the separation. In the long discussion which ensued, he was strongly supported by the German-American Oblates in the western part of the country who were also seeking to establish an ethnic province. It should be mentioned that Father Lamothe added that the new province would be seeking no financial aid or grants from the old province to set up the necessary houses of formation.

The final decision was left up to the general administration. After consulting with the Congregation for Religious, the superior-general, Bishop Dontenwill announced in a circular letter dated March 1, 1921, that from that moment on the Houses of Plattsburgh, Saint Joseph of Lowell, Notre Dame de Lourdes of Lowell, as well as the residences and outposts of Aurora, Kansas, Egg Harbor and Fond du Lac, Wisconsin, would form part of a new vice-province, which would be known as the Saint Jean Baptiste Vice-Province of Lowell.

After a trial period of three years, the superior-general and his council would decide on its definitive erection as a province. In Lowell, such a wise and opportune decision to form an ethnic vice-province could only be received with joy by the parishioners. No one was surprised that Father Turcotte was named as the first vice-provincial. He was known to be pious, faithful in visiting the sick, or devoting himself to the duties of the confessional where he spent long hours. He was altogether suited to direct the first steps of the newborn community.

The Fathers, with the backing of the people, got to work immediately, taking as their motto: "Heaven helps those who help themselves." In the very first year of its existence, the small Franco-American vice-province established two houses of formation. In June 1922, the novitiate of Our Lady of Grace opened its doors in Hudson, New Hampshire, and in September of the same year, Father Edouard Carrier, its superior and founder, escorted, "as a shepherd leading his flock," thirty-five young Franco-Americans from Lowell to the new Saint Joseph Juniorate in Colebrook, New Hampshire. From their opening, it was understood that these two houses were to be Franco-American and bilingual. Concerning the juniorate, Father Turcotte specified:

> Young Franco-Americans, this juniorate is for you. It calls you to the service of the Lord, so that many of you will come to prepare yourselves to become missionaries, and then work for the evangelization of your own people in the United States.

The Franco-Americans of New England, by means of their press and societies, made clear their enthusiasm for this initiative, on both the religious as well as on the "nationalistic" or ethnic level. The financial and moral backing of the people contributed significantly to the success of these newly founded endeavors.

In Lowell, the parishioners of Saint Joseph's were eager to provide their pastor-provincial with a tangible sign of their esteem and appreciation. On December 31, 1923, New Year's Eve, 700 persons gathered at the C.M.A.C. hall to present Father Turcotte, from the school children and the parish societies, with the sum of $4,051.05 for the undertakings of the new vice-province.

The three-year trial period having passed, the joyous news was received from Rome, in May 1924, that the vice-province of Saint Jean Baptiste was now officially and canonically erected as a province with all the customary privileges and rights. After reading this decree, the Fathers of Saint Joseph's went to the chapel where they broke into song with a hymn of praise and jubilation. The future now opened before them a fertile apostolate field, replete with consolations and merit.

It should be mentioned, in parenthesis, that the experience of the Oblates served as an example and inspiration to other communities of priests. The Marists of New England, unable to obtain permission to found a purely ethnic province, succeeded, nevertheless, in 1924, in establishing the territorial province of Boston. This allowed them to group together all the French-speaking houses. The La Salette Fathers, by opening a juniorate in Enfield, New Hampshire, in December 1927, also founded a Franco-American province.

In 1916, the Redemptorist priests of the Ste-Anne-de-Beaupré province in Québec had wanted to establish a French-speaking house in New England to preach missions and help the Franco-American parishes. After consultation with the American provincial, it was decided instead, in 1917, to station permanently two French-speaking priests at the Redemptorist Shrine of Our Lady of Perpetual Help in Boston.

By the time of its official foundation in 1924, the Saint Jean Baptiste Province had already acquired a new parish. Ever since the opening of the Moody Street bridge in September 1896, which gave access to the eastern part of Pawtucketville, that section of the city near the Textile School resembled an immense construction site. It was an entirely residential area, served by electric street cars connecting it to downtown via Moody Street (University Avenue today). The Franco-Americans in Little Canada were eagerly buying lots there to build cottages for themselves or smaller tenement blocks accommodating three or four families. The area became so heavily populated that people began to call it *Haut Canada* (Upper Canada) since it was north of the river from the Moody Street Little Canada. The men of that neighborhood met at the *Club Social de Pawtucketville,* founded in 1897. In 1909, there were 2,593 Franco-Americans living in Pawtucketville. The question of a separate parish had been debated at different times without reaching a successful resolution. Starting in January 1913, the men of the area decided to meet in the hall of the Social Club to look for the means of obtaining a French parish of their own. At that meeting, the most influential men of Pawtucketville were present: Walter J. Alexander, Joseph E. Lambert, Rodrigue Descheneaux, Frédéric Thériault, James St, Hilaire, Elisée Rochette, Urcisse Larue, Alfred Leblanc, Delphis Robert, Spiridon Lippé, L. C. Gélinas, Charles R. Daoust, Josephat Sawyer, Oliva Brunelle, Joseph Payette, Louis Napoléon Milot, Arthur St. Hilaire, Adélard Rivet, Joseph F. Montminy, Joseph Harvey, Rosaire Tourangeau. As a result of these meetings, the men decided to address themselves directly to the archdiocese, and so, in October 1915 an official request for a French parish in Pawtucketville was drawn up. Joseph Payette, Josephat Sawyer, and Oliva Brunelle delivered the petition in person to Cardinal O'Connell and were named as a permanent committee to keep an eye on the progress of the proposal.

The cardinal initially put off the decision. It was only in December 1920, that he resolved the matter by entrusting to Father J.B. Labossière, the pastor of St. Louis, the responsibility for adding a parish chapel to the little school on Fourth Avenue. The news arrived like a thunderbolt. Pawtucketville would have its parish, but it would be served by diocesan priests.

The Oblates at Saint Joseph's, who had never encouraged that separation for fear of harming existing parish institutions, did not hide their apprehensions at such a decision. They were concerned not only for the parish, but they feared that the new province could be weakened thereby. Discreetly, they advised their Pawtucketville parishioners to send the cardinal petitions requesting that he stop the separation from Saint Joseph's, or at least ensure that the new parish would be served by the Oblate Fathers. The faithful were faced with a dilemma, for though they wanted to have a parish of their own, they did not want to be separated from the Oblates. The vast majority petitioned to be served by the Oblate Fathers.

In the first week of January 1921, Father Labossière ordered the start of construction for a chapel annexed to the school building. The work was progressing when the pastor ran out of funds and the cardinal found himself short of priests. The chapel, though built in haste and without frills, had nevertheless cost $16,000, and the cardinal could not find a French-speaking parish priest to assign to the new parish. Given this situation, the archdiocese turned to the Oblates, and Father Turcotte offered to finish the construction, assume the debt, and provide the necessary priests. The population was jubilant. Divine Providence had brought about the desired solution.

The chapel was finished under Father Turcotte's direction, and on March 2, 1921, he placed it under the patronage of Sainte Jeanne d'Arc. He himself celebrated the first Mass on April 17, 1921. The parishioners felt at home there and began to work unsparingly and with great devotion in raising money to complete the foundation. A bazaar in September 1921, raised $6,248.00. The money arrived just in time, for on November 17, the city of Lowell put up for sale at auction the Moody Street school (University Ave.), built in 1906 at a cost of $35,000. A beautiful school, with six classrooms, evaluated at the time at $50,000, it was sold to Father Turcotte for $13,000! Sainte Jeanne d'Arc now had its schools and its church. On December 30, 1922, by a decree of the cardinal, the mission became Sainte Jeanne d'Arc parish. The residence of Mr. Avila Sawyer, on White Street, was purchased for $3,500 in January 1923, and converted into a rectory. Father Léon Lamothe, the new pastor, settled in with his two curates, Fathers Charles Dénizot and Aurélien Mercil. The parish had 818 families, amounting to 3,727 people. The eight classrooms, six on Moody Street and two on Fourth Avenue, were educating 463 children. Due to the lack of space, about one hundred of them continued to attend Saint Joseph's. By January 1925, the $30,000 debt had been completely repaid.

The existence of a new parish stimulated a construction boom in Pawtucketville. By the beginning of January 1924, fifty-three new families had been added. One construction company had just sold 700 lots in the Rivermont section, on the east side of Moody Street, and another was preparing lots on land situated on the west side of Moody Street, near West Meadow Road. All of this construction, along with the attractiveness of the area, were to make of Sainte Jeanne d'Arc one of the most prosperous parishes in Lowell.

In his numerous occupations, Father Turcotte relied heavily on the support of the Grey Nuns and the Marist Brothers for the smooth functioning of the schools. But these two communities were not exempt, in their own right, from the ethnic questions that troubled the 1920s.

On June 20, 1921, Mother Saint-Albert, superior-general of the Grey Nuns, received in Ottawa an official letter from Cardinal Dougherty of Philadelphia announcing that henceforth, by a decree from Rome, all the houses of the Grey Nuns in the United States would be separated from the mother house in Ottawa to form a new English-speaking congregation to be called The Grey Nuns of the Sacred Heart of Philadelphia. The English-speaking nuns, encouraged by certain bishops, had asked for this new foundation in response to their difficulty in recruiting new candidates in the United States, given the fact that the general administration was French-speaking, and also that the formation of new aspirants took place in Ottawa, in Canada, thus, outside of the United States. Also at stake were the different ethnic philosophies of the two groups.

The surprise at this unexpected turn of events was just as great in Lowell as it was in Ottawa. According to the decree, Saint Joseph's school now became part of an Irish congregation. The French-speaking nuns who did not want to belong to the new congregation were free to return to the mother house in Ottawa. They would be replaced by English-speaking nuns.

Father Turcotte was surprised by all this, for he was not expecting to see his schools transferred to an Irish administration. Since all the nuns at Saint Joseph's were French-speaking, they wanted to continue belonging to the Grey Nuns of Ottawa. At the same time, they were reluctant to leave their Franco-American students. Sister Sainte-Léontine had been in Lowell for thirty-eight years, and many others had spent long years serving the Lowell children.

On June 22, 1921, the sisters of Saint Joseph convent decided to remain attached to Ottawa. On July 16, the mother general, to obey the decree from Rome, gave the order to evacuate the convent. The sisters, with heavy hearts, sought refuge at their summer house in Tyngsboro. One week later, the Fathers closed the convent and removed the Blessed Sacrament.

Mother Saint-Albert, the Superior General of the Grey Nuns, – seated in the middle of the first row – photographed at St. Joseph's convent during her visit to Lowell in 1925.

No one had wanted this change which jeopardized the Franco-American future of the parochial schools. Seeing the schools of Saint Joseph, Sainte Jeanne d'Arc, Notre Dame de Lourdes, and St. Pierre, in Plattsburgh, threatened in this manner, Father Turcotte met with the Marist Fathers of Haverhill and Bishop P. Garand of Ogdensburg, New York, who were themselves facing the same dilemma.

Having reflected on the matter, Father Turcotte went to Mother Saint-Albert to suggest appealing to Rome requesting that the Franco-American houses in the United States remain attached to the mother house in Ottawa. To everyone's great joy, the Vatican agreed to the supplication, and on August 11, 1921, the elated sisters returned to take possession once again of their convent on Moody Street.

The Marist Brothers, from the time of their arrival in Canada in 1885, and in the United States in 1890, had seen their works prosper to such an extent that in 1913 the authorities had established an American province with headquarters in Poughkeepsie, New York. Although, at the time, the majority of the brothers in the province were French-speaking and the Franco-American houses in Lowell, Lawrence, Haverhill, Massachusetts, and Manchester, New Hampshire, continued to receive brothers from France and Canada, it was clear that in the future, it would be necessary to recruit more heavily among young Franco-Americans. This recruitment would have to be followed by a solid bilingual education. But the increasing number of English-speaking vocations was making French studies at Poughkeepsie ever more difficult. So, it was decided, after a good deal of insistence by the New England brothers, to open a Franco-American bilingual juniorate. Brother Florentius of Lowell was delegated by the provincial authorities to seek out a suitable location. In June of 1921, he purchased the 200-acre Tyng property in Tyngsboro, Massachusetts, for $15,000. The Marist Brothers were happy to note that the site of the new juniorate was only a few miles from the Oblate novitiate in Hudson, New Hampshire.

Construction began immediately in the summer of 1922, and on Sunday, October 12, 1924, the magnificent Marist juniorate of Tyngsboro was solemnly blessed. It was built of brick and granite in a fine-looking French style. The Saint Joseph parishioners noticed with pride that a large percentage of the first class of students were boys from their parish, and that the new provincial, Brother Léo (Emile Brouillette), elected in December 1921, was also a son of the parish. The Tyngsboro juniorate would continue to serve the community for many years, and its vast gardens provided a pleasant site for the annual conventions of the *Association des Anciens Élèves des Frères Maristes de Lowell* as well as the *Fédération des Sociétés d'Anciens Élèves*.

The foundation of this juniorate greatly pleased the Franco-Americans of Lowell for the Marist Brothers were very much loved by the population. The care which they brought to their teaching, the strong but fatherly discipline which

The community of the Marist Brothers at St. Joseph.

200

they enforced, and the religious spirit which they instilled in their students were greatly appreciated by the hundreds of men for whom this teaching, the only one they would receive, had to last a lifetime. The formation of boys was the only apostolate of these brothers, and they were marvelously successful at it.

All this attention directed towards the schools and to teaching, was not merely foresight on the part of teachers impelled by a duty to preserve the Catholic faith and the French language, it also derived from a truly aggressive concern on the part of the people, who wanted to survive culturally in a hostile environment. The twenties were a critical period for Catholic and ethnic teaching in the United States.

Following World War I, an intense wave of Americanization swept over the country. With increased immigration from Europe and other countries, the League of Women Voters, the Daughters of the American Revolution, and politicians of every stripe demanded the abolition of the teaching of foreign languages in the schools, and insisted on the Americanization of all "foreigners." General Leonard Wood, a candidate for the presidency of the United States, set the tone with his motto: "One Flag, One Language." Everywhere, and at all levels, federal as well as state, an offensive was mounted against Catholic schools by promoting laws forcing them to submit to public control and to suppress foreign languages.

It didn't take long for the Church and ethnic groups to react to these anti-Catholic efforts. The Smith-Towner Bill in Washington, which aimed at government control of all schools, was defeated only after running into massive resistance. In Lowell, the priests of the parish mobilized public opinion and kept the population on the alert, in concert with "national" societies and the press. State Representative Henri Achin took up the cause in the Legislature, and the societies sent delegates and petitions whenever necessary. The Jackson, and later, Chamberlain Bills, introduced in the Legislature in 1919, sought to limit the teaching of languages to one hour per day and to restrict the autonomy of parochial schools. The Franco-Americans of Lowell joined with their confreres in Lynn, Fall River, Worcester, and other cities to defeat these measures.

The political reality now became evident to everyone. The need to elect Franco-Americans to public office, be it in Lowell or in Boston, was being clearly felt. The parishioners of Saint Joseph understood this and saw to it that Henri Achin was re-elected, and that one of their own be on the School Board and the City Council.

In 1905, Joseph H. Hibbard (Hébert) was elected to the Massachusetts House of Representatives and in 1908 to the State Senate, the first Franco-American from Lowell to hold these offices. Henri Achin began his legendary career when he was elected to the State House of Representatives in 1912. He would be re-elected until his retirement in 1936.

On September 17 and 18, 1922, *La Fédération Catholique Franco-Américaine* held its convention in Lowell. The delegates exhorted the Franco-Americans to "resist by all legitimate means any and all attacks on the primordial right of parents regarding the life and the education of their children."

The president of the federation, Attorney Eugène Jalbert of Woonsocket, Rhode Island, sounded the convention's theme: "What we want is to live our own lives; in other words, to remain what God has made us, in the fullness of our rights, rights which are natural as well as constitutional." Father Turcotte, speaking in the name of the St. Jean Baptiste Province, committed the Oblates by stating: "We are with you to the very end." *Abbé* Lionel Groulx, director of *L'Action Française* of Montréal, seeing this firm collective aspiration, could only conclude by saying about the Franco-Americans: "Your funeral is not yet for tomorrow."

In their desire to transmit their cultural heritage to their children, the parishioners were up against not only public opinion and the politicians, but also the Catholic hierarchy which was pushing its own centralizing tendency to encourage assimilation. In reacting to all of this public pressure, the bishops kept insisting on the Americanism of parochial schools. They standardized the curriculum while limiting the extent of foreign languages in school programs. The bishops, mostly Irish-Americans, were following a policy of peaceful assimilation. as set forth in the *Catechism of Catholic Education,* published in 1922 by the National Catholic Welfare Council:

> The language of the Catholic school is English. In some Catholic schools the teaching of a foreign language is allowed. . . . In all Catholic schools the basic language is English. The Catholic educational policy is to insist that all subjects be taught in English, not excepting religion.

Teaching religion in a foreign language could be allowed, but it was understood that this was only a temporary expedient, expected to be phased out one day. The aim was the disappearance of foreign languages as soon as it became practical and possible to do so. Of course, not all the bishops and diocesan administrators were active in accepting this formulation regarding ethnicity. However, some of them adopted this policy unreservedly and with an excess of zeal that, too often, bordered on fanaticism.

In 1919, a priest, William Hickey, whose family name was the same as that of the archdiocesan superintendent of parochial schools, became bishop of Providence, Rhode Island. Given his authoritarian and unyielding temperament, his assimilation policy brought the Franco-Americans of that State to the brink of schism. From 1923 to 1929, he triggered the *Sentinelliste* Movement in Rhode Island which gradually embroiled a large part of New England in a controversy of religious and "nationalist" claims.

In Lowell, as in the rest of the archdiocese, the population remained quite calm as far as religion was concerned. The tolerant and fair attitude of Cardinal O'Connell in matters relating to the Franco-Americans—some even went as far as to say pro-*Sentinelliste*—and the love of the Oblates for their people, avoided all misunderstandings. The *Sentinelliste* movement in Lowell manifested itself especially in a renewal of "nationalistic" activity in the political and cultural spheres. This was accompanied by a close surveillance of the ethnic integrity of the established institutions and societies. The *Croisade No. 1* (Crusade No. 1), as its name indicates, was the first local branch in New England, of the secret society with ties to the movement. It had hundreds of members and carried a lot of weight at City Hall.

The Franco-Americans of Lowell, well-aware of what was happening in Rhode Island, supported their confreres in the conflict. A few Oblates even sent secret contributions to sustain the newspaper *La Sentinelle* of Woonsocket. On May 15, 1927, six to seven thousand people gathered in Dracut to hear Elphège Daignault and Phydime Hémond, the two principal orators of the Sentinellist struggle.

Within this atmosphere of intense ideological activity, the schools and other parochial activities continued to flourish. In September 1919, the parish bought the tiny house on James Street, near the convent, and turned it into two classrooms. The purchase and the exorbitant cost of renovating the house amounted to $8,000! The following September, this little School of the Sacred Heart for five-year-olds, contained 200 children, 80 in one classroom, and 120 in the other. From then on, the small building next to the church, which had served as a school, was given over to the St. Vincent de Paul Society and the Sewing Circle for the poor. The opening of the large Sainte Jeanne d'Arc School, in 1922, made it possible to relieve the Saint Joseph schools of part of their troops of children.

Naturally, there were always a few aggravations which had to be endured. Father Hickey visited the parochial schools again in November 1919, and insisted that the teaching be given in English for almost the entire day, instead of only half the day. Again, Father Turcotte intervened to protect the integrity of the bilingual program, and to insulate his teachers from all outside pressures.

The single most significant educational event of the period was without a doubt the reopening of Saint Joseph High School. The Marist Brothers, who worked diligently at maintaining their school, had long dreamed of re-establishing the high school, ever since their first effort in that regard had failed in 1907. The Fathers also wanted to see this foundation, but could not find the means to finance it. In 1916, Father Belle, during his canonical visit, made known his concern for the religious formation of boys after they ended their primary education, and insisted that a religious society be formed to bring them together. The *Ligue du Sacré-Coeur,* founded in 1916 for these young men, was as good an answer as was possible at the time, to meet these needs for continuing formation.

The pastor and the brothers were also aware that not enough young Franco-American men completed their primary education, or went on to secondary education. So, the Fathers and the brothers, as their predecessors had done, used every means possible to counteract the attraction of employment in the mills and the salaries paid there. Every month, Father Turcotte and the director of the boys' school visited the classrooms to distribute honor cards. *Le Clairon* published the long list of monthly honorees to impress both parents and students. Graduation ceremonies were always the occasion for motivational speeches and the distribution of many gold, silver and bronze medals. The success of *L'Association des Anciens Élèves* (Alumni Association), alongside the example of the business and professional men who led this association—Attorney Arthur L. Eno, a founder of this alumni group, would be named a judge of the District Court in 1927—finally paved the way for the high school. The Alumni Association's powerful body, composed of 500 members, which assisted the brothers and their projects by sponsoring various annual activities, especially dramatic presentations, to raise money, took it upon themselves to provide the money needed for a high school.

With the backing of these alumni, the brothers opened a freshman year of the new school in November 1920. The classes incorporated the French system of descending numeric identification and were divided as follows:

I — Upper Primary Education: 1st year of high school

II — Primary Education:

1st Class	=	8th Grade
2nd Class	=	7th Grade
3rd Class	=	7th Grade
4th Class	=	6th Grade
5th Class	=	6th Grade
6th Class	=	5th Grade
7th Class	=	5th Grade
8th Class	=	4th Grade
9th Class	=	4th Grade

III — Elementary Education:

10th Class	=	3rd Grade
11th Class	=	3rd Grade
12th Class	=	3rd Grade
13th Class	=	2nd Grade
14th Class	=	2nd Grade
15th Class	=	2nd Grade
16th Class	=	2nd Grade
17th Class	=	1st Grade
18th Class	=	1st Grade
19th Class	=	1st Grade

The cast of *Le Bossu de l'Abbaye* in March 1924 with Brother Francis, F.M.S. seated in the middle.

In the following year, 1921, Brother Florentius added a second year of high school, with a total enrollment of thirty-two boys in the two classes. They were somewhat cramped for space, but everyone got along well, so it didn't seem to matter. The parish, proud of its high school, kept it going by organizing a flurry of activities. Raffles, whist parties and, especially, dramatic plays, organized and directed by the brothers or alumni members, supplemented the money needed for tuition and for supplies. *Le Bossu de l'Abbaye* (The Hunchback of the Abbey), a play presented in March 1924, brought in $407.93 for the school.

Never had there been so much publicity touting the benefits of education as during these very optimistic years. Attorney Eno, after his elevation to the judge's bench, gave this address to the high school students:

"You are the architects of your future. Have a very clear concept of what you want to be. Give your efforts a guiding idea, and then strive for that goal with all your intelligence and with all your heart."

The tenth anniversary of the foundation of *L'Association des Anciens Élèves,* observed with great pomp on February 12, 1922, gave additional proof of the benefits of education, for most of the distinguished alumni of the school spoke in turn: State Representative Henri Achin, City Councilor Joseph A. N. Chrétien, the provincials, Father Turcotte and Brother Léo, Attorney Arthur Eno, and optometrist J. Montminy. The entire event was reported in the columns of *L'Étoile* by another alumnus, Edmond Turcotte, who rose to the post of editor in 1924, before leaving for Canada where he became a high-ranking member of the diplomatic corps. The Lowell postmaster, Xavier Délisle, was also an alumnus of Saint Joseph.

One of the first graduating classes of the St. Joseph Junior High School, c.1922.

Every year the brother director sent a circular letter to the parents of the primary school graduates, promoting the advantages of higher education at Saint Joseph's and pointing out the deficiencies of the program at Lowell High School, among others, in the teaching of French. "French, as taught in the high school, is of no practical value and is rather a complete waste of time for our French Canadians." Little by little, the number of young men completing elementary school began to increase—forty-five in 1926—as well as the enrollments in the high school. For the time being, the high school was limited to two years, leaving open the option of adding two more years later on. The graduates were given a junior high school diploma. Most of these students transferred to Lowell High School to complete their studies.

At about the same time, the brothers' residence, at the corner of Moody and Pawtucket Streets, which had always been somewhat overcrowded, was badly in need of repairs. In the summer of 1921, the pastor hired Mr. Rodrigue, a contractor from South Lowell, to upgrade the building at a cost of $10,000. The roof was raised to make room for a third story which was to serve as a dormitory, and such improvements were made that the brothers could announce to everyone: "The Reverend Oblate Fathers have done things in an imposing manner." Spacious rooms, a vast study hall, a pleasant site, and shaded garden, all of this made the residence one of the most appreciated in the Marist Province. Theatrical presentations, although very numerous at that time, not only on the parish stages where for a time they were occurring monthly, but also in Lowell's public theaters, where many traveling troupes from Canada performed, did not eclipse for all that the attendance at musicales. The Franco-American taste for music expanded in many directions.

The great success of the celebrated French singer Théodore Botrel in Lowell, in 1922, served to confirm the popularity of singers, choirs, orchestras, and bands, as well as piano and violin studios.

The organist and choir director at Saint Jean Baptiste church had been the composer, Louis Napoléon Guilbault who directed the Guilbault Piano Academy – *L'Académie de Piano Guilbault* – located directly across from the church. Now, in October 1922, the Oblates invited one of the most eminent organists in New England to Lowell. Rodolphe Pépin, after having been the organist at the Cathedral of St. Boniface, in Manitoba, was at the time serving in that position at Saint Louis de Gonzague parish in Nashua when he accepted the invitation of the pastor of Saint Joseph's to come to Lowell. In addition to being blessed with a fine musical talent, Rodolphe Pépin had received a thorough musical education. Besides his duties as the parish organist, he established the Sainte Cécile Chorale, bringing together the best Franco-American voices of Lowell. In 1925, he spent a year in Paris to study under the great masters Bonnet, Dupré and Poitiron. Upon his return, the Franco-Americans of Lowell enjoyed the full benefit of his musical knowledge. Musical soirées, concerts, and sung Masses, worthy of the largest churches

The parish library and store later renamed *La Librairie Baron,*
after Fr. Baron's death.

in the land, were the delight of the parishioners, who were enchanted with their organist.

But, lest the impression remain that parish life revolved mainly around theatrical and musical presentations, it must be added that the parish library contained 2,000 volumes on the most diverse subjects. Under the direction of the learned Father Baron, and his team of *Les demoiselles de la Bibliothèque,* the *Propagande des Bons Livres* (Diffusion of Good Books) had become one of the most important French-Catholic bookstores in the United States. The purpose of the undertaking was to "provide good books in the least expensive way possible," in order to exercise "a real apostolate through good reading." Their 1925 catalog listed more than 6,000 books for sale, not counting the novels which, incidentally, were also sold in drugstores. Father Baron's specialty was to establish and increase the number of Franco-American parish libraries. The endeavor also included a store for the sale of religious articles and a bookbinding service. In addition, the *Bulletin Paroissial* kept the general public informed about all this every month, while fostering a liking for reading.

Anchoring all of these thriving ventures, was a healthy and vibrant parish family spirit, based upon a very active spiritual life. The spirituality of the parish suffused all the societies and gave strength to all their endeavors and hopes.

Les Enfants de Marie, Les Dames de Sainte-Anne, Les Anges Gardiens, La Ligue du Sacré-Cœur, Les Hommes de la Sainte Famille, Les Demoiselles de Notre-Dame-de-Lourdes, Les Tertiaires, etc., all worked at their own sanctification and that of their neighbor. Each year, on the third Sunday in May, the Enfants de Marie undertook their annual public procession and pilgrimage to the grotto at the orphanage, under the direction of Father Graton. The *Anges Gardiens* and the *Dames de Sainte-Anne* as well as the other societies, all held their respective annual retreats in preparation for Easter. Every year the members of the C.M.A.C. held their general Communion, followed by their impressive pilgrimage to the cemetery. Even the children between six and ten years of age had their Easter retreat, which was well-attended and listened to with attention. The general five-week mission, preached in May 1923, by Fathers Viaud and Lewis, who succeeded one another with homilies and exhortations, ended on Palm Sunday with 2,000 people at each of the two Masses, one for the men, the other for the women.

The processions on the Feast of the Blessed Sacrament, which resumed at this time, took place annually on the grounds of the orphanage. The repository was placed at the grotto, and later on, at the home for the elderly. Thousands of people were thus able to give public expression of their devotion to the Eucharist and the faith that united them.

Piety ran deep and prayer was unceasing, as witnessed by the great number of religious vocations that came from the parish, and by its support of the foreign missions. It has often been written that the surest indication of the religious spirit of a people is their attachment to the work of the missions. The parishioners, nourished by the spirituality of a missionary congregation, understood the great beauty and the sublime nature of the work of evangelization. Between 1899 and 1922, Saint Joseph parish contributed $38,063.73 to the Society for the Propagation of the Faith, the largest amount donated by a parish in the archdiocese. In 1924 alone, $6,422.23 was contributed to the Society, along with the names of 124 perpetual members. This does not include the parishioners who adopted orphans in China and belonged to the different mission confraternities. Ever since its foundation, the parish had accorded a very special welcome to visiting missionary bishops. On the occasion of his visit to Saint Joseph's in August 1923, Bishop John Forbes of the White Fathers was on the verge of tears when he was presented the sum of $800 for his missions in Uganda.

The interest in foreign missions was not limited to prayers and almsgiving. Many parishioners entered religious orders as missionaries. Alice Marin entered the Carmelite nuns at Hanoi in Indochina, Vietnam today; her brother, Jesuit Father Georges Marin became a missionary in China; Rose Anna Paradis joined the White Sisters, Missionaries of Africa, in Tanganyika. Father Joseph Leclerc also took the road to China. These are only a few examples, and to them should be added the names of those who became Missionary Oblates. Saint Joseph parish was living its own missionary epic, one which, as shall be seen later, had even finer hours in store.

The spirituality of the parish was also able to share in the joy of the Sacrament of Holy Orders. On the first Sunday in July 1924, Father Edouard Ducharme, O.M.I., a native of Worcester, was elevated to the priesthood by Bishop Louis Rhéaume, O.M.I., of Haileybury, Ontario. This first ordination at St. Jean Baptiste would not be the last since it was now the mother church of the Franco-American Province. As such, parishioners could henceforth participate in the finest hours of the new province. The next ordination took place on June 27, 1926, when Bishop Ovide Charlebois, O.M.I., vicar-apostolic of Keewatin in the Northwest Territories of Canada, conferred the priesthood on Arthur Lemire, O.M.I., a child of the parish. This ordination of another young priest for the province also marked the beginning of the grand celebration of the 100th anniversary of the pontifical approbation of the Constitutions and Rules of the Missionary Oblates of Mary Immaculate. The ceremonies, which lasted three days, June 27, 28 and 29, were brought to a close at the Lowell Auditorium. The purpose, following a plan launched by Frank Ricard, was to honor the

Oblates with a public demonstration of affection and congratulations.

A large number of clergy gathered from all over New England, with Bishop Bunoz, O.M.I., vicar-apostolic of the Yukon, and Bishop Charlebois, O.M.I., sat on the stage. They were joined by the officers of the general committee: Joseph H. Guillet, president, Arthur L. Eno, secretary, Arthur Beaucage, assistant secretary, and Frank Ricard, treasurer. The spokesman for the committee expressed the affection felt by the Franco-Americans of Lowell for the Oblates in the following terms:

> The voices of twenty-five thousand French and Catholic souls are here this evening to convey to you, along with their wishes for everlasting prosperity, and long life in God's service, the heartfelt expression of their attachment, their gratitude, and their love.

The destiny of the people was closely intertwined with that of their pastors. As a visible token of this union of hearts and wills, a check for $6,000 was presented to Father Turcotte, the proceeds of a fund drive among the people.

That year of the Oblate centennial, there were fourteen Oblates in residence at Saint Joseph's, to serve 11,000 parishioners. Father Eugène Turcotte was superior, pastor, and provincial of a community that included Fathers Augustin Graton, Armand Baron, Avite Amyot, Louis Nolin, Joseph Emery, Athanase Marion, Adolphe Fortier, Félix Vachon, Louis Bachand, and Emile Bolduc, along with Brothers Ovide Levasseur, Alexandre Bedell, and Louis Desjadons. The schools provided an education for 2,000 children and the orphanage for 300. In addition to this, yet another foundation had successfully come into being.

Father Campeau had expressed the desire, often repeated by his successors, to open a home for the elderly, in order to complete the work of the orphanage. The care of orphans and of the elderly are the basis of evangelical charity. Children in the first stages of life were linked with the elderly at the sunset of their lives, in their need for love and consolation. No other commitment was as dear to the hearts of the parishioners. They all understood the needs and miseries of the elderly, as described by the pastor in the following words: "These persons whom age has brought too far along in life for them to be self-sufficient and who are too near to the grave and to eternity to be left only to their own failing strength."

In Lowell, at the time, the care of the elderly was not the industry it has become today. Generally speaking, older persons remained within the family circle, either with their children or with relatives. Many families included grandparents, an Aunt Rose or an Uncle Joseph. Other aging persons, without families, or abandoned by them, lived by themselves, or rented a room with a

The *Hospice Saint Joseph* home for the elderly, on Pawtucket Street.

charitable family or in a boarding house. The most desperate cases ended up at the city's Poor Farm. There was no Catholic institution in Lowell to fill this gap in the city's social services.

Father Turcotte launched his project and funds immediately began to accumulate. The Sainte Cécile Chorale, at its first public concert, on January 2, 1924, held at the Lowell Auditorium, contributed more than $3,000 to this endeavor on behalf of the elderly. The profits of the following year's concert were also donated to the same cause. The women of the parish were outstandingly creative in finding ways to raise money. Besides the usual whist parties, they organized cake sales in Gagnon's Department Store on Merrimack Street. The "French ladies" had lost nothing of their technique in the art of pastry-making. Sales of their products brought in amazing sums—$725 for instance, in 1926. A penny sale, the first of its kind, attracted large crowds to the C.M.A.C. Hall.

While the money was being collected, the cardinal gave his approval to the proposed home. Divine Providence once again provided an ideal site. Joseph Marin, an eminent parishioner, had died in 1920. His widow, Joséphine, now elderly and sick, wanted to sell their magnificent brick residence on Pawtucket Street, which included land extending down to the bank of the Merrimack River. The property, contiguous with that of the orphanage, was an ideal location for a home for the aged. When Mrs. Marin learned of the pastor's wishes, she refused all other offers. On September 11, 1922, she sold the entire property to the parish for $25,000, a price much lower than its actual value.

Pawtucket Street, which had been the chic old neighborhood of stately houses, with wide lawns, inhabited by wealthy Yankee families, became, in the twenties, almost entirely Franco-American, as the old families gradually moved out. Pawtucket Street and upper Merrimack Street would, for many years to come, be the residential area of wealthy parishioners.

The parish now had its home for the elderly, but where would one find religious women to manage it? Once again Divine Providence came to the rescue. In May 1924, the Sisters of Charity of Québec, the same nuns as at the orphanage, accepted to administer the new foundation. On September 13, 1924, Sister St. Célien arrived in Lowell to take up her duties as superior. The situation which faced the enterprising nun was not a promising one. The totally empty house needed major modifications to convert it into a rest home for the elderly. Everyone set to work, and laborers moved the alterations along as quickly as they could. Sisters St. Nil, Ste. Agnès d'Assise, St. Louis de Montfort joined their superior, and a few months later Sister St. Aldémar arrived. Since the house was devoid of furniture or other supplies with which to start out, the parishioners came to the rescue with an outpouring of donations: checks, curtains, bedspreads, chairs, beds, pillows, bureaus, and even jars of jam for the kitchen. Sister superior, astonished at this massive display of charity, had this

The Sisters of Charity of Québec, foundresses of the St. Joseph Hospice.

to say about the parish spirit: "It would seem that an expressed desire becomes a formal order." The C.M.A.C. donated an altar worth $200 for the chapel, and a pious woman personally embroidered all the altar cloths.

Finally, on Wednesday, November 3, 1924, when almost everything was ready, Father Turcotte sang the first Mass in the chapel of the St. Joseph Hospice and blessed the home. In December, the first elderly woman was admitted, Miss Exilda Bilodeau, a poor parishioner from Saint Louis parish, who was crippled and had been bed-ridden and racked with pain for thirty-five years. She was a model of patience and resignation, and became legendary in the parish for her saintliness and goodness of soul.

The home for the elderly quickly drew to itself compassion from all sides. The pastor, happy to see the success of this venture so dear to his heart, made many visits to his "elderly ladies" upon whom he lavished his care. *L'Union Saint Jean Baptiste d'Amérique* sent a check for $200 from its headquarters in Woonsocket, Rhode Island. There was no end to the goodness and kindness of the parishioners towards the sisters and the resident ladies. One woman even offered her services as a cook for two weeks, in fulfillment of a vow she had made. In July 1925, the orphans did their part by bringing eight of the women with them on a picnic. The establishment prospered, as the family spirit of the parish opened up a large place in its heart for this new arrival among the parish institutions.

For the moment, the house was fairly comfortable with its private and semi-private rooms, in addition to its dormitory and a dining area on each floor. However, the limited size of the residence allowed for only fifteen women who, if they could, had to pay at least $5.00 per week. The parish had made a down payment of $5,000 to purchase the home, and borrowed $20,000 from the bank. By the summer of 1925, the debt had been reduced by $10,000. It was now foreseeable that one day a larger and more modern structure could be built to accommodate both men and women. Everything seemed possible in this atmosphere of generosity and commitment.

Bereavement often mingles with joy. On May 24, 1927, the parish lost one of its most illustrious old priests, Father Avite Amyot, at the age of 83. He had spent forty years in Lowell, serving the Franco-American population as a good and charitable worker in the vineyard of the Lord. Bishop Dontenwill, superior-general of the Oblates, who was in Lowell at the time, presided at his funeral, which took place in an atmosphere of profound mourning felt by all.

The priests of the parish were growing old, and soon there would be a succession of funerals, but recruits were on the way. Since the ordination of Father Lucien Brassard in 1921, the year the province was founded, the number of men had increased by twelve priests and three lay brothers. By 1926,

Engraving of the establishments of St. Jean Baptiste Province, prepared and widely distributed on the occasion of the one hundredth anniversary of the approval of the Oblate Constitution and Rules, in 1926.

PANORAMA DES ETABLISSEMENTS
DE LA PROVINCE ST-JEAN BAPTISTE OMI
1826 ~ 1926

1 L'EGLISE ST. JOSEPH
2 L'EGLISE ST. JEAN BAPTISTE
3 COLLEGE ST. JOSEPH
4 COUVENT ST. JOSEPH
5 PRESBYTÈRE ST. JOSEPH
6 RESIDENCE DES PERES MARISTES
7 RESIDENCE DES SOEURS GRISES
8 ORPHELINAT FRANCO AMERICAIN
9 HOSPICE ST. JOSEPH

10 EGLISE NOTRE DAME DE LOURDES
11 PRESBYTÈRE NOTRE DAME DE LOURDES
12 RESIDENCE DES SOEURS N-D-L
13 EGLISE STE. MARIE
14 EGLISE STE. JEANNE D'ARC
15 ECOLE STE. JEANNE D'ARC
16 PRESBYTÈRE STE. J. D'ARC
17 NOVICIAT DE HUDSON, N.H.
18 JUNIORAT DE COLEBROOK, N.H.

214

the province numbered thirty-four priests, ten brothers, sixteen scholastics, and a large number of novices and students at the juniorate. This successful growth had given the provincial extra work, with the result that, in January 1928, the parishioners learned with regret that Father Eugène Turcotte was resigning as pastor of Saint Joseph, so that he could devote himself entirely to his duties as provincial.

The news was disheartening, but everyone was consoled by the fact that he would continue to reside in the rectory, and therefore be accessible and attentive to the needs of his people.

Father Turcotte would guide the province until 1933 when his superiors named him pastor of Sainte Jeanne d'Arc parish and then to a succession of important positions. In his later years, he would spend his last days at d'Youville Manor, the successor of his humble hospice of years past. He died on January 16, 1968, at the age of 92, surrounded by the Fathers of the Saint Jean Baptiste Province.

At a concert in his honor, held on February 16, 1928, the Sainte Cécile Chorale sang the following lines which are so very appropriate:

> *Vous avez notre meilleur souvenir*
> *Nous chanterons en votre honneur : Vivat Semper!*

(Our finest memory is yours to have,
We shall sing in your honor: *Vivat Semper!*)

23. Saint Joseph Hospital

Throughout the 1920s, so prosperous and so full of enthusiasm, there were, nevertheless, premonitory signs of the great debacle which accompanied the Crash of 1929 and led to the economic Depression, the greatest the country has ever known. During World War I, the textile industry in Lowell had enjoyed a boom which prolonged its prosperity for a certain length of time. In 1919, the Hamilton Manufacturing Company had one of the largest weaving rooms in the world. The acme of post-war prosperity had been reached in 1921, when the number of spindles in the Lowell mills amounted to 1.2 million while there were 26,000 cotton looms in operation. Yet, already this prosperity was beginning to wane for, starting that same year, competition from the South increased rapidly.

To this competition, should be added the demands of the unions, unenlightened management, heavy State taxes, and the long distance from raw materials. All of these factors contributed to the ruin of the cotton industry in Lowell. In 1926, the Hamilton Company closed its doors. In 1927, the Massachusetts Cotton Mills and then the Tremont and Suffolk Mills followed suit. That same year, the Appleton Mills moved to South Carolina. In 1928, the Bay State Cotton Mills disappeared. In all, 10,700 people lost their jobs. These closings were only the first in the total disintegration of the city's principal industry. From 1920 to 1930, the population of Lowell declined from 112,759 to 100,234. In 1940, only three textile mills remained, of the eleven that had been founded at the beginning of the nineteenth century. The decline was irreversible and the cotton mills of the city of spindles would one day be only a memory of the past.

The parishioners of Saint Joseph adjusted as well as they could to these harsh realities. In January 1928, nearly two years before the Wall Street Crash, they were preparing to receive Father Louis G. Bachand as their new pastor.

Father Bachand was the son of Joseph Jérémie Bachand and Lumina Comeau. He was born in Clyde, Kansas, on August 27, 1888. His parents were sturdy Canadian pioneers who had been the first to go to that fertile region around 1870. Quite soon, other immigrants from Québec joined the Bachands, to form a small, fairly prosperous Franco-American agricultural community. Young Louis grew up on the family farm with his four brothers and five sisters, two of whom became nuns.

After elementary school, he decided to follow in the footsteps of the Oblates who at that time were ministering in Kansas and Nebraska. He entered the Oblate juniorate in Buffalo, then pursued his studies in the congregation's various institutions of formation, and was ordained on May 28, 1915, by

Fr. Louis Bachand, O.M.I.

William Cardinal O'Connell in Boston's cathedral. After one year of ministry in his home State, he was assigned to Saint Joseph parish in Lowell as a curate, where he remained from 1916 to 1928.

His superiors in Lowell were able to observe him closely. Very energetic, unwavering in the service of God, he also revealed himself to be a fine administrator. To his work as bursar of the parish, from 1922 to 1928, he brought such dedication and skill that he seemed to be the obvious choice to become pastor. He was also very open to the ideas of the time, while giving proof of his deep convictions and strength of character, proclaiming the truths of faith and the role of the Church in modern society. His stands, though not always popular, were the product of serious reflection and his desire to promote the welfare of the Church and the people of Christ.

Father Bachand took a firm grip on the reins of the parish, concentrating his efforts at first to completing the educational work begun by his predecessor.

217

Convinced of the importance of Franco-American schools, he would declare, in 1937, at the Second French-Language Congress, held in Québec:

> Destroy our schools and everything will fall apart. The generation coming up will no longer know French. Our newspapers will cease to be published, our societies will soon be at death's door, our priests will have to choose either to preach in English or give up their parishes to English-speaking priests, and sound the death knell of our survival.

The high school was looked upon as playing an essential role, that of forming an élite capable of achieving the highest positions in American society without, however, forgetting the Catholic and Franco-American values drawn from the heart of the family. The role of the high school, he continued, was " . . . to implant in the souls of our young people more light and more strength in order to immunize them further against the enemies of their religion and their race."

So as to highlight the sacred mission of the schools, in June 1928, the diplomas were granted for the first time during a solemn High Mass in Saint Jean Baptiste church. That evening, at the play directed by the Brothers, the pastor announced that in September 1928, a third year would be added to the boys' high school, and, in 1929, a fourth. It was also announced at the sisters' end-of-the-year play that the first year of a high school for girls would be started that September.

The enthusiastic response of the parents was immediate. *L'Association des Dames Éducatrices Franco-Américaines* and *Le Conseil Sainte-Thérèse de l'Union Saint-Jean-Baptiste d'Amérique* sent the first checks to the sisters, to give the high school "a good start." In April 1929, the alumni gave the Brothers $1,000 for their high school. Even the children were thrilled. Irène Potvin, a student at the girls' school, won $2.50 in gold at a raffle, and voluntarily donated the money to the high school fund.

At the opening of the school year, in September 1928, twenty-one young women enrolled in the new St. Joseph High School for girls, under the direction of the Grey Nuns. That first year, the classes were held on the top floor of the Moody Street School. The following year, the classes were moved to the little yellow house at 227 Pawtucket Street on the grounds of the orphanage, close to the home for the elderly. At first, the bilingual program offered only classical subjects, but with time a complete commercial course was added. The graduates from the orphanage were admitted free of charge to both the girls' and the boys' high schools. In spite of the Depression, the girls' school prospered, and on June 12, 1932, the first diplomas were granted. There were ten graduates: Lorraine Roberge, Gertrude Boucher, Gracia Paradis, Germaine Héroux, Irène

St. Hilaire, Gilberte Gaulin, Lilliane Boucher, Irène Blazon, Olivette Lachance and Annette Dumont. Three of them: the Misses Blazon, G. Boucher, and Héroux joined the Sisters as Grey Nuns, and one of them, Miss Paradis, became a White Sister of Africa.

A third year was added to the boys' high school, and everything augured well for adding a fourth year. However, as happens to the "best laid plans," problems arose. The economic crisis struck and the parish income diminished. The pastor was then forced to make rather difficult decisions that were not always popular. In 1928, there were nineteen Brothers teaching in the school, and nine women lay teachers. The salaries of the latter were necessarily higher than that of the religious men and women. In addition to this, there were more vocations among the Sisters than the Brothers.

Brother Francis, the dynamic director since the year 1922, wanted to modernize the school. He had already introduced many innovations, one of which was a complete sports program. He wanted to build a major extension for the high school, at the corner of Decatur Street, which would have incorporated the parish hall whose construction was being contemplated. His plan necessitated the purchase of several properties, and the erection of a footbridge over Decatur Street. Brother Francis convinced the Alumni, bringing them around to his way of thinking, and had plans drawn up by an architect, all of this without really consulting the Fathers. Father Bachand found the plan both

The women lay teachers at the boys' school, the *Collège,* in 1927. They taught the young boys in the begining classes.

219

unrealistic and impractical, told the brothers so and categorically refused to go along, without giving too much consideration to their susceptibilities.

All of this made the decisions which the pastor had to take, far more difficult for, following long and animated negotiations between the rectory and the Marist administration in Poughkeepsie, it was agreed that Brother Francis would be transferred, that the third year of the boys' high school would be eliminated, that the salary of the brothers would be reduced, and that the first four grades of the school, a total of six classes in all, would be turned over to the Grey Nuns who could teach boys while the brothers were prohibited from teaching girls. As a result, the Brothers' community was reduced from nineteen to thirteen.

In July 1931, the continuing Depression led to the complete closure of the boys' high school. This resulted in the departure of the beloved *Frère Vétérin,* the founder of the high school, who had been teaching in Lowell for thirty-one years. It was a harsh blow for the alumni and the children of the parish, for the charity and goodness of spirit of this brother had become legendary. During class time, he would walk through the corridors of the school with a heavy strap in his hand, waiting to teach disruptive students a lesson. But when the boys who had been expelled from their classrooms came before him, more often than not, they received a piece of candy and some paternal advice instead of the anticipated licking.

This departure recalled the emotions felt by the parishioners in 1928, when Sister Sainte Léontine, the *bonne maman* of the boys' kindergarten, left Lowell after teaching there for forty-five years. People were deeply attached to these teachers who spent so many years sacrificing themselves and doing so much good without considering their own comfort or their own material needs. Their reward and their joy had to be found in prayer and the certainty that they were accomplishing God's will. God alone knows the heroism of these souls who were so faithful in His service and to His love.

The brothers and the parishioners found it difficult to resign themselves to the loss of the boys' high school, for this course of studies had often given proof of the excellence of the teaching dispensed there. The program was more demanding and more complete than the one being offered at Lowell High School. On December 18, 1929, Principal Harris of Lowell High sent the brothers this unsolicited homage, which is reproduced here from a French translation of the time:

> The students of your Saint Joseph School that you sent to us in September for their fourth year of high school have given us full and complete satisfaction in their conduct and their work. In their studies, they are among the best. You can be justly proud of this excellent group

of young men, for they are a credit to the school and to the teachers who have succeeded so well in their task as educators.

I consider it to be my duty and I am happy to make this testimony public. May my words of appreciation be an encouragement and a consolation for the teachers who devote themselves with such zeal to the formation of youth.

Last August, when these same students came to my office to enroll, they immediately impressed me favorably by their reserve, good manners, and courteous answers. Now that I have seen them at work, I can assure you that reality surpasses what I had been expecting from these young men.

When these same boys received their diplomas from Lowell High School in 1930, six of them were declared to be "star scholars": Omer Descheneaux, Henri Fournier, Armand Laroche, Gérald Leblanc, Georges Parent, and Louis Sicard. It took many prayers on the part of the brothers to keep themselves from becoming dejected upon seeing their high school program collapse after so much effort on their part.

While accepting the harsh economic realities of the time, the parishioners were determined to reopen the high school as soon as the financial situation stabilized. In spite of everything, in September 1932 the sisters' school still enrolled 771 students taught by fifteen nuns. The boys' school had 452 students taught in the lower grades by five nuns, along with three lay teachers, and in the upper grades 350 students were taught by nine brothers. The girls' high school had 70 students, taught by three nuns. The orphanage sheltered 238 children under the care of twenty-six nuns and six lay teachers.

The parish family spirit remained positive, in spite of the crisis, and social ties were more easily maintained with the opening of the parish hall. Given the proliferation of evenings of dramatic presentations and soirées, Father Turcotte, taking up the dream of his predecessors, had wanted to provide the parish with a spacious and modern parish hall. Everyone agreed that the old hall in the *collège,* which went back to Father Garin's day, was no longer adequate for the needs of the times. So, on January 2, 1921, the cardinal having given his approval to the project, the pastor and his flock began raising funds in all the usual ways: bazaars, raffles, etc. A special monthly collection was even added for this purpose begining in March 1925. Once the money had been raised, Father Turcotte handed the project over to his successor.

Father Bachand chose the site, and on December 7, 1928, construction began in the schoolyard next to the collège, facing Merrimack Street. The new hall, which would have seating room for one thousand people, turned out to be one of the most modern in the city, with a stage fitted out with props and the most modern projectors for sound movies that were available at the time. The grand opening took place on October 20, 1929. The hall was filled to the rafters when Father Bachand turned and spoke the following:

Here is our parish hall, large, spacious, modern. It is the result of your generosity and bigheartedness. Accept it with the same deep joy that I experience in placing it in your hands. May it always be what we have made it: an ideal place for your parish gatherings, an attractive social center where, in an atmosphere of happy friendliness, you will learn to know and love each other better for your collective good, and for the glory of God and that of the valiant nationality of which you are the worthy sons.

To inaugurate the hall, the organist, Mr. Pépin, had composed a sweeping *Passion du Christ* based on the grand pageants of Europe. At first, it was feared that this dramatic work would be too difficult to rehearse and present. But to everyone's joy, it was an enormous artistic success, so much so that it was repeated ten times in the space of one year. Postcards were even published with representations of the principal tableaux. This drama, in five acts and ten tableaux, included the Sainte Cécile Chorale and the best dramatic talent in the parish:

Jesus – Achille Gaulin	Thomas – Léo Pintal
Mary – Mrs. Dewey G. Archambeault	Phillip – Albini Desrochers
Mary Magdalene – Mrs. Yvette Vallières	Matthew – Germain Normandin
Veronica – Marguerite Bourgeois	Judas – Frank Filiatreault
Claudia (Pilate's Wife) – Arthémise Hotin	Simon of Cyrene – Lucien Pelletier
Servant girl – Cécile Vincent	Centurion – Olivier Pagé
Angel – Cécile Labrie	Soldier – Roger Racette
Pilate – Elzéar Côté	Balbus – Aldéric Coderre
Caiphas – Edouard Desrosiers	Selphia – Arthur Germain
Annas – Wilfrid Jacques	Dathan – Rosario Baillargeon
Sadoc – Léon-M. Côté	Malchus – Rodolphe Richer
Manasses – Arthur Paquin	Barrabas – Lucien Sanscartier
Simon – Edouard Grégoire	Holy Women – Mmes. C. Coté,
John – Raymond Baril	N.-J. Pichette, Eugénie Soulard,
James – Stanislas Paquin	G. Grégoire

The hall having been properly inaugurated, there followed a profusion of plays, bazaars and soirées. Mr. Pépin's inexhaustible zest led him, with the assistance of the men from the church choir or the Sainte Cécile Chorale, to mount an abundance of comedies and concerts. Even the Fathers dabbled in the playwright's art, as when Father Arthur Lemire presented *Pauvre mémère* (Poor Grandma), the product of his own pen, in 1932.

The new hall thus became the family center for the parish. Only the very large gatherings would now be held at the municipal auditorium, or in the assembly hall at Lowell High School.

The parish was debt free. Since 1917, it had succeeded in liquidating its enormous debt burden. The $20,000 that had to be borrowed to build the hall was easily repaid within ten years. The entire construction had cost $32,800 plus $5,000 for the projection room. The last $5,000 were accounted for separately for they represented the receipts raised by Father Baron's Saturday and Sunday movies for the school children.

Fr. Armand Baron, O.M.I.

Father Baron, who had always been interested in propagating the faith through the press, had, very early on, seen the possibilities of an apostolate through film. As soon as he had arrived in Lowell, in 1905, he had begun giving lectures which he illustrated with the help of a magic lantern. But with the development of the movie industry and the proliferation of small five-cent theaters, he realized the powerful attraction of motion pictures, not all of them good, and their effects on school children. At first, he began by presenting a few religious films from time to time in the school hall, while at the same time Father Watelle was waging war from the pulpit against the movies being shown downtown.

Having come to the realization that not all films had to be on religious themes, but could be enjoyed so long as they were inoffensive, he began to show movies on Saturday or Sunday afternoons. As with everything he undertook, success smiled on his efforts. The audiences grew and grew. The apostolate of *la bonne presse* (the good press) was now expanded to include the apostolate of the good cinema. To those who criticized the showing of movies and too often asked, "Why are we having motion pictures?" he would respond, "We are fighting bad movies by promoting those that are not offensive." He welcomed with great joy the declaration by Cardinal Verdier of Paris regarding this kind of apostolate: "Catholics who are involved with the cinema are doing beautiful work; we offer them our congratulations and our most ardent wishes for success." Finally, he must have experienced an intense emotion upon reading Pope Pius XI's encyclical on *The Christian Education of Youth* in which the Holy Father strongly recommended the promotion of wholesome cinema.

As a result, the nickels accumulated and the hall was able to afford state of the art sound movie projectors. As soon as the films began to show signs of a growing popularity, young Father Lucien Brassard, who was the parish bursar, was given the responsibility for the work since Father Baron already had his hands full. Soon, even the adults began to enjoy the good motion pictures presented in the parish hall for, as Father Baron wrote:

> Businessmen, workers, students, whoever I may be, I have the absolute right, I have a human right to legitimate entertainment. Furthermore, I need to have it, caught as I am in the rough stranglehold of my work, my cares, and boredom, which is the greatest of burdens.

The Fathers as a group selected the films and reviewed them before each showing to the public. They considered this to be another part of their ministry in this ever-changing twentieth century:

> Briefly put, we must choose among the films. That is what your priests are doing for you before the movies are offered. To provide you with good entertainment is a continuous concern, an enormous task and we are glad to do it.

The parish, thus launched into the avant-garde of the century, success surpassed all expectations. Father Brassard was heartily engaged in the enterprise, and even began taking home movies whenever he could. The greatest American movies were shown on the screen of the parish hall and even "talkies" from France were screened. At the height of the Depression, the income from the motion pictures was applied to the support of the schools, and this revenue in and of itself was sufficient to keep the schools going satisfactorily. The apostolate of wholesome cinema continued to bear fruit for many long years, and would disappear only after World War II.

The spiritual life of the parish family continued to move forward. The grotto at the orphanage was always filled with people. Novenas, triduums, pilgrimages, processions on the feast of Corpus Christi, and devotions during

May, were all expressions of popular piety. Ordinations were held every year on a regular basis in Saint Jean Baptiste church, followed by visits of missionary bishops seeking prayers and funds. And there was also always a place for the unexpected. On February 22, 1929, Archbishop Forbes of Ottawa presided at a High Mass of thanksgiving, at the request of Attorney Guillet, to mark the occasion of the favorable solution of the Roman Question. Guillet, who had been a pontifical Zouave, enrolling at the age of seventeen to defend the Pope, had lived long enough to see the Holy See liberated from all political entanglements with the establishment of the Vatican State. The worthy attorney died in 1931.

There were many bereavements during this period. First, Father Félix Vachon died on May 1, 1928, at the age of fifty, and on the following July 13, Father Augustin Graton, who had been ministering in the parish since 1903, passed away. These were grievous losses, for Father Vachon had been the energetic director of the Sainte Marie chapel in South Lowell, where he had laid the foundation for a new church building, and had already opened the church basement for worship. As a former missionary, his zeal and faith knew no bounds and he easily communicated his enthusiasm to his flock. Father Graton, of fond memory, accomplished the work of three. At Father Fournier's death, he had inherited the latter's special ministry to the poor and the sick. His Holy Hour every Tuesday, and on the First Friday of every month, his religion classes in the girls' school, his instructions to the *Enfants de Marie,* and his advice, in short, his love of souls made Father Graton, who was universally loved, mourned by everyone at the time of his death.

Father Graton's death occurred in Montréal, where he had gone for surgery. At that time Lowell had only one Catholic hospital, Saint John's. Franco-Americans, beginning with the bazaars of 1889 and 1892, contributed regularly to the support of the hospital. But this institution had always had the disadvantage of being entirely English-speaking, and too small to accommodate the very large Catholic population of Lowell. The poorer parishioners, of necessity, frequented the non-Catholic Corporation Hospital, where treatment was free of charge for the poor who worked in the mills.

As a consequence of this, the priests and parishioners of Saint Joseph had dreamed of one day founding a Franco-American hospital. But the idea seemed so audacious that no one dared think about it too seriously, for starting a hospital required quite a considerable sum of money.

In 1840, the association of the cotton mill corporations of Lowell had purchased the former princely residence of Kirk Boott, the founding mill agent of the city, to turn it into a hospital. The Lowell Corporation Hospital, the first industrial hospital in the United States, dispensed to the mill workers all the care they needed at a very low cost. Those without means were treated free of charge. The mills absorbed the deficit. Directed by the most eminent physicians of the region, this hospital had quite soon become one of the best institutions of its kind in the country. In 1887, a school of nursing had been added. From 1840 to 1930, 62,137 patients were treated at the hospital.

The closing of the mills and the dismantling of the corporations seriously weakened the financial stability of this venerable institution. In the face of accumulating deficits, the directors decided, in 1927, to put the hospital up for sale at the price of $200,000. Mr. Joseph A. Légaré, one of St. Joseph's most eminent parishioners, now came forward. He was a philanthropic industrialist, former secretary to Congressman Butler Ames, former postmaster of Lowell, and respected advisor to the agents of the mills. It was he who suggested to them that the hospital be offered for sale to the Oblates. Since it was located at the corner of Pawtucket and Merrimack Streets, and only a five-minute walk from the rectory, it would be a magnificent acquisition for the parish.

But the Fathers found the price to be out of their reach, and the cardinal, for his part, refused to grant his permission, objecting that one Catholic hospital was enough for Lowell. However, the proprietors, already feeling the effects of the Depression, and not finding any buyers, lowered the price to $150,000. Légaré tried again. The Fathers were interested, but the cardinal refused once more, objecting to the enormous debt that would be incurred by them.

Not wanting to let go of his idea of a Franco-American hospital for Saint Joseph parish, Mr. Légaré decided to take the matter into his own hands, using the best means at his disposal. He made the rounds of the offices of the cotton mills' treasurers, and thanks to his many useful contacts, he was able to convince the directors, one by one, to offer the hospital to the Oblates as an outright gift. After all, he reasoned with them, the hospital had served the Lowell population

Joseph Légaré

for ninety years, and so it would be a shame to see an institution of such public usefulness disappear. This hospital had been the pride of the city, and of the Yankee industrialists who had sustained it for so many years. Wasn't it better to give the hospital to those who could continue it, rather than to see it end up in the hands of auctioneers? What could be a grander philanthropic act on the part of the mill owners, he argued?

This approach succeeded. After three years of negotiations, the transfer took place. The hospital became the property of the Oblates as a free-will offering. The former owners took on the $15,000 debt that remained to be paid for recent repairs to the institution. In return, they simply asked that the hospital continue to function for at least ten more years. And so it came about that for the sum of one dollar, the parish acquired a 108-bed hospital, and a school of nursing, completely fitted out, furnished, and debt free. Mr. Légaré's dream had come true. He died in 1938, respected by everyone.

The parishioners could hardly believe it. Father Bachand, Father Turcotte, the provincial, the cardinal, everyone moved quickly to accept this generous gift. On Friday, October 31, 1930, Father Bachand, Mr. Légaré, and Judge Eno went to Boston for the transfer of titles. Father Baron could truthfully write, "Let us thank God, the Author of all good inspirations, for this remarkable grace to our parish, which will be of special benefit to the entire Franco-American population of Lowell."

As soon as he received the first intimation of the agents' decision, the pastor hastened to Canada to offer the administration of the hospital to the Grey Nuns of Ottawa who had extensive experience in this kind of work. They accepted on October 22, and on Saturday the 25th, Mother General Saint-Bruno, accompanied by Sister Joséphat, superior of the Ottawa General Hospital, arrived in Lowell for a visit of the establishment. On November 15, 1930, Father Bachand presented the first contingent of nuns, who had arrived from Ottawa the night before, to the doctors and the women directors of nursing. The nuns were Sister Saint Alphonse Rodriguez, superior, Sisters Sainte-Françoise, Saint-Yves, Odélia, and Norman. The greetings were courteous and everyone on either side was eager to please.

The nuns set to work with all their usual diligence and dedication. Changes were made for the better in many departments; visiting hours and daily schedules were reorganized; the outside clinic was expanded. Religious services were quickly put in place. These included daily Mass, communion and confession available to the patients at all hours, and all the time, in addition to retreats for the nurses and the nuns. Before very long, three other nuns joined the personnel to look after the school of nursing and patient care. The old Yankee doctors couldn't believe their eyes upon seeing all this activity and burst of benevolent energy, nor could they withhold their admiration and joy.

The hospital was without debt, but also without capital, and so was in need of tangible revenues. The nuns and the pastor launched a fund-raising campaign with the raffle of a Chevrolet car as the prize. The former directors, who had donated the hospital, and who were more than delighted at this turn of events, presented the nuns with $8,000, the amount owed by former patients up to that point. The cardinal sent $1,000, and, in spite of the economic crisis, the first campaign, in December 1930, brought in $12,000, which was allocated to the administrative budget.

On February 15, 1931, the hospital received its charter of incorporation and officially became Saint Joseph Hospital. Its first Board of Trustees included Father Louis G. Bachand, president, Father L. Brassard, treasurer, Sister Saint Alphonse Rodriguez, secretary, Sister Norman, Father Armand Baron, Father Emile Bolduc, and Joseph Légaré. The Board of Directors was made up of Father Bachand, Father Brassard, and Sister Rodriguez. Doctor Joseph Lamoureux became the chief of physicians.

Thus did the hospital start out on its new course, and the population of Lowell benefited from the proverbial Christian charity of the Grey Nuns. The good that was accomplished during those Depression years can never be measured. Following the example of their foundress, Mother Bruyère, the nuns were unstinting in sparing no effort of their time and dedication. The hospital, without any support from the government, depended solely on the generosity of its personnel and the people.

At the large *Jour d'offrandes* (Day of Offerings) for the benefit of the hospital in May 1931, under the direction of Mrs. Clarina Morier, R.N., and a team of women, the nuns published a list of "suggestions" for gifts: "Any object useful in a hospital will be accepted: Money! Linen: sheets (63 X 108), blankets, bedspreads, pillowcases, towels, hand towels, baby clothes; Preserves of all kinds: jellies, jams, fruit; Vegetables: fresh or canned; Electrical appliances: flat irons, light bulbs, toasters, etc. Coal is an important item."

In 1931 alone, the hospital gave free care to 12,145 people (out-patients and in-patients) who required 644 operations and 3,500 laboratory tests. This was in contrast to the 6,722 who paid for the services. In the kitchen, the nuns provided 7,172 meals for the poor and homeless.

The sick came to the hospital in great numbers and improvements continued to be made in the form of repairs and additions to the facility. So much so, that at the tenth anniversary of Saint Joseph Hospital in 1940, the personnel consisted of seventeen nuns, twenty-two registered nurses, and sixty-two nursing students serving an average of 101 patients per day. What a change from the fall of 1930, when the first five founding nuns, upon arrival,

St. Joseph Hospital

were faced with a total of fifty-nine patients cared for by eight nurses and twenty-three students.

Everyone was pleased with the success of the hospital which indirectly caused unexpected anguish. In October 1930, *L'Étoile* in announcing the news of the transfer of the hospital to the Oblates, had quoted the following from an interview with Father Bachand:

> It is quite possible that the elderly in the Saint Joseph Hospice will be lodged in a section of the hospital. This would permit us to use the home for other purposes.

The word spread: "They're closing the home for the elderly!" This news was all the more startling since the last payment on the loan for the facility had just been made, leaving it debt free. But it was Father Bachand's intent to put the hospital on a better financial footing by annexing the home, and combining the gifts he received, thus enabling him to earmark them for the hospital which he hoped to turn into a hospital-hospice as in Canada. However, it became apparent that the union of the two was not feasible, and, since expanding the home was out of the question, Father Bachand came to the conclusion that the hospice had to be sacrificed for the good of the hospital, alerting the mother general in Québec of his decision. As early as December 1930, the nuns, with heavy hearts began to return the elderly to their families, or to place them in other institutions. Miss Bilodeau was placed with the Grey Nuns in Cambridge. The home for the elderly closed its doors in January 1931.

This decision, reached rather hurriedly and in secret, did not please most people. It was openly criticized by many as lacking in judgment. But, faced with a fait accompli and the growing poverty caused by the economic crisis, the parishioners accepted the sad situation and order was restored. Nevertheless, the memory of the "little home for the elderly" remained vivid, and in 1945 Mr. Amédée Archambault gave a house on Pawtucket Street to the sisters of the orphanage. His intention was that it become a hospice for the elderly. But the house was ill-suited for this purpose and the plan collapsed. It was only in 1960, with the construction of D'Youville Manor on Varnum Avenue, that a home for the Franco-American elderly in Lowell once again became a reality.

Times were difficult as the crisis deepened still further. In 1932, the Lowell Trust Company and the Middlesex National Bank failed and closed their doors. The following year, the great shoe-shop strike foreshadowed the departure and disappearance of this industry from Lowell. Half of the city's working-class population was unemployed, and 25% of the families were dependent upon public welfare.

The parish experienced its share of suffering. Families were moving away, the collections were diminishing, and pew rent was no longer taken. The nuns in the convent spent their free time making small gifts out of almost nothing for their students who would not be receiving anything else at Christmas. The orphanage, seeking help, launched a campaign for donations in the fall of 1932. Some gave clothing, others food, and the more fortunate offered money. Somehow, the nuns succeeded in balancing the budget. At the 25th anniversary celebration of the orphanage, in May 1933, two thousand people, gathered at the grotto, burst into prayers of thanksgiving for the past and supplications of hope for the future.

The family spirit, one of marvelous harmony and collective faith bequeathed to the parish by its founders, was solid, and continued to bear fruit in spite of everything. Novenas and pilgrimages took place as before and the societies and religious confraternities, 4,180 members strong, remained stable and active.

The atmosphere of understanding and agreement which reigned between the Oblates and the parishioners was again made clear when Father Bachand returned from Europe. He and Father Turcotte had attended the General Chapter of their congregation in 1932. On Tuesday, October 18, one thousand people filled the parish hall. Delegates from the societies, school children, orphans, and workers rubbed shoulders as they pressed to get in to welcome their returning pastor. Father Bachand, entering the hall, to the strains of "O Canada," played by the C.M.A.C. band under the baton of Mr. Lebrun, was at pains to control his emotion. Moved to the core, he listened to the speeches, compliments and songs. But when two young girls from the school presented him with a check for $1,025 for the parish, his pastoral heart understood at once all the sacrifices and generosity that had made this gift possible. Frank Ricard put into the following words everyone's love and esteem:

> In our midst for more than seventeen years, and our pastor for several years . . . we have learned to love you and deeply appreciate you . . . Dear Father, this large gathering this evening, so enthusiastic and friendly, proves to you that my words are the true expression of our innermost feelings.

Happy to be back among his parish family, and profoundly touched by all these praises, Father Bachand could not help but think of his predecessors and his religious family which had been laboring in the Lord's vineyard at Lowell for more than sixty years.

Still exhilarated from his voyage to Rome and the General Chapter, the pastor's heart was radiant with zealous idealism. The Oblate Congregation was thriving on all sides, and Father Bachand had been able to see for himself the impressive extent of the missionary work so wished for by Bishop de Mazenod. Nearly half of the 4,465 Oblates, in March 1933, were toiling in mission countries. Eighteen wore the miter of an archbishop or bishop, and one was a prince of the Church and primate of the Canadian hierarchy, Cardinal Rodrigue Villeneuve of Québec .

The books of Bishop Duchaussois spread the story of the heroic exploits of the missionaries in the Arctic region of Canada, and everywhere the Oblates had earned the reputation of looking after the most difficult and the most abandoned missions, whether in Africa, North America, or Ceylon, now known as Sri Lanka.

The parishioners of Saint Joseph, who were always very close to the Church's evangelical spirit, wholeheartedly shared the zeal of their Fathers and enrolled by the hundreds in the Missionary Association of Mary Immaculate, an international union of prayers dedicated to supporting the Oblate missions.

The coming of venerable missionary bishops to Lowell had been regular occurrences, and the almost legendary generosity of the parishioners had never failed them. As proof of this, a passage in the memoirs of Bishop Grouard, the elderly prelate of Athabaska-Mackenzie in Alberta, Canada, describes a beautiful example of faith. The incident had taken place in Lowell, during a visit with Father Garin and reads as follows:

After High Mass at Saint Joseph's church, I was told that someone wished to see me in the rectory parlor. Having gone there, I found a young man with his wife who was holding an infant in her arms. This man said to me:

– Your Excellency, we were not ready to respond to your appeal in favor of your missions when you made it, but, as soon as we returned home, we thought, my wife and I, that we could offer you our small contribution.

He then presented me with a five-dollar bill, and added, taking out his watch:

– Maybe this watch could be useful to you, so please accept it.
– But, my dear man, I answered, you have already given me a beautiful gift and I do not want to deprive you of all your belongings.
– Oh, it isn't much, he replied.

Then he took a package from under his arm and handed it to me.
– If you would accept this also, it would please me very much. It is a suit which I bought for my wedding, and for which I no longer have any use. Please take it if it can be of use to you.
– Oh! This is really too much, I exclaimed.
– No, Your Excellency, it is not too much for the favor we are about to ask. You see our little boy. Well, we are asking you to pray for him so that he can go through life without committing a mortal sin!

I was moved to the very depth of my soul, and tears came to my eyes. I was overwhelmed with admiration at seeing such a strong faith, and accepted what the young Canadian couple was offering so generously, and with such a saintly motive.

The result of this episode was revealed only in October 1933 during the visit of Bishop Joseph Guy, Bishop Grouard's successor. The worthy prelate had related the above incident to a large audience, and a few days later, he received the following letter, written by someone who had been present when he spoke:

To His Excellency Bishop Guy, O.M.I.

Your Excellency,

Since His Excellency Bishop Grouard died in your arms, it seems to me that you would be happy to receive a photograph of the child whose parents requested His Grace's prayers and blessing, so that he would never commit a mortal sin.

All of them have passed away from this world. Mrs. Corriveau was the first to go. After being a widower for two years, Mr. Corriveau married a young woman of high Belgian nobility who had immigrated to the United States because of a reversal of fortune. She was a true Christian, dignity personified. So often she would say: "What a sweet boy is this little Candide!" The child was then four years of age. Alas, this second mother would be laid to rest next to the first one, one year after the marriage.

The child was taken to Canada to live with paternal aunts who took care of him until his father married a third time a few years later. Candide entered the seminary and only came to Lowell at vacation time. Mrs. Corriveau (a Miss Deschênes from Québec) never tired of praising Candide. She would often say to us that he was a perfect child. When he fell ill with tuberculosis, he was sent again to the countryside, with his aunts, where he died as one predestined for heaven. According to the priest who assisted him at the end, the young man had never sullied the white robe of his baptism.

Mrs. Corriveau, who is now deceased, is the one who gave me this memorial card, telling me the facts that I have related above.

Respectfully,
A former parishioner of Saint Joseph parish

The parish often had the opportunity to participate closely in the missionary experience. In July 1933, there occurred an event which could have come from the first centuries of the history of the Catholic Church. The Oblate Bishop of Basutoland [Lesotho since 1966], had launched an appeal for missionaries. The young Saint Jean Baptiste Province responded immediately by sending to the missions its first priest to be so designated. The Grey Nuns of the Cross, impelled by the same ideal, named one of their number from Saint Joseph convent for the African mission.

Bishop Joseph Bonhomme, newly consecrated Bishop of Basutoland, came to Lowell, and on Sunday evening, July 30, took place the beautiful and ancient missionary departure ceremony. Bishop Bonhomme presided from his throne in the packed church as the obediences for the two new missionaries were read, one for Father Georges Saint-Jean, and the other for Sister Marie du Calvaire. After the appropriate homily, Father Saint-Jean advanced with a traveler's staff in his hand, in accordance with the Gospel text, and stood on the first step of the altar as a procession of Oblate priests, diocesan clergy, Marist Brothers, and the altar boys filed past, each in turn to kiss his feet. At the same time, Grey Nuns from their four convents in Lowell, as well as a large number of women religious from other communities, advanced, each individually kissing Sister Marie du Calvaire's ring, the mark of a bride of Christ the Savior. The Fathers and sisters sang alternate verses of the hymn *"Partez, hérauts de la Bonne Nouvelle"* (Go forth, heralds of the Good News).

Bishop Bonhomme explained their assignment as follows: "We are leaving, not in search of honors or riches, but to conquer souls for the glory of God, the triumph of the Church, and the honor of our homeland." After these words, the ceremony ended at the foot of the altar with Benediction of the Blessed Sacrament.

In the fall of 1933, ceremonies of a totally different kind were being prepared. The intense pride of the parishioners in their parochial schools, along with the acknowledged success of these Catholic and French institutions, would finally have the opportunity to be made public before the whole city. The decision had been taken to mark the fiftieth anniversary of the founding of the Moody Street school with as much pomp as possible.

A great many battles had been fought, sacrifices made, and rebuffs endured to ensure the success and the flowering of the schools. Since the day when Father Garin's plan for a school had been rejected, so much ground had had to be covered in order to arrive at the vast schools and convents of St. Joseph parish at the time of this commemoration. Saint Joseph, one of the most important parishes in New England, and the mother parish of a province of Franco-American priests, was duty bound to mark this anniversary with impressive celebrations.

With this in mind, the cardinal archbishop of Québec, the cardinal archbishop of Boston, and the ambassador of France to Washington were invited to Lowell.

The idea of inviting an ambassador from a foreign country to an ethnic anniversary in Lowell seemed rather daring and Cardinal O'Connell hesitated somewhat, given the complexity of the delicate international situation at the time. But Father Bachand's usual savoir-faire dispelled all fears, and the plans advanced without a hitch.

First of all, a large umbrella committee was set up, covering all the sectors of parochial life. The nuns launched the appeal to form an *Amicale* (Alumnae Association) of their former students to help in the preparation of the celebration, and to serve as an ongoing support organization for the works of the sisters.

The first meeting, held in July 1933, was attended by two hundred alumnae. The superior, Sister St. Benoît Labre, presented her agenda and then proposed to move on to the election of the first-ever officers of *L'Amicale Saint-Joseph*. Mrs. Clarina Morier was elected president, Mrs. Albina Skalkeas, vice-president, Miss Berthe Desmarais, secretary, Miss Cécile Vincent, treasurer. Elected as councilors were: Mrs. Albertine Beauchesne, Mrs. Joseph Gagnon, Mrs. Angéline Ninteau, and the Misses Rose Anna Gagnon, Irène Messier, and Angéline Perron. The recruiting committee was made up of Misses Rose Anna Gagnon, Estelle Landry, Annette Dumont, Hélène Généreux, Marie Ange Rivet, and Mrs. E. Soulard and Mrs. Alma Laurin.

The celebrations, orchestrated with such care, lasted three days, from Sunday, November 5 to Tuesday, November 7, 1933. The brilliant success of the festivities exceeded all expectations.

On Saturday, the 4th , *L'Étoile* published a special commemorative issue of sixteen pages, containing many photographs. On Sunday morning, the 5th, Bishop Guy, bishop of Grouard, officiated at the High Mass for the alumnae and distributed a thousand communions. That afternoon a reception was held in a packed parish hall for Mother Saint-Bruno, superior general of the Grey Nuns. That evening 3,000 people filled the municipal auditorium for a solemn reception in honor of Cardinal Villeneuve, O.M.I. of Québec .

On Monday morning, the 6th, the cardinal ordained Lauréat Savard, O.M.I., a son of the parish, to the priesthood. In the evening the cardinal and his retinue—his secretary, the rector of the Québec seminary, and a Knight of the Holy Sepulcher—along with numerous clergy from all parts of New England, joined the nearly 2,000 spectators who had gathered in the Lowell High School auditorium for the official welcome of the French ambassador to Washington, André-Marie Lefebvre de La Boulaye.

On Tuesday morning, November 7th, in a church filled to the rafters, all the splendor of the Catholic liturgy was on display at a Pontifical High Mass, celebrated by Cardinal Villeneuve. Cardinal O'Connell presided from the throne, with Bishop Guy, the Russian Archbishop Vladimir Alexandroff, and the French ambassador in the sanctuary. Two hundred priests were in attendance in the middle aisle.

That evening, a gala banquet closed the grandiose festivities with 800 people in attendance at the municipal auditorium. The orchestral and choral music harmonized with the eloquent speeches to make this evening an unforgettable one, the worthy crowning event of so much work and elaborate preparations.

While the festivities were splendid, thanks in great measure to the personalities assembled there, and all of the well-orchestrated events, the speeches delivered at them, and the sentiments they gave expression to should not be overlooked. Some details of the most interesting ceremonies and some excerpts from the more outstanding speeches are added here to provide an idea of the quality and spirit of the jubilee.

The dominant theme of the celebrations, from the opening ceremony, was the triumph of religious and ethnic values. In his welcoming address to Cardinal Villeneuve, Judge Eno trumpeted the leitmotiv, on a note full of emotion and pride:

> The churches, some rather modest, others spacious and beautiful, that we have built at the expense of sacrifices of all kinds, the many educational and charitable institutions which we have established and sustained for the benefit of our children and the survival of our faith, the benefit societies that we have founded and maintained to preserve our traditions, all speak eloquently of the often heroic devotion of our clergy. They also reveal the tenacity of our efforts and labors, along with the ambition to remain faithful to the religion of our forefathers, to perpetuate on the soil of the Great Republic the characteristics of our race, and to exercise in it that share of influence that is coming to us in this adopted land. We sense quite rightly that it would be wrong for us to shirk the sublime mission that Divine Providence has assigned to us, in having us be born under the star-spangled flag.

However, being on American soil, the practical and political aspect could not be forgotten. Father Bachand, at the closing banquet, made it a point to give his audience the following clarification concerning the Oblate Franco-American schools in Lowell:

> The history of our schools is very revealing in its results. Today there are 4,467 children in attendance. We Americans always like to talk in terms of dollars, perhaps a little too much so. Whatever the case may be, each student in the public schools costs the city a little under 100 dollars per year. It would then not be an exaggeration to say that our schools, with their 4,500 students are saving the city $300,000 to $350,000 per year. Catholic and bilingual from their birth, our schools are still so after fifty years.

If the commemoration was meant to be the apotheosis of the Moody Street school, it was also a glorification of the Franco-American Woman who had passed through that school. Mother General Saint-Bruno, speaking to her alumnae, traced for them a picture of the valiant woman involved in religious social action, as an invaluable help to the parish clergy and called upon to cultivate, in the vast field of the lay apostolate, the solid Christian principles learned at Saint Joseph school. Cardinal Villeneuve took up the same subject, adding all the weight of his authority as a cardinal and the Primate of Canada:

Good Christian women, preserve the heritage which Canada bequeathed to you in the century of the beautiful Catholic and French tradition. . . . Rejoice at this jubilee. Your souls are like the block of marble upon which the engraver inscribes. The letters which have been marked out there have become the golden letters of benediction from heaven. You have a vocation, it is to be apostles of Christian education, the flowers and models of virtue, by fulfilling the great role of the woman in the Church and society.

Each event of the jubilee bore its own special and unforgettable mark, but for many persons, one of them, among all the others, would be remembered with affection. Lowell was no stranger to French culture, but the reception extended to the French ambassador struck the imagination by the exquisiteness and quality of its presentation. The songs, the music, the skits, and the speeches revealed an innate love for, and a special pride in the French language and culture which were like a little treasure, a particular heritage, to be painstakingly preserved in one's heart of hearts, and that was brought out into the open on this evening, to be revealed to the ambassador of the mother country. Father Baron, speaking in everyone's name, carried the audience along with him in lyrical and nuanced flights of eloquence which proclaimed all the feelings nurtured for such a long time:

Ah, M. *l' Ambassadeur,* one has to be Canadian and French, or have lived, as I have, for a long time in the midst of these people, to understand our pride, our happiness in having you here with us! You represent France for us, "the most beautiful kingdom after heaven," as our fathers used to say.

Further on, he gave more precision to his thinking, by referring to one of the dominant themes of the jubilee:

Oh! French language, the language of diplomacy, philosophy, literature, and international politeness. It is you, your charm and your beauty that we are celebrating these days as we observe the glorious fiftieth anniversary of our Catholic Franco-American schools. It is the language that has brought the most luster to Catholic oratory. After 200 years of separation from the mother country, it is still you that we hear sung in our schools, and on the lips of the Canadian child when he says his prayer, or recites his catechism. It is, no doubt, a charming exaggeration, to say, but how many times have I heard it: "I know English better than I do French, but I say my prayers in French, because it is only in French that one prays well."

In closing, he ended with the following assessment:

> Of itself, *M. l' Ambassadeur,* the fiftieth anniversary of schools can possibly seem elsewhere to be a rather ordinary and inconsequential occurrence. But here, it is highly meaningful, and you have understood this well. We are celebrating fifty years of unceasing labor, loyalty to an ideal, constantly renewed sacrifices, and vigilance ever on guard. We are celebrating the triumph of the French spirit, the love and fidelity that France can inspire in the souls that it touches.

For his conclusion, Father Baron recited the poem *Ode à la France* which had been composed by Father Nolin for the occasion. Father Baron's address had been interrupted by repeated applause at almost every sentence, and at the end the audience rose to give a standing ovation to the priest from France who loved them so much. The ambassador then expressed his personal gratitude to both Father Baron and Father Nolin.

The evening unfolded in an atmosphere of utmost merriment and refinement. French culture, on these grand occasions, was that of the great classical seventeenth century, noted for its grace and delicacy of expression. The warbling of the little orphans in the skit prepared by the nuns, the witticisms in Dr. Lamoureux's speech, followed by the great verse drama *La Fille de Roland* (Roland's Daughter), all accompanied by songs, imparted to the evening an aura of nostalgia and feelings which have remained alive in the hearts of those who were present.

The overall impression of these festivities on the distinguished visitors was revealed clearly through both their official and non-official declarations. The learned M. de La Boulaye, an expert on the French contribution to the founding of the United States, had this to say to his Franco-American brothers and sisters:

> Thus, it is up to you, as American citizens, to be the representatives within your country of what French civilization and its qualities have contributed to a country which is united to France by so many memories and historical ties. For, in spite of certain disagreements which have arisen over the course of time, our qualities, our defects also, are really the same as yours.

From Lowell, the ambassador traveled to Lawrence, where a triumphal reception awaited him, along with the renewed homage of affection on the part of Franco-Americans for France, geographically distant, but close to everyone's heart.

Cardinal Villeneuve, an Oblate, who in his younger days had preached retreats at Saint Joseph parish, expressed his love for his Oblate confreres in Lowell and their parishioners, and in his address, he sought to express his aim to support to the fullest extent the aspirations of the Franco-Americans, with all the authority of a cardinal archbishop and primate.

> Be worthy of the best among your ancestors. Be worthy of your blood, for it has often been spilled in defense of the Church. Be worthy of your name which adorns so many memorable places in this great country of the United States. Be worthy of your language; it has disseminated so much faith and heroism for the last one thousand years. Be worthy of your civilization which can add an element of such vivid clarity and great nobility to the treasure of thought and moral values of your Republic. But, be worthy especially, and above all else, of the heroic and unchanging faith of your ancestors. No sacrifice can be too great for the preservation of your religion, no self-denial should scare you away. Leaning on the rock of Peter, obedient to the voice of the pastors of your souls, loyal to that star-spangled flag which, henceforth, will protect you and your sons, you must pursue on this soil the virtuous and apostolic route traced for you by Divine Providence.

Since this was his first official visit to the region, the eminent prelate saw fit to bring the same message of fidelity to Franco-American institutions and clergy in other centers. At Presentation Academy, in Hudson, New Hampshire, and at Sainte-Anne Academy, in Marlborough, Massachusetts, he exhorted the young women, the mothers of tomorrow, to remain faithful to their Catholic and French mission. At a private meeting with the clergy in Sainte-Marie rectory in Marlborough, he expressed himself clearly on the obligations of the Franco-American clergy. Everywhere, he attempted to provide support and encouragement. Later on, in his many succeeding visits to New England, he would prove his unfailing love for the Franco-American people.

Cardinal O'Connell, who was a friend of French culture, and who liked the Franco-Americans, also had a word to say to the Lowell members of his archdiocese. Very much aware of the preparations for the celebration, and very happy concerning the results of the festivities, he wished to give the parishioners of Saint Joseph, and all the Franco-Americans of his diocese, a token of his esteem. To do this, he chose a very impressive setting.

At the end of the Pontifical Mass, he rose from his throne under a baldaquin and came forward in the sanctuary. Saint Jean Baptiste church was resplendent with scarlet velvet hanging along its walls, and draped with banners displaying the papal colors. The congregation, which included 200 priests, many of them Irish, pastors from Lowell and elsewhere, listened attentively.

The cardinal, a former Vatican diplomat, and who had often been the spokesman of the American bishops, spoke first in French, from his prepared text:

This zeal, of which I speak, the French-speaking Catholics of this parish, like those of every other parish in the city, have notably exhibited it by their full and loyal obedience to the teachings of the Church in matters of the education of youth, and also, I am happy to proclaim it, by giving witness to their attachment to the language and traditions they have inherited from their distant ancestors.

After his presentation in French, the elderly prelate, so as to be understood by his Irish confreres, put aside his written text and freely paraphrased it in English. This allowed him to speak more easily, and, several times seeking to express his personal feelings toward his loyal Franco-Americans, he plainly stated: "I love them."

The memory of the Lowell festivities remained vivid with him for a long time, and often afterwards, when His Eminence was questioned on this subject, he would reiterate: "I love those good people."

In Washington also, the recollection of the jubilee persisted. M. de La Boulaye had said in Lowell: "Retain your love for France and it will not forget you." He kept his word. In March 1934, the Oblates of Saint Joseph's parish received a letter announcing that their provincial, Father Bachand, had been made a *Chevalier de la Légion d'Honneur* (Knight of the Legion of Honor), the most prestigious decoration granted by the Republic of France. Once the initial surprise had passed, the official installation ceremony took place during a splendid reception in the parish hall on February 18, 1935.

A few months later, in August 1935, Cardinal O'Connell was also decorated by France, with the title *Grande Croix de la Légion d'Honneur* (Grand Cross of the Legion of Honor) for services to France and to humanity.

As time went on, with the usual torrent of activity at Saint Joseph parish, it was inevitable that changes would be made in the personnel. In the summer of 1933, Father Turcotte, aware of his advancing years, had passed on the responsibility of being provincial to younger shoulders, more capable of handling the increasingly complex administration required by the times. The obvious choice was Father Bachand who became the second provincial of the Saint Jean Baptiste province.

Father Bachand resigned immediately from his important post as superior of the Saint Joseph residence, a responsibility he delegated to Father Emile Bolduc, once he had overcome the latter's humble protestations. Father Bachand continued, nevertheless, to function as pastor until July 1934, at which time he presented his successor to the parish.

24. Beloved Father Emile Bolduc

Emile Bolduc was born in Lowell on March 16, 1896, the son of Zéphirin Bolduc and Clara Houde. He was the third child in a family of thirteen. He showed signs of having a priestly vocation at quite an early age, and the pursuit of this calling would one day lead him all the way to the Philippines. Emile was assiduous in his studies and a model of obedience. He liked to say to his teachers: "I have to study a lot so that I can become a missionary some day."

Following in the footsteps of his older brother Joseph, already an Oblate priest, he applied for admission to the juniorate in Buffalo. This was the first step that would lead him all the way to ordination at the Washington scholasticate on June 14, 1923. He celebrated his first Mass in the old Saint Joseph church, attended by his brother who also gave the homily.

His first assignment was to Saint Jean Baptiste parish, near the priests he had known growing up. At that time, there were elderly Oblates living there who were veterans of parish ministry. This close contact with the pioneer Oblates in the United States proved to be a valuable experience for this ardent and zealous young priest. Kind, gentle, and pious by nature, Father Bolduc was able to develop his spiritual life under the tutelage, and by emulating the example, of these old missionaries who fully lived the community life of their vows. Living side-by-side with Fathers Amyot, Graton, Nolin, Baron, Marion, Dénizot, Turcotte, etc. the young priest grew in strength and blossomed, in conforming to the model of the Missionary Oblates.

Forty-five years later, in 1968, Father Bolduc, a veteran of thirty years of preaching in the foreign missions, candidly acknowledged the following:

> What gave me a good start was the community life that was observed so well here at Saint Joseph. It was difficult at times, but I had the example of the oldest of them. This got me off to a good start and it has served me well my whole life.

Community life, based on the observance of the Holy Rules of the Congregation, closely resembled that of a monastery. Monthly retreats and lectures on theology, total silence in the evening, prayer in common, obedience to the superior, all of this fostered a spirit of religious solidarity, so necessary for a community of priests.

Father Anthime Desnoyers, the assistant-general who had come from Rome for a canonical visitation in 1934, wrote in his report: "At Saint Joseph, I found fervent religious, zealous priests. and an orderly community." Further on he added:

> It has often been said, since Saint Paul, that an apostle without an inner life is like a resounding gong or a clashing cymbal. The Oblate who ceases to be a religious and a man of God to throw himself headlong into

the works of the ministry squanders his life painfully, only to lose his soul and with it an infinity of other souls. Thanks be to God, this is not the kind of Oblates that I have found in this residence.

What is obvious at first glance is the positive spirit that reigns in the community; a spirit of charity, solidarity, collaboration, mutual support. The members are united and devoted to their excellent superior who himself expends his energy for his community and his flock with a zeal that is almost excessive.

The "excellent superior" mentioned here, in 1934, was none other than Father Bolduc himself for, within ten years, his superiors had quickly recognized the faith and remarkable devotion of the young priest. The parishioners, for their part, who always kept an attentive eye on the young curates, declared without hesitation: "He is a saint."

Wherever there were down-and-out or sick people to be helped, he could be found at their side. His free moments, some called them his enjoyment, were spent visiting the sick or helping the poor. His confreres were at pains to ensure that he got enough rest, since he was so much "on the go," by the bedside of a sick person, or offering encouragement to the head of a household who was unemployed. It was said that he knew every parishioner in Little Canada by his or her first name.

The story is told about his Communion visit, one winter day, to the bedside of a sick parishioner who was unemployed. He found the poor man surrounded by his wife and children who were in tears. In this unheated apartment, the man was nailed to his bed by a very bad case of the flu. To add to all this misery, an employer had offered him a job that was to begin on the next day. This was the first offer he'd received in weeks. Father Bolduc sized up the situation, paused prayerfully for a moment, and said in a low voice: "This is not God's will." The words were heard by the young acolyte who accompanied him. Father then raised his hand, blessed the sick man, and said quite simply to him: "Tomorrow you will go to work." The next morning the worker awoke fully cured, and reported for the job awaiting him. The doctor, who arrived at the apartment a short time later with an ambulance to bring the patient to the hospital, could not believe what he was told, and so he went to the place of employment to see for himself. The doctor then declared that there was no possible explanation for this healing.

After Father Graton died, Father Bolduc inherited his entire phalanx of sick people and penitents, which he added to his own numerous protégés. He was the confessor of the nurses and patients at the hospital, director of the Anges Gardiens and the *Ligue du Sacré-Coeur,* all the while preaching occasional retreats and conducting triduums.

Fr. Emile Bolduc, O.M.I.

The love and praise of the parishioners for their young assistant priest never waned. Fortunately, his kind heart and smiling humility were unassailable, as was his faith in Christ the Redeemer. Affectionate, with a simplicity of manner, and being down to earth, he was everyone's older brother. His honest, simple and open manner of speaking drew the young as well as the elderly close to him. Having grown up among the Irish of the Belvidere section of Lowell, he was fluent in English and felt at ease with everyone.

However, a very special place was reserved in his heart for children. Like Christ, he loved children and was constantly sought out by them. Father Bolduc could never walk down Merrimack Street, or in the streets of Little Canada, without attracting a troop of children around him. You had to see him in the schoolyard and with the *Anges Gardiens,* one of them suspended from his arm while another was hanging onto his cassock or his suit. Nor was it rare to find him playing baseball with the older boys. Each of his visits to the orphanage was like a family celebration. The following message, on the back of a holy card, distributed to the school children for Christmas 1937, helps us understand somewhat how he related to children:

Dear little parishioner,

Christmas delights everybody, especially children. It is their holiday. The long vacation, the shop windows, the Christmas tree, the lights in the windows, the gifts, the candy, it's almost a dream. Oh! I was forgetting Jesus. It's really true, Christmas is His feast day; without Jesus, no Christmas. I know that you will not forget Jesus since on Christmas Day you will go to Communion and receive Him in your heart, which is more beautiful and warmer than straw; since you will pray at the manger to thank Jesus for your gifts and promise Him that you will be very good during the year 1938.

Have you noticed that in the Christmas Story, Saint Joseph knocked on doors and that people did not answer; they wanted to have nothing to do with Him. Today there are still homes that do not want Jesus. That's easy to see: no prayer, no Sunday Mass, blasphemies against Jesus and quarrels. Ah! At your house it's not like that. There is a crucifix on the wall. Before Jesus on the cross we forgive one another, put up with one another, we make sacrifices, we say our prayers, and we learn our lessons. At Christmastime, we speak of the manger, we sing hymns, we think of the poor.

My dear child, make gifts of prayers on Christmas Day; pray for your parents, for work, for peace, for the parish, for the school and for

your most devoted,
Father Bolduc, O.M.I.

When he was named superior of Saint Joseph Residence, in 1933, he did everything he could to refrain from accepting the honor. But there was nothing to be done. The Fathers acclaimed him joyfully and eagerly, for they knew that in him they had found a holy religious with a fatherly heart. His additional nomination as pastor in July 1934, surprised no one, and older parishioners, who had seen a great many types of priests and pastors, were unanimous in their judgment: "Father Garin has returned among us," which was no small compliment.

The new pastor had been pondering for a long time some ideas on what constituted the good health of a parish and now that he was pastor, he lost no time in transforming them into action. He believed that family spirit was the key element for the success of a parish. Everyone had to feel united to the rest, accepted by all and an important part of parish life. In order to achieve this, more soirées and other activities within everyone's reach would be organized. Father Bolduc also felt that more attention needed to be paid to the development of the schools. One of his deep preoccupations was the religious education of children at home and in the schools. As to the heart of this Catholic action apostolate—the spiritual life of the parish—an effort would be made both to deepen and to broaden it. Novenas, Forty-Hour Devotions, religious processions and hours of adoration needed to be attended by more people and improved upon. He also felt that everyone should better understand the Mass. The parish should not be allowed to rest on its laurels, but always be ready to live and preach its mission of truth. The pastor had drawn up this plan for himself and, with his usual energy, he threw himself wholeheartedly into the effort.

First, more activities and social gatherings were needed. In July 1934, *La Societé de la Sainte Famille* organized "a huge parish picnic" which attracted 3,000 people. Musical evenings and the showing of movies succeeded one another in the parish hall. Whist parties outgrew their usual meeting places, so that a new approach was tried out in October 1936, called "home bridge." Each family received a certain number of tables of card players for whist or other games, with the goal of turning it into an evening of good honest fun. All of this greatly pleased the pastor, but he wanted something still more widespread. He envisioned large gatherings where everyone could come together to enjoy themselves free of charge. From this hope came the idea of soirées and later the *semaines paroissiales* (parish weeks).

He set out to bring together, each year, either at the municipal auditorium or in the parish hall, as many parishioners as possible to report on parish activities and accomplishments during the preceding year, in the form of exhibits and kiosks. To make this sort of parish fair more entertaining, skits, movies, and singing were provided, along with gymnasts from the *collège* who gave performances.

At the beginning of the evening, Father Bolduc welcomed everyone and then provided an explanation or commentary on each kiosk—the convent school, the collège, the orphanage, the *Dames de Sainte-Anne,* the missionary kiosk, one on religious art, vocations, etc. After allowing time to view the exhibits, the entertainment began. Father Nolin, who was honored in February 1936, along with Father Baron, captured the spirit of these celebrations with this poem:

> *Chers amis, n'est-ce pas qu'elle est belle la fête*
> *Qui vient vous réunir ce soir?*
> *Qu'il est beau ce spectacle, éloquent interprète,*
> *Qui vous invite à venir voir!*
>
> *(Dear friends, is this not a beautiful feast*
> *That brings you together tonight?*
> *How beautiful this spectacle, eloquent interpreter*
> *Which invites you to come and see.)*
>
> *C'est des membres si chers d'une grande paroisse*
> *La joyeuse réunion,*
> *Voulant que toujours plus se maintienne, s'acroisse*
> *L'esprit d'accord et d'union.*
>
> *(It is for the members so dear of a great parish*
> *The joyous reunion*
> *Wanting that always and more so*
> *Be maintained and grow*
> *The spirit of harmony and unity)*
>
> . . . .
>
> *Oui, spectacle enchanteur, sans tristesse et sans ombre*
> *Dans cette salle, où tout sourit,*
> *Où des anciens amis, venus en si grand nombre,*
> *La vieille amitié refleurit!*
> *(Yes, this enchanting spectacle, devoid of sadness or shadow,*
> *In this hall where smiles abound,*
> *Where old friends in such large numbers come together,*
> *And old friendships bloom again!)*

These parochial soirées, starting from the first one in January 1935, which attracted 3,000 persons, to the last one in February 1939, two days before Father Bolduc's departure, fully realized his ideal of collective harmony.

Deeply preoccupied with the question of schools and religious education in such changing and troubling times, he kept a watchful eye on their well-being. The need of a high school for the boys had become more and more pressing, and it became a priority among his projects. In fact, this was the first task he undertook as a pastor. He, who had consoled the brothers in their darkest hours, now became the instrument of Providence for rebuilding the work done away with by his predecessor.

He began by reassuring the Marist Brothers' administration, who were somewhat reticent, given their problems with Father Bachand. Then he announced to the parish, in the summer of 1934, that the first year of the high school would open in the fall. He had to be somewhat daring to undertake such a foundation in the midst of an unemployment crisis, but he believed that pastoral needs took precedence over purely financial considerations. He presented the problem in the following manner:

> Since our Religion is a living one, adapting to circumstances and adjusting to requirements, each year offers its share of new problems. The Fathers who administer your parish rack their brains to resolve them. No one can doubt that the need of the day is a Catholic high school for boys, as for the girls. Today, our young people must wait until they are eighteen or twenty before they can find employment. What can they do in the meantime? Must we abandon our young people to the streets, or to schools that are neutral, public, and indifferent? These young people are at a critical age, but they are destined to become the heads of Christian households. Father Garin, in his day, built schools for a few grades because children then began to work at ages twelve and fourteen. Today, however, children stay in school till the age of eighteen, and it is up to us to provide for them.

In order to find the necessary money and teachers, Father Bolduc modified the conditions for admission to the schools. Beginning in 1934, the *Collège* St. Joseph would no longer accept boys from other parishes. Since the foundation of other Franco-American parishes, most parents enrolled their children in the school attached to the parish where they lived. Many, however, had continued to send their boys to the *collège,* wanting them to be taught by the Brothers. As a result of the pastor's decision, an entire class could be eliminated, and one more Brother became available. It was clearly understood by everyone, however, that the new high school would be happy to accept boys from other Franco-American parishes in the city, as had been the custom all along in the girls' high school.

In order to save money, it was also determined during the summer of 1936 that the sisters' school would no longer accept children under the age of six. A kindergarten was set up for those younger than six, under the care of a laywoman, to whom each child was to pay 25 cents per week. In answering the objections of parents, as well as the worries of Sister Superior, who would be forced to send back the younger children, Father wrote:

> If we are taking these measures, it is so that we can save money for our high schools, for it is less risky to leave a five-year-old at home than to have big boys of sixteen or seventeen on the streets or in public schools.

The Freshman year of Saint Joseph Boys' High School opened in September 1934 with thirty-seven students. Each September another class was added, so that by September 1937, the high school had reached its full complement of four years with a total enrollment of 103 students. What a joy it was for the pastor, along with the parents, to applaud the graduates at the commencement ceremony in June 1938, when twenty Seniors received their diplomas from Saint Joseph's. The graduates were: Emile Aubé, Lionel Thériault, Roland Létourneau, Henri St. Arnaud, Hervé Châteauneuf, Albert Marcotte, René Beaucage, Roland Bourgeois, Raymond Gagnon, Henri Ostiguy, Dolor Tousignant, Robert Roy, Paul Lemire, Robert St. Hilaire, John Martin, Origène Allard, Clifford Harvey, Marcel Lacourse, André Poirier, and Léo Richard. Besides teaching in the high school, the Brothers continued to teach in the sixth, seventh and eighth grades of the grammar school, always referred to as the *collège* in French.

The financial burden of these schools was quite heavy, considering that in the fall of 1937 there were more than 1,950 children in the schools, including the orphanage. At the elementary level, the students in the upper grades, called the "academic classes," paid 25 cents per week, while the other grades gave 10 cents. If there were several children from the same family, the oldest paid 10 or 25 cents, according to the grade, while all the others paid 5 cents. In the high school, the students paid 25 cents per week and rented their books at an annual fee of $2.50. Fortunately, the other Oblate parishes that had students enrolled at Saint Joseph's High School paid 25 cents per week to the parish for each of them, to help defray the costs. The majority of the children at the orphanage depended on the parish, so it was only by means of an annual house-to-house "harvest" by dedicated women volunteers that the needs of the orphans could be met. This collection began on September 30, the Feast of Saint Thérèse of Lisieux.

The pastor, faced with the constant need for raising money. Especially to maintain the schools, always called upon the generosity of the people and their family spirit which were legendary. It was generally known that many children in both the elementary and secondary schools could not afford to pay their school fees. Each student cost the parish $15.00 per year to maintain the schools, etc. The times were hard, and the pastor never insisted. He would explain the need, then leave the rest to Divine Providence and the good will of the people. He was especially sensitive about embarrassing anyone, so in January 1935, he did away with the custom of publishing the annual tithing report in which the names of the people were listed, along with the amount they had contributed to the general annual collection. Extreme poverty lurked everywhere. In the summer of 1935, 45% of the families in Lowell were on public assistance, "relief" as it was called. That same year Saint Joseph Hospital served 3,799 free meals to the poor, and treated 11,749 people who were unable to pay. This was in contrast to the 6,915 patients who paid for services.

Father Lucien Brassard, the intrepid bursar and organizer of the movies, struggled each month to make ends meet in the budget, often without succeeding in doing so. In the spring of 1938, when it came time to pay the teachers their minimal salary, the parish coffers contained but a meager $8.10.

Following the lead of his predecessors, the pastor promoted bazaars, soirées and, as in Father Watelle's day, outdoor fêtes on the orphanage grounds. On March 20, 1935, the first Bingo was held in the parish and repeated quite regularly from then on. Father Baron, who was a perceptive observer, had this to say about the new game: "Luck is a sorceress; those who have not been favored at first do not lose hope and keep returning to place themselves under its capricious spell."

As a rule, the pastor preferred activities which gave people the chance to have fun together without feeling obliged or pressured to contribute money. It was up to each one to give what he or she wanted to, or could afford. At parish soirées a basket was sometimes circulated. The outdoor celebration on the orphanage grounds, held from September 1 to 6, 1937, realized a profit of $1,450. A bazaar which took place from November 17 to 22 brought in $1,620. And finally, thanks in large measure to the Sunday movies—afternoons for children and evenings for adults—the parish was able to get through the years of the Depression without accumulating debts or crippling any of the established institutions.

The hard times did not even prevent certain small improvements from being made, such as the conversion from gas to electricity in the girls' high school in 1935. The number of Marist Brothers having decreased from eighteen in 1922 to ten in 1935, it was decided to transform the former hospice for the elderly on Pawtucket Street, which had remained empty and had become the home of the sexton, Eugène Trudel, into a new residence for the brothers. This move would free their large residence on Moody Street, so that it could become the new site for the girls' high school, which up to that time had been rather poorly lodged first on the fourth floor of St. Joseph's School on Moody Street and then in the small yellow house on the grounds of the orphanage. On August 22, 1935, the brothers moved to the brick building on Pawtucket Street, and the carpenters began the work of transforming their old residence. In a very short time everything was ready, and the girls' high school was at long last able to take possession of its own school. The nuns lived on the third floor, thereby removing some of the congestion at Saint Joseph's convent.

St. Joseph Girls' High School at the corner of Moody and Pawtucket Streets.

Father Bolduc's ministry was based upon realism. He knew full well that the formation given in school necessarily had to go hand in hand with a solid Christian formation in the home. There were limits to what the school could accomplish, and it was up to the parents to see to the religious practice of their children. The "mamas" of the parish, the *Dames De Sainte-Anne* had to become catechists and apostles in their homes, for:

It is surprising how many six-year-old children arrive in September knowing almost nothing about Jesus and prayer. How many children pray before and after meals? If they are not grateful to God now, later on they will be ungrateful towards their old parents. In the marriage ceremony, the young couple is exhorted to bring up their children for

250

God, to be heirs of heaven, rather than of this world. This exhortation is very quickly forgotten.

The good that needed to be done was urgent and necessary "in these days when amusements are so frequent and take up so much of everyone's time." Family life was being bombarded by the noisy, aggressive and "modern" American culture. The problem concerning youth could be stated as follows:

> For too long our young people have allowed themselves to be guided by what is fashionable. Everyone follows the custom of the day: "parking," "road house," illicit love affairs. . . and too often a premature family, and a forced marriage, with its embarrassment, shame and quarrels, in a young household off to such a bad start. This attitude is encouraged by the theater, the "Love Story Magazines," the "Sex Books," and who knows what else.

The pastor found his remedies for the ills of the day in the papal encyclicals, and in his own pastoral experience. While still promoting the spirit of family solidarity, he believed that healthy social activities had to be provided for young people while at the same time developing their sense of Christian responsibility. In short order, the leisure time of the young was besieged from all sides by the pastor's projects: sports programs were encouraged in the boys' school—baseball, basketball, and gymnastics—then came publicity and promotion of the parish library, plays were presented by both high schools, and a greater variety was sought in the choice of films for the parish hall, e.g. those of James Cagney, etc., were added. The choir of 125 voices from the collège and the high school, under the direction of Brother Constantin, grew in scope to a remarkable extent, and sang regularly in concerts on the radio.

The pastor also looked for something new. After consulting with Mr. Albert Bergeron, the parish expert on semi-military marching units, the Fathers organized one marching group for the boys' high school and another for the girls' school. A separate one was even set up for the altar boys. The popularity of the marching units increased so rapidly that it was decided to hold a rally with a parade in June 1937, on the feast of Saint Jean Baptiste. Father Bolduc rose to the podium at the reviewing stand on North Common, to congratulate the Lowell Franco-American marching units for their fine spirit of discipline and healthy enjoyment in the context of a well-understood American civic pride.

In January 1937, within this same context of American civic spirit, Brother Paul Ambroise, with the help of Judge Eno, organized Troop 5 of the Boy Scouts of America with sixteen members. Within three months, the numbers doubled, and Merit badges in translation were given to the best bilingual members of the troop. Their camping experience during the summer was a great success in spite of the rain.

Spirituality for young people had to be brought up-to-date and even better adapted to the needs of the hour. The great Pope Pius XI was preaching justice and Catholic Action to a world sliding more and more towards war. In 1925, Canon Joseph Cardijn had founded a youth movement in Belgium called *Jeunesse Ouvrière Catholique* (J.O.C) (Young Catholic Workers) whose aim was the evangelization of the young in working-class environments by instilling in them a committed and militant evangelical spirit. The movement had spread beyond the borders of Belgium, and throughout the Catholic world with phenomenal rapidity. By the 1930s the J.O.C. had enrolled hundreds of thousands of members and Pope Pius XI raised it to the status of the model of effective and modern Catholic action.

The energetic pastor, always ready to seize upon an occasion where some good could be accomplished, had wanted for quite a while to organize the young workers of the parish. As a resourceful and enterprising person, he went to the work sites, the factories and mills, to see at close hand the working conditions of his parishioners. He asked questions and observed as he looked in on offices, weave rooms, and warehouses.

In the summer of 1935, Father Bolduc gathered a few young women together to speak to them about the movement and what young workers had to face in the mills and elsewhere. These young women invited their friends to join them, and,. after studying the question, they decided to form a J.O.C. section in Lowell. They held an election on January 13, 1936, and elected their officers: president, Miss Délia Thellen, vice-president, Miss Marie Anne Moisan, secretary, Miss Jeanne Champagne, and treasurer Miss Corinne Jean. This Saint Joseph group from Lowell was the second J.O.C. circle in the United States. The first had been started at Sainte-Marie parish in Manchester, New Hampshire. The motto: "Proud, Pure, Joyous, Conquering" became their watchword. During the first month, Father Bolduc gave two lectures to the group to get them off to a good start, one on communism, and the other on euthanasia. The *Jocistes* met twice a month at the girls' high school and quite soon there were forty members.

The pastor also worked at rejuvenating the old *Ligue du Sacré-Cœur,* founded in 1916 for the benefit of unmarried young men. There were lively discussions on the role of the man in the family, and the need of the young for Catholic social action. This group was the first to organize hockey games in the parish. They also began a small publication in November 1938, called *Le point d'interrogation* (The Question Mark). It sold for three cents per copy.

At that time the C.M.A.C had a great many young men and young workers in its ranks. The society had an Oblate chaplain, but there was no spiritual program as such, except for the annual communion and the pilgrimage to the cemetery. On Tuesday, March 23, 1937, the officers convened a special meeting of the young members, at the request of the pastor. Father Bolduc spoke to them about the need to organize and spread the example of an active Christian life in their milieu. It was up to them at the C.M.A.C. to give the example and form J.O.C. circles. Father H. Lalande, S. J., general chaplain of the *Fédération de la Jeunesse Catholique Française,* as the guest of honor, exhorted the young men to become lay apostles, ardently devoted to Catholic Action. In spite of these efforts, however, the attempt to form a masculine section of the J.O.C. was not successful as such, and so the pastor had to fall back on the organizations already in place.

For the school children, the *Croisade Eucharisique* (Eucharistic Crusade) began to be discussed. This was a movement of religious formation for children that centered on devotion to Jesus present in the Host. Without being set up as an official society, the benefits and graces to be obtained from being faithful to Holy Hours and adoration of the Eucharist were explained to the children. Young Laurier Grégoire, a boy of ten at the orphanage, was held up to the children as a model of virtue. Converted to the Croisade, he had died heroically, on November 12, 1938, as a result of acute peritonitis. There was also young Jacqueline Dubois, a model of piety, whose death on December 27, 1930, at the age of nine, had been truly a saintly one. There was even a question of publishing her biography, written by Fr. Narcisse Cotnoir, O.M.I.

The deep yet well-balanced spirituality of Father Bolduc extended into every aspect of parish life. He knew that without prayers and sacrifices there could be no effective social action, or truly Catholic family life. The spiritual strength of the parish was found at church. Concerning the First Friday devotions he wrote:

The first shepherd in the parish is Jesus in the Host. He lives among us. He wants to listen to our joys and our prayers. He wants our love. Our hearts must turn to Him, especially on the First Friday of the month, a day consecrated to the Sacred Heart. The Blessed Sacrament remains exposed all day. The adorers are few in number. Sometimes Jesus is almost alone. What should we do? First, think about it.

How? Here is one suggestion. Let's divide the day, and each category must do its part. We know that the parochial school boys come at 10:30. The girls come at 1. So let's invite the men of the *Sainte Famille* to come from 9:30 to 10:00; the tertiaries from 11:30 to noon; the *Dames de Sainte-Anne* from 2 to 3, and the *Congréganistes* from 4 to 5, on their way home from work. The boys in the Ligue can come from 6 to 6:30. In the evening, at the Vigil Hour, each family from the parish should be represented.

If each society becomes interested in this there will be more adorers present before Jesus in the Host.

The times were perilous, so more prayers and sacrifices were needed. Communism had a stranglehold on Russia, and was driving the anarchist government in Spain where priests, religious, and the Catholic faithful were massacred in great numbers while an atrocious civil war was killing thousands of persons on both sides. In Germany, the Hitler regime was stifling any semblance of democracy and pushing Europe towards war in the name of a fanatic nationalism. The fascist government in Italy was causing grave concern regarding the peaceful future of that country and foreshadowing somber days ahead.

In the United States, the economic situation was improving very slowly. Unemployment was causing a degree of anxiety for the government, and favoring agitation by the Socialists. In 1937, in Lowell, where there were still a great many workers without employment, with what fervor and what sincerity the young first communicants of the parish repeated this part of a prayer of thanksgiving prepared for them by Father Eméry Lyonnais:

> And then you know, little Jesus, I have a good papa and a good mama; that's quite understandable since you're the one who gave them to me. They are sad because the times are hard and papa has no work. At home, we have to eat; we need clothes because it's cold; we also need heat; and all of this costs money. Could you please give work to papa, and I'll take care of having you thanked by everyone at our house. And then, don't forget either to give good health to papa and mama, my little brothers and little sisters, and to me too. And then also there are the nuns at the school who have prepared my little heart to make its First Communion: I don't want you to forget them. so I ask you to see to it for me that they are rewarded, for you know well that I can't do it by myself.

God seemed to be putting the world to the test, even the elements conspired with the general misery. Early in March 1936, the Merrimack River overflowed its banks and the worst flooding in the history of Lowell devastated two-thirds of the city. Property losses reached seven million dollars and 133 deaths occurred. Most of the parish was spared, except for a few flooded cellars in Little Canada and the accidental death of Mr. Alphée Morin, who drowned while trying to retrieve lumber from the river. However, as a precautionary measure, some one hundred persons sought shelter in the parish hall for a few days. The Fathers and the Red Cross provided the necessary clothing, food and bedding. Two years later, the Hurricane of 1938 wreaked so much havoc that the city of Lowell had to be placed under martial law.

Throughout all of this, the pastor continued to exhort the faithful to pray and offer acts of reparation. On October 31, 1937, the day when the new liturgical feast of Christ the King was celebrated, he renewed the consecration of the parish to the Sacred Heart and re-introduced one of Father Watelle's pious practices. At the end of the Act of Consecration, some forty little children, carefully trained by Father Lyonnais, knelt in a semi-circle at the foot of the altar, to repeat before the Sacred Host in the monstrance, the invocations and promises whispered in their ears by their devoted chaplain.

The closed retreat movement encouraged a spirit of prayer and spread the best principles of Catholic Action among the families. The first groups of men had left as early as the summer of 1933, for a weekend at the Natick scholasticate. The women's groups went to the Presentation of Mary in Hudson, New Hampshire. Eventually, the *Ligue des Retraitants* was formed in February 1939.

The fiftieth anniversary of the Third Order, celebrated in September 1937, at the grotto, the traditional location for the Order's ceremonies, provided the occasion to highlight once again the great spiritual benefits obtained by those who were affiliated to this Franciscan confraternity. Over a span of fifty years, 5,000 parishioners had enrolled in its ranks, an average of one hundred persons per year. On this anniversary, twenty-seven new members joined, twelve men and fifteen women donned the habit and the cincture. That evening, a movie was shown on the life of Saint Francis.

The grotto at the orphanage, as a privileged place of prayer, continued to nourish the piety of the people and it remained one of the central points of the spiritual life of the parish. Each year the Corpus Christi procession, the gathering of the *Enfants de Marie,* the closing ceremony of the school children's retreat, which included the distribution of scapulars, were held there. The twenty-fifth anniversary of the grotto, in the fall of 1936, attracted crowds during the week of preparation, and 1,500 people took part in the candlelight procession on Sunday evening, September 7.

In spite of the financial crisis, the zeal for the foreign missions did not diminish. An army of devoted men and women canvassed the length and breadth of the parish throughout the year. Under the direction of Father Edouard Carrier and young Father Armand Morisssette, the sewing circles, the stamp savers, the organizers of whist parties, those who knitted sweaters, and groups of young school children were all gathered together under the banner of the important *Association Missionnaire de Marie-Immaculée.* In January 1935, the association brought out the first issue of its monthly missionary magazine:

L'Apostolat des Oblats de Marie-Immaculée. It was an American edition of the Québec publication of the same name.

Missionary departures continued to be observed with great ceremony. On July 22, 1934, people gathered in the church for the departure of Father Gérard Chouinard, a newly ordained child of the parish, who was leaving Lowell for the distant missions of Mackenzie, in the Canadian Far North. Sister Sainte Théodorine, from Saint Joseph convent, daughter of the late Joseph Lamoureux, had spent nine years among the Cree of Fort Albany, in James Bay. She had returned to Lowell to restore her health, and as soon as she had recovered, she returned to the Far North, in August 1934.

The parish had always retained its place of honor on the itinerary of missionary bishops passing through New England. Bishop Arsène Turquetil, vicar apostolic of Hudson Bay, and Bishop Pierre Fallaize, vicar apostolic of Mackenzie, each preached in turn at Saint Jean Baptiste, and held out their hands towards the *Association Missionnaire.* The A.M.M.I., as it was called, mounted a vast missionary exhibit in the parish hall from April 26 to 30, 1936, highlighting the accomplishments of Oblate missionaries all over the world. Throughout these days, people crowded around to see paintings, view the kiosks and photographs depicting the work of evangelization going on in Ceylon, Africa, Indochina, and the Canadian Far North. After viewing them and hearing accounts of lives given over so heroically to Christ, everyone, priests and lay persons, left the hall uplifted with admiration for missionaries.

Father Bolduc, as we have seen, was assisted in his pastoral work by a remarkable group of priests. Father Alphonse Breault was just beginning to show his great talent as a retreat master. Father Eméry Lyonnais was revealing his special gift for praying with children. His First Communion preparations, followed by public acts of thanksgiving with the children at the foot of the altar became legendary. His very famous prayer of thanksgiving, quoted earlier, brought tears to adult eyes. Read aloud, they were meant to serve as a model and an inspiration for the children:

> Finally, dear good little Jesus, I possess you in my heart. You know very well how happy I am, it's been so long since I wanted to make my First Communion. You too, are happy because I know you love so very much to come into the hearts of little children. Little Jesus, it feels like I'm in heaven this morning, I'm so happy. It is so good of you to come down into my soul this way. To thank you, I will make lots and lots of little sacrifices. As long as you bring me to heaven with papa and mama, I'm ready to do everything you want. Thanks a lot, little Jesus, for having me make my First Communion, thank you as big as the Church.

Father Arthur Parent organized the altar boys into a veritable religious confraternity, with Saint Tarsicius as their patron. This saint was the first martyred altar boy for having protected the Eucharist from profanation by the pagans. The altar servers in the parish had their own annual retreats, and special spiritual direction. They also had a semi-military marching group as a leisure activity, and Father Parent's famous "commandments" to guide them:

ASSOCIATION DES SERVANTS DE MESSES
COMMANDEMENTS
(ASSOCIATION OF MASS SERVERS COMMANDMENTS)

1
L'acolyte suppléera
A l'église dignement.

1
The acolyte will assist
In church with dignity.

2
Pour Jésus tu serviras
Et jamais pour l'argent.

2
For Jesus will you serve
And never for money.

3
Aux offices tu viendras
Un quart d'heure avant le temps.

3
To all the services you will come
One-quarter hour early.

4
De la nef tu accoureras
Vers un prêtre sans servant.

4
From the nave you will rush
Towards any priest without a server.

5
Tes deux mains tu blanchiras
Et les ongles sûrement.

5
Your two hands you will wash
And surely clean your nails.

6
Tes souliers tu noirciras
En arrière et en avant.

6
Your shoes you will polish black
In the front and in the back.

7
Tes cheveux tu peigneras
Au miroir modestement.

7
Your hair you will comb
Modestly before a mirror.

8
Ton surplis tu baiseras
Ta soutane également.

8
Your surplice will you kiss
And your cassock likewise.

9
Aux services tu mettras
Boucle noire et collet blanc.

9
At services you will wear
Bow of black and collar white.

10
En français tu parleras
Au besoin très doucement.

10
In French you will speak
Very softly, if need be.

11
Ton missel apporteras
Pour y suivre l'officiant.
12
A la messe tu joindras
L'oblation du célébrant.
13
Ton Latin prononceras
En Romain distinctement.
14
Tes fonctions accompliras
Comme un clerc exactement.
15
Le bon Dieu tu recevras
A l'Agnus royalement.
16
En ton cœur tu dresseras
Un autel reconnaissant.
17
La patène tu tiendras
Sous l'hostie assurément.
18
Chez Tharsice imiteras
L'héroïsme du servant.
19
Le bonheur demanderas
Pour le monde et tes parents.
20
Notre-Dame tu prieras
De veiller sur son enfant.
21
Au jubé tu doubleras
Ta prière en la chantant.
22
Bulletin distribueras
Avec zèle et poliment.
23
Le dimanche tu paieras
Tous les dûs fidèlement.
24
Aussitôt tu replieras
Ton surplis soigneusement.

11
Your missal you will bring
To follow there the officiating priest.
12
At the Mass you will join
The celebrant in his oblation.
13
Latin words you will pronounce
Distinctly as a Roman.
14
All your functions you will perform
Exactly as a cleric would.
15
God will you receive
At the Agnus royally.
16
In your heart you will set up
An altar of Thanksgiving.
17
The paten you will hold
Surely there, beneath the host.
18
In Tarsicius you will imitate
The heroism of the server.
19
Happiness will you ask
For the world and your parents.
20
To Our Lady will you pray
To watch over you, her child.
21
When you sing from the loft
Doubled is your prayer.
22
The Bulletin will you distribute
Zealously and politely.
23
Every Sunday will you pay
Faithfully all that's due.
24
Your surplice you will neatly fold
As soon as Mass is ended.

25
Sans retard tu partiras
Un traînard est ennuyant.
26
Sur ton cœur tu porteras
Ton insigne fièrement.
27
Au collège tu seras
Un modèle d'étudiant.
28
Ton foyer tu aimeras
Pour y vivre longuement.
29
Mais ton club tu fréquenteras
Au lieu d'être juif errant.
30
Dans les sports tu brilleras
Et toujours honnêtement.
31
Tes loisirs tu rempliras
De musique aux airs prenants.
32
En vacances tu camperas
Un scoutisme rayonnant.
33
Ton Eglise honoreras
Et le presbytère autant.
34
En retour tu recevras
Les honneurs dûs à ton rang.
35
Cette gloire chériras
Jusqu'à l'age des vieux ans.
36
Dans les cieux tu rejoindras
L'Acolyte avec l'encens.
37
Près de lui tu serviras
A l'autel du Tout-Puissant.

25
You must leave without delay
For the laggard is a bore.
26
On your heart you will wear
Your emblem with pride.
27
In the schoolroom you will be
A model student.
28
Your home you will love
To live there for a long time.
29
Your club you will frequent
Rather than be a wanderer.
30
In all sports you will shine
And always honestly.
31
Your leisure time will you fill
With captivating musical airs.
32
On vacation you will camp
As befits cheerful scouting.
33
Your Church you will honor
And the rectory quite as much.
34
In return you will receive
The honors due your rank.
35
This glory will you cherish
Until you reach your elder years.
36
In the heavens you will rejoin
The Acolyte with incense.
37
Next to him will you serve
At the altar of the Almighty.

Father Baron continued to do the work of four men. His *Propagande des Bons Livres* sent voluminous catalogs to the four quarters of New England. The *Bulletin Paroissial* which, under his direction had become the organ for the four Franco-American Oblate parishes of Lowell, celebrated its twenty-fifth anniversary in May 1935. Up before sunrise , he retired only very late at night. His motto seemed to be these words of the Curé of Ars: "Let's always work, my brothers, we'll have plenty of time to rest in eternity." In order to stay awake while working in his room, he wrote standing up, in his bed slippers, using a small tablet attached to the wall as his desk.

He was the confessor of the Grey Nuns and the Marist Brothers, as well as the spiritual director of the Third Order, the *Congréganistes—Demoiselles de Notre-Dame-de-Lourdes*. He had unlocked the secret of directing souls with wisdom and knowledge. His homilies, which were simple, yet replete with learning and logic, always based on the "great truths" of the faith, attracted souls to Saint Joseph church, where he had been in charge for many years, and drew them to his confessional, which was always besieged. The *Congréganistes,* who benefited from his wise direction for twenty-seven years, attained such a level of spirituality that a great many young women were moved to consecrate themselves to God by pronouncing a private vow of virginity while remaining in the laity.

It is said that a large number of Franco-Americans in Lowell bear the name of Armand because of the esteem in which the parishioners held Father Baron. In one Little Canada tenement block, three boys were born on the same day in 1910, and each one, according to the testimony of the parents, was named Armand in honor of their beloved priest.

For thirty years he made the parish visitation in Little Canada. It was quite a surprise then, when he didn't show up in 1936. The reason was that, suffering from persistent pain, he had consulted physicians. The news that he had come down with a fatal cancer caused considerable consternation at the rectory. An operation, with little hope of success, became imperative. His physical condition did not prevent him from joining his confrères for their annual retreat in June of 1936. Although rather weak, he wished to prepare for death by following each of the exercises with such attention and piety that the other Fathers, who witnessed his inner peace and outer calm, were profoundly moved. He was a model religious, with a heart of gold, and highly esteemed by the other Oblates, especially his colleagues at Saint Joseph residence who considered him as the "Papa" of the house and anticipated with sorrow the void that would surround them after his death.

He returned to Lowell on June 27, a Saturday, and set about, as was his custom, to prepare, as he always did, his homily for the next day. He mounted the pulpit on Sunday to say farewell to the parishioners, as he calmly, and with resignation, shared with them his medical diagnosis. The parishioners, deeply moved, couldn't believe that Father Baron, with his usual paternal tone and in such a calm voice, was announcing his death. On Monday, he entered the hospital, the operation took place on Wednesday, and on Monday, July 6, 1936, at 5:15 in the afternoon, he gave up his beautiful soul to God, murmuring: "Jesus, have mercy. Jesus, I have confidence in You."

The profound mourning expressed itself in diverse ways. First of all, the funeral was among the most impressive ever witnessed. The "Ladies of the *librairie*" attended, dressed in white, as a posthumous homage to the one who had often told them that death in the Lord should not be observed in black, but celebrated in white, the color of light and the Resurrection. In *L'Étoile* Arthur Milot published a laudatory editorial. The parish bookstore now became *La Librairie Baron.* The August edition of the parish bulletin was filled with letters of praise and testimonials in memory of the great Oblate. Four priests divided the deceased's many responsibilities among them. Father Bolduc inherited a large portion of his outreach to the sick and confessions, in addition to the Society for the Propagation of the Faith. Father Rosario Jalbert became editor of the *Bulletin.* Father Léon Loranger took charge of the librairie, and Father Charles Dénizot assumed the duties of serving Saint Joseph church.

On his deathbed, Father Baron had Father Nolin by his side. Father Nolin, who had served at Saint Joseph church for many years, was the dean of the parish, and patriarch of the province. In spite of his blindness and his eighty-seven years, he continued his daily walks with the help of a faithful companion. He was a familiar figure along Merrimack Street, with his slightly nervous stride, and a good word for everyone. Father Nolin had from his youth always been considered a healer. From his earliest years in the parish the word was passed along by the faithful: "Father Nolin has a gift." He was quite grateful and happy that God was making use of him to heal people. He seemed particularly gifted at curing babies and skin diseases. Whenever people saw an empty baby carriage in front of the rectory, they knew that another young mother had brought a sick child to be blessed by Father Nolin.

His procedure was always the same. He would bring them to the chapel, read a passage from the Bible, and pray for the child to return to health, which happened very often. The only condition he placed was that a Mass be said for the souls in Purgatory. Father Armand Morissette tells how one day as a small child, he accidentally spilled a cauldron of hot soup on his little brother, who later became Father Joseph Morissette. Their mother, beside herself with panic, took the child in her arms and ran to the rectory to see Father Nolin. After the prayer, she asked the priest if the burns would leave scars on the child's body. He answered: "Nowhere will it show." In fact the child healed and no burn marks showed.

Many parishioners remember Father Nolin's ointment for eczema, a product that he invented. *L'Onguent du Père Nolin* (Father Nolin's Ointment) was sold at the Routhier and Délisle Pharmacy on Merrimack Street.

Father Nolin died peacefully, two months after Father Baron, on Wednesday evening, September 16, 1936, at the age of eighty-seven. Only five days before, he had brought his last poem to *L'Étoile,* for publication: *Cinquante ans de journalisme franco-américain: L'Étoile.* It had been written to commemorate the 50th anniversary of the newspaper.

Fr. Louis Alphonse Nolin O.M.I.

The large number of deaths during these years placed a strain on the Oblate Fathers of the young province. The old pioneers were leaving one by one for their other "home" near the Lord. In one year, 1935, death claimed Fathers A. Marion, N. Pelletier, A. Mercil, V. Viaud and A. Fortier. In 1936 Fathers A. Baron, L. Nolin, G. Ouellette, and L. Lamothe passed away, and in 1937, Father Julien Racette. Fortunately, there were many new candidates, and replacements came regularly at the annual ordinations. In the spring of 1938, the Saint Joseph community was made up of Fathers E. Bolduc, as the superior and pastor, L. Brassard, L. Loranger, C. Dénizot, R. Jalbert, N. Cotnoir, A. Houle, E. Lyonnais, E. Fournier, F. Rivard and Brothers O. Levasseur, A. Bedell, L. Desjadons and F. Violette.

But the priests were not the only ones to be mourned by the parish. On May 28, 1937, Mrs. Elizabeth Boisvert died at the age of 85. She had been president of the parish sewing circle for thirty-five years, and the one at the orphanage, for sixteen years. Mr. Pierre Tremblay, director of Saint Joseph Cemetery from its inception, died in 1936.

These years brought many changes to parish life. Among others, the priests had to acknowledge the reduced role of old Saint Joseph church. In 1936, the parish numbered about 8,000 faithful, in 2,000 families. But with the opening of Sainte Jeanne d'Arc parish, as the older Fathers had predicted, attendance at Saint Joseph diminished considerably. With the passing of Father Baron, who jumped with indignation at the mere mention of closing the old church, attendance declined even more.

The *Congréganistes,* who had been among those most attached to Saint Joseph church, and for the longest time because of Father Baron, in the end decided to move also and to hold their meetings and devotions at Saint Jean Baptiste. However, they would not leave without their statue. On December 6, 1936, two days before the Feast of the Immaculate Conception, this old and venerated statue of Notre Dame de Lourdes, purchased at Lourdes in the 1880s, was transferred to a place in Saint Jean Baptiste church, and positioned against the pillar to the right of the main altar. Another statue was purchased for the Blessed Virgin's altar at Saint Joseph.

Morning Masses continued to be offered on weekdays and Sundays at Saint Joseph's, as well as a noon Mass, in addition to the morning Mass on Holy Days for the benefit of the downtown workers. From 1936 to 1938, a group of devoted parishioners sacrificed their evening leisure to clean and repaint the interior of the old church. They included: Arthur Beaulieu, Arthur Provencher, Gédéon Guilmette, Albert Lafortune, Joseph Geoffroy, Mrs. Anna Beaulieu and Miss Minnie Noval. Expenses were paid with money raised from all quarters of the parish with patient tenacity by Miss Marguerite Geoffroy. But, in spite of these efforts, Saint Joseph church was aging and entering a dormant period from which it would not emerge until 1956, when the church was transformed into a shrine and the large crowds and grand religious ceremonies of yore returned.

The distinguished Professor H. A. Jules-Bois, who had lectured at a gathering of *L'Alliance Française de Lowell,* in April 1936, wrote the following about the Oblate Fathers of Saint Joseph parish:

In the evening, I was invited to the mother house of these admirable missionaries, by Reverend Father Baron, a Frenchman who has dedicated his pious activities for many years to the development of spiritual life in this country. In the midst of these monks, who are so cultured, who follow with a very well-informed zeal the progress of the Catholic renaissance in France, I felt as though transported into the very heart of our homeland, where one prays, where one thinks, where one discusses the very greatest problems of art and religion. The hours were as precious as they were edifying, where one has the sense of being reborn, and where the soul spreads its wings!

The Oblate Fathers, who were very well-informed regarding the current French intellectual scene, considered themselves to be among the most fervent supporters of French culture in Lowell. They belonged to the *Alliance Française* which included the intellectual élite, and where the most distinguished professors, like Jules-Bois, and André Morize of Harvard, rubbed shoulders at the podium with Franco-American men of letters like Rosaire Dion-Lévesque and Josaphat Benoit. The Fathers, by importing movies from France and with their tenacious ethnic spirit, helped to maintain the Franco-American character of their parishioners. The presentation of the film *Louis Pasteur* in April 1936, was accompanied by a talk given by Doctor Harsus, of the *Institut Pasteur* in Paris, who was at Harvard on a grant. He was followed by a series of recitations by the Parisian monologuist Miss Arrosa. That evening proved to be a great success while also providing yet more proof of the vitality of French culture in Lowell.

The musical tradition added its component to this vitality. On May 9, 1939, Father Breault presented, under the auspices of Saint Joseph parish, a musical soirée starring Diane Morin, a former parishioner, who was now an opera singer with the Metropolitan Opera of New York. During the winter of 1935-36 the *Folkloristes Franco-Américains,* under the direction of Laurier Sans-Cartier, gave thirteen presentations of their well-received *La Veillée du Bon Vieux Temps* (An Evening of the Good Old Days). This success encouraged them to come out with another in the spring called *Une Noce du Bon Vieux Temps* (A Wedding Celebration of the Good Old Days). Each New Year's Day, the men of the Saint Vincent de Paul Society went from door-to-door singing *La Guignolée,* seeking alms for the poor, an old Canadian tradition.

The two major Franco-American events which stand out in those years were unquestionably the election of Mr. Dewey Archambault as mayor of Lowell, on November 5, 1935, and the *Congrès de la Langue Française* which was held in Québec from June 27 to July 1, 1937.

Dewey Archambault was a respected attorney, a faithful parishioner, and an eloquent and honest candidate. Elected with a majority of 4,000 votes, he turned out to be the only Franco-American ever to be elected mayor of the city by a direct vote of the people. A major campaign of voter registration among the Franco-Americans had been conducted throughout the city, and on victory night all those who were awaiting the results at the C.M.A.C. were delirious with joy. The area around the club was crowded with people, and a spontaneous motorcade drove through the streets of the city while the new mayor spoke on radio Station WLLH.

From there on in, every communion breakfast, every bazaar, every entertainment and every Franco-American observance required the presence of the mayor in a seat of honor. Whenever he spoke, Mayor Archambault praised the civic spirit of the Franco-Americans, and encouraged them to sign up for civil service courses so as to become eligible for the highest administrative and governmental positions. Following his advice, the *Association des Dames Éducatrices* started a series of evening classes for women. Another series for men was given at Saint Joseph High School.

The honest and wise administration of Mayor Archambault won him an easy re-election in November 1937, for another two year term (1938-1939). At the end of his mandate, he accepted the important position of Director of Employment Security for the Commonwealth of Massachusetts.

As a Franco-American mayor, Atty. Archambault was given a choice role in organizing a Franco-American delegation to the Congress of the French Language in Québec, the other outstanding event of those years.

Preparations for this congress energized the French populations of North America, from British Columbia to distant Louisiana. Under the high patronage of Cardinal Villeneuve, who had suggested the idea, the goal of the Congress was to bring together in Québec representatives from every French-language group on the continent in order to establish a balance sheet regarding *survivance,* and lay down a line of conduct for the future. Monsignor Camille Roy, rector of Laval University and a renowned author, who had been appointed president of the Congress, was sent to New England to keep the Franco-Americans informed and encourage them to participate. Every Franco-American center was set in motion. Regional and parish committees were formed under the aegis of a central committee. Lowell was designated as the general headquarters of the Regional Committee for Northeastern Massachusetts. Mr. Rodolphe Pépin accepted the presidency of the region, while Father Léon Loranger, O.M.I. , as secretary for the committee, spoke on the radio each week for two months, to keep the public on the alert and abreast of what was being prepared. The watchwords: "Let us remain Franco-Americans" and "On to Québec," were being spread everywhere.

On Monday evening, April 19, 1937, Mayor Archambault and the members of the regional committee welcomed 3,000 persons from the region who had come to the municipal auditorium to hear the distinguished visitor from Québec. That afternoon, the clergy had had the opportunity to discuss the main topics of the Congress with Monsignor Roy, in the privacy of the rectory. The evening program was for the benefit of the general population. On the following morning, 3,500 school children gathered in the municipal auditorium to hear Msgr. Roy. According to him, the meeting with the children on Tuesday, April 20, was one of the most impressive experiences of his New England tour. From all parts of the city, long lines of children could be seen arriving at the auditorium. They had been prepared by their teachers to receive the message brought from Québec. Father Bolduc introduced Monsignor Roy who spoke movingly to this young audience upon whom rested the future of the "French mission in America," about the doctrine of survivance. His ending was an eloquent summary:

> The French race will continue to live for a long time to come in the United States if young Franco-Americans, faithful to the directives of their parents and teachers, keep and cherish as precious and their most beautiful treasure and their greatest spiritual wealth, this French spirit, which expresses itself in French terms passing through a French heart.

These Congress preparations were a success, and in Québec the Lowell delegation figured prominently and received a substantial part of the honors bestowed. Mayor Archambault delivered the official presentation at the ceremony held at the Champlain Monument, and Rodolphe Pépin was one of the principal speakers. During the study sessions, Father Bachand, Judge Eno and Mrs. Louis Biron, the wife of *L'Étoile's* owner, were called upon to give talks on the various themes of the Congress. Upon his return to Lowell, Father Loranger shared with his Lowell audience the enthusiasm and the positive results of the Congress in these words:

> What were we seeking by going to Québec? First of all, a direct contact with the French-Canadian soul, a bit of national pride, and a sense of our solidarity with all the French groups in America. And all of this, once again, in order to give us the courage to undertake and continue the task already begun, of preserving our French heritage in New England.

The C.M.A.C. celebrated its incorporation as a mutual aid society on May 14, 1939. The festivity, with its great array of activities, was one more demonstration of ethnic solidarity in Lowell. The club had almost 1,000 active members and its resources amounted to $153,276.73. Since its founding, it had paid out $227,192.40 to the families of deceased members or as indemnities to the sick. This association was the strongest French-language society in Lowell, so it was no surprise when Governor Saltonstall and Congressman Rogers attended the gala banquet at the municipal auditorium.

Theatrical productions in French also remained quite numerous at that time, but they were, however, beginning to weaken in popularity under the pressure of evening movies and concerts. Musical entertainment continued to be offered but, more and more, the great plays, which required months of preparation, began to be reserved for extraordinary occasions. All of the great dramas enacted at this time were religious and Catholic in nature, associated with or presented in a special context, such as the series put on during the Lenten season of 1938. The most popular of these religious plays was *Le Père Pro,* the story of the famous Mexican priest-martyr, directed by Father Rivard.

The best-known theatrical presentation of the period came from the pen of Father Armand Morissette, which included songs and dances by Father Ovila Fortier. *L'Association Missionnaire de Marie-Immaculée,* always seeking ways of raising money, approached Father Carrier's young assistant for a play that would attract crowds to the parish hall. At the time, Father Morissette was writing a series of magazine articles on Kateri Tekakwitha, the lily of the Mohawks, who is now beatified. He decided to write a three-act drama, with songs and dances, entitled *Kateri Tekakwitha, ou la Princesse des Mohawks.* Miss Jeanne Héroux interpreted the role of the young Native American. At the first presentation, on May 17, 1939, the hall was filled to the rafters, and so it went for the four presentations which followed.

At the showing of Wednesday evening, the 24th of May, Father Carrier came forward to read to the audience a letter from the superior-general of the Oblates, Father Théodore Labouré, announcing the departure in mid-July of Father Emile Bolduc for the Philippine Islands. The 900 spectators were stunned, not knowing how to react. They then rose in a spontaneous homage, directing their eyes toward the pastor who was seated in the front row. Father Bolduc was deeply moved as he rose to confirm the news in a joking manner for, as he explained later: "I forced myself to be humorous, so that I wouldn't break into tears. Laughter is often a means to keep from crying."

The cast of *Kateri Tekakwitha* on the stage of the parish hall.

The news spread like wildfire. That same evening it was being communicated from door-to-door in the tenements, and the following day the headline in *L'Étoile* read in bold letters: FATHER BOLDUC TO LEAVE LOWELL IN MID-JULY. Mr. Jean O'Beirne, a correspondent for the paper, voiced this opinion, which was that of all the parishioners: "The parish will be losing its pillar! Hundreds of sick persons — suffering harrowing pain in body and soul — will lose their great consoler! Lowell will lose its Curé d'Ars."

For many years this dedicated pastor had dreamed of offering himself to the foreign missions, as had so many of his predecessors. To that end, he had beseeched the superior-general three or four times to be sent to the missions. The telegram had finally arrived. The Oblates had just accepted the Philippine missions, and Father Labouré was in need of missionaries, blessed like Father Bolduc with apostolic zeal. He wrote: "It goes without saying that it is painful for me to leave this parish, but there is so much good to be done out there. Here, I know everyone, I've visited just about every family. In the Philippines I will have to learn a new language, but I'll adjust. The apostolic field is so beautiful."

Young Fathers Georges Dion and Egide Beaudoin also received obediences for the Philippines. The departure ceremony was scheduled for July 12, 1939, at the orphanage grotto. Without going into all of the details, it should be noted that the ceremony was deeply moving for all those who participated. Cardinal Villeneuve came from Québec to preside at this occasion. He was surrounded by 200 priests and religious. The large crowd filled the grounds in front of the grotto, all the way to the sidewalk on Pawtucket Street. After the ceremonies of the kissing of the feet and the cardinal's apostolic blessing, Father Bolduc read in his name, and in the name of Fathers Beaudoin and Dion, an Act of Consecration to Mary, the protectress of the new mission.

Father Bolduc had always said that the parish is a family in which closeness and charity must reign. Once the departure ceremony was over, it was time for the family to say goodbye to its shared father. On the scorching hot Sunday evening of July 23rd, five thousand persons hurried to the auditorium to pay homage to a pastor who had served them for sixteen years. Touched, but smiling as always, Father Bolduc spoke these words of farewell:

> I thank God for having allowed me to remain in your midst these sixteen years. They have been the most pleasant years of my life. I experienced great consolations in my ministry, especially among the sick. God has spoiled me. You received me with so much respect and trust when I returned to my own hometown as a priest. That was not the way they treated Our Lord; much to the contrary, the Jews mocked him saying: "He is only the son of Joseph the carpenter." Then they ran him

out of His town of Nazareth. You, yourselves, have acted quite differently because you have a great spirit of faith. . . . Now I want to thank everyone, without exception, especially the poor who gave me what they themselves needed, which must have pleased God very much. I leave you to go very far away. My work out there will be to pray, and then wait ten, maybe fifteen years, for conversions . . . . But I place my trust in the help of God. I say to you, au revoir, and if it is not au revoir, it will be adieu.

Upon leaving the auditorium, Father Bolduc found a homeless man in rags on the steps. The poor fellow had been too embarrassed by his appearance to enter the auditorium. He had been waiting for almost three hours to bid a last farewell to his friend and benefactor. This incident became a symbolic closure for the ministry in Lowell of this remarkable priest.

A few days later, Father left with his two companions for the distant Philippine missions where his dedication would bring him to new heights of spiritual and apostolic life. Father Brassard, in his closing words at the auditorium, had left the parishioners with this reminder: "Let us thank God for having given us Father Bolduc, and let us remember that we all have the obligation to imitate his virtues."

Jeanne Héroux in the role of Kateri.

25. "Prince of Peace, have pity on us"

Father Bolduc's departure left a void that was difficult to fill. After much prayer and reflection, the provincial found the man who was required for this important and difficult pastorate. It was Father Arthur St. Cyr, pastor of Notre Dame de Lourdes.

Fr. Arthur St. Cyr O.M.I.

Born in Lowell on July 19, 1897, Father St. Cyr was the son of Charles St. Cyr and Victorine Foucault. He had entered the Oblates at fourteen years of age and been ordained to the priesthood in Washington, D.C. on June 14, 1923. He was rather introspective and meditative by temperament and he very much loved to study and teach. While his classmate, Father Bachand had a special talent for administration, Father St. Cyr was of a more sensitive and delicate nature. Immediately after his ordination, his superiors sent him to teach at the Colebrook juniorate, where everyone loved him. He remained there for ten years until the provincial called him to be pastor at Notre Dame de Lourdes parish in Lowell. The appointment was difficult for him to accept since he took no delight in either administration or in the management of finances. However, as a faithful religious, deeply attached to the Rule of his congregation, and understanding the intrinsic value of the vow of obedience, he accepted. At Notre Dame de Lourdes, where he was able to give full scope to his taste for music, he started a parish orchestra and served as its conductor and director.

When he was named to succeed Father Bolduc, he at first experienced some hesitation. The parish was enormous, the activities were numerous, and the administrative complexities almost insurmountable. Moreover, even on the spiritual level, he feared that "his feet wouldn't fit in such large boots." His deep but quiet spirituality contrasted with that of Father Bolduc which was geared towards social and pastoral action.

But, in spite of his hesitations, and always in the finest spirit of submission, he accepted, and assumed his responsibilities in August 1939. The parishioners immediately recognized in him a man of faith and convictions. He was easily approachable, open to everyone, and kindness personified. He delighted in teaching catechism to children and directing souls in the confessional. His repugnance for administration and large organizations led him to delegate many of these functions to his curates, and he very often refused to be photographed for the newspapers. The parishioners loved him for his goodness of soul, and he reciprocated their love. Father Anthime Desnoyers, on the occasion of his canonical visit, noted the fine spirit that reigned in the religious community, as well as in the parish. Much of the merit for this could only be attributed to the "excellent superior," he wrote.

Lowell, in 1939, was recovering from the ravages of the great Depression. Industry was beginning to recover, and even to prosper anew. Yet, this was happening at a time when the situation in Europe was causing very great anxiety for, in September 1939, Hitler's Germany invaded a practically defenseless Poland.

In spite of everything, parish life, as always, continued its ever-expanding development. The days and weeks were filled with financial concerns, social activities, and religious duties. The Parish Week of April 1940, brought in a profit of $3,000; the *collège* drew crowds to its exhibit commemorating the centennial of the death of the founder of the Marist Brothers, the then venerable Marcellin Champagnat who would be canonized in 1999; and in December 1940, a celebration organized to mark the one hundredth anniversary of the foundation of the old Corporation Hospital, which had become Saint Joseph Hospital, furnished an opportunity to take pride in the progress that had occurred during the intervening years. Bean suppers, bazaars, and movies kept the population in a flurry of activity.

French culture, an integral and integrating factor of parish life, was proudly displaying its triumphs. In the spring of 1940, Mr. Elie Lescot, head of the Haitian delegation in Washington, D.C., who happened to be in Lowell on an important mission, gave a lecture to the men of the Retreat League which resonated with faith and patriotism. In May, Dominican Father Joseph Ducatillon, the eminent orator from the pulpit of Notre Dame de Paris, gave a masterly presentation in the parish hall, on modern France.

Musical culture was placed in the limelight when Mr. Pépin's choir earned praise after praise during tours all over New England. The Saint Jean Baptiste choir, under the direction of this distinguished organist, had always been the pride of the parish, and when, in 1940, Professor Pépin was awarded an honorary Doctorate in Music by the University of Tennessee, following the publication of his *Messe de Requiem,* the entire parish shared in the honor.

Popular piety and collective spirituality continued, as before, to be the vital heart of the parish organism. The pilgrimage of the Dames de Sainte-Anne to the shrine of Saint Anne in Fall River, in July 1940, brought together 175 women for the trip. The splendor of the religious ceremonies in Saint Jean Baptiste church, and even the processions of the Enfants de Marie to the grotto, were matter for the religious column in the local papers. People eagerly came from all over the city to visit the sumptuous repository, during the Forty Hours' Adoration.

This well-nourished spirituality was fed from new sources of grace, during this immediate pre-war period. The experiment of the *Mouvement de la Croisade Eucharistique* among the school children proved once again the fervor and sincerity of these youthful souls. Rarely had so much zeal and enthusiasm been encountered.

Envisioned as a school of religious and moral formation, the Eucharistic Crusade aimed to integrate spirituality into the daily life of the child. To achieve this, the motivating words were: "Pray! Receive the Eucharist! Make sacrifices! Be an apostle!" A whole series of religious practices was expected of its members: morning and night prayer, recitation of one decade of the rosary each day in addition to very specific duties: attendance at Mass three times a week, receiving communion at least once a week, and weekly meetings. All lent an apostolic character to this movement and focused the children on sanctifying their days and their milieu.

Placed under the banner of the Sacred Heart, members of the small phalanx of crusaders had different ranks and wore uniforms. The aspiring members, after a period of "novitiate," were admitted as full members at an impressive ceremony in Saint Jean Baptiste church. The chaplain presented each member with a pin in the shape of a red cross, the emblem of the society. Having been fully accepted, the members had the right to wear the official uniform, consisting of a cape—white and red for the boys, white and blue for the girls. The crusaders in their uniforms could now take the special places reserved for them at the hours of adoration and in solemn processions. The most dedicated in the group could reach the rank of apostle which was reserved for the leaders of the movement.

The *Croisade Eucharistique* having been launched successfully, it spread rapidly. Started at the orphanage, in 1938, it was brought to the girls' school in 1939 by Father Arthur Tardif. Two years later, in 1941, Father Eméry Lyonnais organized a group of boys at the *collège*. A rush to join followed quickly thereafter. At the Feast of Christ the King, on October 27, 1940, one hundred and twenty-four young ladies entered the ranks, and the following year, at the same feast, seventy boys, including nine apostles, rallied behind the Eucharistic banner. In December, it was announced that henceforth the small school on James Street would be shared for meetings between *L'Amicale Saint Joseph* and the girl crusaders. The boys would have one of the halls in the basement of the *collège* available for their use.

Activities proliferated and hearts were fired up with a desire to offer themselves for God and neighbor. The girls sold Bibles door-to-door, while the boys solicited subscriptions to the Catholic press. Prayer and self-sacrifice held pride of place. Group consecrations to the Sacred Heart, parades and processions to the grotto, hours of watch before the Blessed Sacrament and the monthly rosary were all part of the customary program of the *Croisade*. The movement had arrived at a propitious moment and injected new vigor into the apostolate among children which, up to that time, had been the responsibility of the old parish societies.

The often heroic nature of these young children in love with God, at times broke through to the general public. The aforementioned Laurier Grégoire edified the other patients at the hospital by singing hymns from the Mass on his deathbed, and in April 1944, the death of Georges Tremblay, a model crusader who was twelve years old, provided many moving scenes, one of which was recorded by Father Eméry Lyonnais on the night of the child's death:

"If Jesus came for you, would you like to go see Him?"

"Oh yes, very much!"

"You aren't afraid to meet Little Jesus?"

"Oh no, I would like so much to be with Him in heaven."

"But if he comes to get you, what will you do with the *Croisade,* you who love it so much?"

"In heaven I'll pray very hard for the *Croisade*."

Father Lyonnais, who recorded these words, left a deep impression on the hearts of these young people. He was a remarkable man and a gifted priest who, like the famous Father Flanagan of Boys Town, had the gift of being able to read the hearts of boys and young men, and to see there all the goodness and wholesome energy seeking to come out and be channeled along paths leading to God. He was always encouraging and always willing to listen. He prayed with "his boys" and taught them to do good wherever they were, without fanfare or exaggeration. Whether engaged in sports or on one of the walking picnics all the way from the *collège* to Red Top Beach in Dracut, or during a weekly meeting in the little basement hall, or at a lecture from time to time, each event was an opportunity to meet one another, to get to know each other, to understand one another, and even, on occasion, to console and to counsel even while walking on Merrimack Street or crossing the North Common. His work with male youth was sincere and profound. He also had a way with adolescents and young adults, as we shall see later.

The *Croisade* among the schoolboys was followed by the *Association de la Jeunesse Catholique* for young men which replaced the former *Ligue du Sacré-Coeur*. Under the stable and vigorous direction of Father Albert Beausoleil, this new association brought together the adolescents of the parish, aiming to provide them with healthy pastimes, as well as a modern and solid Christian education. The association flourished, and in December 1941, the chaplain announced the forthcoming blessing and opening of a new site for their meetings. It was in the heart of Little Canada, where Gariépy's Market had been, at 464 Moody Street, near Aiken.

As this center became more and more frequented, with members flocking to it, the need was felt to enlarge by founding a youth center designed especially for that purpose. There were now over 200 members and the time had come to move forward or begin to decline. As always, Divine Providence provided a solution. The former Club Rio, on Pawtucket Street along the Merrimack River, near the opening of the Pawtucket Canal, was for sale. The building, which was the former boathouse of the Vesper Country Club, would provide a perfect setting with its many large rooms.

The *Centre St. Jean Baptiste* youth center on Pawtucket Street.

Mr. Joseph Faucher, a contractor and influential parishioner, who happened to be Father Lyonnais's cousin, bought the property. After making the necessary repairs, he offered to rent part of the structure to the parish for a minimal fee, as a gathering place for its youth. The boys took possession of their center in the spring of 1942.

When he left for the Philippines, Father Bolduc had said publicly:

I am leaving, but I will not forget the parish where I spent sixteen years of my apostolic life, years which have brought me great consolations. I will collaborate with the *Bulletin Paroissial* and *L'Apostolat de Marie-Immaculée* to tell you about my experiences.

Faithful to his word, almost every month he sent letters filled with personal experiences and commentaries to the *Bulletin* and *L'Apostolat.* He remembered his friends in Lowell while recommending himself and his Filipino people to their thoughts and prayers. His auxiliaries in Lowell, for that is how the school children, the sewing circles, the members of societies, and simple parishioners, all considered themselves, wrote to him regularly and prayed for his missions. The sewing circles and mothers made shirts for the lepers, the school children dropped pennies in a bank on one of the classroom windows, and the *Dames de Sainte-Anne,* helped by the *Congréganistes,* organized penny sales to benefit Father Bolduc's poor people. The A.M.M.I. added its share and Father Carrier was in charge of forwarding packages and monetary offerings. By dint of work and the assistance of his Lowell "helpers" Father Bolduc was able to rebuild the church in Jolo, and construct an elementary school. One day, writing about the little fatigues and adversities encountered in mission lands, he confided:

I have always pondered about life in the missions so that I expected these little inconveniences. I'm surprised to find that there aren't more of them. I also expected that I would soon be forgotten in Lowell, but judging by my mail and what I read in the *Bulletin* and *L'Apostolat,* the parishioners of Saint Joseph seem to consider Jolo as an offshoot. . . as was Sainte Marie in South Lowell. I'm deeply touched by this and I thank the Lord for it with all my soul.

On the day following the great missionary exhibit, in 1936. Father A. Morissette had written the following lines:

The impression remains that these great days were not only an extraordinary celebration which has left a very agreeable memory, but also a new beginning, a forward thrust in the Franco-American apostolic effort. This activity has served as a lighter from which a giant flame has been lit that will continually spread its light and ardor.

The "Franco-American apostolic effort" had become a reality, and would become so even more. The zeal of the Saint Jean Baptiste Province Oblates for the foreign missions was seeking like a force under pressure to expand and spread. This apostolic thrust impacted the entire province and, by extension, it touched the diverse centers in New England affiliated with Oblate works.

The *Procure De Mazenod*, the Oblate mission house on Mt. Washington Street.

To organize this work, ample and centrally located quarters were needed. The blessing of the *Procure de Mazenod* at 46 Mt. Washington Street, took place on Sunday, November 3, 1940. Father St. Cyr officiated, assisted by Father Gérard Chouinard, a child of the parish who was a missionary in Alberta, and Father Prime Girard, the "Apostle of the Eskimos." The house, the former residence of Joseph Légaré, had been bought from his sister Virginie and quickly converted into offices, workrooms and storage space. Father Carrier also installed a sewing room for making liturgical vestments, to which he attached the activities of the missionary circles in Lowell, Lewiston, Maine, Berlin and Colebrook, New Hampshire. In November 1941, another contingent of Oblates embarked for the Philippines: Fathers H. Langlais, J. Bertrand, and W. Bélanger. However, war intervened while they were on their way, so they had to return to Lowell in December.

The war spread with the rapidity of a cancerous infection, threatening to poison the entire world. Prayers, novenas, holy hours were expanded in the hope that peace would be restored, and the United States spared the horrors

276

of war. Throughout all of Peace Sunday, November 24, 1940, the church was never empty. During the great novena that preceded Christmas that year, the Cardinal exhorted the faithful to sacrifice and pray and resort to this prayer: "Divine Child, Prince of Peace, have pity on us, save us."

The following year, what everyone feared became a reality. The whole world was drawn into the conflict when the United States declared war on Japan, on December 8, the day following the attack on the American fleet at Pearl Harbor, on December 7, 1941. Three days later, the country also declared war against Germany and its allies. Nothing could be done, and everyone prepared for the inevitable development of events.

One of the immediate consequences of the declaration of war against Japan was the abrupt interruption of all correspondence with Father Bolduc. Everyone feared the worst, for, without knowing whether he was alive or dead,

Fr. Emile Bolduc, O.M.I., in the Philippines.

everyone realized that he was in a most perilous situation. Father Bolduc himself after the war confirmed that these fears had been well-founded.

Christmas night, 1941. On the day before, although afraid for myself, I had reassured my Catholics. However, during midnight Mass, which Father Clancy was celebrating, the mayor of Jolo came into my confessional to alert me that the Japanese were eleven miles from the city, and that it would be better for us to flee. I passed beside the altar and in a whisper warned the celebrant, who was preaching, to "cut it short."

After Mass I informed my congregation about the situation, and most of them fled to the mountains. I then began to say my three Christmas Masses to the sound of gunshots while a nun encouraged and sustained what was left of the attendance. Then I went to the local hospital where the wounded had already begun to arrive. All the personnel were entrenched behind a wall of sandbags hastily piled up. The Japanese had already entered the town and were pacing up and down the streets armed with machine guns. In spite of all this, I was able to get back to my rectory.

Thanks to friends whom I had among the Japanese, I was able to benefit from a passport for five weeks, and so remained at my post without being bothered. But, as the Americans approached, the situation became more tense for us. Finally, they knocked at my door and brought me to the general headquarters of the Japanese army. The enemy had decided to "round up" all the Americans in the city. During the hours which followed, I really believed that my last moments had arrived. I was placed at the foot of a wall, with Father Clancy at my side. They began by tying our hands behind our backs and a rope was lowered from a window and tied around our necks. We were preparing one another for death when a Japanese officer came. Visibly impressed at the sight of our white cassocks and Oblate crosses, he gave the order to untie us.

Finally, the news arrived that Fathers Bolduc, Dion, Beaudoin and Laquerre from the province, along with other Oblates, were prisoners of war in a Japanese concentration camp. Prayers began to rise towards heaven for their safe return after the war. The missionary circles sounded the call to establish a special fund for the reconstruction of destroyed missions.

It wasn't long before local boys began to leave for the war. Each family in the parish felt a void caused by the absence of a son or a husband. In the large families of Little Canada, young men signed up, five and six brothers at a time. Enrollment declined at the high school since many of the older boys were leaving school to fill the mill jobs left by those who had gone off to war.

In the *collège* each crusader adopted a serviceman from Lowell, chosen by the chaplain, with whom the boy was expected to correspond frequently. Above all, the crusaders promised to pray and offer sacrifices daily for "their" soldier, such as a visit to the Blessed Sacrament with a companion crusader. The *Croisade* accepted this role of intercessor with its usual dedication. In March 1942, with the benefits from a paper drive, they purchased a defense bond and in December they unfurled an honor-roll flag in their meeting hall, carefully updating it with all the names of the parishioners who were bearing arms.

Economic prosperity, which had begun in the years immediately preceding the war, had continued apace as a result of the military buildup, resulting in a far less constricted way of life, one that was more protected from extreme poverty.

The parish could now think about repairing the ravages wrought on its buildings by the passage of time. Much of the work had become urgent to avoid their falling into ruin. During the Depression, nothing had been touched, except what was strictly necessary, and that was usually in the schools. Saint Jean Baptiste church itself had suffered from buffeting by bad weather and the passage of time. No repairs had been undertaken since 1915. The flooring of the lower church was crumbling under the feet of the faithful; water was entering through the roof and windows of the upper church; and the lead in some of the stained-glass windows had deteriorated to the point where it was feared that some of these magnificent art works would collapse. It was estimated that more than $15,000 would be required for repairs. The schools needed an additional $8,000. Fortunately, Saint Joseph church had been refurbished over the course of many evenings by a group of dedicated parishioners who had themselves absorbed the cost.

So, it was decided, at a large parish gathering in October 1941, to commemorate the 75th anniversary of the parish by organizing a campaign to raise funds for the repairs. The war made it difficult to obtain construction materials, but that didn't prevent the projected campaign from moving forward. It was decided to add fifteen cents to the Sunday pew rent, while during the week the societies vied with each other using their imagination and talent to come up with new ideas for fund-raising activities. The campaign did not let up, and as the money arrived, repairs went forward. One year later, in October 1942, the fund drive had brought in $16,349.64, of which $3,016.00 had come from individual pledges, and $4,318.35 had been raised by the societies. The actual cost of repairs amounted to $22,525.06.

Little by little, Saint Jean Baptiste church was returned to its former splendor. It was repainted, the artist Gaston Goyette touched up the frescoes and a tile floor was put down in the lower church. The church seemed as new as on the day of its dedication. On Sunday, October 18, 1942, date of the official reopening, a series of ceremonies and celebrations took place: a Mass for the Women's Alumni Association, a reception of new Crusaders, the initiation of new members into the *Ange Gardien* Society, a triduum to Christ the King, the blessing of a statue of Saint Joseph, etc. The parishioners were duly proud of the results of the campaign to refurbish their church. Little did they know at that time, however, that the Oblates were about to celebrate in Saint Jean Baptiste church one of the most imposing rites of the Catholic liturgy, the consecration of a bishop.

Even before the war, the Oblates had been in diplomatic negotiations with the government of Haiti, concerning the acceptance and development of one of the poorest and most abandoned missions in the world. In April 1940, Mr. Elie Lescot, the Haitian legate to Washington, had written a letter to Father Bachand, requesting Franco-American Oblates for his small and very poor French-speaking country, situated only a little more than one hundred miles from Florida. Clergy from France, who had been looking after the spiritual needs of the Haitian people, could no longer keep up with the needs, especially since the war had severed all connections with their home country. The missionaries who remained were in need of immediate and powerful support.

The consecration on November 21, 1942 of Bishop Louis Collignon, O.M.I. (On the Right) as Bishop of Les Cayes, Haiti. In the Center, Cardinal Rodrigue Villeneuve, O.M.I., Archbishop of Québec.

Father Bachand, very interested in this project, wanted to accept immediately, so he contacted the assistant-general of the Oblates in Canada, who was equally enthusiastic. The superior-general in France also agreed that the project had great merit but. . . . The situation in Europe was very difficult. The war had wreaked havoc upon the Congregation. Several seminaries were closed; many priests had disappeared or were prisoners; others had died in the war; a large number of scholastics had been deported; and in certain parts of Europe no one even knew what was happening, due to the lack of news or means of communication.

The general and his assistants, without denying the advantages, and even the great merit of having missions in Haiti, decided that no decision could be taken until the war was over. In spite of the repeated requests of Elie Lescot, Father Bachand, and the National Catholic Welfare Conference that was supporting the project, the general replied once again that in spite of his wish to see the project succeed, neither he nor his assistants could reach such an important decision because it committed the future of the Fathers in the Congregation. So, everyone had to wait.

Divine Providence, however, always has its own way. To everyone's astonishment, in April 1942, His Holiness Pope Pius XII ordered the Oblates to accept the missions in Haiti. The Holy Father, who had been kept abreast of the situation by the apostolic delegate to Haiti, had settled the matter. The Saint Jean Baptiste Province was forthwith entrusted with the foundation and direction of missions in Haiti.

Elie Lescot, now President Lescot, who was quite prepared to welcome "his" Oblates, had, in accord with the Vatican, designated Father Bachand as Bishop of Les Cayes, a very poor diocese, almost without priests, located in the south of the country. Father Bachand, feeling that his age and health precluded the acceptance of such a post, declined the nomination and proposed instead the young and brilliant superior of the Natick scholasticate, Father Louis Collignon who had been ordained to the priesthood in 1931.

On Saturday morning, November 21, 1942, the Feast of the Presentation of Mary, Saint Jean Baptiste church, filled to capacity, was the scene of a most impressive ceremony. The main choir sang the *Messe à Marie-Immaculée,* composed by Professor Pépin, and dedicated by him to Cardinal Villeneuve. Before a congregation numbering 2,000 faithful, a cardinal, eight bishops, 300 priests and the plenipotentiary minister from Haiti, Father St. Cyr read aloud, in the name of the Holy See, the bulls nominating the new bishop. Then Cardinal Villeneuve, assisted by Bishop Cushing, auxiliary Bishop of Boston, and Bishop Keough of Providence—Louis Collignon was a Rhode Island native—intoned the ritual prayers for the consecration of Father Collignon as Bishop of Les Cayes. The Franco-American province now had "its" bishop as well as "its" missions. The church was magnificent in all its light and color. Many parishioners could not forget that this glorious event was held, day for day, on the thirtieth anniversary of the devastating fire of 1912.

It was with justifiable pride that the following words appeared in the *Bulletin:*

> This magnificent temple, erected and renovated by dint of so many sacrifices, was now receiving a quite unexpected reward. The bishop's consecration could have taken place in a great cathedral in Boston, Providence, New York, Washington, or Port au Prince—but it took place in our home, in our own church. God be praised for it!

The honor bestowed on the parishioners, by having a Franco-American bishop consecrated in their church, also reflected on the entire Franco-American population. The Saint Jean Baptiste Province, which had been made possible by the almsgiving and prayers of Franco-Americans in order to serve their people, was now seeing its dedication and its missionary zeal crowned with approval and encouragement. Due to their loyalty to the faith and culture of the pioneers of New France, the Oblates, and the Franco-Americans of New England were now being entrusted with the task of spreading the Catholic faith in another French-speaking country of the Americas. In accepting this responsibility, the Oblates were aware of undertaking work which God had chosen since the Holy Father himself wanted this mission.

The good to be done in Haiti was immense, and so they set to work immediately. Missionary Circles, established from Maine to Connecticut, undertook to raise funds, and to have their members pray for the success of the new mission. France-American pastors lent their pulpits for the annual tour by the missionary preachers and allowed special collections. Each year the ordinations in the spring always provided a contingent of young Oblates who left to join their confreres in the distant missions of Les Cayes. Bishop Collignon, who was at his See as early as December 1942, lost no time in organizing the construction of chapels, schools, and dispensaries. He and his colleagues visited the most remote areas of his diocese, which by 1944 were served by fourteen Oblates.

Haiti, at the time the world's only black republic, now shared the love and zeal of a tiny American minority, itself little-known. When Dantès Bellegarde, the plenipotentiary minister of Haiti to Canada, addressed the Alliance Française in Lowell, in 1944, he could refer quite appropriately to the "very strong bonds" that united Haiti to the Franco-Americans.

The campaign for the 75th anniversary of the parish was approaching its end, when, in February 1943, Father St. Cyr received an obedience naming him provincial to replace Father Bachand, who would soon be returning once again

Dantès Bellegarde, Minister Plenipotentiary of Haiti to Canada – seated in the middle – photographed with the directors and distinguished guests of *L'Alliance Française* **of Lowell in 1944.**

as pastor of Saint Joseph. The new provincial was taken somewhat by surprise, but he accepted this new responsibility with resignation. His health, weakened by illness, had led him to the hope of returning to the quiet life of the seminary. But the time for this was not yet at hand, and so he began to exercise his new functions.

He remained as pastor for the moment, and it was as provincial-pastor that he presided over the closing ceremonies of the 75th anniversary in May. The fund-raising campaign had been a real success. All the repairs and alterations had been made without incurring any debts. Everything had been paid for in cash as the money had come in. In that same month, the anniversary of the very first Mass was being orchestrated, always within the limitations imposed by the war. On Wednesday, May 12th, the Feast of the Solemnity of Saint Joseph, the pastor celebrated a Mass for the children, exhorting them "to walk in the footsteps of those who had come before them, imitating their virtues, and following their examples, especially their beautiful spirit of faith and great love for the Church."

That evening a compact crowd filled the parish hall to hear the great Franco-American baritone Camille Girouard and the other artists, at a grand musical celebration for the jubilee. At the point in the program entitled "Homage of the parishioners," Atty. Dewey Archambault presented Father St. Cyr with an expensive gold and silver chalice, embellished with precious gems, that had cost more than a thousand dollars. A check for one thousand dollars and a voluminous spiritual bouquet accompanied the chalice. On Sunday, May 16, a solemn High Mass of Thanksgiving was offered at Saint Joseph church. Presided by Bishop Marc Lacroix, vicar-apostolic of Hudson Bay, it was celebrated by Fathers St. Cyr, Eugène Labrie, Lucien Brassard, and Léon Loranger, all children of the parish. The church was jammed, in spite of the absence of the great organ, which had been sold to Notre Dame de Lourdes parish in October 1941. The Saint Jean Baptiste master choir gave a brilliant rendition of the Mass of Saint Joseph by Ravanello.

In August, Father Bachand assumed his duties as pastor, with all his usual energy. For the past ten years he had been dealing with the most difficult problems brought about by the Depression and the Haitian question. This new pastoral charge seemed more of a rest to him compared with that of provincial.

Father St. Cyr, helped by the advice of Father Bachand, gave himself wholeheartedly to the work of being provincial until July 1948, when he resigned because the responsibility was becoming too burdensome for his failing health. He was assigned to become superior, and later professor, at the Bar Harbor minor seminary. There he was able to spend his last years happily in a peaceful environment. He died abruptly on June 26, 1957, following a heart attack, and was buried in Saint Joseph Cemetery, next to his Oblate confreres.

Father Bachand first chose to complete a project dear to the heart of his predecessor. On the evening of the 75th anniversary concert in the parish hall, Father St. Cyr had expressed the wish that the gift received at that soirée be placed in a fund to install a marble altar in Saint Jean Baptiste church, to honor the memory of the soldiers from the parish who had died on the field of battle. The existing altar was a wooden structure recovered from the ruins of the fire, and refurbished or redecorated many times since then. It would certainly be preferable to replace it with a permanent altar, one more in keeping with the style and dimensions of the church. The altar would thus be a monument worthy of the many lives given up for the cause of justice.

In the fall of 1943, Father Bachand presented the plan for the proposed altar to the parishioners. Of grand proportions, surmounted by a dome resting on four marble columns, it would be luxurious and impressive. Those who wished to do so were encouraged to add ten cents to their seat money on Sunday mornings. It was also promised that the names of those who contributed ten dollars or more would be inscribed on parchment and then sealed in the stone under the altar. The proposal received widespread approval, and the money began to trickle in slowly, a little each week. At one point the archdiocesan authorities threatened to prevent the erection of the proposed altar, arguing that with its separate columns it was a cathedral-like altar. Father Bachand got in touch with the cardinal who intervened and had the project approved as presented.

The dreadful war was continuing its devastations and each family had either a son, a husband, or a relative in the army, or in one of the other military services. On May 30, 1943, the Alumni Association unfurled a large service flag on the façade of the *collège* Saint Joseph in honor of their members who were bearing arms. A year later, Father Bachand commissioned two service flags from the artist Marie-Jeanne Huot, who was a seamstress making liturgical vestments at the Procure de Mazenod. One of these two flags was placed over the main altar in Saint Joseph church and the other at Saint Jean Baptiste. They served as constant reminders of the need of prayers and sacrifices, for an end to the war and a return to world peace.

Just as during the First World War, continuous prayer was the order of the day. There were Holy Hours, vigils before the Blessed Sacrament, novenas, and pilgrimages to the grotto to nourish everyone's hope and grace. Father Bachand had a large honor roll placed before the Sacred Heart altar, in the lower church of Saint Jean Baptiste, making it a Victory Altar. In June 1944, on the 25th anniversary of the consecration of the parish to the Sacred Heart, Father Bachand, at the foot of the Victory Altar, renewed that consecration; he encouraged the faithful to rededicate their homes to the Sacred Heart and to lead therein a more intense Christian life, so necessary for peace and harmony in the family and in the world.

Some of the Fathers maintained an extensive correspondence with the servicemen. The letters from the front contained magnificent examples of heroism and loyalty which in turn spurred the parishioners to pray. Some letters found their way into the pages of the *Bulletin Paroissial* or the columns of *L'Étoile,* like the following excerpts published in the *Bulletin:*

"Reverend Father: I want to thank you for the blessing you gave me before my departure. It did me a lot of good. I left the rectory with confidence, and I'm sure I'll be protected in my engagement . . . ."

"The change from civilian to military life was tough, very tough. Many times at night as I went to bed, my mind would fly to Lowell and my loved ones, and the tears would begin to flow, only to be buried in a very hard mattress. And then I would say the rosary on the beads that Father X gave me, and I would ask the supreme general for courage and perseverance. Now life is improving from day to day, but my heart still remains 'chez nous' . . . ."

"Since I've been here, I recite my rosary every night before going to bed, and every morning when I get up. I always have my rosary handy and I pray whenever I march without a gun, etc. I have it in my hand at this moment while writing to you. I wish you would tell this to my family. Since I left I haven't sworn or blasphemed, and since I've been here, I've received communion three times. When I go to confession, I say my sins in English, but the prayers in French. . . . They seem impressed to see that a Canadian, who does not know his prayers in English, goes to confession just the same. . . . I've promised Saint Anthony $5.00 if I am accepted into the radio engineering school. Please help me to have my request granted. . . ."

"I'm happy to be wearing the uniform for my country. I have a duty to accomplish and I'll be here until it is. I'm asking you to help me do this in your prayers. I have great confidence in you. This duty that I am called to do is a big job, and, with your prayers and God's help, I will accomplish it, so that one day in the future I can return home to my family and my fiancée, safe and sound. I think of these things every day. And I know that with God's help I will return home after the war. Our duty may be hard and terrible, we know that, and we must make sacrifices.—We have left our parents—but not for long. We have been chosen to defend our country, and that we shall do, even if we have to give our life. Many

The Victory Altar with the Honor Roll in St. Jean Baptiste's lower church.

have done so already, and others will do it in the future. But we are determined. . . ."

Often letters received by the parents were published:
My dear parents:

Even if I lived to be a hundred, I couldn't spend a more beautiful day than today. The Catholic Marines left this morning by truck for a church on the other side of the harbor. Needless to say, I was one of them. When we arrived, there were so many trucks of all kinds that ours had to park a half-mile from the church. The church was so packed that some Marines couldn't even get inside and had to remain standing all around on the grounds.

When the chaplain entered the sanctuary the choir sang an Ave Maria. In the United States, those who are used to going to Mass regularly don't know how to appreciate it. There are even some who are very neglectful. They have to be pulled out of bed for them to go. But here, it's very different and we would like to attend more than once a week. Since I've been in the Marines, seven months now, I've attended Mass in auditoriums, theaters, etc., but I never missed on Sunday through my own fault. But this was the first time that I had the happiness of attending Mass in a church, and I could have cried like a child. I still have tears of joy at this moment.

There were five lines of Marines to go to the communion rail, and the communions lasted from fifteen to twenty minutes, distributed by two priests. At the elevation, instead of ringing the bells, a bugle played. After Mass, I asked the sergeant if I could remain there all day; he gave me permission and I stayed. The next Mass was for the native people. The priest who said this Mass was Father Dumais, from Van Buren, Maine, who studied with the Marist Fathers in Bedford, Mass. He arrived here only last week, and after Mass I went up to speak with him. He invited me to have lunch with him, and it was a great pleasure to eat with one of our priests.

When I returned to camp I found all your letters and your package. I am very happy and I thank you very much. Don't worry, I'm as safe here as in the United States. I've just spent a day that I'll never forget, I'm eager to see my new friend again, and I ask God to bless you all.
Your soldier of Christ,

Paul

The candor and sincerity of some of these letters move one to tears:
. . . This morning around 8 o'clock I left the Camp to go to the large

287

white church on the other side of the bay. I had with me all my gear plus my laundry bag full of good things.

I walked about four miles before being picked up by a truck that dropped me off right at the church door, around 10 o'clock. I entered the church, said my rosary, and made my Way of the Cross. I then learned that there would be no Mass since there was only one, and it had been said at 7:30 in the morning.

I was very sad because I had come all this way on an empty stomach so that I could receive Communion. To console myself I went to visit the nuns at this place. I gave them my bag along with everything it contained, and some money for Saint Anthony. The one who greeted me was so pleased that she was crying. The superior and another nun then came to see me. One came from France, the superior, and the other from Montréal. I told them that I was a Franco-American and that I could speak French, but not as well as they could. They spoke a very beautiful French. But, I understood everything they said and I replied in my own French, for they hadn't spoken to a Frenchman for the past 3 years.

. . . They asked me what brought me to them. I told them it was love of the Blessed Virgin and God. They found it admirable of me to have come all this way to receive God. When I told them that I had not eaten for twelve hours, they told me to go find the priest and tell him my story, that's what I did. I was very well received. He even made me kneel on the altar steps to give me Communion. Gosh! It was the first time that I received Communion on the altar steps. It's an honor that few have had.

. . . He then told me to go to the Sea-Bees, a little farther down the road, to put something into my stomach. I don't believe that the best restaurants in N.Y. could have served me a better dinner!

To return, I walked about three miles; I got a ride for part of the way, and then walked another two miles to reach my camp. I was so pleased with my day!

One morning in June 1944, bells and sirens announced to the citizens of Lowell that the Normandy invasion had begun. People filled the churches. At the morning Masses the Communions were beyond counting. During the day the school children were brought to the church in groups to recite the rosary, and at night, prayer services attracted a very large number of the faithful.

Father Bachand continued to encourage the parishioners to be as brave and courageous as the soldiers, and to place their confidence in the God of Armies and the Sacred Heart. Father Rodolphe Smit, the herald of the Blessed Mother, spread the devotion to Mary, as Mother and Patroness of the Afflicted. Too often, the pastor and his assistants had the sad duty of bringing the dreaded news to a family that one of its members had been killed or was missing in action. At such moments, nothing could be done but to unite their suffering to that of the bereaved family.

Victory in Europe in the month of May 1945, gave rise to the hope that the war with Japan would soon be over. On August 15, the Feast of the Assumption, Japan surrendered. The world was at peace after six years of conflict. In Lowell, bells and sirens announced peace to the wild cheers of the crowds. The Blessed Sacrament was exposed all day in Saint Jean Baptiste church, and that evening people gathered before the Altar of Victory for a solemn ceremony of Thanksgiving.

The unveiling of the veterans memorial altar had taken place at the Christmas Midnight Mass, in 1944. The following May, the month when the European conflict ended, Bishop Guy presided at the solemn blessing, and sealed in the altar stone the list of contributors, and the names of the men from Saint Joseph parish who had borne arms in the war up to that moment. By the end of the conflict 1,325 parishioners had served in the armed forces of the country and thirty-eight had died. The commemorative marble plaque in French, behind the altar, reads as follows in English:

The inauguration of the WWII Veteran's Memorial Altar, Christmas Eve, December 25, 1944. The parish's service flag hangs above.

289

Saint Joseph Parish
— 1868 —   Lowell, Massachusetts   — 1943 —
Founded and Directed by the
Missionary
Oblates of Mary Immaculate

Commemorative Altar
Erected
By the Parishioners
On the Occasion of the
75th
Anniversary of the Parish
In
Memory of
Their Servicemen
In the War of
1941

Inaugurated
On
December 25, 1944

The new Romanesque-style altar, which had actually cost almost $20,000 instead of the $9,000 that had been projected, is very impressive because of its monumental proportions. The baldaquin, gilded at first, before being adorned later with a superb fresco representing the Holy Spirit, surrounded by the symbols of the four purposes of the Mass, and the eight Beatitudes, rests on four marble columns imported from the French Alps. The altar itself, sculpted in American marble rests on steps of marble from Italy. This choice of three marbles, besides adding great artistic richness to the altar, also illustrates the parish's desire to express symbolically the three wellsprings of Franco-American Catholic culture.

A few parishioners, comparing the monumental style of this altar with the smaller and more "intimate" proportions of the old one, with its many statues of saints and a beautiful bas-relief of the Last Supper, regretted the change. In general, however, most people considered the new altar as the perfect crowning for the festivities of the 75th anniversary of the parish and the restoration of Saint Jean Baptiste church.

Shortly before the end of the war, the news spread like wildfire that Father Bolduc and his Oblate companions had been liberated. In March

1945, the *Bulletin* published a letter from the former pastor announcing his forthcoming return to Lowell for a well-deserved rest. After three years of internment by the Japanese and an absence of six years, Father Bolduc was returning to Lowell!

Immediately, Father Carrier, the A.M.M.I. and the parish societies began to prepare a grandiose reception for him of the type that the Lowell people could organize so well. On Sunday evening, April 22, 1945, the crowd flocked to the municipal auditorium to welcome back Father Bolduc and two of his prison companions, Fathers George Dion and James Burke. The program proved to be as impressive as the departure ceremony had been. Diane Morin-Dubé, accompanied by a Franco-American orchestra directed by Charles Bélanger, sang Gounod's Ave Maria, while a combined chorale, made up of the choirs from the various Franco-American parishes, sang patriotic hymns.

When Father Bolduc rose to speak, applause exploded from all corners of the hall. His first words expressed the emotion gripping him: "It is a dream to see such a beautiful reception after so many hardships. To see so many friends is a dream, a resurrection."

Father Carrier then rose, and presented Father Bolduc with money for his Filipino missions: $285 collected from the orphans, $170 from the altar boys, $290 from the boys' school, $500 from the girls' school and a $10,000 check representing all the money gathered by the *Association Missionnaire* since Pearl Harbor. Everywhere in the parish, Father Bolduc's visit became the occasion for receptions and celebrations. At the *collège,* at the girls' school, at the orphanage, short skits and addresses were prepared. Father, as was his wont, found time to visit the sick in the hospital, make the rounds of families in Little Canada, and even play in a baseball game at the North Common with the boys of the *collège.*

His return to the Philippines, on November 4, 1945, was again the occasion for more tears and regrets. In leaving, he expressed this parting wish with the school children: "I hope that some of you will come to take my place when I am too old to do God's work."

After the war, the apostolic endeavors of the parish in favor of the missions regained their usual vigor. Sewing circles multiplied, raffles were held regularly, and the energies shared between the Philippine missions and those of Haiti kept a large number of enthusiastic workers busy in Lowell as elsewhere in New England.

In Lowell, Saint Joseph parish often won the golden palm for its works of charity. In collections for polio or paper drives, the children of St. Joseph's schools were frequently first, even ahead of schools with a larger enrollment. For years, their contributions to the Society for the Propagation of the Faith or the Holy Childhood kept the school children among the top-ranking benefactors of these good works.

The parish never hesitated to mobilize whenever an urgent need arose. For instance, during the clothes drive for the needy people of Europe, in the fall of 1944, the parishioners contributed five tons of clothing. Similarly, the national campaign of food for Europe, in December 1945, aroused so much enthusiasm that the parish sent to the Lowell railroad station 150 cases including 7,075 items of canned goods.

In spite of the sufferings and privations it brought, the war, by a curious reversal of circumstances, occasioned a wider extension of Franco-American culture.

As early as 1939, Father Bolduc, then a member of the Lowell U.S.O., had noticed the ever-increasing number of French sailors who came to Lowell hoping to meet young women who spoke their language.

These sailors, serving on French ships docked for repairs in the ports of Boston or Portsmouth, New Hampshire, were generally very young and without religious support. The pastor delegated young Father Armand Morissette to look after their spiritual welfare.

Before long, Father Morissette's ministry expanded for, as the war developed, ships arrived more frequently. In April 1943, Lowell and the parish received the official visit of the officers of two ships tied up in Boston, *Le*

Fr. Armand Morissette, O.M.I., standing in the middle, with a group of French sailors. In the rear are members of the French American War Veterans in their uniforms.

292

Fantasque and *Le Terrible*. In the summer of 1944 *Le Triomphant* spent eight months in Boston. Commander Gilly, a close friend of General de Gaulle, often came with his sailors to visit the city.

This contact of young French military personnel with the Franco-Americans of Lowell was a most fortunate one. Dances were organized at the U.S.O. on Appleton Street, and receptions were held at the Saint Jean Baptiste Center. Sailors were received in homes for a meal. A contingent of children from the orphanage was even driven to the harbor to visit aboard the ships.

Father Morissette performed his ministry to the military, and other French citizens, with such zeal and dedication that, for all practical purposes, he became almost the non-official French ambassador to the region. France—that is to say Free France—deeply touched by the welcome extended to its sailors, and grateful to Father for looking after their spiritual well-being, decided to elevate his ministry by according it an official rank.

In November 1944, after the departure of *Le Triomphant,* General de Gaulle's government, in conjunction with the religious authorities, named Father Morissette chaplain of the French Navy in the United States, with the rank of captain. He was the only American citizen to be part of the French Navy. One of his first "official" functions was to marry Désiré Milliner, a French sailor, to Claire Gagné, a parishioner, in Saint Jean Baptiste church, on February 19, 1945.

This indefatigable chaplain's dedication to his ministry knew no bounds. Consequently, in 1945 the French government honored him with the *Médaille Militaire* and in 1949, made him a *Chevalier de la Légion d'Honneur.* He was the third Oblate of the province to receive such an honor. Father Léon Loranger had been made a *Chevalier* in 1947 and Father Bachand in 1934.

Once the contact with France had thus been established, there occurred a veritable deluge of activities and French visits to Lowell. *L'Alliance Française,* two of whose principal officers, Judge Arthur L. Eno and Antoine Clément, editor of *L'Étoile,* had been decorated with the *Palmes Académiques,* in 1938 and 1939 respectively, continued its French cultural evenings, at which the most learned French intellectuals in the country gave lectures: André Morize, Count Jéhan de Noue, Louis Rougier, Jean Seznec, André Frère, etc.

On January 25 and 26, 1945, Professor René de Messières, regional president of France Forever, presided at the inauguration of the local chapter of this organization, whose purpose was to tighten the bonds of friendship between France and the United States, and to support the cause of General de Gaulle. One of the activities of this chapter was to host a grand reception for the French Ambassador to Washington, Henri Bonnet, in October 1948. It was with pride that the members spoke of the courageous role of the secret agent "Paul," who was the Franco-American soldier, Edwin Poitras of Lowell. Working with the

Fr. Armand Morissette, O.M.I., in his French navy uniform.

French resistance movement, he had prepared the occupation of the South of France by the Allies.

No celebration was complete without the presence of a representative from France at the table of honor. The French consul to Boston, Albert Chambon, and his vice-consul Baron Louis de Cabrol, were frequent honored guests at Franco-American festivities.

Saint Joseph parish, with its many important annexes, also received its share of attention. On May 14, 1946, Monsignor Georges Chevrot, a preacher at Notre- Dame de Paris, gave a vibrant lecture in the parish hall on Catholic France. The following week, Roland Rondel, chancellor at the French Consulate in Boston, attended the annual procession of the *Enfants de Marie* at the orphanage grotto. Then, this same diplomat, accompanied by Raymond Massiet de Tremours, a special envoy from France, visited the parish institutions. In April 1947, Monsignor Joseph Guérin, another of the great homilists from Notre-Dame de Paris, preached on the major themes of current spirituality from the pulpit of Saint Jean Baptiste church. That same month of April 1947, the youngest general in the French army, Guillain de Benouville, also visited the institutions of Saint Joseph parish. In September 1948, the

Petits Chanteurs de la Côte d'Azur came to add their sweet strains to the concert of French friendships that were proliferating in the city of Lowell.

The Franco-American ethnic spirit was very much alive, but also in full transformation. The social evolution of the group, in addition to the dislocations caused by the war, would bring about many changes in their manner of seeing and their behavior.

The large-scale theatrical presentations had all but disappeared from the parish stage, having been replaced by concerts and movies: fifty-five double-feature showings, or 110 films each year, could be seen in the parish hall. On March 21 and 22 , 1945, the Paul D. Renaud theatrical company from Montréal presented the major drama *La Passion du Christ* in that same hall, but this was an exception. Apart from the annual play presented by the girls' high school, and the one by the boys' high school, the French theatrical tradition at St. Joseph had all but died out.

The vogue of evening concerts, however, was at its height. In June 1944, the parish learned with sorrow that its devoted organist, Rodolphe Pépin, was leaving Lowell, after more than twenty years at Saint Jean Baptiste church. He had accepted the position of organist and choirmaster at the shrine church of Our Lady of Perpetual Help, Mission Church, in Boston's Roxbury section, one of the leading liturgical positions in the country. His replacement, Charles Bélanger, was eminently qualified. Son of the organist at Sainte Marie church in Lewiston, Maine, Charles had been a child prodigy, having played the organ from the age of six. He had earned an advanced degree in music from the Pius X Institute in New York. For his debut in Lowell, he presented a grand, unforgettable Pops Concert in Saint Joseph Hall on November 27 and 28, 1944. The program included the Saint Jean Baptiste Orchestra, assembled for the occasion, the chorus from the girls' high school, the small choir from the *collège,* and operatic arias sung by Diane Morin-Dubé. The concert was one of the greatest musical successes of the war years.

Changing attitudes affected other areas of parish life as well. The *Bulletin Paroissial,* which celebrated its 35th anniversary in May 1945, was breathing its last. Printing costs kept going up and fewer readers bought it. Each month the publication had to face a considerable deficit. Even *L'Étoile* was suffering from the economic and social conditions. By March 1943, the newspaper, which had been a daily, was forced to become a tri-weekly, published three times a week.

To modernize the *Bulletin,* and make it more attractive, the directors, beginning with the September 1941 issue, adopted a large magazine format with the cover in color. In March 1943 other improvements were made with the addition of color on the inside pages and a comic strip section. The editors succeeded in producing a modern periodical of thirty-two pages which sold for 10 cents an issue. But in spite of all these upgrades, the *Bulletin* no longer held the same appeal as before. Faced with continuing deficits, publication was halted with the June 1946 number. To keep the parishioners informed of weekly events, a four-page weekly bulletin was begun, which continues to be published.

The war also had a profound effect on the moral and spiritual life of the people. The dislocation of families, the military experience of brutality, the return of the servicemen to civilian status, juvenile delinquency, were all problems that had to be faced in the second half of the fifties.

Cardinal O'Connell died on April 22, 1944, at the age of 85. It was the end of an era. His successor, Archbishop Richard Cushing who was enthroned on November 8, 1944, was faced with the mission of adapting the Church of his densely populated diocese to the new conditions brought about by the needs of the hour. There was not only the question of reintegrating the veterans into the fabric of social and family life in their old environment, there would also be the future question of the exodus of people from the cities to the suburbs and the subsequent need for new parishes and institutions.

One of the first administrative decisions taken by the new archbishop was to change the name of Saint Joseph parish. Although this parish had originally been placed under the patronage of Saint Joseph, it had Saint Jean Baptiste as its principal church. The Lowell Lithuanians also had a Saint Joseph parish, founded in 1908. To avoid confusion, it was decided to change the name of the Franco-American St. Joseph parish to Saint Jean Baptiste, thereby allowing the Lithuanians the sole use of the name Saint Joseph. The parishioners were none too pleased with this change that went counter to tradition, but logic and good sense prevailed, and Saint Jean Baptiste became the new patron of the parish.

For Archbishop Cushing these administrative decisions were of lesser importance at the time. The religious situation of the archdiocese and the spiritual well-being of his flock were more pressing.

It was the opinion of certain chaplains that military service "had corrupted the morals and religion of American youth," and they provided revealing statistics to support this observation: only thirty percent on average of the Catholics in the armed forces attended Mass on Sunday, and only forty percent of American Christians under arms were faithful to their religion. Already, at the end of the thirties and the beginning of the forties, a rise in juvenile delinquency and a materialistic outlook had been observed. The need to organize the laity for the work of evangelization and the conversion of society had become more and more imperative.

To this end, Archbishop Cushing first ordered each parish in the archdiocese to form a Holy Name men's society, whose aim was to serve as a countervailing force to "paganism" in all its forms. "Our men must take the offensive through positive action by practicing what they believe," stated the cardinal. The post-war world needed direction and examples to follow, and Christianity had to organize itself accordingly. In December 1945, Joseph A.N. Chrétien assumed the presidency of the Saint Joseph Chapter, and the members attended the rally in Boston on the 16th of December to receive the Society's watchword.

The archbishop sent letter upon letter and issued as many directives, but these somber reflections on the moral state of society were not news to the Oblates. As we have seen, as far back as the thirties, they had discerned the need for increased Catholic Action and a popular approach to pastoral ministry. Following the recommendations of the Holy Father, the general chapter of the Oblates in 1938 had given the highest priority to Catholic Action geared to the people, and had urged the whole Congregation to develop cores of informed and believing Catholics. The end of the war allowed the Oblates to accelerate the efforts at evangelization already in place, and to seek to bring about new ones.

Father Lyonnais, alongside his work with the *Croisés,* had wanted, from the time of his arrival in Lowell in 1937, to find a way of curbing the increase of juvenile delinquency by giving young people direction and the healthy friendship they needed.

In 1939, he had offered his services to the Lowell Police Department as a counselor, and had succeeded in turning around the lives of many young people. Always wanting to do more, he decided, in 1944, to go right to the heart of the problem. He went in search of gangs and groups of young people who were planning mischief. After gaining the confidence of the leaders, he launched a movement called *Jeunes Étudiants Chrétiens.* On Sunday afternoons, he brought the young people together in a private home and led a Christian assembly where he counseled, encouraged, and, if need be, scolded the participants. His formula for success was a simple one: "Resorting to force will get you nowhere. Gentleness, patience, work, and prayer can win over all hearts." Observing his successes in this difficult apostolate, the city authorities made Father Lyonnais a probation officer of the court. This allowed him to go further and get even more involved with families and troubled households. Only God knows how many controversies he was able to settle, and how many boys he helped out along the way. His apostolate bore fruit until the time of his death in 1959, although at a slower pace after 1950. To boys and young men of Lowell, he was a reliable friend and a faithful counselor in Christ's image.

The schools at that time were flourishing. In November 1942, the fiftieth anniversary of the founding of the *collège* Saint Joseph and the arrival of the Marist Brothers in Lowell was celebrated with as much solemnity as was possible during wartime. It consisted of a general reunion of former students with a High Mass on Sunday, November 1st, followed by a gala banquet at

Fr. Emery Lyonnais, O.M.I., with a group of boys in 1946.

the C.M.A.C. that same evening. Inspired by this model, in October 1943, the Grey Nuns celebrated a triple anniversary: the sixtieth anniversary of the girls' school, the fifteenth anniversary of the girl's high school, and the tenth anniversary of the founding of *L'Amicale Saint Joseph* with a Mass, banquet, and the usual convocations. These celebrations would be crowned by an unexpected surprise: the election the following year of a former student, Aurore Drapeau, Sister St. André Corsini, to the office of superior-general of the Grey Nuns of the Cross of Ottawa. Another former student, Marie-Louise Guay, Sister Paul Emile, became the historian of the Congregation and published a well-received biography of their foundress, *Mère Bruyère.*

The schools at the time were financially solid. The *Dames de Sainte-Anne* organized a gigantic penny sale each year for the benefit of the schools, and the *Congréganistes* helped the administration's budget with the profit from their huge bridge party held in various homes. In April 1944, the Lafayette Club donated $3,000 to modernize the chemistry laboratories in the two high schools.

In 1944, the parish numbered 2,277 families, comprising 8,603 parishioners, including 1,470 school children. In the fall of 1944, there were 595 boys in the *collège,* 485 girls in the girls' grammar school, ninety-three students in the boys' high school, 141 in the girls' high school and only fifty-six in the public schools, including Lowell High. This was, however, considered to be fifty-six too many, so the pastor hastened to emphasize once again that the school was an extension of the family, and a necessary complement to the Catholic education received in the home. Besides, wasn't it true that most cases of juvenile delinquency came from the students of "godless" schools? The duty of parents was clear, the children had to be sent to the parochial school at all cost. The following year, the number of children in the public schools had been reduced to twenty-five.

The problem of juvenile delinquency preoccupied many people at that time. To counteract this problem, the Catholic Youth Organization was established more widely in the schools. The C.Y.O. was a national movement aimed at organizing healthy leisure outlets for youth. Father Roland Lavallée had introduced the organization in the parish in the early 1940s. Since then, he had put together a baseball team which, along with the teams from Sainte Jeanne d'Arc and Notre Dame de Lourdes parishes, belonged to the Lowell C.Y.O. League and competed in the League tournaments during the summer months.

Always in keeping with the aim of helping young people, the parish bought, on January 7, 1946, the property on Pawtucket Street that it had been renting from Joseph Faucher. The parish had been paying rent for the use of a large hall in the building, but Father Bachand wanted to purchase the building to give the center more scope. Father Eugène Fournier, the bursar, took the matter in hand. Mr. Faucher sold the property to the parish for almost $12,000. Saint Jean Baptiste Center thus assumed its definitive form. An ice-skating rink was set up on the adjacent grounds, and during the winter it became one of the most frequented places in the parish. The interior was converted to include a banquet hall, meeting rooms, a lounge with jukebox and cantine, all the facilities needed to turn it into a comfortable and modern social center. Except for the skating rink, the center was reserved exclusively for boys.

For their own meetings, the girls of the parish always had at their disposal the small room in the former school, right next to the church. It was open for them every Thursday evening from 7:30 to 9:30.

Besides being the director of the C.Y.O., Father Roland Lavallée was also responsible for the J.O.C. Under his enlightened leadership, the association of young Catholic workers assumed a new lease on life, concentrating especially on marriage-preparation programs. It had been felt for some time that marriage education was inadequate and not realistic enough.

The return of the soldiers from military service, and the changes taking place in the American social structure, required more than ever the start of a solid formation program based upon Christian and Catholic values. It was decided to adopt a program of courses developed by the *Jocistes* in Canada who had studied the question extensively. Their program was adapted and made compatible with the American milieu. In the autumn of 1945, the Lowell J.O.C. presented to the public a *Service de Préparation au Mariage* which consisted of a fifteen-week course of lectures given once a week by Fathers Bachand, Loranger, and Lavallée, along with the nurses Clarina Morier and Simonne Généreux. This lecture series was given at first only to women and consisted of the following topics:

1—The contemporary situation—Remedy: marriage preparation
2—Choosing fiancés and husbands
3—Christian love and happiness
4—Dating and engagement
5—Masculine and feminine psychology—The ways a woman can understand a man
6—Economic preparation
7—Marriage is a Sacrament
8—The marriage ceremony
9—The legal and civil aspects of marriage
10—Feminine and masculine anatomy
11—The marriage act—pregnancy and birth
12—Hygiene—venereal diseases
13—What is allowed and what is forbidden in marriage
14—The first years of marriage
15—Social and family problems—Solutions. Conclusions.

The *Jociste* movement thus continued to grow, and in July 1946, the Lowell *Jocistes* had the pleasure of receiving a visit from Canon Joseph Cardijn who was on a lecture tour throughout North America. This priest, who was the founder of the worldwide movement, encouraged the Lowell members to continue along the path they had chosen, and to develop even more fully their initiative in the field of marriage preparation. The program had been launched on a trial basis, but its success was such that within a few years other series of courses were offered for men, and later for coed groups. Even after the dissolution of the J.O.C movement in Saint Joseph parish, around 1958, the marriage-preparation courses continued under other auspices.

Ministry to adults assumed as many diverse forms as the pastoral situation required. Through the Holy Name and other parish societies, the Fathers faced the needs of the day with appropriate teaching and moral direction. The Librairie Baron bookstore and the parish library displayed the most recent books and magazines from France and Canada. In the fall of 1948, a comprehensive program of religious instruction was set in motion. Starting on Sunday,

October 24, 1948, an insert each week in the parish bulletin gave answers for a question which had been announced the preceding week. The answers came after a discussion period in the homes and in gatherings of the associations. This was a kind of adult catechism which touched upon the most contemporary problems: "What do you think of Christ?. . . Is he God? Can we read the Bible? Is civil divorce permissible for Catholics? Can a Catholic be a Communist? Can Catholics marry outside the Church?" etc. After ten weeks, the series of questions and answers were bound together in booklet form, to be sold at the Librairie Baron. The printing and binding of these brochures were the work of Brother Robert Béliveau in the small parish print shop over the sacristy. The campaign ended on May 15, 1949, with the binding of the third and final series of questions and answers.

Father Bachand led the parish with care and prudence. All the *oeuvres* were well directed and supervised. The parish was debt-free, and by 1947, there was even $25,000 in the bank for unforeseen emergencies. The rectory was home to twenty Oblate Fathers and Brothers, all busy with parish or provincial ministry. Father Anthime Desnoyers, in his canonical visit of 1947, could not do otherwise but declare that Saint Jean Baptiste had maintained "its glorious reputation as a model for parishes."

Much of this flourishing state of affairs was due to the zeal of its priests but, as Father Desnoyers emphasized, a debt of gratitude was also owed to the "precious collaborators" of the Fathers: the Oblate Brothers. Sacristans, porters, secretaries, carpenters, painters, printers, and handymen, they worked behind the scenes and gave their lives to support the work of the priest by their prayers and their dedication.

The presence of the Oblate Brothers at the heart of the parish, which was often as humble and hidden as their work, did not always leave a trace in the archives. Yet, on July 13, 1948, one of the brothers who died at Saint Jean Baptiste had left a deep impression in the hearts of all those who had known him. The one everyone called *le petit Frère* (the little Brother), Brother Ovide Levasseur, was the model of a Brother and Oblate religious. He had been serving in the parish since 1900, and had been there to help at every step of the way, doing the varied work required by the growth of the parish. He had founded the small print shop in which he spent his free time. His goodness of heart, in addition to his gentle and welcoming humility, touched everyone with whom he dealt. The young Fathers could not help but be moved at seeing him each night when, old as he was, he would kneel at the feet of the superior to receive his blessing before retiring. His death, at the age of 72, left a deep void at Saint Joseph residence, as it did within the parish family.

On May 16, 1943, Brother Alexandre Bedell, a member of the Saint Joseph community for more than 35 years, had also gone to his eternal reward.

Father Bachand, always surrounded by everyone's respect and esteem, had come to the end of his second three-year term as pastor. His years of service to the parish and to the province could have filled more than one life. In August 1949, his superiors judged that he should have a well-earned rest, and named him bursar of the parish. He was 60 years old. The new pastor, Father Gérard Chouinard, began his duties that same month.

26. Father Henri Bolduc
Saint Joseph Shrine

Fr. Gérard Chouinard, O.M.I.

Father Gérard Chouinard came to Lowell from Fort McMurray, Alberta. Born in St. Elie d'Orford in Québec, on May 30, 1906, the son of Gustave Chouinard and Amanda Langlois, the family immigrated to Lowell shortly after the birth of Gérard. His elementary studies completed at the *Collège* Saint Joseph, he entered the Oblate juniorate in Colebrook in 1922.

Ordained to the priesthood in 1933, he was sent to the missions in the Canadian Far North, becoming the pastor at Fort McMurray in 1934. In addition to his parish ministry, he managed to have a hospital built while looking after both the material and spiritual needs of the region's Native peoples.

After spending ten years in this harsh environment, his health failed and he had to return to Lowell to recover his strength. As soon as he regained his

The St. Jean Baptiste Parish altar boys in 1950. Seated in the middle at left is their Chaplain, Fr. Roland Bourgeois, O.M.I., and at right, the Pastor Fr. Gérard Chouinard, O.M.I. At the far right, is Sister St. Alain, S.G.C. (Gertude Rondeau) at the far left, Sister Cécile de la Croix, S.G.C. (Cécile Duquette).

health, his superiors assigned him to Saint Jean Baptiste parish as a curate, in August 1948. In July of the following year, he became pastor.

Of an affable and joyous nature, he quickly adapted to his new responsibilities and, following in the footsteps of his predecessors, he became the friend of the poor and the sick. His goodness had a deep effect on the parishioners. His term of office, though short, was not devoid of events.

On November 1, 1950, Pope Pius XII proclaimed the dogma of the Assumption of Mary while announcing a Holy Year for 1951, with a solemn closing to be held at Fatima. The same year as this long-awaited Marian proclamation, President Truman ordered American troops to Korea to defend its population from the Communist invasion. The country was once again at war. As the soldiers marched off to combat, the parishioners had to accept once again the cross of sacrifice and prayers for peace. The new pastor shared the anguish and sufferings of his parishioners undergoing the terrible ordeal of another war and joined his prayers to theirs.

Having assumed his duties as pastor, Father Chouinard participated with hearty gusto in the cultural life of the parish. The Polyphonic Choir of Mr. Bélanger, the organist, continued to delight the parishioners with his *Fantaisies Musicales* and evening concerts. But, in the winter of 1951, Mr. Bélanger announced his departure for Florida, where he had been invited to become the organist at the cathedral in Miami.

Faced with the task of locating another choir master and organist, the pastor soon found his man in Maurice Pépin, son of Rodolphe, a graduate of the Boston Conservatory of Music and Boston University. Maurice brought to his new position his fine talent as both a musician and a pedagogue. He assumed his post in January 1952, and set out to carry on the long and rich musical tradition of Saint Jean Baptiste.

The bonds of friendship between France and the parish remained strong. In 1949, Saint Joseph Hall was selected for the American premiere of the important French film *Monsieur Vincent.* The movie created such a stir that it had to be shown several times. Later, it moved on to the screens of New York and Boston. Jacqueline Du Bief, the Parisian star of the "Ice Chips," while on tour in Boston, and looking for a friendly and French-speaking place to practice her skating, came regularly, in March 1950, to skate on the Saint Jean Baptiste Center rink. *Les Petits Chanteurs de la Croix de Bois* from Paris, who came to Lowell in October 1950, as part of the Parker Lecture series, accepted the hospitality of parishioners' homes during their stay, and in return sang at the High Mass at Saint Jean Baptiste. In that same month of October, the French fishing vessel *Bassilourd* docked in Boston. Its Captain Richer asked the parishioners, in the name of France, for toys and clothing for French children at

Christmas. Needless to say, the response was bountiful and generous.

Friendship for France was demonstrated with great pomp when Bishop Markham, the auxiliary Bishop for the Lowell region, celebrated a solemn Mass at Saint Jean Baptiste on May 6, 1951, commemorating the second millennium of the city of Paris. Enhanced by the presence in the congregation of the Consuls Chambon and Lapierre and delegations of the Franco-American societies, the celebration remained a memorable occasion in the French annals of the city. As a gesture of gratitude for this event, Father Armand Morissette, France's military chaplain and the coordinating mastermind of the celebration, was invited to Paris, in October 1951, by the French government. The honor of this official visit, in appreciation for his many years of dedication to France and its people, was also shared by all the Oblates and the Franco-Americans of Lowell who had remained faithful to their heritage over the years.

The French-language allegiance of the parishioners also manifested itself towards Québec, the cradle of the Franco-American immigrants. The appeal issued from Québec for the Third Congress of the French Language, slated for June 1952, gave rise, once again, to increased public awareness. The regional committee followed the same organizational plan as for the previous Congress, while the indefatigable Antoine Clément, editor of *L'Étoile,* wrote multiple press notices and gave talks on the radio. Thursday afternoon April 24, 1952, Monsignor Fernand Vandry, rector of Laval University, came to Lowell where he spoke at a rally convened at the municipal auditorium to pass on the watchword to his Lowell brethren. Dignitaries and the people, religious and lay, listened attentively to his vibrant message entitled: "The Providential Vocation of the French People in America." Having sanctioned the message, Fathers Chouinard and Jules Guy, as well as some forty delegates left Lowell by chartered bus in June to attend the Convention in Québec.

This trip to Québec was one of the last acts of the young pastor for he was diagnosed soon after with cancer and had to resign in August 1952, at the end of his first three-year term. After two quiet years of rest, he seemed sufficiently recovered to be appointed pastor of St. Pierre's parish, in Plattsburgh, New York. But it proved to be too much for his health. In June of 1955, he was rushed to St. Joseph Hospital, where he died on June 19, at the age of forty-nine. His solemn and very moving funeral was held in Saint Jean Baptiste church on June 22, the twenty-second anniversary of his priestly ordination in the same church.

Father Chouinard's successor was Father Henri Bolduc, also a child of the parish. Born on August 9, 1910, the son of Israël Bolduc and Tharsile Lauzon, he started his schooling at the *Collège* Saint Joseph and then studied in the various houses of formation of the Saint Jean Baptiste Province of the

Oblates. Ordained in June 1936, his first obedience was that of bursar at the Hudson novitiate. From there, he was sent to Notre Dame de Lourdes parish as both curate and bursar. In 1943, he was assigned to the Natick scholasticate as professor and bursar. In his next two posts, first at Saint Jean Baptiste, and then in Colebrook, New Hampshire, he added the position of propagandist to his other accomplishments. He arrived at Saint Jean Baptiste as pastor in September 1952 and immediately set to work.

Fr. Henri Bolduc, O.M.I.

Blessed with strong administrative and personal qualities, Father Bolduc brought ingenuity and originality to his new position. He was straightforward and direct, unafraid to grab hold of a difficult situation and bring it to a successful conclusion. Once he gave his word, he followed through by every means possible. Under his guidance, parish life expanded remarkably on all fronts.

Father Bolduc arrived at a propitious time for the parish which was entering a difficult and complex period. Grave problems needed to be solved and many transformations had to be implemented to prepare a strong future.

The Korean War ended on July 27, 1953, and the troops returned to the country. That year the bridge on Aiken Street was renamed the Ouellette Bridge, in honor of Joseph Ouellette, from Saint Louis parish, killed in action in 1950. He had been awarded a posthumous Congressional Medal of Honor in 1951. On Thursday afternoon, September 10, 1953, the city held a hero's welcome for Sergeant Alfred Laurent, a parishioner of Sainte Jeanne d'Arc. He was the first Lowell citizen to be freed from a Communist prison, where he had been detained for thirty-seven months.

Lowell's industry never recovered from the upheavals of the post-war years. In 1947, the industrialists of the city had announced that with the end of World War II they foresaw an uncertain future, at best, for the few mills still operating in spite of the gigantic collapse of the 1920s and 30s. The Korean War had delayed the inevitable, but history now ran its course. In 1955, the huge Merrimack Mills, reorganized in 1952, and employing 1,800 people, closed their doors. The Boot Mills followed suit in 1956. Of all the old textile mills in Lowell, only one, the Lawrence Mills, remained open. Electronics and a host of small industries took up some of the slack, but, in spite of everything, the population of Lowell — from 1950 to 1960 — diminished from 97,249 to 92,107 persons.

The parish, for its part, was beginning to feel its age. Located in a timeworn part of the city, many facts had to be reckoned with. First of all, families were not as large as before. Then, young couples were no longer interested in inhabiting the old tenement blocks, preferring to live in their own homes in the suburbs. Thus, from 1950 to 1955, the parish census showed a reduction from 2,534 families encompassing 8,908 individuals to 1,876 families numbering 7,394 individuals. By 1955, it was no longer necessary to sell tickets for the Christmas Midnight Mass. At the dawn of urban renewal, in 1960, the parish totaled 1,519 families containing 6,455 individuals.

Faced with these realities, Father Bolduc worked out a plan of action which first sought to ensure the stability and the future of the parochial schools. The professional competence of the schools was at a high level and enrollment continued to be one of the strongest in the city. In 1955, the schools received 1,243 children, 645 boys and 598 girls. Although three-fourths of the high school students came from other parishes, Saint Jean Baptiste parish itself had 1,002 of its own children in the schools. The budget amounted to $50,000. Although both the professionalism of these schools and enrollment in them were excellent, the physical condition of the buildings left a lot to be desired.

For the 75th anniversary of the parish, the old school structures had been repainted and refurbished, but all these buildings dated back to the nineteenth century. This time the interiors had to be reconstructed from top to bottom, in order to be more in conformity with the requirements and pedagogical theories of the day. The classrooms had to be modernized, making them more airy and bright. New desks were needed, new laboratories, new libraries, etc.

Father Bolduc, with the help of his bursar, Father Donat Morrissette, undertook a vast campaign of repairs. The parish was aging, the population was diminishing, but immediate action was imperative to ensure the future of the schools and the success of the enterprise. The pastor called together a committee of representative men of the parish to explain his program to them.

The modernization campaign, as he saw it, would extend over a four-year period and would probably cost over $100,000. If each month one dollar per family were collected by going from door to door, enough money could be raised in four or five years to make needed repairs each summer, as the money came in. This could be done without accumulating debt and without interfering with the school program. After some thought, the men found this program to be both reasonable and practical. The work would begin in the *Collège* Saint Joseph which housed the eighth grade and the boys' high school. The men would form a Parish Committee made up of 200 men and women volunteers. Each member would be responsible for visiting ten families per month. The pastor assumed the responsibility for describing the project to the parishioners from the pulpit, and for coordinating its implementation.

Successfully launched, the committee was able to raise $2,249. 95 during the first month, October 1955; and 1,037 parishioners promised to donate one dollar per month. The November collection brought in $1,837.00 and the total for the first twelve months was $18,572.04. The carpenters went to work and by the end of August 1956, they had finished the reconstruction of the six classrooms on the first floor of the *collège*. From the start of the campaign in October 1955, to Father Bolduc's departure in August 1958, the parishioners donated $43,010.15. The entire first floor of the *collège,* and about half of the second had been completely renovated. It would then be up to his successor, Father Donat Morrissette, to complete what had been undertaken, and begin the renovation of the elementary school.

As the parish aged, so too did the rectory which was already old in 1887 when it had been purchased. One morning, as the Fathers came down from their rooms for morning prayers in the chapel, they noticed that during the night the wall in one of the parlors had bulged, and the ceiling had dropped. The engineer who was consulted concluded that a special Providence had been watching over the Fathers, for, according to him, they could have found themselves in the cellar some morning, buried in the ruins, since the whole front of the house was on the verge of collapsing.

The engineer's advice was heeded, with the result that in the summer of 1956, the necessary repairs were undertaken, with the asistance of the lay brothers. The front of the house, which was the oldest part, was reinforced with cement pillars and iron posts in the cellar. Steel beams and iron columns were set in place on the second floor, to support the weight of the third. Taking advantage of the situation the parlors of the first floor were refurbished with oak woodwork and acoustic ceilings. This was a considerable improvement over the old visiting rooms with their glass partitions where everything could be seen and sometimes overheard!

In 1958, it was time to undertake badly needed improvements to the convent of the Little Sisters of the Holy Family. There were now eight nuns living in these quarters, but hardly any changes had been made to the convent since its construction in 1907. For the time being, running water was added to more rooms, and the dormitories were divided into small rooms, leaving more extensive alterations for a later date.

Saint Jean Baptiste rectory, in January 1956, housed twenty Oblates: Fathers Henri Bolduc, Donat Morrissette, Roland Bourgeois, Eméry Lyonnais, Roméo Ferland, Roméo Murphy, Normand Fillion, Emile Rossignol, Charles Dénizot and Brothers Louis Desjadons, Robert Béliveau, Donat Joyal, all of whom were assigned to parish ministry; and in residence were Fathers Eugène Turcotte, Edouard Carrier, Achille Lhermitte, Égide Beaudoin, Marcel Généreux, Joseph Débergh, Léo Staves, and Raoul Chabot.

As of July 1954, the rectory had ceased to function as a provincial house, for with the expansion of the province and its activities, the provincial, Father Ferdinand Richard, and his assistants, had been obliged to find a more spacious and convenient center of administration. They had chosen a beautiful twenty-three room home in the Nesmith Street residential section of Lowell. In the summer of 1954, the provincial administration transferred to this new site. One of the first visitors to the new residence was President Paul Magloire of Haiti on February 7, 1955 while he was touring this country.

The Oblate missions were expanding. In 1954, the Saint Jean Baptiste Province had 126 priests, forty of whom were in Haiti, and the Missionary Association counted 4,350 members. *Le Missionnaire Oblat* had replaced *L'Apostolat* as the society's publication in July 1953. Published in the United States by the province itself, this new periodical kept the public informed of Oblate works and needs. In a single year, the Procure de Mazenod, later known as the Oblate Foreign Missions Office, sent $30,000 and 300 cases of clothing and useful objects to the missionaries. All of this came from the dedication of the missionary circles and the members of the Association.

This generosity of the people was not restricted to the Oblate missions in Haiti. In September 1955, Bishop Plumey, from Cameroon, in Africa, preached from the pulpit of Saint Jean Baptiste church in favor of his country. He was profoundly moved by the generosity of the parishioners. Before him, in February 1955, Bishop Mabathoana from Léribé, in Basutoland (now Lesotho), had also benefited from the generous Christian spirit of the parish.

The Oblate spirit during these years was being implemented in many new places. One development, among others, came from Canada. In 1952, Father Louis-Marie Parent, O.M.I. had founded a secular institute for young women called the Oblate Missionaries of the Immaculate Conception. The new institute grew very rapidly—in 1957 after only five years it had 676 members.

These young women, who took annual vows, wore a lay habit and accepted any work in society wherever their lived example could help spread the love of Christ.

Given these conditions, it was only natural that this type of Institute would seek to establish itself in Lowell. On December 1, 1956, Father Parent sent four of these Oblate missionaries to the city to open the first house of the Institute in New England. The four pioneers—Gabrielle Lachance, Yvette Roberge, Jeanne Dumont, and Simone Lessard—took up residence at 355 Pawtucket Street, in the house owned by the nuns of the orphanage. They began to work as sacristans, two of them at Saint Jean Baptiste, and the other two at Saint Joseph church. As their society became known, candidates flocked to them. In 1958, they moved to 56 Fairmont Street, which became their center for recruiting throughout New England. That same year, another Oblate Missionary of the Immaculate Conception, Jeannette Lambert, became the receptionist at Saint Jean Baptiste rectory, while another became secretary at the Procure de Mazenod, in 1960. The provincial house had one of these committed young women as a housekeeper, beginning in 1957, and another became the secretary for the Oblate Vocations Office in 1959.

This flowering of activities was not confined to the Oblates. It extended also to the work of the Grey Nuns. On May 30, 1954, Archbishop Cushing came to bless the new central building of Saint Joseph Hospital. This was the beginning of an expansion plan that would last for the next twenty years and in the end would provide the hospital with totally new and modern facilities. The number of admissions increased constantly, while the school of nursing was granting about twenty diplomas per year. More and more elaborate services were being demanded and provided. According to the expansion plan, the older wooden buildings of the Corporation Hospital would be demolished in stages, and replaced, one section at a time, with new brick structures. The whole would eventually be connected in the form of a "U" with the main body of the building and entryway on Pawtucket Street. Once this central section had been inaugurated, new east and west pavilions were projected.

Although the old Saint Joseph Home for the elderly had closed, the reasons for its existence were still present, with an even greater urgency and necessity. Everyone felt its absence deeply. In November 1955, Father Bolduc penned these words about the lost *hospice:*

> Ever since that time, the population has regretted the disappearance of this institution, and, under the current conditions, the call for another has become almost a clamor. At the present time our plans are not sufficiently finalized to announce anything definite, but before long we hope that the desire of the older generation will be satisfied.

As a matter of fact, Father Bolduc had been working on this problem since 1953. He had turned first of all to the Grey Nuns of Québec, who could not accept for lack of personnel. He then entered into negotiations with the Grey Nuns of Ottawa, who were most receptive. In 1950, their general administration in Ottawa had erected their establishments in the United States into an autonomous province, under the patronage of Saint Joseph. They had transformed a residence on Rolfe Street in Lowell into their provincial house and formation center, which they named Mount Saint Joseph. The new province was seeking ministries for the dedicated commitment of its sisters. Recruiting was going very well. The province was flourishing. In Saint Jean Baptiste church, on Thursday morning, July 26, 1955, Archbishop Cushing presided at the bestowing of habits of the first postulants in the Saint Joseph Province of the Grey Nuns.

In 1956, Mother Saint André Corsini, having ended her mandate as superior-general, became the provincial superior of the Saint Joseph Province. She was a Lowell native, from Saint Joseph parish, and very much in touch with the feelings of the people regarding a home for the elderly. With Father Bolduc, she began actively seeking a solution. In November 1955, the nuns had purchased, under very advantageous conditions, three farms totalling seventy-three acres at the west end of Varnum Avenue, in Sainte Jeanne d'Arc parish. This was the site selected by Mother Corsini and her assistants on which to build the much longed-for nursing home, as soon as the necessary permissions and funds could be obtained.

Saint Joseph Province continued to develop. In 1957, when the Commonwealth of Massachusetts requisitioned the property on Rolfe Street for the expansion of Lowell State College, the provincial administration moved to 25 Fairmont Street, very near to the residence of the Oblates of the Immaculate Conception, and behind the Oblate provincial house, on Nesmith Street. The following year, in May 1958, the nuns acquired a magnificent property in Framingham, Massachusetts, which they transformed into a novitiate and house of formation.

The 1950s were years of intense Marian devotion. As we have seen, in 1950, Pope Pius XII had defined the Dogma of the Assumption of Mary. As a follow-up, in 1953, he published the Encyclical *Fulgens Corona,* which declared 1954 as a Marian Year, in honor of the centennial of the proclamation of the dogma of the Immaculate Conception by Pius IX. The centennial celebration, in 1957 and 1958, of the apparitions of the Blessed Virgin at Lourdes, closed a decade of Marian ceremonies.

As Oblates of Mary Immaculate, Father Bolduc and his associates applied all their zeal to ensure the success of these events within the parish. First, on September 8, 1953, the feast of the Birth of Mary, the pilgrim statue from

Fatima spent three days in the parish. Thousands of people crowded into Saint Jean Baptiste church to pray before the statue and take part in the Marian hours preached by Father Marcel Généreux. Many families, in addition to participating in the devotions at church, insisted upon enthroning a statue of Our Lady of Fatima, Queen of Families, in their homes. The pastor seized upon this tide of Marian devotion by consecrating the parish to the Immaculate Heart of Mary, as Father Turcotte had done before him to the Sacred Heart of Jesus.

The grand celebrations of the Marian Year required extensive planning. The Oblates of the Saint Jean Baptiste Province set up a central office called *Le Service du Centenaire* in order to coordinate all the events. Under the capable leadership of Father Marcel Généreux, this bureau, through the Fathers, launched a Crusade of Rosaries. Throughout all of New England and Haiti 16,319,535 rosaries were recited for the Pope's intention and for "the triumph of Mary Immaculate in the world."

In Lowell the grotto at the orphanage was selected as the regional center for Franco-American pilgrimages during the Marian Year. Each Sunday, from May to August in 1954, a large group came — there would be fifteen pilgrimages in all, one for each mystery of the rosary. The services, which included a blessing of the sick, Benediction of the Blessed Sacrament, and veneration of relics, attracted the faithful in droves. Four thousand persons were present for the closing triduum, held from August 13 to 16, to participate in the crowning of the Virgin and to take part in the candlelight procession. On this occasion the pastors of the five Franco-American parishes of Lowell collectively offered their respective parishes to Mary.

The hundredth anniversary of the apparitions at Lourdes was observed in 1958. A solemn triduum was held in the parish from December 6 to 8, and pilgrimages by the various societies to Notre Dame de Lourdes church, which had been designated by the archbishop as a privileged church to obtain the indulgences of the centennial, succeeded one another.

Along with all the events surrounding this Marian epoch, the parish shared in the significant honor of another event related to Mary. On March 28, 1958, while the Fathers were at dinner, a package arrived at the rectory by special courier. It was immediately brought to the addressee, Father Joseph Debergh, who opened the package to a burst of applause for it contained the first copy of a new book *Our Lady of Beauraing* written by Father Debergh in collaboration with Don Sharkey. It was the first book of great significance on this subject published in the United States.

After World War II, the Oblate Province in the southern part of Belgium, which was devastated and in ruins, sent Father Achille Lhermitte to the United States for the purpose of raising money to help in the reconstruction of their houses of formation. Having arrived in Lowell in October 1946, Father

Lhermitte founded the Our Lady of Grace Society, whose purpose was to offer for sale in the United States, holy cards, religious art, and especially visual aids for religious instruction, imported from Europe. The project thrived under his care and became a huge success. He was a good priest, humble and devoted, and very intelligent and a skilled organizer. As the clientele continued to increase, Father Joseph Debergh arrived from Belgium in October 1947, to assist his colleague in the enterprise. Both priests lived in the rectory and set up their office in the basement of the Eno residence, on Race Street. Later, they moved to the first floor at 784 Merrimack Street, only a few steps from the church.

Fathers Lhermitte and Debergh, Belgians by birth and both Oblates of Mary Immaculate, had a very deep devotion to the Mother of God, particularly to her as Our Lady of Grace, or as she was better known in their homeland, Our Lady of Beauraing. Beauraing is the name of the little village in Belgium where the Blessed Virgin appeared thirty-three times to five children from November 1932 to January 1933. Devotion to Our Lady of Beauraing was almost unknown at that time in the United States. So, Father Debergh decided, shortly after his arrival in this country, to spend what free time he had, giving lectures and talks on the subject of these apparitions. In a short span of time, the message of the Virgin with the Golden Heart began to spread, attracting followers. Before long, the apostolate of Our Lady of Beauraing outgrew the time Father Debergh could devote to it. It required a separate organization. In 1950, with the help of two young women from the J.O.C., Doris Poisson and Ursula Belley, he founded the Pro Maria Committee, and affiliated it with the committee at the sanctuary in Belgium.

The sale of holy cards prospered to such an extent that, beginning in 1952, Father Debergh had to take on the role of a traveling salesman. Father Lhermitte managed the office and the shipping while Father Debergh spent five to six months each year on the road throughout the country. In the evening, having completed his rounds, he spread the word about Our Lady of Beauraing by means of slide shows, evenings of prayer in private homes, and radio talks. The result was a flood of requests to join the *Union Mariale de Beauraing,* a prayer association directed by the guardians of the sanctuary, and administered in the United States by the Pro Maria Committee. So, the publication of his book, in 1958, was the joyous crowning point of his dedication. It was also a major step forward towards the great day when Our Lady of Beauraing would be universally known and loved in the United States.

The parish and its institutions were flourishing, but there were, nonetheless, some disturbing shadows in the picture. With his good judgment, and a perceptive eye, Father Bolduc could write in 1955:

From a spiritual point of view, we still have a good core of fervent parishioners who can be counted on for full cooperation. Their faith is still strong and their Catholicism is sincere and steadfast. We notice, however, a marked difference from thirty years ago. Home life is not as solid, separations and divorces are becoming more numerous, even civil marriages after divorce are increasing noticeably.

Statistics backed up these observations. From 1952 to 1955, the records show that the number of persons who did not fulfill their Easter duties increased from 275 to 347, while the number of unblessed marriages grew from 222 to 326. Also, Little Canada itself was aging. Certain run-down areas were emptying little by little and attracting only transients and undesirables. The lower section of Moody Street, and other fringe areas, were seen as being disadvantaged and even disreputable.

Mass attendance and the frequenting of the sacraments had remained stable while participation in the old devotions like the Holy Hours on Tuesdays, First Friday services, nightly rosary, triduums and annual retreats, tended to diminish. The Tuesday Holy Hour of Adoration and Reparation, begun in 1911 by Father Watelle was attended on certain nights by only seventy-five persons. Meeting with the Fathers, the pastor reluctantly decided to hold the Holy Hour once a month only, on First Friday evenings.

The Church at large in those days was looking for answers to the pastoral problems noted by Father Bolduc and posed by a more and more hectic and agitated modern life. Pope Pius XII, as head of the Church, introduced several remedies, especially in the areas of liturgy and social teaching. In 1957, he modified the laws of fasting and abstinence to allow more of the faithful to receive Holy Communion. Fasting before Communion was reduced to three hours for solid food and one hour for non-alcoholic beverages. He ordered numerous changes in the rites of Holy Week and other days of the year, to allow more laity to take part. In his encyclicals and teachings, he made clear pronouncements on the important questions of the day, and on the means to be taken to confront the evils of the times.

The priests at Saint Jean Baptiste went along wholeheartedly with this liturgical renewal. The pastor and his associates made the recommended adaptations and decided to attempt a new approach to the annual retreat of 1957. First, they did away with the old formula of separating people into categories by sex and age that had always existed, and substituted a new one of a general retreat for everyone that included biblical readings and the singing of the Gélineau modern Psalm arrangements. These services were held twice a week and lasted throughout the Lenten period. The Fathers brought in famous preachers of the time to conduct this new type of retreat. For Lent in 1958, they brought the celebrated Dominican Father Dumas to Lowell. Although these sessions were well-attended, this new approach did not have the hoped-for success, so the priests found it necessary to revert to a modified version of the former annual retreats by category.

During this same period, the old parish societies began to show their age. Presence at meetings and monthly exercises, although still good, was diminishing. But the societies were still strong in numbers. The *Dames de Sainte-Anne* for married women, had 900 active members in 1956, the *Congréganistes de Notre Dame de Lourdes* for single women had 400; the Third Order of men and women had 200 members enrolled in its ranks. The Holy Name Society for all men, married and not, which had absorbed the *Ligue du Sacré-Coeur* and *La Sainte Famille* totaled 650 members. The *Enfants de Marie, Anges Gardiens,* and *Croisade* had become societies for elementary school children.

With the changes in lifestyle, the old confraternities had to alter the type of their activities. After 1958, there were no more stage plays or movies, and hardly any concerts. The parish cinema was no match for television or the local movie houses which themselves were featuring cinemascope and stereophonic sound to keep their customers. The final Sunday evening movie for adults was shown in the parish hall in January 1955. At the request of the parents, the Sunday afternoon films for children continued until January 1956 when they also ceased for good. The last two films to be shown in the parish hall were *Journal d'un Curé de Campagne,* a French film based on a Georges Bernanos novel, which was presented by the Holy Name Society, in December 1956, and the famous *Song of Bernadette* shown on December 7,1958, in honor of the centennial of the Lourdes apparitions.

Stage plays, which for quite some time had been limited to the annual high school presentations, stopped completely after 1958. Only the Saint Joseph School of Nursing continued for some time longer to present an annual play in English.

With the departure of Charles Bélanger as organist, the musical orientation of the parish began to change. Liturgical music and sacred songs replaced popular concerts. Very few of these were held in the hall and they were mostly religious in nature. For all practical purposes, the tradition of popular musical entertainment had ended and would only be resurrected with movies and plays for the celebration of the centennial of the parish.

Father Bolduc, who had studied music, was interested in deepening the choir's knowledge of liturgical and religious music with Maurice Pépin. Upon arriving, the latter had immediately begun the task of modernizing and repairing the organ. Under his direction, 790 new pipes were added in 1952, bringing the total to 3,000. At a cost of $10,000, a modern console was installed with three new keyboards, seventy-two stops, and twenty-one valves. The whole was interconnected with twenty-two miles of wiring and 2,926 silver contacts. The organist had hardly begun his duties when, as a born educator, he resigned from his post in the summer of 1954 to become a music teacher at Dracut High School.

His successor, Professor Paul-Emile Letendre, arrived in the parish with impressive professional credentials. He held a Bachelor's degree and a Licentiate in Music from the National Conservatory of Music in Montréal, and was a graduate of the *Schola Cantorum* of the University of Montréal. He had been organist at the cathedral of Sherbrooke and at the cathedral of Saint John in New Brunswick, before coming to New England and to Lowell. Beginning his new duties in September 1954, he presented, on the following April 3, *The Seven Last Words of Christ* by Dubois, sung by the augmented Saint Jean Baptiste choir. It remains justly memorable. He was a man of great talent who brought together musically gifted parishioners. With them, in 1956 and 1957, he organized a choir among the members of the Holy Name Society, as well as a choir school for young boys. This school, an initiative dear to both Professor Letendre and the pastor, became affiliated with *L'Union Mondiale des Petits Chanteurs de la Croix de Bois* and they followed the model of the *Petits Chanteurs*. The *Petits Chanteurs de Saint Jean Baptiste,* made up of twelve boys, quickly became renowned. When they sang with the full choir, other parishes envied Saint Jean Baptiste. Father Bolduc, who was extremely enthusiastic about the success of the group, had the joy of hearing "his" little singers join their voices to those of the *Petits Chanteurs* of Paris.

On September 18, 1956, *Les Petits Chanteurs de la Côte d'Azur* had presented a concert in the parish hall that was very well received. In 1957, the famous *Petits Chanteurs de la Croix de Bois de Paris*, under the direction of Monsignor Fernand Maillet, announced a world tour to mark their fiftieth anniversary. By chance this tour began in Lowell. On Sunday morning, January 27, the *Petits Chanteurs* from Paris sang at the High Mass, joined, on this occasion, by the *Petits Chanteurs de Saint Jean Baptiste.* Never had the parish been so proud.

The changes in the social activities of the parish began to require modifications to the physical plant. The *Dames de Sainte-Anne,* as noted earlier, remained numerous and active, although there was a slight increase in the average age of its members. Besides their annual card parties, they raised funds by hosting bean suppers. The men of the Holy Name also organized card parties, and held outdoor barbecues.

It became more and more evident that the old St. Joseph Hall required refurbishing, but especially that it needed to have a kitchen and a cloakroom, – eating cold beans with one's hat on one's knees was far from being appealing.

In July 1957, the *Dames de Sainte-Anne* and the *Congréganistes* began to make new drapes for the hall's windows, and the men of the Holy Name Society undertook to repaint the interior. By the end of summer, a cloakroom had been installed, thanks to the fund-raising efforts of the men, and a new kitchen, thanks to those of the women.

Activities for the young always presented a certain degree of difficulty to organize. But now, starting in July 1956, dances were held in St. Jean Baptiste Center on Friday nights from seven o'clock until eleven, always under the surveillance of the Fathers.

The J.O.C. tended more and more to limit its activities to recruiting for marriage preparation courses. Yet, in December 1953, they raised enough money to present the city with a lighted crèche painted on wood for the grounds of City Hall. This gift to the city of its first municipal Christmas manger signaled a symbolic last gesture of the J.O.C. for, after 1958, the group dissolved.

The old *Association des Anciens Élèves du Collège Saint Joseph* celebrated its final activities in a grand fashion. On November 2, 1952, shortly after Father Bolduc's arrival, the members marked the fortieth anniversary of their foundation. Harmony among the members of the aging association and their attachment to its ideals were manifest in the procession to Saint Jean Baptiste church, the splendid banquet at the Rex restaurant, the beautiful souvenir booklet and the presence of many brothers and dignitaries from out of town at the commemoration. The May 1953 banquet, organized to celebrate the fiftieth anniversary in religious life of Brother Louis Viateur, provided the alumni with an opportunity to demonstrate, in an even more personal manner, their affection for "their brothers." That evening, Brother Louis Viateur, surrounded by the members and officers of the Association, received the insignia with rosette of an *Officier de l'Instruction Publique* from the hands of the French Consul, François Charles-Roux. This honor, as well as the evening celebration, were representative of the Catholic and French ideals of the past generations of Saint Joseph's students. Theirs had been a formation imbued with an ethnic, patriotic, and religious vision that had nourished several generations of Franco-Americans and produced outstanding results. Businessmen, religious, professionals, priests, workers, and heads of families had acquired during their elementary school years the fundamental components of a formation that had borne lasting fruit for them all their lives, and at all levels of American society.

The work of the Marist Brothers in the education of the young received yet another mark of appreciation in 1957 when Brother Stéphane received the *Palmes Académiques* from France, for a lifetime of service to education and the promotion of French cultural life in New England. Yet, in spite of past glories and present support, the old ideals of the *Anciens Élèves,* which had once flourished, failed to be passed on to a new generation, the fruit of different times. Faced with the difficulty of recruiting new members, and given the lack of interest even of a new generation of Brothers, the Association was dissolved in 1956.

None of the transitions or social transformations, which took place in the 1950s, were as painful or as difficult to face as those affecting the role of the French language in Franco-American life. *L'Étoile,* which for economic reasons had been publishing only twice a week, would cease publication entirely on August 9, 1957. That same year, on Friday, March 29, the final meeting of the Lowell chapter of *L'Alliance Française* took place. The last French play was presented by the high school girls in the spring of 1957. At the *collège* the final curtain had already fallen in January 1954. A last effort by Brother Louis Viateur to present one more production, in 1956, collapsed for lack of interest on the part of the boys. The few columns still written in French also disappeared from the school paper, *The Lookout.*

Some efforts at turning the situation around were attempted, however. The *Locale Tancrède Blanchette,* a local chapter of the *Artisans* fraternal society began an annual French spelling bee among the parochial schools in 1956. In a short time, the idea caught on, and the contest spread to all the Franco-American centers throughout New England, with regional competitions being held. These spelling bees remained very popular for quite a while. About

Brother Louis Viateur, F.M.S.

this time the *Artisans* of Manchester, New Hampshire, started a French essay contest among the schools which also expanded throughout New England, including Lowell.

The *Fédération Féminine Franco-Américaine,* including its Lowell affiliate, launched a region-wide biennial French Oral contest, in 1953. The closing competition among the finalists from the various regions of New England was held at Assumption Preparatory School in Worcester.

Thanks to these diverse initiatives, many of the young people of the period could derive benefit from their heritage and take pride in carrying it with them joyfully into the future.

The loss of *L'Étoile* was deeply felt, it was sorely missed, and could not be made up for at the time. For any local news in French, people had to fall back, for better or worse, on the small newspaper *L'Écho,* published monthly by the C.M.A.C. The most fervent in favor of French subscribed to *Le Travailleur* of Worcester, a literary weekly of international renown.

The question of the French language, its teaching, and the way it was spoken by the young, was a pressing concern for the pastor, preoccupied with the well-being of the parish and its various works. In the parish, all the preaching, services, and the teaching of catechism were done in French. In the schools, it was becoming more and more evident that the French language was less understood than it had been, and that teaching it was becoming more difficult.

Father Bolduc decided to invite the pastors of the five Franco-American parishes to a Friday, November 16, 1956, 9:30 a.m. meeting at the rectory, in an attempt to solve, or try to find a solution to the difficult language problem. Present at the meeting were Oblate Fathers Eugène Labrie from Sainte Jeanne d'Arc, Lucien Brassard from Notre Dame de Lourdes, Victor Alexander from Sainte Marie, along with the diocesan priests Georges Duplessis from Saint Louis and Paul Martin from Sainte Thérèse in Dracut. Each of these parishes had a parochial school and was sending its students to Saint Joseph's High Schools. Saint Louis also had a high school academy for girls. Father Bolduc compiled a summary of the discussions at the meeting for the parish archives:

The question of the day is the teaching of catechism and French.

a) The catechism is less understood because of French. Should it be taught in English, with English textbooks? And the prayers? Do the children understand what they are saying? From their confessions, it seems that the children understand very little.

b) As for French, how successful are we in teaching it? It is clear and has been noticed that the children understand it less and less, and speak it very badly, with a few exceptions. This is due for the most part to the lack of practice within the families. Today the children instinctively speak to us in English. Shall we continue to teach them a grammar that presents difficulties and which, according to many, makes the students develop a dislike for French with the result that the children refuse, or hate to speak it.

As for the catechism, all agree on the fact that concessions will have to be made, because knowledge of the truths of their faith comes before the practice of the French language. According to everyone, we have arrived at the point of decision. Will we teach this subject only in high school or in the grade school also? And what shall we do about the prayers? In both languages? Opinions differ and we are not fully qualified to make any pronouncement on the possibility of achieving good results by teaching in both languages.

Where French is concerned, it was suggested that it be limited to "Conversational" French so that the young generation can continue to understand and even speak it somewhat well. Here again, the question arises of teaching it.

Resolution: In order to arrive at a more enlightened decision, we resolve to call a general meeting with the major and local superiors of our teaching communities, as well as the school principals and directors of studies, so as to discuss the matter with the pastors. After this consultation, we will be able to arrive at a course of action that will bear fruit and also guarantee the success of the teaching in our schools, while ensuring the future of our Franco-American parishes.

The planned plenary meeting was held, as announced, on Sunday, December 9, at two in the afternoon in the girls' high school. All six pastors were present, except for Father Alexander, who could not be there, plus the principals of the elementary schools, the superiors of the communities of Saint Jean Baptiste, Sainte Jeanne d'Arc, Notre Dame de Lourdes, the provincial directress of studies of the Sisters of the Assumption, Sister Louis Robert, provincial directress of studies for the Grey Nuns, Sister Sainte Célestine, delegated by the mother provincial of the Grey Nuns, Sister Hélène de la Croix, principal of Saint Joseph High School, Brother Conrad, director of the Collège Saint Joseph and Brother Louis Viateur. The following is the text of the report as written by Sister Sainte Estelle, who was chosen as secretary:

As requested, Sister Sainte Célestine, S.G.C. read the report of the special meetings held by the Grey Nuns, and Sister Saint Léandre, S A.S.V. summarized the conclusions arrived at by the Sisters of the Assumption.

The discussion was opened and proceeded as follows:

Reverend Father Lucien Brassard (Pastor of Notre Dame de Lourdes): Insisted strongly on a bilingual education throughout the course of studies and suggested the writing of a bilingual textbook for the teaching of Religion. "If necessary, let French replace Latin," he said, "it is a part of the formation!"

Father Georges Duplessis (Pastor of Saint Louis de France): Argued that we are in a country where English is the principal language and the other languages become secondary. Therefore, for the good of the child, he should be given a vocabulary with which he will be familiar. Teaching religion in two languages would be confusing to him. Therefore, religion should be taught only in English throughout the elementary and secondary schools. Prayers, however, should be taught and learned only in French.

On the subject of teaching the French Language, the traditional method is meaningless. Since the main thing is to speak French correctly and understand it, the method of "Conversational French" should be adopted at least up to the fourth or fifth grade.

Brother Louis Viateur: "According to my personal experience from 53 years of teaching, French today is a foreign language in our milieu. The traditional method of teaching French is a waste of time." He advises using "Chardenal" as a text which he has been using successfully for two years. A survey in the boys' high school revealed that ONE out of 180 requested that religious instruction be given in French. At the elementary level, it could be done in the two languages as need be.

Father Paul Martin (Pastor of Sainte Thérèse in Dracut): Recommends bilingual education. His objection to the exclusive use of English in grammar school is that it gives rise to another problem: understanding the sermons in church. For the high school level, he suggests a bilingual textbook, but the teaching in English.

Brother Conrad Joseph, director: Suggests the teaching of religion in English in the high school, and in French in the elementary grades, with English if necessary.

Father Eugène Labrie (Pastor of Sainte Jeanne d'Arc): Suggests that in the parishes where one sees the possibility of its being done, that the pastor ask for the cooperation of the parents on this highly important question.

The nuns state that they are ready to comply with the decisions of the pastors.

Father Henri Bolduc then summed up the items on the agenda and read the report of the decisions taken:

A.   The teaching of Catechism:
    1) High School:
        a) An English textbook, explained in French while teaching;
        b) The choice of a text left to the directors, after mutual consultation;
        c) Prayers should be taught in both languages.
    2) Elementary School:
        a) French or English text, according to the individual need of the student;
        b) Prayers in both languages, or the decision may be left to the pastor of each parish, according to the difficulties which arise.

B: The teaching of French:
    1) High School:
        a) Adopt the "Conversational French" method with a French-English textbook to be as practical as possible;
        b) Require four years of French, although no student should be failed on account of French. In any case, the new text chosen should eliminate the difficulty.
    2) Elementary School:
        a) French religious vacabulary in the first year;
        b) "Conversational French" up to the 4th grade:
        c) Begin reading in the 5th grade;
        d) Elementary grammar taught in the 6th, 7th, and 8th grades; conversation always;
        e) First Communion in the second year, except in the schools where a kindergarten exists.

In September 1957, the Saint Joseph parochial schools began their school year with 792 children at the grammar school level, and 367 students — of which 105 were from the parish — at the high school level. The schools continued to function well. In 1954, a group of generous laypersons had established a scholarship fund for the high school graduates, more and more of whom were pursuing their education in the colleges and universities of the region.

The only shadow in the picture appeared in January 1956 when the Corporation of the Locks and Canals decided to sell the Aiken Street Park to the Stop and Shop supermarket chain, for the construction of one of their stores. The parish, the residents of Little Canada and the C.M.A.C. objected strongly to this sale because the land had, up to that time, been used as a playing field by the schools and the sports teams of the area, and it was the only park and open space available for sports in Little Canada. Also, many merchants and shopkeepers feared the strong competition on their business, which was already rather limited. Since the land could not be sold without the approval of the city, it was hoped that the City Council would block this sale, and buy the land in the public interest. With that in mind, a delegation of parishioners from Little Canada and the C.M.A.C., joined by the pastor and Father Donat Morrissette, appeared twice before the City Council which decided, however, not to buy the land and allowed it to be sold. To appease the people, the city manager, a few months later, said that the vacant lot at the corner of Bowers and Fletcher Streets would be converted into an athletic field for the high school—a project that never saw the light of day.

At this same time also, a solution appeared for the persistent problem regarding the future of Saint Joseph church, on Lee Street. For years, it had been serving only for a few weekday Masses and on Sunday mornings. Several solutions had been proposed, even the idea of selling it, to provide parking space for downtown stores. But, in the course of a business meeting with Archbishop Cushing, Father Labrie, the provincial, and Father Bolduc had mentioned the possibility of turning it into a shrine dedicated to Saint Joseph, with a Catholic Center in the basement. The idea pleased the archbishop so much that he refused to allow any other solution. As a result, the provincial council decided, in May 1956, to make of the old Saint Joseph church a center of devotion to Saint Joseph the Worker. Situated in the heart of the city, it was ideally suited to accommodate the piety of the workers and the prayers of the numerous passers-by.

Divine Providence seemed to be in agreement with the decision, for on May 1st, 1956, occurred the first observance of the Feast of Saint Joseph the Worker, instituted during the previous year by Pope Pius XII. It was intended as a counterweight to the annual May 1st Communist demonstrations which had become the traditional celebration of the proletariat in Europe.

Father Eugène Noury, who was named director of the shrine, had been present in Rome, in 1955, when this feast was instituted. Zealous and accustomed to challenges, he was the ideal person for the position. He had been the first member of the province to join the military as a chaplain during World War II. Attached to the first Philippine Regiment of the United States, he had not hesitated, for the well-being of his soldiers, to appear before Congress in Washington, to ask for the repeal of certain unjust laws affecting the status of the Philippine soldiers in the United States. His solid and down-to-earth piety was such that in his hands the shrine flourished immediately.

The initial plan was to inaugurate the shrine with a special novena beginning on May 1, 1956, the first anniversary of the institution of the Feast of Saint Joseph the Worker. However, since the archbishop could not be present on that date, the ceremony was delayed for ten days, and set instead for May 10th, the feast of the Ascension. On that Thursday, Archbishop Cushing, before a throng of one thousand persons, including thirty or so priests, and Bishop Collignon from Haiti, proceeded to the solemn elevation of the old temple into a shrine dedicated to Saint Joseph the Worker, patron of working people. At the end of the Mass, celebrated by Father Noury, the archbishop advanced towards the congregation. Very proud of his new shrine, and happy over the role that his decision had played in bringing the project to completion, he addressed the congregation in these terms:

> With this dedication today, Lowell becomes the first city in this part of the country to have a shrine dedicated to Saint Joseph, Patron of Workers. This is fitting because Lowell's spiritual standing, its friendship, its charity, and its friendliness is typified by the many churches which dot its area. Today we inaugurate this central shrine where the workers of the city, from its business area, may participate in various religious activities. Proof of the usefulness of such shrines is given by that to St. Anthony, in the center of Boston, where over 300,000 confessions are heard annually by the Franciscan Fathers.
>
> We could have sold this church over and over again to business interests, but we held on to it with the knowledge that some day it would become a shrine and we realized its value in this respect. We have placed the Franco-American Oblate Fathers in charge of it because they have served here for years and have the personnel to look after your needs, be they for confessions, devotions, or for special services.
>
> We urge you, the working people of Lowell, to send your petitions to Saint Joseph. A greater saint you couldn't have. We don't know a word he ever spoke or wrote, yet, next to Mary, Mother of God, he is the greatest saint in heaven. You and I are all working people and from working families, and Saint Joseph, a worker himself, will look after our needs, if only we take time to ask him. He is the patron saint of the home, the family, of a happy death, and of the universal Church.
>
> Make this your chapel of ease, a sort of central place of worship for you whose duties keep you downtown.

The future confirmed that Archbishop Cushing was right for, as early as the following year, the numbers spoke eloquently of the good being accomplished at Saint Joseph Shrine. In a single year, from May 1956 to the following May 1957, the noonday Mass was attended by 67,853 people, and the Fathers heard 27,214 confessions. In addition to the many Masses and other devotions, such as the exposition of the Blessed Sacrament twice a week,

Benediction five times a week, a perpetual novena to Saint Joseph on Tuesdays and Wednesdays, confessions were heard at all hours of the day. There were also two major special novenas, one on March 19, the feast of St. Joseph, and the other on Labor Day, in September, the day on which the celebration of May 1st is usually observed in the United States. That first year 8,366 people took part in the novena of March 19, while 6,082 did so for the one at Labor Day. Father Noury also founded the Guild of the Seven Sorrows and Seven Joys of Saint Joseph, for women who were willing to accept responsibility for the altar linen and other needs of the shrine. He also instituted the Archconfraternity of Saint Joseph with the reception of the cord of Saint Joseph by the new members, and he obtained the special indulgence for the distribution and blessing of the Saint Joseph scapular.

Although Saint Joseph church had become a shrine, it remained the property of Saint Jean Baptiste parish. On Sundays it functioned as a parish church, with Mass in French. For that matter, so as not to disrupt the religious traditions of the Franco-American population, certain exercises during the week were bilingual, held in both French and English.

Father Noury's position required so much work that Father Robert Paradis was soon assigned to him as an assistant. Also, Fathers Charles Dénizot and Eugène Fournier helped with the Masses. Brother Desjadons, who had been

Fr. Eugène Noury, O.M.I.

the sacristan for many years, continued in that position until December 1956, when two Oblates of the Immaculate Conception replaced him for the care of the altars and the sacristy. Professor Joseph Thibault, who had a considerable reputation in Canada, became the organist. Now close to retirement age, he assumed responsibility for the singing and music at the noonday and evening Masses and for the other services.

As to Brother Desjadons, it should be said that he left a deep impression at Saint Joseph. He had been baptized by Father Garin and entered the Oblates as a brother in 1897. He had spent many years as the custodian of Saint Joseph church, remaining there alone for most of the day. After his death, on April 23, 1965, at the age of eighty-eight, during the refurbishing of the shrine, notes and letters were found which he had written to the Blessed Mother during his long days alone, and tucked into an opening behind one of the statues. One of these notes which is remembered reads simply: "*Ma bonne mère,* today is my birthday. No one remembers it, but you, my mother, know it, and you are close to me."

At the same time that the work of the shrine was developing, the wish for a Catholic Center in the church basement resurfaced. In February 1956, the parish printing press, directed by Brother Robert Béliveau, was transferred there. In December, a bookstore and religious articles shop, an extension of the Librairie Baron, was opened in time for Christmas. It was placed under the able direction of two former employees of Father Baron, Délia Thellen and Lilliane Moisan. Since this store was practically the only one of its kind in the city, it was immediately successful. At Saint Jean Baptiste, the old Librairie Baron continued to operate, managed by Lucienne Bilodeau and Aurore Dion.

Also in 1956, the J.O.C., which had merged with other J.O.C. groups in the city, transferred its activities and meetings to Saint Joseph's. The marriage preparation course, directed by Father Normand Fillion, settled there permanently in 1957 after many moves from one place to another.

The increase of activity at the shrine necessitated many repairs and restorations. The old church had hardly been touched for many years. The side balconies were now condemned by the city, the electrical system was a fire hazard, and all the walls needed re-plastering. The most urgent need was addressed first. In July and August 1957, at a cost of $5,000 the electrical wiring, which had been in place since 1899, was replaced by a more modern system. Part of the money for this undertaking was raised by Mrs. Wilbert Grew who organized an immense card party at the Rex Hall, in thanksgiving for her recovery from injuries sustained in an automobile accident. In the spring of 1958 the balconies were removed and the walls re-plastered. More needed to be done, but the necessary funds were not immediately available.

The population spared no effort, neither time nor resources, to support the shrine. Societies, clubs and individuals competed with each other in undertaking a great variety of activities and projects. There were communion breakfasts, group Masses, card parties, smokers, etc. It was a point of honor, especially for the Franco-Americans, to come to the aid of *la vieille église Saint Joseph* (old St. Joseph church). As time went on, more and more people were finding the shrine to be a haven of peace and prayer. They came from all over the area. During the second year, from May 1957 to May 1958, attendance at the daily noon Mass increased to 92,128 people.

Meanwhile, Father Bolduc had his share of needed church repairs. It had been discovered that major work would have to begin as soon as possible to avoid serious damage to the outside of Saint Jean Baptiste church. The entire masonry of the structure needed pointing, especially the towers, the façade, and along the apse, where there was no mortar left in certain places allowing water to seep down into the walls. The expense would be substantial, but thanks to an obliging contractor, who offered to do the work between his other contracts and spreading it over a longer period of time, all the repairs were completed at a reasonable cost and without accumulating any debt. The work began first on the towers and the façade in the fall of 1957. By the summer of 1958, this part alone was brought to an end at a cost of $7,000. In the fall, work began on the side walls. It was discovered that the drains and gutters were in very bad shape, especially on the Moody Street side and would have to be replaced. Those on the Moody Street side were replaced at a cost of $5,000. It was then decided to finish the rest of the work on the church before replacing the side drains. The parishioners, proud of their church, responded generously to all the needs. Besides, had not Father Léo Deschâtelets, superior general of the Oblates, declared in his December 1954 visit that Saint Jean Baptiste was "one of the most beautiful, if not the most beautiful church of the Congregation"?

In September 1957, Dom Legrain, a French Benedictine monk, came through Lowell seeking funds for the reconstruction of his church, the historic Abbey of St. Benoît-sur-Loire. Escorted by Father Armand Morissette, the French Benedictine's appeal to the generosity of the people did not go unanswered, and he left with concrete proof of the love that united France to Saint Jean Baptiste parish of Lowell.

The spring of 1958 found the parish entering a period of festivities. On May 3 and 4, the *Amicalistes* celebrated the 75th anniversary of the founding of the school on Moody Street, and the 25th anniversary of *L'Amicale Saint Joseph.* The celebrations began on Saturday, May 3rd , in the parish hall, with a general reunion of former students and teachers. On Sunday morning the entire group, comprised of several hundred women and some eighty or so nuns, marched behind a band from the parish hall to Saint Jean Baptiste church for a solemn High Mass, with singing provided by the choir and *Les Petits Chanteurs*. That evening more than 600 guests gathered at the municipal auditorium for a gala banquet. The eighty nuns—who had received a very special permission to eat outside the convent—were seated at a table in the form of a cross, situated at the center of the hall. All the other tables around them were circular and surrounded theirs. This was meant to symbolize the apostolate of the sisters, that of transmitting to their charges the faith drawn from the cross of Christ. The evening and the festivities ended with paeans of praise in honor of these humble daughters of Mother d'Youville and Mother Bruyère.

These celebrations served as a prelude to other even more grandiose tributes to another branch of the Mother d'Youville family. On June 6, 7, and 8, 1958, took place with great pomp the commemoration of the 50th anniversary of the Franco-American Orphanage. The institution was flourishing, with a staff of thirty nuns, who worked very hard, day after day, looking after the children. *L'Amicale des Anciens,* founded in 1933, was also celebrating its 25th anniversary. These alumni provided precious support to the nuns. *L'Oeuvre du Pain* (Project Bread), under the direction of valiant Sister Marie-Eustelle, had hundreds of members.

In 1955, the orphanage was sheltering 198 children, of whom 110 were boys, aged 5 to 12, and 88 girls from 5 to 17 years of age. The grammar school courses were bilingual and the girls completed their high school education at Saint Joseph. That year, there were five of them studying at that level. A large number of alumni, men and women, had entered religious life and, that same year, 1955, Sister Sainte Béatrix d'Assise, S.C.Q., née Béatrice Dégagné, left for the foreign missions in China. It is also worthy of note that it was a native of the parish, Sister Sainte-Christiane, née Albertine Cayer who, as superior of the orphanage at that time, was responsible for these meticulously prepared festivities which lasted three days. On Friday evening, the 6th, Archbishop Cushing, assisted by several members of the clergy, celebrated an open air Pontifical Mass of Thanksgiving. A large square platform had been erected near the grotto for the occasion. The magnificent decorations, the moving and solemn liturgy, the great number of praying faithful, all bathed in the twilight of the day, brought back for many, memories of the great days of old.

On the following morning, Saturday, Father Bolduc celebrated a High Mass for the deceased, at the grotto. In the parish hall that afternoon, the history of the orphanage was reviewed for the public, with the help of a slide presentation. Two of the founding nuns, Sisters Sainte Zoé and Marie du Bon Conseil, were present, thus adding a note of authenticity to the proceedings.

On Sunday, the closing day of the commemoration, Father Joseph

**Archbishop Richard Cushing celebrating, June 6, 1958, the Mass for the
50th Anniversary of the Franco-American Orphanage at the outdoor altar erected
near the Grotto.**

Bouchard, chaplain of the orphanage and the *Amicale,* offered morning Mass
at the grotto for the alumni. In the evening everyone headed for the municipal
auditorium. More than 800 guests filled the main hall as well as the Liberty
Hall for the gala banquet. After the meal, a delegation of some sixty nuns, led
by Mother Saint Nazaire, general counselor from Québec, marched solemnly
to the stage, where they sat to listen to the many talks showering praises upon
them, but what emerged mainly was the gratitude of the population for these
good nuns who, in emulation of Mother Mallet and Mother d'Youville, had
dedicated their entire lives to care for orphans and children in need.

Father Bolduc's work at Saint Jean Baptiste was approaching its end,
with the termination of his assignment. One more accomplishment must be
mentioned, however, which, although more hidden, was no less important.
From the time of his arrival, he had taken it upon himself in his free time, to
assemble and organize the archives of the parish. This work was all the more
important in that it had never been done before. We are indebted to him for
the preservation of a great number of documents. Along with this, he saw to
the completion of a file and general index of baptisms, weddings, and funerals
in the parish since 1868. This was an enormous task, begun by Brother Bedell
in his spare time, to facilitate the issuance of certificates. Hours were spent in
deciphering the handwriting of the older Fathers, which was often illegible.
After his death, other Brothers had continued the work. At Father Bolduc's
arrival, the file was more than half finished. He assigned this task to Paulette

Tremblay, Marie-Louise Simard, and his own sister Marie-Ange Bolduc, whom he trained personally for this type of work. Today, according to the experts and geneologists, this index-file is one of the best and one of the only of its kind in New England.

In August 1958 Father Bolduc accepted a new assignment as bursar and professor in Natick. His stay in Lowell came to an end. From Natick, in 1960, he became superior and bursar at the juniorate in Bucksport. In 1966, he was transferred to the retreat house in Willimantic, Connecticut, and in 1968 he was sent as chaplain to the Holy Cross Sisters in Franklin, New Hampshire. His time at Saint Jean Baptiste had been marked by a great concern for organization and preparation for the future. It would now be up to his successor to lead the parish through the difficult times that lay ahead.

27. Urban Renewal

Father Bolduc's successor, Father Donat Morrissette, had been his bursar. He was ideally qualified for the position since he was well aware of the construction under way, and he also had a rich pastoral experience to his credit.

Father Morrissette was born on March 18, 1897, at Sainte-Sophie-de-Lévrard, Québec, the son of Gédéon Morrissette and Vitaline Roy. His parents had immigrated to Lowell when he was a child, so that he had made his elementary studies at Saint Joseph's. He went to the Joliette Seminary for his secondary education, after which he entered the Oblate novitiate in Tewksbury. He completed his theological studies in Washington and was ordained to the priesthood in 1923.

Fr. Donat Morrissette, O.M.I.

After his ordination he had been in turn professor, bursar, and superior in Colebrook. After that he had been named to Sainte Jeanne d'Arc as curate, and then had spent two terms as pastor, prior to his assignment as bursar at Saint Jean Baptiste. So now, upon becoming pastor of Saint Jean Baptiste, he was already accustomed to having held positions of trust to which he brought his sound administrative sense. He was a humble and devoted priest, even a trifle bashful. It should be noted that his confessional was always mobbed, and that he had no trouble getting along with people.

His first concern as pastor was to complete the campaign for school repairs started by Father Bolduc. On October 15, 1958, he invited the members of the Parish Committee to dinner, and while thanking them for their dedication, he gave them an overview of the situation. To summarize, the campaign had been running for three years, and though it was still yielding good results, the people were beginning to wonder if it would ever end. After some discussion, it was decided to close the major campaign in October 1959, with a promise to put on display an honor roll in the vestibule of Saint Jean Baptiste church, with the names of all who had contributed fifty dollars or more.

A final push for funds was set in motion. The street captains and collectors went to work. There remained only one floor and a half to complete at the *collège*. The October collection brought in $1,117.00, and the one in November, $1,984.00. The people were giving willingly, and construction began once again in November. In February, the honor roll was set in place. The names appeared on movable wooden strips inserted within a frame. The laggards were urged to complete their $50 donation as soon as possible. (This honor roll remained in place until the celebration of the hundredth anniversary, when it was removed during the repainting of the church vestibule.) In October, the committee members made their last rounds. The campaign was declared over. More than 400 persons had their names inscribed on the honor roll. The Parish Committee campaign had raised $60,886.80 in four years.

Even so, the third floor of the *collège* was not yet finished, and the construction of a new science laboratory alone would cost $6,000. The pastor took it upon himself to announce at all the Masses that, starting in February 1960, there would be a second collection once a month to pay for school repairs in order to finish the work in the collège and begin what needed to be done in the elementary school. The money thus continued to arrive in the parish coffers.

On April 11, 1960, a valuable boost came from the Lafayette Club. Its members presented the pastor with a $5,000 check to help defray the cost of the laboratory in the boys' high school. Thanks to this gift and other monies raised by the parish societies, the reconstruction of the *collège* interior was successfully completed. On Sunday, December 4, 1960, the whole parish was invited to visit the building, in order to see for themselves what had been accomplished. Father Morrissette's letter to the parishioners summarizes it well:

> Saint Jean Baptiste parish is proud to open the doors of the *Collège Saint Joseph* to you, so that you can see and note the changes that have been made over the past four years, thanks to the generosity of the parishioners and their friends.

> Everything has been accomplished without incurring a single debt, and we now have a very new, modern school, comparable to the finest in the city of Lowell.

The reconstruction of the school had cost $77,149.92. This modernization came at an opportune time, for the applications for admission were increasing more and more.

In the summer of 1961, fifty-three boys received their high school diplomas, the largest number since the school began. At the opening of the school year in September, the eighth grade — the last year of elementary schooling — was transferred to the Moody Street school. The high school enrollment rose to 257, the following year it went up to 290, and in September 1963, it had reached 316.

The boys' high school being finally in good shape for the future, the time had come to focus on the old Moody Street school which, in September 1961, enrolled 341 boys, 315 girls and 91 kindergarten children. The carpenters went to work on January 31, 1961. New floors had to be built, a library had to be installed, offices added, etc. The pastor noted in the codex for that day: "The work at the school on Moody Street is beginning on this feast of Don Bosco, the friend of children; we therefore place this work under his protection."

Once the project was underway, the needed money had to be found, as always. One of the means to raise funds this time was the planning of a large parish festival. The idea seemed a good one, since it had been years since the last undertaking of this kind. The festivities were to last one full week, from Tuesday April 11, 1961, to Monday the 17th. Each parish priest was given "his" specific activity: Father Nelson Boucher, the responsibility for a roller skating party at the Hi-Hat Roll-Away; Father Emile Rossignol, the Holy Name's evening of Bingo; Father Joseph Bouchard, the *Dames de Sainte-Anne* Bean Supper; Father Normand Fillion, the closing reunion and ball at the Commodore Ballroom, organized by the *Congréganistes;* the pastor, the huge Parent Teacher Association (PTA) fair.

The evening dance at the Commodore was the highlight of the festival, for that evening, a young lady would be crowned as "Miss Popularity" of the parish. After a number of beautiful young ladies had been selected from among the prettiest in the parish, each parishioner, in return for a small donation, could cast a vote by ballot for his choice for the title.

The entire affair was an enormous success. Over one thousand persons were present at the Commodore on April 17, for the closing. When the moment arrived, Miss Jacqueline Clermont won the "Miss Popularity" crown. Madeleine Dumais and Suzanne Landry were the second and third choices. A great success on all counts, the festival provided a week of joy and merrymaking, in addition to contributing $5,000 to the repair fund.

To support him in the work of modernizing the schools, Father Morrissette had known how to find the needed financial backing. Yet, he was also aware, from his acquired experience, that the schools needed other types of sustenance, just as important, if not more so. As pastor of Saint Jeanne d'Arc, he had presided over the founding of a group of parents interested in the role of the school and who wished to support the nuns in their work regarding the intellectual and spiritual formation of their children. Several parishes already had a Parent Teacher Association, and the time had come for Saint Jean Baptiste to try to form one also.

On October 28, 1959, he called a meeting of women likely to be interested in such an activity. They met in the small hall on James Street. The idea was favorably received, and on January 5, 1960, the first major meeting of the Saint Joseph PTA was held in the parish hall. Of the 126 persons present — all of them parents of children in the elementary school on Moody Street — 93 became members that very night. Two months later, with an active group of 131 members, the first officers were elected. Mrs. Robert Descôteaux was chosen as president. The other officers were: Mrs. Marcel Bourassa, vice-president; Mrs. Hector Clermont, secretary; Mrs. Hervé Hardy, treasurer; Mrs. Robert Hardman, responsible for publicity.

As soon as it was formed, the new association embarked on various activities. It wasn't easy at first. Each parish association had it own "method" or formula for raising funds. The PTA, beyond its work with the nuns and children, had to find its own approach, at a time when the fund for repairs to the school was on everybody's mind. Card parties were the rage at the time, but the Holy Name Society were the masters of these evenings. Their thematic evenings, such as the "Giant Balloon" or the "Carnival of Valentines," with a thousand players and hundreds of prizes, could not be improved upon. Their only rivals in this domain were the Congréganistes, who could match them in card-party expertise. The Dames de Sainte-Anne for their part, had long ago earned the golden palm with regard to Bean Suppers.

The PTA finally settled on the concept of the "Country Store." This was a kind of bazaar-flea market with diverse items sold, along with Monte-Carlo and Bingo in the evening for the adults. In November 1961, the country store brought in $1,625! The Bingo, or Blitz as it was called, to bypass the state laws prohibiting Bingo, had been a hit. The following year at the Country Store, on November 7, 1962, the entire evening was given over to this game, with even more amazing results. It didn't take long for the PTA to arrive at a decision on this matter. Starting on Friday, November 23, 1962, the PTA would sponsor a Blitz party every Friday evening in the St. Joseph Hall. With its 237 members, it had become one of the most active groups in the parish. They could now get down to business. The beginnings were modest. The first evening brought in a mere $246. But in time Blitz became a veritable mania. On February 1, 1963, the evening showed a profit of $819.19, for 332 players! It was the rage of the day, so much so that in May 1963, the PTA was able to present the pastor with a $15,000 check for the schools. The Blitz fever was not limited to Saint Jean Baptiste. The whole area was taken up by it. Even Rivier College, in Nashua New Hampshire, sent buses into Lowell during the week to pick up players. With time and given its success, the PTA had to form a separate and distinct committee for running the Blitz. It was named *Le Comité d'Aide aux Écoles,* and it is through this committee that the profits were transferred to the parish.

In this flurry of activity surrounding improvements to the school, the contribution of the children themselves should not be forgotten, since it was perhaps the most touching. Their offering, made up of savings, small raffles and penny sales, helped to complete the repair project. Justifiably proud, Father Morrissette rose in the pulpit on September 16, 1962, to announce that the twelve classrooms and the new library in the Moody Street School were now totally restored. In a short time, they then started on a new music room, a cafeteria, and the office of the directress. The books for the library arrived in March 1963, and in May everything had been installed. The renovation of the elementary school had cost almost $55,000. It was a success. The older parishioners could hardly believe their eyes when they saw the beautifully restored school.

For the moment, the girls' high school was left as it was. A major renovation had taken place in 1935, and other improvements had been made in the recent past. The school itself continued to function well. The enrollment maintained a steady average of 160 young women. In 1963, it even increased to 189. Later, when certain changes were proposed, it was too late. Urban renewal was causing uncertainty regarding the future of the school.

The pastor had been immersed in repairs from the start, and he had not yet come to the end of it all. Work on the rectory and Saint Jean Baptiste church still needed to be finished. In July 1960, a contract for $10,600 was signed, so that workmen could finish pointing the masonry on the outside of the church. The walls on the Moody Street side were all that remained to be done and this was completed in a short time. As for the gutters and drains on the side walls, the project to replace them was put off till later.

As if this weren't enough, Father Morrissette still had to settle the problem of the Saint Jean Baptiste Youth Center. The center no longer paid for itself and failed to attract the young as it had in the past. The habits of young people were changing, and, except for the skating rink in winter, which had always retained its popularity, the activities at the center seemed no longer in vogue. To make matters worse, the main hall could no longer be used for dances and banquets because the floor had become too weak to support the weight of a large gathering. Finally, the decision to sell was taken. On May 4, 1960, the old Saint Jean Baptiste Youth Center was sold to Patrick Plunkett for $13,710.00. He immediately converted it into beautiful apartments.

The *Petits Chanteurs de la Croix de Bois* from Paris returned to Lowell as the guests of the Parker Lectures on November 30, 1958. As in the past, the young boys were housed in the homes of parishioners, and also, as was their custom, they sang at the High Mass on Sunday morning. The following year they came again in September, but this time the program was slightly different. In addition to their usual musical offerings, they gave a concert in the parish hall for the general public, under the auspices of the Dames de Sainte-Anne and another one in the parish hall exclusively for the nuns of the city and the surrounding area. This 1959 tour was their last, but memories of the *Petits Chanteurs de la Croix de Bois* of Paris remained dear to the hearts of the parishioners of Saint Jean Baptiste for a long time.

Official France did not forget its distant cousins in Lowell. On Thursday, February 26, 1959, Robert Valeur, plenipotentiary minister at the French Embassy in Washington, accompanied by Baron Charles de Pampelonne, consul-general of France in Boston, made an official visit to Lowell and its Franco-American institutions. They visited, one after the other, the orphanage, the rectory, and other foundations and, in the evening, the local chapter of France Forever held a gala reception for them at the C.M.A.C. Hall, to which they invited all the most ardent Francophiles in the city. The warmth of the welcome, the impressive attendance, the singing and the stirring speeches were all reminiscent of the great evening receptions of the past. Unfortunately, this splendid evening was to be the last activity of the local chapter of France Forever, for soon thereafter, the group dissolved.

On September 14, 1959, Saint Jean Baptiste church was filled with children and nuns. Father Morrissette was celebrating a High Mass of Thanksgiving to mark the beatification in Rome of Mother d'Youville. All the activities of her daughters were flourishing.

In May 1959, the construction of d'Youville Manor for the elderly had begun. On the following August 3rd , in Saint Jean Baptiste church, Cardinal Cushing presided at the religious profession of ten new Grey Nuns for the Saint Joseph Province. That afternoon, the first symbolic shovelful of dirt was dug for the construction of the new wing of Saint Joseph Hospital on the Salem Street side. On February 3, 1960, another group of young Grey Nuns pronounced their vows, this time in Saint Joseph church.

The entire population was in a celebratory mood, on Tuesday June 21, 1960, when Cardinal Cushing was present for the solemn dedication of d'Youville Manor. At last, the home for the elderly, that had been desired for so long, had become a reality. And what a residence it was! Built according to the best gerontological theories of the time, it in no way resembled what had existed before. The structure extended on one floor starting from a large chapel, and was surrounded by a green park-like field. The rooms, grouped into pavilions, were bright and airy. The facility could accommodate 150 people in all, 125 of them in private rooms. There were even, and this was rare for the time, private rooms for married couples. The presence of an Oblate priest in residence, as well as the many nuns in the personnel, ensured attention to religious care. Needless to say, the manor was fully occupied as soon as it opened, and a long waiting list was established. As an honor to the young Saint Joseph Province of the Grey Nuns, the new d'Youville Manor was selected as the site to install the large painting of the glorification of Mother d'Youville, which had served as part of the beatification ceremonies at Saint Peter's Basilica in Rome. It was a Grey Nun of the Cross of Ottawa, Sister Jean-Marie, S.G.C., Rosalie De Blois from Haverhill, Massachusetts, who had received the last miracle needed for Mother d'Youville's beatification. She was healed of blindness.

The new wing of Saint Joseph Hospital was dedicated on November 20, 1960. This new brick construction, at the corner of Salem and Pawtucket Streets, added eighty-six rooms and a new emergency room. Only one other extension, on the Merrimack Street side, remained to be built. The School of Nursing celebrated its 75th anniversary with a Mass and banquet on June 24, 1962.

All the enterprises seemed to be prospering at this time. The small Lowell community of the Oblate Missionaries of the Immaculate Conception also had its joyful moments. On January 25, 1960, their founder, Father Parent, came to Lowell with Jacqueline Lemay, a quite well-known Oblate from Cap-de-la-Madeleine, in Québec, where she had earned a reputation as a singer at the Canadian shrine. The young woman, accompanying herself on the guitar, gave a concert in the parish hall. On Tuesday evening, February 2, 1960, in Saint Jean Baptiste church, Father Parent presided at the vows of seven young women for the institute.

The Oblate Fathers themselves had their share of celebrations. Nine young Oblates were ordained to the priesthood for the Franco-American province on June 24, 1959. One of them, Father Roger J. Lamoureux, was a child of the parish. Seven more were ordained in September 1960. The new retreat house in Willimantic, Connecticut, was solemnly blessed on October 16, 1960. It followed in the tradition of the existing retreat centers in Augusta, Maine, Hudson, New Hampshire, and Manville, Rhode Island.

The family spirit of the parish was still quite strong. Evenings of entertainment, meetings, and celebrations provided, as always, opportunities to meet and understand one another, while the life of prayer, the liturgy experienced together, united everything, giving meaning to it all and providing a sense of belonging. One of the best examples of this "parish" Catholic life was the Holy Name Society of the period. The list alone of the variety of their undertakings, demonstrates the extent and spirit of its activity. Encouraged by their dynamic chaplain, Father Emile Rossignol, the Holy Name men reached into all sectors of parish life: card parties, a bowling league for its members, picnics, annual pilgrimages to shrines in Québec and the United States, and participation in regional Holy Name activities such as Masses, communion breakfasts, etc. They also formed their own choir to sing at Holy Name services, organized a parish Blood Bank in 1962, and, starting in 1959, published a monthly bulletin, *La Voix du Saint Nom*. All of this was the expression of a strong and united Christian family spirit.

The Holy Name was only one example of the intensity of this parish life. This spirit of mutual aid and charity, the products and proof of a well-directed spiritual life, was very much alive. Paper drives, rag collections, penny sales, and sewing circles fostered the regular cadence of activities in favor of the poor. For their part, the women of the *Association de Marie-Immaculée* dutifully attended to the needs of the Haitian missions.

Father Emile Rossignol, O.M.I. with a committee of men from the Holy Name Society.

On October 13, 1959, an unusual event bolstered everyone's sense of solidarity with the foreign missions. It came in the form of a visit from Father Emile Bolduc who had returned to Lowell from the Philippines, to preach on behalf of his missionary endeavors. He had no sooner arrived "home," as he called Saint Jean Baptiste, than he resumed his old habits of visiting people at home and calling on the sick. He was available to all, without a trace of uncomfortableness. He preached at all the Masses, detailing the needs of his mission with his habitual good nature and openness, and the people responded as usual, joyfully and with open hearts. Asked to give the homily at the annual pilgrimage to Saint Joseph Cemetery, in October, he touched every heart so much that when he left to return to the Philippines, on December 2, 1959, the chronicler at the rectory wrote: "It was with great regret that we saw Reverend Father Emile Bolduc, O.M.I., return to the Philippines . . . on Wednesday, December 2nd. Everyone wants him because his edifying and joyful presence is so pleasant, and his services are so precious."

Saint Jean Baptiste remained the foremost parish of the province, and, in fact, at the heart of all its endeavors. A report prepared for the superior-general in 1959, summarizes it this way:

> This mother parish, and administrative center of the Province for more than 30 years, is the most important of our parishes in the United States. The Saint Jean Baptiste religious house accommodates a personnel of 17 Fathers and 3 Lay Brothers . . . The parish serves 1,683 domiciles and 7,424 parishioners.

Then, after reviewing the parish components: its buildings, schools, orphanage, hospital, etc., the report concludes:

> From the spiritual, religious, priestly, and apostolic points of view, the parish and religious house of Saint Jean Baptiste in Lowell produce a remarkable output, meritorious and glorious for the Province and for the Congregation.

The future, however, was worrisome. Throughout the United States, the fate of large cities was a source of anxiety. Aging and dilapidated neighborhoods, often sparsely populated, home to extreme poverty, were like a cancer. Local businesses were fleeing these areas and city administrators worried a great deal about the diminishing city revenues. In this atmosphere of general malaise, mayors and governors looked to Washington for a solution. As often happened at that time, the solution was a massive infusion of federal money. Called Urban Renewal, this program entitled each city to receive the money needed to demolish blighted areas, with the intent of rebuilding there on a more modern and profitable basis. In Lowell, the first Urban Renewal project, which took place on Church Street, although displacing hundreds of families, was declared a success. The second anticipated project would be on a much larger and more ambitious scale.

Certain parts of Little Canada, as we have noted, had become quite run-down, and even almost abandoned. Deserted tenements and quasi-vacant mills were becoming more commonplace. The reputation of lower Moody Street, with its taverns and run-down buildings was not improving. The population of the district had been diminishing steadily since 1950. For all these reasons, the next Urban Renewal project would be called "The Northern

Canal Urban Renewal Project." It was aimed at Little Canada.

It was generally acknowledged that there were indeed many derelict buildings in Little Canada, especially near the mills, and everyone was in agreement that there were improvements to be made on lower Moody Street, but they were certainly not in accord with the project as it was being proposed. The plan was to demolish much more than a few old buildings here and there and some time-worn mills.

The intention was to raze just about everything between Merrimack Street and the river, an area covering ninety-six acres. Of the 325 buildings in the designated sector, more than 200 would have to be torn down. In 1960, there were 2500 people living in that part of the city. Of that number, more than 520 families, that is to say a large majority, would have to be moved and provided with new housing. The owners would have to sell their property to the government. The entire project would cost $6,370,820. Three-fourths of this amount would be paid by the federal government, and the remaining quarter by the city and the Commonwealth.

To replace all of these demolished structures, the intent was to build a civic center near the City Hall, as well as a new police station, a central fire house and, facing the city's high school, on the other side of the canal, a new school building. In the northern part of the affected acreage, Lowell Technological Institute planned to put up a number of dormitories. A new post office was also considered. Finally, in the section near Saint Jean Baptiste church, parallel to Moody Street, would be the residential part of the project, where beautiful brick apartment buildings were foreseen.

For all of this to be realized, however, the project had to be approved by the citizens at a public hearing to be followed by a favorable vote of the City Council. The final word would then have to come from Washington. For the time being, the most important element was the approval of the citizenry, or at least the absence of opposition on its part, especially from the people who lived in Little Canada.

To achieve this end, the media, the press, and radio were mobilized to present the project in its most favorable light. At the very beginning, however, in order to leave nothing to chance, the city planner, Charles Zettek, along with the banker Homer Bourgeois, approached Father Morrissette twice, the last time on October 17, 1960, in Mr. Bourgeois' office at the Union National Bank, to explain the proposed project to him. According to them, the work would only momentarily disturb the parish for, following the construction of new apartments and the refurbishing of the few old ones that would be allowed to remain, a stable and lasting population would settle there. Former parishioners, who wished to return to the neighborhood, would have the first choice of these apartments.

Father Morrissette accepted this reasoning although not without reservations. In the Community Codex for New Year's Eve, he noted:

> The year will soon be over; we have had our ordeals and our consolations throughout its duration. New problems now confront us. Let us ask God to grant us the graces to surmount all obstacles which could damage the accomplishment of His will for us.

The pastor knew all too well that any opposition would have been in vain. Later, to a group of small businessmen who wanted to form an association to have certain parts of the project modified or abrogated, he simply declared that there was nothing to be done. To the city in general, the plan was presented as an extraordinary godsend. Millions of dollars from Washington, the certain rise in property values with the corresponding increase in taxes, calculated at more than 400%, new municipal buildings, in a word, progress! To be opposed was unthinkable, almost impossible, and not tolerated.

The clubs *Passe Temps* and *Citoyens Américains* along with A&L Taxi Company tried to obtain an exemption so as to remain where they were. Only the *Passe Temps* was successful. For their efforts they were massacred by the press and radio and treated as "obstructions to progress." The venerable Lowell Historical Society, which, for its part, tried to protect certain very historic and important corporation housing on Dutton Street, was treated more politely, but encountered, nonetheless, closed doors and deaf ears both at the local and state levels.

On August 7, 1962, the pastor attended the public hearing at City Hall and gave his approval. The City Council voted unanimously in favor on the 28th, and on March 28, 1963, Washington approved the entire proposal.

And so began this unfortunate project, which would last much longer than anyone thought or wanted, and produced only very few of the promised results. In addition, human nature being what it can be, suspicions and accusations of theft and corruption, which swirled around it from the start—some went so far as to say since its inception—could never be ruled out. To this day, any valid and objective investigation of the matter seems to be impossible. One thing is clear, the city's tax revenue from the project did not increase one cent and the beautiful brick apartments were somewhere along the line turned into ugly and unsanitary concrete apartment blocks, with no one knowing just how it had happened.

From the human point of view, and the respect owed to people, this was the darkest of events for the parishioners, replete with injustices and suffering, the depths of which only God knows, and that He alone could console or forgive.

On December 31, 1961, Father Charles Dénizot, the last of the French-born Oblates, died at Saint Joseph Hospital. His birth had taken place on June 28, 1880 at Saxon-Sion, in the diocese of Nancy, and his parish was the Oblate Shrine of *Notre-Dame- de-Sion*. During the French government's persecutions of religious communities, at the beginning of the twentieth century, he had had to leave France and so he was ordained to the priesthood in Rome in 1903. In all he had spent forty-five years at Saint Jean Baptiste of Lowell, from 1910 to 1923, and from 1929 to 1961.

Death had also struck down Father Eugène Noury. On the morning of May 20, 1961, the eve of Pentecost, the word spread that Father Noury had suffered a heart attack on the previous afternoon, and had died during the night. He was only forty-nine. The parish was plunged into grief. Saint Jean Baptiste church was hardly large enough to receive all the people who wanted to attend the funeral. Father Noury, who was a good and dedicated priest, was mourned for a long time. The incomparable thrust that he had given to St. Joseph Shrine had placed this ministry on a solid and lasting base.

His successor, Father Normand Fillion, continued the work as it had been envisioned, and so he proceeded with the installation of the stained-glass windows. Father Garin had regarded such windows as being an unnecessary luxury. He had never had any installed except in the sanctuary. All other church windows had been clear ones from the beginning. Father Noury believed, however, that to facilitate prayer and contemplation, especially in the heart of the city, the outdoors had to be left outside. Since Saint Joseph church had become a shrine, where workers and busy passersby sought a moment of peace and meditation, the soft glow from the windows would serve to enhance their devotion. Scenes from the life of Saint Joseph were selected as a theme for these windows, with the first in the series installed on October 1, 1961. Since there were many donors, the second window was put in place on the 5th of the same month. The windows were designed by the artist Richard Belley, a former resident of Lowell and the brother of Fr. Bernard Belley and Ursula Belley.

The installation of the stained-glass windows gave rise to a most extraordinary event. There were two locations in the body of the church, directly over the confessionals, which had been reserved for subjects other than the main theme, the life of Saint Joseph. Many suggestions had been made, when one day a generous benefactor, who wished to remain anonymous, came to Father Fillion offering to pay for a window honoring Notre Dame de Beauraing. The offer was immediately accepted. Yet no one could suspect what was being prepared for the dedication of this window. The donor having provided the airline ticket, on November 28, 1964, Albert Voisin, one of the children who had seen the Blessed Mother, was brought from Beauraing. The following day was the thirty-second anniversary of the first apparition of the Blessed Virgin on November 29, 1932. The solemn blessing of the window thus took place on November 29 in the presence of one who had seen the Blessed Virgin thirty-three times!

In 1965, the last window was put in place in the church.

To keep their pastoral ministry up-to-date, and to meet the needs of the day, the Fathers reached certain decisions and undertook some important initiatives. Their ministry to the young was greatly in need of renewal since the successes of the forties and fifties because the world had greatly changed.

Photo – Pro Maria Committee

Albert Voisin, of Beauraing, Belgium, on the left, with the painting of the window of Our Lady of Beauraing. The artist Richard Belley is on the right.

In 1962, the Saint Jean Baptiste CYO was founded, as part of the Catholic Youth Organization of the archdiocese. Also, after careful consideration, it was decided to combine the *Dames de Sainte-Anne* and the *Congréganistes* into a single society for the women, somewhat based on the model of the Ladies' Sodalities that existed in other parishes. The age difference among the members of each of these societies had become almost imperceptible, and the aims of both groups were practically the same. On Wednesday evening, October 24, 1962, the officers of the new *Association de Marie-Immaculée* were elected: Mrs. Alice Lefebvre, president; Irène Desmarais, vice-president; Mrs. Francis Dubé, first assistant; Mrs. Adélard Rheault, second assistant; Mrs. André Ouellette, secretary and archivist; Marie Péloquin, corresponding secretary; Mrs. Joseph Letendre, treasurer; Pauline Desruisseaux, assistant treasurer; Mrs. Hervé Kérouac, publicist; Mrs. Rose Racette and Mrs. Elphège Proulx, sacristans; Mrs. Arthur Provencher, choir director; and Mrs. Hervé Joly in charge of the *petit prêtre* (little priest) effort, a work supporting vocations to the priesthood and seminarians. The activities went on unchanged: bean suppers, card parties, and what was becoming the rage, Mystery Rides, filled month after month.

It was in the area of religious education that the most had to be done. This question was drawing more and more attention from the Church and from diocesan authorities. In 1961, there were 248 children from the parish in the public schools. Half of this number did not attend the religion courses that were being offered for them by the brothers and the nuns. Religious formation was a cause of great concern at the diocesan level, especially the means to be taken to extend religious instruction to adults as well as to children. It was also time to give laypersons the role due to them in the matter of religious instruction. To this end, in August 1962, Cardinal Cushing ordered each parish in the archdiocese to set up a Confraternity of Christian Doctrine (CCD).

The pastor of Saint Jean Baptiste appointed Father Nelson Boucher as director of this undertaking. His mission was to set up an executive committee and form lay teachers. The CCD needed to have the participation of everyone at every level of parish life, from the priests to religious men and women, to laymen and women, and the children. As it was presented to the parish, the movement would be composed of active members, responsible for teaching, titular members—children or adults—who would take the courses or who would participate in discussion groups for adults and associate members, who would support the effort through their prayers and their work.

Starting in November 1962, Father Boucher met regularly with a group of laypersons to prepare the ground for the program. In the spring of 1963, a general appeal was made to the entire parish for members in each of the three categories. By March, a religion course was begun at Saint Joseph shrine for adults interested in becoming teachers in the program. In September 1963, everything was ready to start. The Saint Jean Baptiste parish CCD introduced its program for public school children. At the end of the first month, there were ninety children enrolled at the grade school level, and sixty high school students. They were taught by fifteen lay persons, two priests, and one nun.

The confraternity was canonically erected at an official installation of the executive committee by Father Russell Novello, the diocesan director of the CCD, on Sunday, November 10 in St. Jean Baptiste Church. By the spring of 1964, the organization was complete. Richard Violette was president of the executive committee; Robert Dastous, vice-president; Lucille Labrie, secretary; Raymond Perreault, treasurer; André Ouellette and Gérard Lacroix, headed the teachers' committees, assisted by Léa Paquin and Mrs. Arthur Eno; Mrs. Richard Violette and Mrs. Betty Davis were in charge of parent formation; Irène R. Desmarais and Jeannine Tousignant headed the discussion groups; Arthur Malo was responsible for home visits, and Armand Laroche was in charge of the apostles of good will. In all, the CCD personnel involved more than ninety persons. Such a well-established organization could only prosper, and with time it reached every level of the parish.

On Friday, October 5, 1962, Father John Jadaa, superior of the Fathers of Saint Basil scholasticate, in Methuen, was invited by the Holy Name Society to celebrate an Oriental Mass according to the Byzantine rite in Saint Jean Baptiste church, on the occasion of their monthly communion. The dialogue mass was conducted in French and communion was offered under both species. The singing in Arabic at communion time called to mind a very new vision of the Catholic Church for the large number of parishioners who were present. This Mass was symbolic in more ways than one since it was intended, as announced, to mark the opening in Rome of the Second Vatican Council. Few parishioners knew what a council was, and some even asked why it was a *concile* rather than a *conseil*, *concile* in French being the ecclesiastical term for *conseil*. Both mean "council." Nevertheless, the events were followed with prayers and a great deal of interest.

The official opening of the Council took place in Rome on October 11, 1962. The school children watched the opening pageant on television after having attended Mass that morning, to add their prayers to those of the Catholic world.

Rather quickly, the changes mandated by the Fathers of the Council, especially those affecting the liturgy, began to be felt in Lowell. In the spring, slowly, and for special occasions, Dialogue Masses with French responses were introduced. Certain parts of these Masses, the Gloria, the Creed, etc., were recited in French by the faithful, while the prayers reserved to the priest remained in Latin.

On Sunday, February 16, 1964, it became official. From that date forward, all Sunday Masses would have responses in French and a homily at all the Sunday and Holy Day Masses. In order to facilitate the participation of the congregation, a group of men were selected as directors of prayer. On Sunday, May 3, it was announced that the long prayer recited by the priest during the distribution of Communion was being done away with. The faithful were advised to simply respond "Amen" when the priest said *"Corpus Christi"* as he presented the Host.

This was only the beginning. The Fathers did all they could to keep abreast of developments. Bishop Henri Routhier, O.M.I., vicar-apostolic of Grouard, in Alberta, Canada, on his way home from Rome, between sessions, in April 1964, stopped in Lowell. He was able to speak at length with the Oblates about events at the council. The professors from the Natick seminary, for their part, gave regular lectures in the various houses of the province to keep everyone up-to-date.

Parish life continued on its course. On February 13, 1963, the old Librairie Baron, after more than fifty years at Saint Jean Baptiste, transferred its business to Saint Joseph Shrine. The old books in the parish lending library were sold or given to the parishioners. That July, the young women of the Oblate Missionaries of the Immaculate Conception were faced with recruiting and especially formation problems, and had to abandon their services in the rectory and sacristy. Later, in 1966, amid the difficulties of the post-conciliar years, they found themselves obliged to close their house on Nesmith Street and bring to an end their apostolate in Lowell.

It was at this time also that the Franco-American Orphanage had to re-evaluate and greatly modify its services. The Commonwealth of Massachusetts, which, by then, was appropriating to itself more and more charitable social endeavors, decided that, in the future, orphans and other state wards would fare better if placed in families rather than in institutions. In many cities, orphanages closed their doors, but in Lowell, the sisters' orphanage was turned into a boarding school, in 1963.

On May 26, 1963, Memorial Sunday, Cardinal Cushing presided at the dedication of a new entrance gate, and commemorative monuments, at Saint Joseph Cemetery. This burying ground had become one of the most important in the region. There were 25,525 persons buried there by 1955. Under the capable direction of Father Brassard, it was also one of the most beautiful and best administered. This new entrance was only the first step in an overall plan of reorganization. The new administration building and the great bell tower, were blessed on October 18, 1964. Finally, on October 9, 1966, the cardinal returned for the blessing of the large commemorative chapel, which was the high point of the renewal.

Father Morrissette's term as pastor was approaching its end, but he still had his heart set on repairs to the residences of the Grey Nuns and the Marist Brothers. The brothers themselves had in the summer successfully renovated a good part of their home, and had even transformed their cellar into a recreation room, but there was still more work to be done. The repairs at the sisters' convent were more urgent. It was an old building, in quite bad shape, and in need of major repairs. First of all, new rooms were needed to replace the old dormitories. And then, there was the question of toilets. The students' restrooms, situated in an annex near the school, were no longer usable and needed complete restoration. Therefore, it was decided to build, as quickly as possible, an addition to the convent along James Street. The ground floor would include a garage for the sisters' automobile, and restrooms for the school. The first floor would contain eight private rooms and a solarium. All of this would cost $70,000. The pastor had the plans drawn up, but his term came to an end before he had time to sign the contract. In August 1964, he was named by the provincial as a curate and bursar at St. Peter in Plattsburgh. The storm that had been brewing, under preceding pastors, was now about to burst over his successor.

28. A Weighty Responsibility

Fr. Anatole Lessard, O.M.I.

The provincial named Father Anatole Lessard, a former missionary and spiritual director, as pastor of Saint Jean Baptiste parish. The new pastor was born on February 17, 1917, in Les Grandes Bergeronnes, Québec, the son of Odina Lessard and Alberta Larrivée. He studied in Oblate houses of formation in Québec and Natick, and on June 11, 1944, he was ordained to the priesthood by Bishop Melançon in his home parish of Sainte-Zoé. He left almost immediately for the missions in Haiti. However, a different future was in store for him, as his health could not withstand the Haitian climate. He had to return to New England and become integrated into the Saint Jean Baptiste Province, first as a curate at Sainte Jeanne d'Arc parish in Lowell where he remained until 1960. He then became spiritual director at the Bucksport juniorate. After a time as director and bursar of the Saint Charles house of studies in Washington, he returned to Lowell as pastor of Saint Jean Baptiste.

With this, his first pastorate, Father Lessard was accepting a heavy burden. The future was uncertain and all the apprehensions of his predecessors seemed on the point of becoming realities. The full onslaught of Urban Renewal was descending upon the parish. The future of the schools was threatened. The question of utilizing the French language needed to be settled. And, with all this, the reforms of Vatican II had to be integrated on a continual basis and made comprehensible to the parishioners. But, being good-hearted and charitable towards the poor, he valiantly got down to work.

First of all, he signed the contracts already prepared by Father Morrissette for the addition to the convent. The small old school on James Street near the convent was demolished and construction began. In May 1965, *Le Comité d'Aide aux Écoles* donated $60,000 towards the total cost, with receipts from the Bingo. Around August of the same year the extension was completed. Father Lessard immediately opened the doors of the convent to the parishioners for a general visit. Next to the new and comfortable annex, the condition of the old convent was scandalous to behold. The stairway to the second floor was pulling away from the wall, the plaster was peeling, the electrical wiring was piercing through the walls and the bathrooms were as primitive as could be. The overall effect shocked those who saw it. The needs were clearly evident and the nuns' dedication, to avoid saying their deprivation, was now manifest to everyone. It was decided on the spot to begin the huge task of repairing the building. As always, the parishioners, both men and women, set about the work of renovation. Card parties were held and all sorts of activities organized to raise the needed funds. *L'Amicale Saint Joseph, L'Association de Marie-Immaculée,* and the Holy Name Society did their part, while *Le Comité d'Aide aux Écoles* contributed large sums to the project. Some men even volunteered to do the plastering and painting. When all was finished, the renovation of the old convent alone had cost over $40,000. The end result was encouraging for everyone. The nuns now had a modern, salubrious, and comfortable convent, with individual rooms for each sister.

The first phase of the Urban Renewal Project was not yet complete in 1966, but already a very large number of families had departed. There were 1,386 families in 1963, which included 3,981 persons. In 1964, the number of families was down to 980, and this number continued to decrease as the purchases and demolitions went forward. By 1965 there were 820 families, and 736, in 1966. In a single year, the Holy Name Society lost 200 members. According to the estimates of the authorities, before the completion of this first phase, another one hundred or so families would be obliged to leave the parish. Of the parishioners who remained, many were elderly and on Social Security. The enrollments in the grammar school diminished from 440 in 1963, to 263 in 1967. While there were 159 baptisms in 1963, there were only fifty-three in 1966. The two high schools had only seventy-two parishioners in the total of 395 students. The shock to parish life was enormous and profound. No one dared predict the future. One thing was certain, however, the parish had to be maintained. In Father Lessard's own words: "Should we despair and give up? Certainly not."

Fortunately, the spirit of the parish remained good, and faith continued to be strong. According to Father Lessard: "Saint Jean Baptiste can be presented as a parish with a strong spiritual life. There is a phalanx here of older men and women, married or single, who are true saints." The proof of this beautiful spirit of faith came in November 1965 when Father Romeo Murphy, chaplain of the Holy Name, launched an appeal to form a nocturnal adoration society for the men. On the spot, sixty men signed up to pray before the Blessed Sacrament, in the rectory chapel, on every First Friday, from 10 o'clock in the evening until 6 on the following morning. It was edifying for everyone to see these men deep in prayer, replacing one another during the wee hours of the night. In all about eighty men participated.

In spite of the difficult circumstances, the missionary spirit did not diminish either. For missionaries passing through, the parish continued to be as generous as ever. Bishop Edwin Pinto, S. J., of Ahmedabad, India, preached at all the Masses in June 1965. He collected $800 and the promise of correspondence from many parishioners. In January 1966, Bishop Paul Seitz, M.E.P., of Kon-Tum, in Vietnam, spent some time at Saint Jean Baptiste parish. Everyone was very sympathetic to him, given the tragic events in that country where the war was raging. The situation in Vietnam was on everyone's mind, especially in Saint Jean Baptiste parish, where the war touched close to home. On September 9, 1965, the church was the scene of the young soldier Donald Arcand's funeral, the first parishioner, and the first Lowell citizen, to be killed in that faraway war.

The privileged missions, however, were always those in Haiti. The comings and goings between Haiti and Lowell were constant. Missionaries coming home to visit their families; others there for a rest, or to make an appeal for their mission. Some lay persons even traveled to Haiti to visit the priests they knew. So, it was not surprising that Divine Providence allowed one of its deserving sons to make a final return to Saint Jean Baptiste. On July 27, 1966, Bishop Louis Collignon, O.M.I., fell ill and died unexpectedly while at the Oblate Mission House in Paris. His body was first brought to Lowell for a very solemn funeral service at St. Jean Baptiste on August 5, celebrated by Bishop Ernest Primeau of Manchester, New Hampshire. It was quite moving for the funeral of the so loved Bishop to take place in the very church where he had been consecrated and among the people who had faithfully accompanied him with their prayers and support over the years.

From Lowell, his body was transferred to Les Cayes where a mass of people awaited him in deep sorrow. The president of Haiti, François Duvalier, upon hearing the news, decreed that Bishop Collignon would be accorded all the honors of a state funeral *"des funérailles d'état."* The bishop whom the people had named *"l'homme au bon coeur,* the man with a good heart," was laid to rest in the crypt of the cathedral near those he had loved and served for twenty-four years.

As soon as he arrived in the parish, Father Lessard had realized the need to address the question of using English in the celebration of the sacraments. Everything was still being done in French, even though religion was now being taught in English in the schools, and in spite of the fact that a growing number of people, especially the young, hardly understood French. One day, a woman parishioner had approached Father Donat Morrissette, asking him: "Father, when are we going to have Masses in English? My son has married a girl who doesn't speak French, and it's difficult for her to come to a Mass in French." The pastor's reply says a good deal about this generation of priests who could see with such sorrow French disappearing from the old parishes: "Don't be afraid, *Madame,* after me it will happen soon enough."

Painful as it was, the decision could no longer be put off. The good of souls required it. First off, a trial run took place on Sunday, September 27, 1964. Without announcing it, the 5 o'clock early morning Mass and the 8:15 children's Mass, were celebrated in English, except for the Latin parts that were still compulsory. It was only on Sunday, October 25, after a change in the schedule, that Father Lessard made the official announcement.

Starting next Sunday, we will have two Masses in English: at 8:15 and 11:00. There will still be an 8:15 Mass in French at Saint Joseph's.

Circumstances oblige us to offer a few Masses in English. During the parish visitations, we have spoken of this problem to a great many of our parishioners. They have understood and supported us in this decision.

We preach to be understood—and a good number of our people do not understand French, or understand it very little. These people— especially the young—who are our parishioners, and who come to our church, have the right to receive religious instruction, and it is our duty to give it to them. And, the only way to give them this instruction is to speak to them in English. We know that some of you will be saddened by this decision; we are, also. But, we must not forget that there will still be five Masses in French each Sunday.

My very dear friends, we must first be concerned with the good of souls. Our charity, our desire to help and our intention to bring about the reign of Christ the King must overcome our personal interests and ambitions. By refusing a Christian education to those who do not understand French, and yet are our own people, we are doing them serious harm. Our charity forbids us from doing this.

My very dear friends, even at the price of a few inconveniences, let us all work together for the good of souls and the parish.

Franco-American patriotism was still strong, however, and French culture, still lively. A Richelieu Club for men was founded in Lowell in

September 1963, with the express purpose of giving the members an opportunity to express themselves in French, and to promulgate the language. On April 29, 1965, the club sponsored *Le Tréteau de Paris* from France which performed the famous play *L'Annonce faite à Marie* by Paul Claudel, the Catholic playwright. The C.M.A.C. celebrated its 75th anniversary, on Sunday, December 6th, 1964, in a grand manner, and entirely in French. The decision to insert English at Mass, the very heart of the parish, was not an easy one, and it was criticized by some as the beginning of the end, and even as a betrayal of the work of the founders. In general, however, the people understood, and so the parish entered the era of bilingualism. On Christmas Eve, 1964, there were two Midnight Masses, one, the High Mass in French in the upper church, and another in English in the lower church. From that time on, the annual retreats were preached in both languages.

These changes came at a most auspicious time. The reforms prescribed by Vatican II were becoming more and more elaborate and the complete disappearance of Latin was only a matter of time. In October 1964, it was announced that from that moment on, all the sacraments had to be administered in the language of the people, and participation in the responses of the Mass became compulsory. In March 1965, the parish published two small booklets, the size of a missal, to be taken home, which contained the text of all the responses to the Mass in French and in English. At Christmas, in 1964, the priest offered the Mass facing the people for the first time. The nuns helped to rehearse and lead the faithful in the singing. In very little time the congregation became accustomed to the changes, singing and responding with ease.

The reduction of the Eucharistic fast to one hour before Communion also facilitated attendance at Mass. In March 1965, an evening weekday Mass at 7 o'clock was intoduced. Success was immediate and proved that the decisions of the Council were well-founded, and that Saint Jean Baptiste parish had been properly prepared to assimilate them. According to the rectory chronicler:

> The parishioners are numerous at the evening Mass. Almost everyone sings and responds to the officiating priest. There is a sermon every evening, and many receive Holy Communion. The people are beginning to enjoy active participation in the Mass. They have a better understanding of the liturgical actions, and feel that they are really participants in these liturgical acts.

> We have had small booklets printed, with the cardinal's approbation, in French and in English, to facilitate participation at holy Mass, and to have the text according to the new translation.

The ecumenical spirit, one of the most beautiful fruits of Vatican II, gave rise to a new type of event in the history of the parish. On the first Sunday after

Easter, April 25, 1965, the doors of the church were opened wide for a grand open house with guided tours. Carefully prepared by Father Nelson Boucher, the members of the CCD, and a committee of more than seventy people, it drew a crowd of both Catholics and Protestants. Each visitor was given a handout explaining the history and works of the parish, as well as the prayer of Pope Paul VI for church unity.

As noted earlier, the Grey Nuns provided loyal support to the Fathers in their work of liturgical renewal, and they participated actively in the renewing of catechesis and in leading the singing at Mass. Their own works continued to develop. In 1965, they added a new wing to D'Youville Manor on Varnum Avenue, to serve as a provincial house and residence for the elderly sisters. The house on Fairmount Street was closed.

Cardinal Cushing blessed the new wing at Saint Joseph Hospital, the Homer Bourgeois Pavilion, on September 16, 1966. Situated at the corner of Pawtucket and Merrimack Streets, it had been built at a cost of four million dollars. The former Ayer Home, on Pawtucket Street, was purchased and transformed into a residence for the nuns.

To show their gratitude, the sisters joined enthusiastically in April and May 1965, in the celebrations for Father Louis Bachand, honorary president of the hospital, on his 50th anniversary of ordination. Sister Louis Robert prepared a magnificent memorial album for the occasion. On April 28, the sisters honored him in their new provincial house. At his Jubilee Mass on May 16, in Saint Jean Baptiste church, a large number of sisters and delegations of nurses and students were in attendance. There was another celebration, on the next day, at the hospital. Unfortunately, Father Bachand did not live long enough to see the rest of the hospital expansion. He died very quietly three months later, on August 12, having reached the end of his long religious life. The nuns named their new residence at the hospital Bachand Hall in his memory.

These years also saw the expansion of another religious community, this one more hidden, less visible to the public. The Little Sisters of the Holy Family, so beloved by the people for their humble and self-effacing work, and for their spirit of prayer, decided to open an American house of formation. They officially opened their American novitiate in April 1965, in a spacious house that had been a doctor's residence, on Andover Street. To help them out, a group of parishioners organized a card party and other activities for their benefit. A first group of the Little Sisters took the habit and pronounced their initial vows in Saint Jean Baptiste church on Sunday, July 10, 1966.

Urban renewal continued to disturb the parish in many ways, but in the area of finances it wreaked havoc. Expenses were increasing while revenues continued to decline. If it hadn't been for the generosity of the people, income from Bingo and the societies, along with the money from Saint Joseph Shrine, there would have been no way to make ends meet.

The repairs at the convent had cost over $40,000 and the annex $70,000. New repairs were made to the *collège*—the remodeling of the gym and the restrooms at a cost of over $30,000. Soon the parish hall would have to be redone, and the lower church repainted for the approaching centennial. Several thousand dollars would be needed for all this. While facing all these extra costs, the ongoing expenses still had to be met.

The pastor was doing his utmost, using all possible means to stabilize the finances. He appealed first of all to the generosity of the people. He explained the need to utilize the envelope system for the church collection, and urged them to be even more generous. A monthly collection was added for the schools. The Holy Name, the *Association de Marie Immaculée* as well as the PTA and other parish societies doubled their activities. The pastor announced that only the children whose parents were registered in the parish and utilizing the envelopes would be admitted in the grammar school. For poor families, the problem did not arise, since the parish would pay, as it always had. In 1966, the schools were $10,192.48 in debt.

The generosity of the parishioners was truly touching. While the regular collections for 1964 had brought in a total of $43,401.48, those of 1967 increased to $54,204.59, all this in spite of the constantly diminishing number of parishioners. The Bingo, and the income from Saint Joseph Shrine, helped to make up the deficit and pay for the extra expenses. In 1966 the *Comité d'Aide aux Écoles* contributed $36,000 to the parish. The vigil lamps from Saint Joseph Shrine brought in nearly $16,000.

While the finances were of grave concern, the parish managed to get itself out of this tight spot, and hoped there would one day be an end to all the repairs. But there was another problem, far more serious and more urgent which had to be faced. The urban renewal area included the site of the girls' high school, which was set for demolition. Another location would have to be found for it, or the school would have to be closed. Father Lessard and his advisors considered several solutions, but none of them could be carried out. As a last recourse, the Marist Brothers were approached about accommodating the girls on the first floor of their school, and leaving the rest of the building to the boys.

The idea didn't appear to be practical, and so the Brothers refused. In the meantime, the director of education for the Brothers, Brother Patrick Magee, came to the school for an official visit in November 1965. At that time there were 295 boys in the school, taught by nine Brothers and two lay teachers.

After his visit, Brother Magee insisted that other changes be made to the school building, and that more lay teachers be hired so that the school would be in conformity with the educational program of their Congregation. Since Father Lessard could not accede to these demands he was forced, with regret, to find his own solution.

According to their constitutions, the Brothers could not teach girls, while the Grey Nuns had no such restrictions concerning boys. Also, the personnel of ten nuns, already teaching high school, was sufficient to dispense with the need for more lay teachers.

The required permissions having been obtained, Father Lessard announced his decision to the public on January 6, 1966. In the fall of 1966, Saint Joseph High School would be placed under the direction of the Grey Nuns of the Cross, who would teach both boys and girls. To avoid disrupting the students, the brothers would give up their classes one year at a time until their final departure in 1969. Considering all the circumstances, the departure of the Marist Brothers, and the merger of the two high schools was the most practical and reasonable solution.

The news hit like a bombshell. A storm of protest lashed out at the rectory and the pastor's head. Students picketed the rectory. There were articles in the newspapers, hate letters were sent to Father Lessard, protests were addressed to the chancery and the cardinal, squabbles ensued and insults were hurled. But the pastor remained firm and the parishioners understood his reasoning. The majority of the complaints came from outside the parish. In 1963, there were students from twenty-eight different parishes attending Saint Jean Baptiste Parish's High Schools. What many did not want to understand was that Saint Joseph High School was not a regional high school, but a parish one which accepted outside students. All the costs of maintenance, repairs, and the teachers' salaries were the responsibility of Saint Jean Baptiste parishioners. Therefore, since he was their spokesperson, the pastor's decision was rightfully their decision. The storm subsided, and in July the girls' high school moved to Merrimack Street.

It was with regret that the Marist Brothers left Lowell, and it was also with sorrow that the people saw them go. On June 6, 1967, a special High Mass, followed by a gala banquet at the Speare House, marked the 75th anniversary of the arrival of the brothers in Lowell, and the 150th anniversary of the founding of their congregation. The speeches, the large attendance, and the warmth of the greetings were a reminder of the good old days of the *Anciens Élèves* and provided the Franco-American population of Lowell with an opportunity to thank "their brothers" one last time.

With the hundredth anniversary of the parish fast approaching, the pastor, realizing that more work had to be done, undertook to complete the repairs in time. The parish hall had become inconvenient to use. The floor of the hall had always been on an incline toward the front to accommodate the viewing of plays and movies, but this slant was far from being practical for bean suppers and Bingo. Everything had to be redone in the kitchen and the restrooms, and air conditioning was now a necessity. Work began in January 1967. The floor was leveled. New toilets and a new kitchen were installed, while air conditioning and other amenities were added. In all, the cost of these changes amounted to a little more than $20,000, but the hall had been modernized and made very comfortable just in time for the celebrations. The ladies of *L'Association de Marie-Immaculée,* ever faithful, contributed $1,000 to the project. The men also did their share. Most of the balance was covered by the *Comité d'Aide aux Écoles.*

Now that the hall was ready, the churches had to be touched up. The entrance portico of the upper church had to be repainted, as well as the inside walls along the side aisles, up to the cornices. To go higher would have required specialized and expensive scaffolding. The lower church, which was utilized for weekday services, needed to be renovated to bring it in line with the new liturgical directives of Vatican II. The priest now had to celebrate Mass facing the congregation and a special chair for the celebrant near the altar also had to face the faithful. The Blessed Sacrament had to be reserved apart from the altar of the Holy Sacrifice.

Father Lessard consulted with his curates and got down to work while appealing to the generosity of the people. The needed changes were undertaken as the money became available. It was with genuine sorrow that the people saw the altar of the Sacred Heart disappear—so many of them had prayed there during wartime. They also grieved to see the great marble altar, which had been installed in the sanctuary by Father Garin, also removed. Others regretted seeing the statues of Saint Francis and Saint Claire taken from the sanctuary. But it was necessary to move forward. The statue of the Blessed Virgin was moved to the right of the nave, and the old penitential cross placed in the center of the renovated sanctuary, behind the presider's chair. The Blessed Sacrament was now located at a beautiful altar on the right of the sanctuary, prepared especially for that purpose. To complete the remodeling, the sanctuary floor was covered with blue carpeting, and a new sound system was installed.

No centennial celebration could ignore Saint Joseph church, which was at the very heart of the history and of so many memories connected with the parish. The venerable church was continuing its generations-old mission as a haven for immigrants. At the start of the twentieth century, Polish and Lithuanian immigrants had been welcomed there as had the French-Canadians before them. Now, in the sixties, the Cuban refugees and the Puerto Ricans were finding there a spiritual home.

Since 1964, the Hispanic Catholics of Lowell had been meeting in the basement of Saint Joseph Shrine, just like their predecessors of other nationalities had been doing in years past. Father Léo Guillemette had been placed in charge of the Spanish ministry at Saint Joseph in September 1964. When he left for the missions in the fall of 1965, he was replaced by Father Gilbert Dubé.

Saint Joseph Shrine still required a considerable number of repairs. The balconies had been removed, the walls redone, as well as the wiring, and a thousand other odd jobs had been completed, but the floor and the pews now needed to be replaced. The floor had long been condemned, and was unsafe in certain spots The nearly hundred-year-old pews had had their day, and they now needed to be replaced.

Work got underway with splendid results—a sturdy tile-covered floor and fine pews of smooth polished oak were put in place. The church had become very beautiful once again, inviting even, for a great many pews had been removed, allowing for more space. All of these changes had cost over $50,000 and were paid for mostly by the receipts from the shrine, and by the many donors who paid for the pews or contributed to the construction fund.

Everything was now ready for the centennial.

29. The Centennial

Fairly early on, the broad outline of the centennial celebration was drawn up. The committee in charge had been set up by July 1967. It was composed of an executive board, headed by Father Lessard as honorary president. The members were André Ouellette, president; Mrs. Hervé Hardy, vice-president; Mrs. Georgette Élie, secretary; Armand Tousignant, treasurer; Father George Lessard and Richard Santerre, historians. A general committee was made up of the delegates from the various parish societies: Délia Thellen, from the *Association de Marie Immaculée;* Mrs. Robert Descôteaux, from the *Comité d'Aide aux Écoles;* Richard Violette, from the Confraternity of the Christian Doctrine; Arthur Malo, from the Legion of Mary; Gérard Plamondon, from the PTA; Gérard Tremblay, from the Holy Name Society; Robert Perreault, from the Scouts; Mrs. Lionel Péloquin from the Third Order; Ferdinand Rousseau, from the Saint Vincent de Paul Society. Later a promotion committee was added with Paul Blanchette, Roland Paquette, Albert Daigle, and Louis Bergeron as members, while Léon Lamoureux and Marguerite Lyons made up the publicity committee.

Certain key decisions were taken from the very start. First, the celebration would take place during the week of April 21 to 28, 1968, to commemorate the arrival of Father Garin, in April 1868. Then, the parish commemoration would be distinct from one planned for the fall, to mark the centenary of the arrival of the Oblates in Lowell. It was also decided that, as much as possible, the celebrations would take place in French. The invited guest of honor would be Father Emile Bolduc, who would come from the Philippines to take part in the festivities.

Each sector of the parish would have the opportunity to play its part in the events. There would be something for everyone. It would truly be a *fête de famille* (a family celebration) as the pastor often said. At last, the program was finalized and presented. On Sunday, April 21, at Saint Joseph Shrine, there would be a concelebrated High Mass, with Cardinal Cushing presiding; this would be followed by a family gathering in the parish hall, to greet Father Bolduc and the Oblate Fathers. On Monday, there would be a French movie, *Mon Oncle* (My Uncle) by Jacques Tati, at the parish hall; on Tuesday, a *Soirée du Bon Vieux Temps* (A Good Old-Fashioned Evening), directed by Arthur Paquin; on Wednesday, a grand historical pageant *Cent Ans de Gloire* (One Hundred Years of Glory) presented by the school children; on Thursday evening, a concelebrated Mass for the deceased of the parish, followed by a second presentation of *Cent Ans de Gloire;* on Friday, a huge centennial Bingo; on Saturday evening, a family night with dancing in the parish hall; and on Sunday, April 28, a High Mass to close the centennial, with a gala banquet that evening at the Speare House.

Publicity began to circulate immediately. By March the committee began to sell, at the church doors and in the schools, insignia buttons specially designed by Marie-Jeanne Huot for the occasion, displaying the Centennial emblem. A beautiful illustrated bilingual flier containing the program was printed for popular distribution to the people in the parishes, in the pharmacies, and at other locations.

The historical committee worked closely with the promotion and publicity committees. The *Lowell Sun* published long articles on the history of the parish and the events to come. Antoine Clément, former editor of *L'Étoile,* who had become the "apostle of Franco-American centennials," though not a committee member, took care of press releases to the French newspapers, including *L'Action* of Manchester, New Hampshire, and *Le Travailleur* of Worcester. All over New England, the Lowell centennial was being talked about.

In its work, the historical committee took special care to highlight the person and accomplishments of Father Garin. At Saint Joseph Shrine, along the side walls of the nave, large panels were set up with photographs showing the activities of Lowell's first Oblate. As its contribution, the Saint Jean Baptiste Province had marked the approach of the centennial by arranging for the publication of a biography of Father Garin, *L'Inoubliable Fondateur* (The Unforgettable Founder), by the Oblate historian, Gaston Carrière, of Ottawa.

The official opening of the centennial year was observed on Sunday, January 7, 1968. Fifteen priests, all of them sons of the parish, gathered around the altar to concelebrate a Mass of Thanksgiving. Shortly after, the 800 tickets for the banquet went on sale.

On April 17, the *Lowell Sun* headlined on its front page: "Fr. Bolduc Comes Home." As soon as he arrived, the calls and visits started. No one had forgotten him.

The great week began with an unexpected surprise. *La Presse* of Montréal had sent Lysiane Gagnon, a star reporter, to Lowell, to write an in-depth article on the Franco-Americans of the city for their Sunday Supplement.

The events opened in an atmosphere of joy and enthusiasm. The grand pageant *Cent Ans de Gloire,* written by Sister Louis Robert, S.G.C., involved more than 300 children, from the elementary and high schools, as narrators, actors and singers, along with almost all of the nuns from the convent! The living tableaux, the playing of pre-recorded testimonials, the shared narrations, and the dozen or so impressive illustrated historical panels displayed

Fr. Emile Bolduc O.M.I., on the stage of the parish hall.

along the walls of the hall represented an almost unimaginable amount of work. To perpetuate the memory of this pageant, the text and the names of the participants were published in an illustrated souvenir booklet entitled *Cent Ans de Gloire.*

The *Soirée du Bon Vieux Temps,* presented by Arthur Paquin and his group of amateurs was one of the revelations of the week. The joy, the good-natured fun, and the artfulness of the presentation so captivated the audience that people hated to leave. Everyone had the same thought: "When will we have another one?" Lysiane Gagnon wrote the following about the soirée in her article for *La Presse:*

> They sang songs, old songs, with many in the hall joining in the refrain.
>
> Each one comes to the microphone with his little number: a song, a tune on the guitar, a violin selection, a funny story. And all of this is entirely and purely French-Canadian: this liveliness, this warmth, this manner of telling a joke, the small glasses of wine making the rounds on the stage (for they were recreating here a typical Christmas *réveillon* [the festive meal which follows Midnight Mass] of rural French-Canadian life) . . . . The accent of the actors is that of Montréal, with some slight differences. The voices are those of church singers, beautiful sonorous voices, and on key. At the microphone, references are made to people in the parish, inside jokes, to which everyone laughs, because all these people know one another. Racy stories are told, and the members of the

clergy, seated in the front rows, burst out in hearty laughter. "As 'you know who' would say, ... But . . . we are at home, here!"

Yes, we are at home.

Shortly after the presentation, the actors decided to form a permanent troupe: *La Troupe du Bon Vieux Temps* with Arthur Paquin as the director. The actors who participated in this evening, which has remained memorable, were: Mrs. Joseph Côté, André Ouellette, Léa Paquin, Achille Boulanger, Roger Sauvageau, Arthur Paquin, Jean Lavoie, Mrs. Marie Louise Grenier, Mrs. Blanche Larmand, Mrs. Yvonne Lagassé, Mrs. Georgette Elie, Mrs. Roger Sauvageau, Mrs. Arthur Paquin, Mrs. Florida Mailloux, Mrs. Jean Lavoie, Annette St. Pierre, Gislaine Sauvageau, Joseph Côté, Osa Hébert, Raymond Paquin, Roland Paquin, and Pierre Descôteaux.

The closing banquet provided, with great pomp, the last words for the celebration. Eight hundred guests assembled at the Speare House. Enthusiasm and joy were very much in evidence. The program, capably handled by the master of ceremonies, Stanislas O. Paquin, followed the traditional model of the grand celebrations of the past. Father Anatole Lessard spoke for the parish; Congressional Representative Bradford Morse, for the United States; Attorney-General Elliott Richardson, for the Commonwealth of Massachusetts; Mayor Robert Maguire, for the city of Lowell; Father Raymond Tague, their provincial, for the Oblate province; Homer Bourgeois, president of the Jeanne d'Arc Credit Union, for the parishioners; and Father Emile Bolduc, as the guest of honor. Congressman Morse and Attorney-General Richardson spoke easily in French, to the delight of the audience. Singing provided by the Oblate scholastics from Natick, and the *pot-pourri* of Canadian airs by the tenor Gérard Brunelle, added a nice touch to the evening.

Father Bolduc summarized the spirit of the celebration, and the long history of Saint Jean Baptiste parish. He spoke of the accomplishments of Father Garin who had wanted to help the "Canadians" in their spiritual, social, and even material lives, and how "he went about doing good" wherever he passed. His successors had tried to do the same and Father Bolduc added that he was happy to see that Spanish immigrants were being helped at Saint Joseph Shrine. He was glad also to note that there were now young Oblates to continue the work of Father Garin. His remarks were received with thunderous applause.

In June, the three local councils of the Union Saint Jean Baptiste: Carillon, J.N. Jacques, and Ste. Thérèse, wishing to mark the hundredth anniversary of the celebration of the feast of Saint Jean Baptiste in Lowell, held a concelebrated High Mass, followed by a banquet at the Speare House. To commemorate the event, a brochure by Richard Santerre was published entitled *L'historique de la célébration de la fête Saint-Jean-Baptiste à Lowell, Mass., de 1868 à 1968.*

The parish celebrations were now part of the past, but the preparations for the centenary of the arrival of the Oblates were ongoing. The arrival of the Oblates in Lowell had marked an important step in the expansion of the Congregation in the United States, and as such it was agreed that the festivities should be of some consequence. A group of influential laymen had been working on this commemoration for some time. They had invited the superior-general, Father Léo Deschâtelets, Richard Cardinal Cushing, and Thomas Cardinal Cooray, the only Oblate cardinal at the time, who was Archbishop of Colombo, Ceylon, to preside at the event. On Wednesday afternoon, September 18, a concelebrated High Mass was held in the Memorial Auditorium. Cardinal Cushing gave the homily, and that evening, at the Speare House banquet, Cardinal Cooray spoke of the Congregation and its far-flung works. Father Deschâtelets, ill at the time, was the only one who could not be present. The attendance of so many people, as well as the presence of the assistant-general of the Oblates, Father John King, the five American provincials, and those from Eastern Canada, were in themselves an eloquent testimonial to the important work accomplished by Fathers Garin, Lagier, and their successors.

The grand centennial celebrations had now all come to an end, but in the hearts of the parishioners and the Franco-Americans of Lowell, nothing could erase the history of the good accomplished, or the memory of their own lives spent in the midst of a loving community, centered on Christ, and nourished by a deep sense of respect, peace, and joy.

EPILOGUE
From the Centennial to the Present

The celebrations of the parish's centennial were a great success, and following the events, there was a renewed sense of confidence and hope in the parish. Daily life proceeded as it always had, and was full of activity.

On October 24, 1969, Fr. Armand Morissette celebrated the funeral Mass for Jean Kerouac, popularly known as "Jack" Kerouac. Born in Lowell and baptized at St. Louis de France Church, he had become a world-famous author and, with the publication of his book *On the Road,* the father of the "Beat Generation." Poets, novelists, "beatniks," and admirers arrived from all over the country, in addition to a swarm of media, to remember him and pay homage to his memory. His childhood friends, many of whom figured prominently in his books, would never forget the author who had grown up with them and gone on to such acclaim.

The once-grand celebration of St. Jean Baptiste Day on June 24, the patronal feast of the French Canadians, had declined and now passed almost unnoticed. Armand LeMay, a young city councilor who would later become mayor, wondered why the Franco-Americans did not have an official public observance of their heritage, like some other ethnic groups in Lowell.

At Councilor LeMay's urging, a group of Franco-American business and professional men called a meeting, on April 30, 1971, at the Lafayette Club, to discuss the matter. As a result, the Franco-American Day Committee was formed, with delegates from every club and association in the city. The committee took as its emblem, a round seal with the American flag in the center, the French flag on the left, and the Québec flag on the right. On Sunday, June 20, a memorial Mass, celebrated by Fr. Armand Morissette, was broadcast on WLLH Radio from St. Jean Baptiste Church. Then, in keeping with a resolution passed by the City Council proclaiming June 24, Franco-American Day, the Québec flag was flown from City Hall on Thursday, June 24. Following the reading of the proclamation and the singing of the national anthems, a reception was held in the mayor's Reception Room to unveil the portrait of former Mayor George Ayotte. In the evening, over five hundred people attended a festive banquet at the Speare House. The *Lowell Sun,* for its part, devoted the entire back page of its June 24 edition to the history of Lowell's Franco-American population!

This renewed annual celebration generated an enormous amount of enthusiasm and creativity. In 1972, the Canadian consul general in Boston, François X. Houde was invited to speak at the banquet, and Richard Santerre's illustrated brochure, *The Franco-Americans of Lowell, Massachusetts,* a brief history of the community, was published, and an evening of Québec cinema was added to the festivities. At the flag raising, a portrait of former Mayor Raymond Lord was unveiled.

All of this, combined with interviews on the radio, ample newspaper coverage and a positive and joyous reception on the part of the community, led the committee to expand its activities further and soon the members changed the committee's name to the "Franco-American Week Committee" to reflect the new and enlarged program. There were now musical evenings, cinema, *Soirées du bon vieux temps,* and an event for almost each night of the week. The grand banquet of 1973 had as its invited guest, the Canadian ambassador to Washington, Marcel Cadieux.

The pastor of St. Jean Baptiste Parish, Fr. Joseph Debergh, in consultation with the parish council and the parishioners, proposed that the celebrations include an annual St. Jean Baptiste parish festival with the closing Mass held at St. Jean Baptiste on the concluding Sunday of that week. The parish, after some negotiations, was able to obtain from the urban renewal authority, the vacant lot extending the length of Aiken Street from Merrimack to Moody, opposite the church, to serve as a parking lot. This enabled more people to come to church as well as providing space for flea markets during the festivals.

When Armand LeMay, who became mayor in 1974, proposed to the committee that a public monument to the Franco-American people of Lowell be erected as a lasting memorial of their contribution to the Mill City, the idea

The Franco-American Monument in front of the Lowell City Hall.

was unanimously accepted. Discussing the matter with the city manager and particularly, the placement of the monument, LeMay was struck when the manager, looking out his window, pointed with his hand and said, "Why not there?" indicating the front lawn of City Hall!

On June 24, 1974, after the flag raisings, accompanied by the anthems, the Franco-American monument was officially inaugurated. Situated close to the front entrance of City Hall, the monument is formed of a granite base with the seal of the committee in color in the center and a simple inscription in French and English, "In honor of the Franco-Americans of Lowell, Mass. June 24, 1974." The base is surmounted by a large bronze bell.

Urban renewal had created a few new streets, particularly in the area of City Hall, to connect with the new post office and fire and police stations. The Lowell City Council, on November 14, 1969, had approved the naming of a small street in front of City Hall, Arcand Drive, in honor of the young soldier from St. Jean Baptiste parish who had been the first from Lowell to give his life in Vietnam.

The new Franco-American monument faces Arcand Drive.

*   *   *   *   *   *   *

All of this activity helped stimulate new ideas and bring about new possibilities. One parishioner, Raymond Barrette, who had long believed that a new Franco-American newspaper for Lowell could succeed, founded in February 1975, the French language *Le Journal de Lowell*. A monthly, distributed free of charge, supported by advertisers and later on with paid mail subscriptions, the paper prospered and filled a long-felt need. Eventually, it was continued by Albert V. Côté and his wife Barbara.

The energy and optimism manifested at this time were not confined to the Franco-American community, although they were important elements in the events that were to shape an emerging Lowell where a different spirit was now developing. The mindsets in Washington and Boston had begun to change and urban renewal was now considered a colossal failure. Some of the largest Urban Renewal housing projects in the country, considered unliveable, had to be dynamited and razed. New approaches and new ideas would be needed to save the nation's older cities.

In Lowell, the massive destruction of the Northern Canal project and with it some of the city's most historic buildings left lingering regrets. In particular, the demolition of the corporation boarding houses on Dutton Street and other historic buildings caused many to doubt the value of what had been done and the little profit to the city that resulted from it all.

Led by some forward-looking members of the community and a prominent educator, Dr. Patrick Mogan, new plans were drawn up. In 1972, a bill was introduced in Congress to create in the city, the country's first urban national historic park, in recognition of Lowell's importance in the industrial history and development of the United States. By establishing this park, the preservation and restoration of Lowell's remaining historic buildings and districts became an essential component in explaining and showing this past to those who would be drawn to the national park. Lowell's history and culture had become an asset to be protected and promoted.

Events unfolded quickly. On June 5, 1978, Congress passed Public Law 95-290, creating the Lowell National Historic Park. The Commonwealth of Massachusetts, following suit, also developed a plan to aid its older cities.

In preparation for the country's bicentennial, the state had decided that tourism, based upon cultural heritage, could help cities economically. Heritage awareness and preservation became important tools to ensure economic revival. In 1975, the Commonwealth of Massachusetts created the Lowell Heritage State Park. To facilitate the functioning of these new institutions, a Lowell Historic Preservation Commission was established.

Soon, funding for both parks began to pour in, and in 1983 the center of Lowell was declared by law, the Lowell Downtown Historic District with specific boundaries, thus protecting its buildings from demolition in addition to providing information and access to the study of the past. Many buildings were restored to their original appearance and some, built over the canals, were removed to restore the original setting. Visitor centers were opened and tours given by park guides.

It was a new world for the people of Lowell. Old mill workers even volunteered to help run demonstration looms in the first museum.

The city government, for its part, also found new ways of doing things. The Lowell Housing Authority, in partnership with the state and federal governments, began to transform old abandoned mills and historic properties into elderly subsidized housing and later, private developers would follow suit by turning mills into apartments and studios, a process that continues to this day.

Many of these ideas were very forward looking for their time, and just as in the mid-nineteenth century, prominent Europeans came again to visit the "mile of mills." Charles, the Prince of Wales, was among those who came to see how Lowell had transformed an old industrial city into a new, viable model for the present day. He stated that he had come to Lowell because England had many old industrial cities that were in a situation similar to that of Lowell and it was encouraging to see how new ideas and new solutions could save them.

*   *   *   *   *   *   *

In the summer of 1970, Fr. Myles Cyr became pastor of St. Jean Baptiste parish. Fr. Lessard would return to Ste. Jeanne d'Arc where he later died, on January 29, 1999. Upon becoming pastor, Fr. Cyr, who was kind and gentle of manner, would have to deal with the difficult circumstances that were now facing the parish. The full force of urban renewal had by then taken its toll and the parish population had declined significantly. In 1969, there were 702 families in the parish, a total of 2,937 people. The Hispanic immigration to Lowell remained steady and the parish boundaries included the areas where many Spanish-speaking families were able to find housing.

The financial situation became difficult when the company carrying the parish's fire insurance decided that it would no longer issue that type of policy, thus forcing the parish to obtain its coverage from the Archdiocese of Boston at a cost of about $27,000 per year, three times the amount that it had been paying before. Fr. Cyr paid what he could and left the rest as a debt to the diocese.

Of more immediate concern, however, was the situation of the high school. With the departure of the Marist Brothers and the transfer of the school to the Grey Nuns, the school had become St. Joseph Regional High School and, it was hoped that it would become financially self-supporting. In fact, the school was not meeting its expenses and parish funds had to make up the difference.

Almost half of the students were from other parishes. The old system of having the parishes pay a subsidy to the school for each of their parishioners who attended, was no longer functioning. Some parishes were generous, others less so. Fr. Cyr presented the matter to the parish council which suggested a convocation of the parents. Homer Bourgeois, the president of the Jeanne d'Arc Credit Union, presented the matter clearly: unless tuitions were paid and unless the school could be organized on a sound financial basis, it would have to close.

After some discussion, it was decided that the school would be made completely independent from the parish and fully responsible for its expenses. A separate corporation was established with its own board and the school property was leased from the Oblates for $1.00 a year.

The financial situation was thus stabilized and Fr. Cyr was able to return to the day to day ministry of the parish.

The parishioners of St. Jean Baptiste were very generous in their love and devotion to the parish and were a constant source of support and assistance to each other and to the pastor. Bean suppers, bingos, meetings, excursions, in addition to the new activities of the Franco-American Day Committee all helped to encourage pride and solidarity. But it was the spiritual life of the parish that gave to all the strength and the inner joy that united them.

Fr. Cyr resigned as pastor in the summer of 1972 and was assigned to St. Joseph Shrine where his brother Fr. Roger Cyr was director. There he would spend nearly ten years ministering to the hundreds of people who came every week to the shrine. He would afterwards join the Oblate Mission Band as a missionary, laboring mostly in northern Maine.

Fr. Joseph Debergh succeeded him as pastor. Well known by the parishioners and well liked, he lost no time in undertaking the work at hand.

Following the reorganization of the high school, it was clear that something similar had to be done for the grammar school. Urban renewal had removed all the residential buildings from Moody Street to the river and the housing units built to replace them were neither as numerous nor were they well built.

Enrollment at the grammar school was low and the finances were a struggle, as were those of the parish in general. In March 1976, Fr. Debergh called a meeting of the parents and the parishioners to present the situation to them. The parish could no longer subsidize the school and some form of reorganization was needed.

Everyone agreed and a finance board, really a school board, was set up to watch over the school and its needs. The board consisted of the pastor, the principal, representatives of the teachers, and twelve parishioners, some of whom had to be parents of students. The decision was a good one and would turn out to be a godsend. As for the finances, tuition was raised considerably and a businessman from the parish, Albert Daigle, devised a plan that, over the years, would raise more that $250,000 for the school and the parish.

In accordance with his proposal, a VIP-1000 Club was set up. Essentially a lottery, the club consisted of a monthly drawing on the last Monday of the month. The "members" – up to a maximum of 1,000 – paid $5.00 a month and the first prize winner received $1,200 and nine other winners won smaller amounts. A monthly newsletter, containing the results as well as upcoming news regarding special anniversary raffles, was sent to all who enrolled. It was an enormous success. People joined in large numbers, some even from other states.

In 1958, when the last repairs to the church had been made, it was discovered that the copper gutters on both sides of the church needed to be replaced. But it was decided then to wait until later to undertake the needed repairs. Unfortunately, the matter was completely forgotten until it was noticed that there was increasing water damage in the upper church. An inspection revealed that not only did all the copper gutters need to be immediately replaced, but the decorative copper railing running along the crest of the roof as well.

The cost would be enormous, but the work needed to be done. After the repairs were finished, the parishioners, ever generous and through hard work, managed to pay much of the cost but there remained a substantial debt. Unfortunately, the fresco of the wedding of Mary and Joseph, over the door leading to the sacristy, had been lost due to water damage.

*   *   *   *   *   *   *

From the founding of St. Joseph Shrine, the director and the priests assigned to its ministry had lived at St. Jean Baptiste rectory. As the shrine and its programs continued to develop, it was hoped that it could be established as an independent community. In 1975, the mill-era boarding house adjacent to the church came up for sale. The Oblates purchased the residence and St. Joseph the Worker Shrine became a separate community with Fr. Roger Cyr, as director, and Frs. Myles Cyr, Bernard Belley, and Albert Martineau as its members. At the time of the establishment, Fr. Roger Cyr was able to donate, as a gift to St. Jean Baptiste, $40,000 from the shrine funds to help pay off the remaining debt from the roof repairs.

The newly established residence at the shrine was in the historic district and so the building's exterior was restored to its original appearance and later, after the closing of the Jordan Marsh department store, the other adjoining boarding house, which had been used as a warehouse, was also purchased and restored. Today, the attached houses are called the André Garin Residence for those Oblates who are serving at the shrine or have retired there.

Once again, the parish, with God's help, had met its needs and continued its mission, a mission that was soon to be affirmed in an extraordinary way. Pope Paul VI, on October 19, 1975, beatified the founder of the Oblates, Bishop Eugene de Mazenod, bringing into worldwide prominence the order and its purpose, *"Evangelizare pauperibus misit me"* "He has sent me to evangelize the poor."

February 17, 1976 would mark the 150th anniversary of the order's pontifical approbation as a religious congregation. A grand celebration of the anniversary was planned for Sunday, February 15, 1976, at St. Jean Baptiste church where both the order itself as well as the Oblates' work for over a hundred years in Lowell would be honored. There were six Oblate parishes in Lowell, in addition to St. Joseph Shrine and a parish in Tewksbury; all would participate. It was decided that it would be a joint celebration by both Oblate provinces, the Eastern Province of Our Lady of Hope, and the St. Jean Baptiste Franco-American Province.

Sunday, February 15, St. Jean Baptiste church took on its most festive appearance. There were flowers, banners and, for the occasion, the full-length oil portrait of Bishop de Mazenod was brought from the community room of the rectory and enthroned before the pulpit where it could be seen from every part of the church.

The church was full, even the balconies. The archbishop of Boston, Cardinal Humberto Medeiros was the principal celebrant with Bishop Joseph Ruocco, the two Oblate provincials, and the pastors of the Oblate parishes as concelebrants. Father Debergh welcomed the congregation that included the mayor and a delegation of city officials. Lowell was also celebrating its 150th anniversary, the sesquicentennial of its incorporation as a city.

In his homily, Cardinal Medeiros pointed out that both the city and the Oblates had grown together and helped each other for over a hundred years. Deeply appreciative of the Oblates' ministry, he prayed:

> May your light so shine before men that they will see your good works and give praise to the Father. That is what you ought to do. It is what you have tried to do. It is what you are to try to do.
>
> May this anniversary of your sesquicentennial be an occasion for rededication to the Gospel ideal, to the ideals of your Founder, and the ideal of Mary Immaculate.

Over the years, Lowell had given more vocations to the Oblate Congregation than any other city in the world. In 1978, there were 114 Oblates of Mary Immaculate who were born in Lowell.

At the Offertory procession, on an embroidered pillow, Fr. Garin's Oblate cross was carried in honor and presented to the Cardinal. The humble missionary through whose hands God had worked so marvelously, had not been forgotten.

Seated in a place of honor in the congregation was a small group of laymen, who, for their meritorious service to the order, had been named Honorary Oblates of Mary Immaculate: Léon Lavallée, John F. Reilly, Sr., Lillian M. Sullivan, Victor D. Généreux, Edward M. Gilbert, Assunta M. Gilbert, Thomas M. Pellerin and Homer W. Bourgeois. Léo King, Rose Morin, Laurent Béliveau, Yvon Bourassa, Napoléon Pelletier, also Honorary Oblates, were not present. At the conclusion of the Mass, Mayor Leo Farley read a proclamation making Tuesday, February 17, 1976, Oblate Day in Lowell.

The Mass had been deeply moving and would not soon be forgotten. The music alone had been magnificent. The Immaculate Conception choir and the St. Jean Baptiste choir were exceptional. Selections from Haydn's

Masses and from Handel, settings from French liturgical music and the new hymn *"Evangelizare, Alleluia! Pauperibus misit me!"* sung with trumpet accompaniment led all to deeper prayer. As one member of the congregation confided, in tears, *"C'est pas souvent qu'on voit une messe comme ça."* "It isn't often that we see such a Mass."

In celebration of the beatification, a statue of Bishop de Mazenod, imported from France, was placed in the lower church. Later, a specially commissioned statue was placed in the sanctuary of St. Joseph's Shrine and weekly novena prayers begun. On December 3, 1995, Bishop Eugene de Mazenod was canonized a Saint by Pope John Paul II.

Fr. Debergh was always conscious of the parish's history and the deep wounds inflicted by urban renewal. He had retrieved the granite front step from the pharmacy which had stood at the corner of Aiken and Merrimack Streets and had it carved and placed on the same spot, at the entrance to the parking lot the parish had succeeded in obtaining. He organized the annual parish festival in June to coincide with Franco-American Week, and joined with enthusiasm in the many developments taking place in Lowell.

One day, watching the demolition of the last block of the apartments on Moody Street, it came to him that there was no monument to preserve the memory of all those who had lived and toiled in "Little Canada" and contributed so much to Lowell.

So, in June 1977, he announced that the Notini Brothers, whose company had been relocated to the Merrimack River side of the Northern Canal, where the heart of Little Canada had once stood, offered to let a Franco-American monument be built on a piece of their property which had been the corner of Hall and Aiken Streets.

Fr. Debergh outlined his plan in an article in *Le Journal* and hoped that the dedication could take place during Franco-American Week, on June 26, the day of the parish festival. He added that he would be grateful for any donations received. Money poured in from everywhere and the letters gave evidence of how moving the idea proved to be.

From Lowell:
>*J'ai lu dans le journal la belle nouvelle qu'on aura un monument pour nous, les Canadiens, juste où je suis née . . . .*

>(I read in the newspaper, the beautiful news that we will have a monument for ourselves, the Canadians, exactly where I was born. . . .)

Je vous envoye un chèque. . . . J'ai tenu un magasin au coin des rues Tucker et Ward pendant 47 ans . . . .

(I am sending you a check. . . . I kept a store at the corner of Tucker and Ward Streets for 47 years. . . .)

From Pelham, NH:

Ma mère a grandi dans le Petit Canada et j'ai gardé de bons souvenirs des visites que nous faisions aux parents qui vivaient là . . . Mes félicitations à ceux qui ont eu l'idée de placer un monument là dans le but de rétablir les liens entre le passé et le présent.

(My mother grew up in Little Canada and I have good memories of our visits to the relatives who lived there . . . My congratulations to those who had the idea of placing a monument there for the purpose of re-establishing the bonds between the past and the present.)

From Canada:

L'idée d'ériger un monument souvenir au coin des rues Aiken et Hall rappellera aux jeunes générations l'ardeur au travail de la généreuse jeunesse fière et honnête, de citoyens courageux au travail. J'ai peiné pendant six ans au Lawrence Hosiery Mills et à 19 ans j'étais en forme pour répondre à l'appel à la vocation religieuse. J'ai fêté 60 ans de vie religieuse en 1974 . . . Une ancienne de Lowell. Je me souviens.

Sœur Emma Milot, s.p.

(The idea of erecting a memorial monument at the corner of Aiken and Hall Streets will remind the younger generations of the zeal at their work of the upright, proud and honest youth, of citizens undaunted by work. I labored for six years at the Lawrence Hosiery Mills and at 19 years of age, I was fit to answer the call of a religious vocation. I celebrated 60 years of religious life in 1974 . . . A former Lowellian. I remember.

Sister Emma Milot, s.p.)

And from a "non-Franco-American":

Little Canada. It is a terrific idea, and truly worth every cent. The way Lowell is tearing itself apart; no one would have any landmarks to speak of . . . Please accept my little token toward your projected plans and good luck for its completion.

Franco-American Week in June 1977 included a different kind of remembrance of Little Canada. Friday, June 24, was sunny and pleasant as the participants in the grand parade assembled at the corner of Aiken and Merrimack Streets. Led by the police, the Lowell High School band and

373

the members of the *Club des Citoyens Américains* color guard, followed by the grand marshal, Arthur Paquin and his wife, the parade set out along Merrimack Street. The march included committee members, priests and sisters, parishioners, choir members, and *L'Equipe du Bon Vieux Temps* who would perform in the plaza next to City Hall. In the midst of this imposing column was the statue of St. Jean Baptiste that had survived the fire of 1912, carried aloft on the shoulders of the proud parishioners.

That evening, at Ste. Jeanne d'Arc Hall, the musical soirée included a performance by the celebrated Beaudoin Brothers, Louis and Wilfred, from Vermont, and Louis' daughter Lisa. Recognized as being among the most famous fiddlers in the United States, they had played at Jimmy Carter's inauguration as president. The Beaudoin brothers, now living in Vermont, were born in Lowell and grew up in Lowell's Little Canada. Louis Beaudoin's first memories, as he explained, were of his father playing his violin at home or at the numerous soirées and marriages in Little Canada. His father often played, late into the night, with his fiddler friends.

At fifteen, Louis had decided that he also wanted to be a fiddler, and he explained how his father would play for him and how his mother would sing melodies and songs until he learned them by heart.

As the Beaudoins and young Lisa both played and danced the old jigs and reels, the audience of four hundred was transported to another time and to the Little Canada that had been. Some in the audience even got up and spontaneously began to dance!

Unfortunately, the bronze plaques for the monument were not ready in time and the blessing and dedication took place only on Sunday, October 2. Fr. Michael Lauzé blessed the monument, Brother Richard Côté read a prayer, and Robert Couillard and Germaine Lemire addressed those assembled. Arthur Paquin led the people in singing O Canada and God Bless America.

The simple granite monument, surrounded by a small wrought-iron fence, is both meaningful and moving. There are two bronze plaques on the granite monument.

The upper plaque reads:

<u>LE PETIT CANADA – LITTLE CANADA</u>

EN SOUVENIR DES CANADIENS DE LANGUE
FRANÇAISE ET DE LEURS DESCENDANTS,
LES FRANCO-AMÉRICAINS, QUI ONT VÉCU
ICI. NOS CŒURS N'OUBLIERONT JAMAIS
LEUR COURAGE, LEURS SACRIFICES, LEUR
FOI, LEUR FIERTÉ.

1875 – 1964

ON THIS SITE GREW THE HEART OF THE
FRANCO-AMERICAN COMMUNITY. HARD
WORKING FRENCH CANADIANS CAME TO
FILL THE MILLS OF LOWELL AND BUILD
A TRADITION OF FAITH, GENEROSITY,
AND PRIDE.

JE ME SOUVIENS! – LEST WE FORGET!

On both sides of these inscriptions runs a band with the list of the streets partially or completely destroyed by urban renewal:

AIKEN – CABOT – CHEEVER – COOLIDGE – HALL – MELVIN – MONTCALM – PAWTUCKET – PERKINS – SUFFOLK – TUCKER – WARD

The following is a translation of the French text on the plaque:

IN MEMORY OF THE FRENCH-SPEAKING
CANADIANS AND THEIR DESCENDANTS, THE
FRANCO-AMERICANS WHO LIVED HERE. OUR
HEARTS WILL NEVER FORGET THEIR COURAGE,
THEIR SACRIFICES, THEIR FAITH, THEIR PRIDE.

The lower plaque reads:
1977
ERECTED BY
THE FRANCO-AMERICAN PEOPLE
AND
THE OBLATE FATHERS OF
ST. JEAN BAPTISTE PARISH
THIS STONE COMES FROM ONE OF THE
LAST BLOCKS OR LARGE WOODEN
APARTMENT HOUSES TO BE TORN DOWN

Fr. Debergh, taken suddenly ill, was not able to be present for the dedication, and died soon after, on October 6, 1979. A very kind and sincere man whose sufferings during the war had brought him close to the people, he was deeply mourned.

The Little Canada Monument on Aiken Street, near the Northern Canal.

His compatriot, Fr. Achille L'Hermitte, O.M.I., had died February 25, 1969, while shoveling snow in front of the rectory. He collapsed and died at the foot of Fr. Garin's statue.

Fr. André Houle, who was named as Fr. Debergh's successor, arrived in November 1977. The parish continued its routine life until March 1980 when the Grey Nuns, faced with a serious lack of vocations, announced to the pastor that sadly they were no longer able to staff St. Joseph's elementary school. The news came as a considerable shock. The sisters, who had founded the school in 1883, were well loved and respected by all.

Fr. Houle and the parishioners called several public meetings to discuss the matter and see what could be done to save the school, since there was no question in anyone's mind that it be allowed to close.

Since the school board was functioning well and there were already a number of lay teachers at the school, it was decided that the school would continue to operate with lay teachers and a lay principal and administrators. The transition went smoothly. The new principal, Mrs. Donna Garabedian, began her duties in August 1980, succeeding Sister Alice Tellier, the last sister to be principal.

In the early summer of 1980, Fr. Houle was named associate pastor of St. Mary of Lourdes parish, in Lincoln, Maine.

His successor, Fr. Arthur Obin, arrived in the parish on July 1, 1980, just after the departure of the sisters from the school and convent. Not long afterward, he was approached by members of the Hispanic Catholic community. Although they were numerous in Lowell, they had no place to meet or to organize classes, or even an office for a secretary. As a result, Oblates who ministered to them found it difficult to organize activities.

The Hispanic community asked if perhaps an arrangement could be made for them to use the now empty St. Joseph convent. The building had been completely renovated in the 1960s and the new addition had private rooms that could be used for small retreats.

The pastor immediately called a meeting of the parish council and put the matter before them. Given the fact that the parish now had a large empty building that it was responsible for maintaining, the proposal seemed both reasonable and desirable. Having discussed the matter, the council decided to grant the request with the stipulation that the Hispanic Community be entirely responsible for the upkeep of the building.

All parties having agreed, the Missionary Oblate Hispanic Center opened its doors. Father Obin had the corridor connecting the convent with the school removed, a sad reminder of the recent ending of an era.

The sisters had left the elementary school, but they were still at the high school as well as at St. Joseph Hospital. Among the people there was a desire to thank them for all they had done and were still doing for the people of Lowell. Since the elementary school had opened on November 12, 1883, it seemed appropriate to plan a grand celebration for November 12, 1983, the centennial of the sisters' arrival.

The festivities began on October 23, 1983 at a special Mass attended by the sisters, their students, and many alumni. The closing banquet of Saturday, November 12, was held at the Speare House, with Atty. Louis Eno serving as master of ceremonies. The entire evening was a heartfelt and well-deserved tribute to the Sisters of Charity of Ottawa, the name they now used instead of Grey Nuns of the Cross.

The committee also paid homage to the Marist Brothers who had founded the boys' elementary school and staffed it for 75 years. Brother Dennis Dunne, FMS, the provincial of the Poughkeepsie Province, in a moving letter, thanked God for all the blessings received over the years by the Brothers and students, both at St. Joseph and in faraway lands:

> The Marist Brothers during their stay at this school were blessed with good vocations.
> Our association with the Oblate Fathers has blessed the work of the Brothers and was responsible for the rapid development of our work in the educational arena for the Church. It was Father Bolduc who invited the Brothers to the Philippines in 1948. He and his fellow classmate, Brother Louis Omer Duprez, Provincial, were responsible for the eventual

establishment of schools and colleges placed under the protection of Mary, the Notre Dame School System. The Brothers continue to promote this far-reaching school system which flourishes under the direction of our native brothers.

* * * * * * *

In the printed program for the banquet, Fr. Obin, in his congratulatory letter, wrote concerning the student body at St. Joseph elementary school:

> The surnames of students are no longer only French. They now read like the League of Nations. However, they are today, like in the early years, the most recent immigrants to the city of Lowell and to the parish community.

St. Joseph's continued to serve the poor and the most recent immigrants to the area who now came from many countries. But Fr. Obin was not aware of how prophetic his words would prove to be.

Lowell was at the start of what would soon become another of a series of profound transformations in its history. Following the war in Vietnam, a number of refugees from Southeast Asia and particularly Vietnam had arrived in Lowell, many of them Catholic, escaping suffering and persecution in their native land. Soon, in the late 1970s, they were followed by large numbers of Cambodians fleeing from the terror and the genocide caused by the Khmer Rouge. As the terror and then civil war in Cambodia increased, many more fled to refugee camps, eventually arriving in Lowell to start a new life. From about fifty families in 1983, by 2006, they numbered at least 10,000 people according to the U. S. Census, although many put this figure, unofficially, much higher.

When they arrived, they sought housing in many of Lowell's old remaining tenement blocks and apartment buildings, mostly in the Acre, the Highlands, and some in Centralville, and then set about beginning new lives. Industrious and energetic, they followed the path of the other immigrant groups who had preceded them. They bought property as soon as they could and began their own businesses.

Old Notre Dame de Lourdes church on Branch Street, sold when the new church was built, became the site of a Cambodian shopping mall. The Achin Insurance Agency building on Merrimack Street, four doors from St. Jean Baptiste rectory, became a Southeast Asian supermarket and the store next door to the rectory, a Cambodian café.

For the moment, the parish itself carried on as it always had, while seeking to continue its ministry not only to parishioners but to all who came. Fr. Obin was very kind to the poor and the disadvantaged, and helping, unknown to many, both families and individuals who, but for him, would have had nowhere else to turn.

Like his predecessor, Fr. Henri Bolduc, he was also very interested in the parish's history and in the preservation of its archives. He pointed out to the parishioners that 1987 was the one hundredth anniversary of the purchase of the historic Bonney house by Fr. Garin, for a rectory. A celebration was planned with a banquet in the parish hall held on Saturday, November 21, 1987. This was preceded by an open house at the rectory that same evening before the banquet and also on Sunday afternoon, November 22. An exhibit of historic photographs with accompanying explanations had been prepared for the occasion. The banquet also provided an occasion for raising funds for the parish. Almost $10,000 was realized from donations and the program book.

The exhibit had included the framed photographs of the previous pastors of the parish as well as the Oblate cross worn by Fr. Garin himself. One of these pastors, Fr. Emile Bolduc, was very much on everyone's mind. Fr. Bolduc had spent his last years, almost half his life, in the Philippines and was greatly loved by the people, as much as he had been loved in Lowell and for the same qualities, "patience, kindness, humility and zeal" in the words of Archbishop Gérard Mongeau, O.M.I., his superior. Fr. Bolduc had died peacefully on February 8, 1982 at the age of eighty-five.

His legion of friends in Lowell wanted to ensure that his memory would not be forgotten. Since the year 1989 would mark the 50th anniversary of his departure for the Philippines, a committee was formed and Fr. Charles Dozois was asked to write a biography of the beloved pastor in both French and English.

Everyone set to work. Paul Blanchette helped Fr. Dozois with the research and Fr. Bolduc's family and Oblate confrères provided information. To finance the project, a penny sale was held and clubs, associations, businesses, and over 150 individuals made donations, some as memorials to deceased loved ones.

The resulting book was published in June 1989 in time for Franco-American Week and entitled: Charles H. Dozois O.M.I., *Le bon Père Bolduc. Biographie du Père Emile Bolduc O.M.I / Le bon Père Bolduc. Biography of Father Emile Bolduc O.M.I.*

The dedication states simply, *"Il a été prêtre tel que le Christ veut que ses prêtres soient.* He was a priest such as Christ wants His priests to be." In speaking of the anniversary and Fr. Bolduc's ministry in Lowell, Fr. Dozois wrote:

Cette occasion nous a donc paru toute indiquée de vouloir revivre nos meilleurs souvenirs de lui et de les consigner par écrit pour leur donner une valeur durable. Dans une certaine mesure, nous partagerons ainsi avec les générations montantes l'impact qu'il a eu sur nous et ce qu'il représente encore pour nous cinquante ans plus tard. Et, peut-être qu'avec la grâce de Dieu, l'un de nos jeunes se sentira appelé par le Seigneur à suivre la trace de ce Père Oblat, qui est resté une inspiration dans nos vies au cours de toutes ces années. Le Père Bolduc était un de ces Oblats aimants et bienveillants dont la vie était remplie de l'amour de Dieu et du service de son prochain.

And in English:

So, we thought this might be a fitting occasion to relive among ourselves our fondest memories of him and set them in print to give them lasting value. Thus, we will share in some measure with the younger generation what Father Emile meant to us in those years and still means to us a half century later. And, maybe, with the grace of God, someone among our current youth might be inspired to listen and heed the Lord's call to follow in the footsteps of a generous, dedicated Oblate priest who has remained over the years a living inspiration in our lives. Father Emile was a caring Oblate who found his fulfillment in a life of prayer to God and of service to neighbor.

Fittingly, all the profits from the book were donated to the Oblate Foreign Mission House on Mt. Washington Street.

On May 12, 1982, the Lowell Housing Authority dedicated a new residence on Hildreth Street, named Morissette Manor, in honor of Fr. Armand Morissette. Very patriotic and civic minded, Fr. Morissette had spent most of his life in Lowell. His devotion to veterans' groups was legendary as was his deep pride in being Franco-American.

Almost from the first issue of *Le Journal de Lowell,* he published a monthly column of reminiscences that became one of the most popular items in that newspaper. But most of all, he was a very kind priest who loved people deeply.

In failing health, he had moved from St. Jean Baptiste rectory to a nursing home and now his numerous friends sought a special way to honor him. One of the main intentions of the urban renewal was the construction of a thoroughfare connecting the University Avenue Bridge to the new post office and the downtown area. Originally called the French Street Extension, it was renamed, on May 30, 1990, by the City Council, the Fr. Morissette Boulevard.

Fr. Armand Morissette died peacefully on October 28, 1991. The parish also wanted to remember him, and so, in the usual time-honored way, a committee was formed and plans were made. On Saturday evening, March 7, 1992, a gala banquet was held in his memory at the Elks Hall. Among the many guests and dignitaries present were Laurent Rapin, Consul General of France in Boston, Hélène Day, Honorary Consul of Monaco, and Laurent Cardinal, Québec's Delegate to New England, who all spoke eloquently and movingly of their admiration and respect for him.

In Lowell, it was a time to remember. The city was continuing to reclaim its history. New parks were being laid out, buildings restored, and monuments erected. A large warehouse on Bridge Street was demolished and a new park created in its place. In June 1988, the park was dedicated to Jack Kerouac

The Jack Kerouac Park on Bridge Street.

and a monument composed of granite monoliths inscribed with passages from his most famous works was installed. Kerouac's reputation was constantly growing and the site as well as his grave in the Edson Cemetery had become sought-out destinations for his admirers from all over the world.

The latter half of the 1980s also saw the refurbishment of the small Veterans Memorial Park on Aiken Street in Centralville facing the Ouellette Bridge. New bronze and granite memorials and a new flagpole were set in place to honor Centralville's veterans.

On January 27, 1990, however, a new monument was added to the park. It contains the following inscription:

Presented This Day, January 27, 1990
to the
Brissette Family
In Honour And Loving Memory
Of Their Brother
U. S. Navy Airman
Normand Roland Brissette
Of Lowell, Massachusetts
Who Died While A Prisoner Of War
At Hiroshima Japan The Day Of The
Atomic Bomb August 6th , 1945

He Will Be Forever Young
For He Has Given Us
His Tomorrows

Dedicated On Behalf Of The
Centraville Memorial
Monument Committee
The Veterans Of St. Louis
Parish And A Forever
Grateful Centraville
Community, Lowell
Massachusetts

Normand Brissette, a former altar boy and a parishioner of St. Louis de France, had joined the U. S. Navy at age seventeen, and died at nineteen. The memorial states that he died the day the atomic bomb was dropped on Hiroshima, but in actual fact he survived for another thirteen days dying on August 19 from severe radiation burns and poisoning.

The U. S. government at the time and for many years kept the cause of his death secret and the fact that twelve American POWs had died at Hiroshima. The family however came to know the truth because another POW, transferred to the Hiroshima area after the blast, had seen young Brissette and promised, after his release, to fulfill the young man's dying wish that he go to his parents in Lowell to tell them of his love for them and of his final hours.

Today, Normand Brissette's memory and those who died with him is remembered at the memorial in Japan and is fully acknowledged by the American government.

By the end of the decade, the state of Catholic secondary education had become increasingly difficult. There were three Catholic high schools in the city: St. Joseph's Regional, Keith Catholic on Stevens Street, both co-educational, and St. Louis Academy for girls in Centralville. In 1987, Keith Catholic announced that it would be closing. St. Joseph's, which was already running annual deficits with a declining enrollment, had been holding some joint programs with St. Louis to help alleviate the situation. Then, St. Joseph's also announced that it would soon have to close.

As it was, many families were transporting their children by bus or car to Central Catholic in Lawrence, Bishop Guertin in Nashua, Notre Dame Academy in Tyngsboro, Presentation of Mary Academy in Hudson and even to St. John's Preparatory School in Danvers.

The viability and survival of Catholic secondary education in Lowell was at stake. When Keith Catholic closed in 1988, all three high schools merged in 1989 becoming Lowell Catholic High School on the Stevens Street site where there was room for expansion. The last classes at St. Joseph's were held in the spring of 1992. The Grey Nuns and the Sisters of the Assumption from St. Louis Academy together with lay faculty worked long and hard to ensure the future of the new school which continues to this day.

Fr. Obin had been pastor since 1980, one of the longest terms as pastor since Fr. Garin. On July 1, 1990, he was assigned as pastor of St. Mary parish in Claremont, N.H. The new pastor, Fr. Michael Lauzé, was no stranger to the parish. As a newly ordained priest, he had been sent as an assistant to Fr. Debergh and it was he who had blessed the Little Canada monument.

The St. Jean Baptiste Province of the Oblates, like so many other small provinces of religious orders in those troubled times, had suffered greatly from the lack of vocations and the shortage of personnel. Already, the Oblates were deciding about the future of their presence at St. Jean Baptiste. Consequently, Fr. Lauzé was named as the administrator of the parish rather than its pastor, a canonical distinction that does not grant the administrator the permanency of a pastor with all of his powers. For the parishioners, canon law aside, Fr. Lauzé was the new curé and everyone was happy with him. Affable, enthusiastic and close to the people, he was much loved during his stay and worked side by side with them through their joys and their sorrows.

The parish had very little money, but the parish spirit was remarkable and there was a burst of activity. Whenever he needed help, Fr. Lauzé would put a notice in the parish bulletin and donations and money would come pouring in. And, as in the past, creative fund-raising efforts succeeded in paying the parish's bills. This was no small feat as they even managed to install a new boiler in the parish hall, paint the lower church and make needed repairs to the grammar school. The parish fire insurance debt, however, was too much to pay at once, so regular payments were made, with the balance left as a debt to the archdiocese.

Pastorally, no one was neglected. Many of the parishioners were elderly and had no way to get to Mass. So, a bus was donated and a driver volunteered to transport them to church. A survey of the parish elderly having shown that they preferred the Saturday afternoon Mass, the bus wound its way through the parish and to the housing for the elderly to pick up its passengers every Saturday. And, a Spanish-language Mass was celebrated on Saturday evenings for the parish's Hispanic population.

The number of parishioners was constantly diminishing, however. Between 1980 and 1990, the parish had lost about 400 parishioners. The families were not being replaced as empty apartments were providing housing for newly arrived immigrants. Since many of the remaining parishioners were elderly, few baptisms and marriages were taking place and the confirmations were held with those at Ste. Jeanne d'Arc because of the low numbers. In 1991, there were twenty-one baptisms and five marriages at St. Jean Baptiste.

It must be added also, unfortunately, that the neighborhood around the church had become one of the poorest in the city and too often an attraction for criminal activity. As the aging property owners sold their apartment buildings and residences, new and often less committed landlords purchased them and often let them deteriorate. Several fires occurred and some properties were even left abandoned, opening the way for unsavory activities. One fire on Decatur Street had left many Hispanic families homeless and resulted in several deaths leading to an investigation of the landlord. Another fire on Merrimack Street had left a building partly in ruins for years. Finally, after repeated complaints from Fr. Obin and then from Fr. Lauzé as well as the parish council and many others concerned about revitalizing the area, the city took action in 1992.

It tore down a number of abandoned and burned-out buildings and began efforts at rehabilitation. As the parishioners had repeatedly stated, there was no reason why, with a little good will and everyone's cooperation, the area could not be reclaimed.

On September 26, 1991, at the request of Fr. Donald Arel, provincial of the Oblate province, and Bishop Alfred Hughes, the vicar-general of the archdiocese, a meeting was called which included Fr. Lauzé, the parish council, the school board, and the school faculty. Fr. Arel announced to those present that the Oblates would no longer continue to staff St. Jean Baptiste parish and would be withdrawing at the end of June 1992. Bishop Hughes said in turn that unfortunately the archdiocese had neither the personnel to staff the parish nor the financial resources to assume its debts. When asked if this meant the closure of the parish, Bishop Hughes answered that no final decision could be taken without an in-depth study of the parish and the preparation of a plan-of-action document, that would give the archdiocese a clearer picture of the situation and the Oblates a reason to reconsider their decision.

As soon as the news was announced to the parish, work began. The general cry of alarm was *"La conservation de notre patrimoine franco-américain et de notre église-mère.* The preservation of our Franco-American patrimony and our mother church."

A large general committee of over fifty members was formed and met on October 2, 1991. Named the Historic St. Jean Baptiste Church Preservation Committee, its function would be to coordinate and see to all activities and projects necessary to save the parish and to prepare the plan of action to be submitted to the Oblate council.

The committee was composed of the following persons: Fr. Michael Lauzé, Fr. George Dupont, Monique Blanchette, Aurore Boissonneault, Alice Brunelle, Michael Brunelle, Denise Châteauneuf, Albert A. Daigle, Dianne B. Daigle, Nicole I. Daigle, Thérèse M. Daigle, Albert A. Daigle Jr., Kathleen Daniel, Irène R. Desmarais, Suzanne Fréchette, Jeanne Gagné, Donna Garabedian, Gérard Geoffroy, Laura Geoffroy, Jeanne Hardy, Robert Lafleur, Estelle Lafleur, Jeannette Langlois, Claire Lemieux, Michelle Lemieux, Denise Marcouillier, Paula Masson, George Motard, David Ouellette, Guy Ouellette, Eugène Paquin, Hervé Paquin, Marthe Biron Péloquin, Bernard B. Péloquin, Cécile Poulin, Richard Provencher, Roger Racette, William Toupin, Armand Tousignant, Gérard Tremblay, Pauline Wagner, Arthur Watson, Isabelle Y. Watson.

Albert Daigle was elected chairman and Estelle LaFleur, recording secretary. Meetings were to be held every two weeks. One of the first orders of business was to address the picture of the financial situation of the parish since the one given by the authorities at the preceding meeting was quite inaccurate.

The parish had a number of short-term, mostly school related, loans and those would soon be paid. The archdiocesan fire insurance debt had been grossly inflated. After much insistence on the part of the committee, the diocese found that, through a computer error, the amount had been increased by $150,000! In reality, the parish owed $153,340.22.

In October, the committee "to insure the continuity" of the church launched a city-wide pledge drive. The basic pledge amount was $1.00 per year, per month, per week or per day over a period of ten years or five years to be paid in advance or upon receipt of a bill or bills issued according to the payment method requested. An immediate success, the drive, by the end of November, had received $117,000.00 in pledges and $7,000.00 in cash. By December, the amount had exceeded $125,000.00.

The committee was occupied in preparing the parish proposal when, unexpectedly in mid-November, a letter arrived from the offices of the archdiocesan school department. The Catholic School Study Committee had reached the conclusion that St. Joseph elementary school should close at the end of the school year, in June 1992. The reaction was swift with a subcommittee set up to try to rescind the decision.

However, the situation of the school was a difficult one. In the fall of 1991, the enrollment was 123 students. The 7th and 8th grades had a combined total of 17 students. In 1983, the tuition had been $450.00 for parishioners and $600.00 a year for non-parishioners in an enrollment of 165 students. By 1991, the tuition was $1,250.00 a year for a child outside the parish and slightly less for parish members.

St. Joseph school, like the high school before it, had become a regional elementary school with students from throughout the city and its suburbs. Lowell was in a period of economic recession. Wang Laboratories, the Lowell-based computer corporation, which at their peak employed more workers than all of the textile mills combined, had begun its slow decline. In 1991, St. Joseph's lost fifty students whose parents had been laid off by Wang. The situation showed no promise of improving. In the end, the decision to close the school would stand. Much to everyone's sorrow, St. Joseph Elementary School held its last graduation, Friday evening, June 5, 1992.

The C.M.A.C. was also feeling its age. Most of the members were elderly and decreasing in numbers. In August 1992, its officers and those of the Association Canado-Américaine of Manchester, N.H., a large Franco-American fraternal society, voted to merge. The ACA assumed responsibility for the insurance policies, and the archives of the C.M.A.C. were transferred to Manchester. The landmark building at the head of Merrimack Street was put up for sale.

In the meantime, working steadily, the committee was able to assemble a comprehensive pastoral proposal for the parish. An in-depth study covering over fifty pages, including financial annexes, the proposal examined every aspect of the parish and defined its mission for the future, both pastorally and financially. Prepared with great care and expertise, the impressive document received the unanimous approval of Fr. Lauzé, the parish council and the committee.

Special emphasis was placed upon the parish's mission to the elderly, the poor and the unchurched. With the economic downturn in the area, the parishioners knew firsthand the needs and sufferings of the people.

On April 1, 1985, at the invitation of Bishop John D'Arcy, the regional bishop, Sr. Jeanne Poor, a Grey Nun of Montreal, arrived in Lowell to establish a shelter for the homeless. Sr. Poor had been the co-founder of Lazarus House for the homeless in Lawrence and was very experienced in ministry to those in need.

A board composed of lay people, religious, priests and a deacon was formed to bring the project to fruition. Sr. Yvette Thibodeau, the director of St. Joseph's Hospital and a member of the board, offered the use of a three-decker apartment building, two doors down from the hospital on Merrimack Street for $1.00 a year.

An army of volunteers from throughout Lowell and the suburbs set about transforming the property and on December 24, 1985, the House of Hope shelter opened its doors, with Sr. Jeanne Poor as director. Homeless men and women and gradually families found there a safe haven and compassionate help.

The House of Hope continued to expand with the growing need until today it owns the original house and two others on Salem Street, all providing care and dignity for the most vulnerable.

The new pastor of St. Patrick parish, Fr. Thomas Powers and Fr. Obin met one day to discuss the situation of the poor. All of the Catholic institutions in the Acre: schools, parishes, convents, and the hospital were experiencing an increasing number of requests for food and help, often from the same people. They decided that there was clearly a need for a food pantry in the area.

Fr. Obin offered the space of the former Librairie Baron in the lower church, with a door opening onto Moody Street and, in January 1989, a board composed of representatives of the Lowell parishes and various community groups met at the rectory to begin implementing the project. Since those needing food came not only from the Acre but from throughout the city, it was decided that the pantry would be placed under the auspices of the Merrimack Valley Catholic Charities.

The first need was for money and equipment. Freezers were donated and installed and money was collected. It was agreed that the food pantry would reimburse St. Jean Baptiste parish for the cost of monthly utilities and any repairs or custodial help needed. The board continued to meet at the rectory and launched a campaign to recruit volunteers to staff the pantry. A search was begun for a full-time director.

Through articles in the press and letters to the parishes, as the opening date approached, food poured in and sixty-one persons, very many from St. Jean

Baptiste parish, volunteered. Sister Marie McDonald, a Sister of Notre Dame, was named director and on November 1, 1989, the Food Pantry of Merrimack Valley Catholic Charities opened.

In the first month, the pantry gave out 177 food orders representing 579 men, women and children. The pantry ran on grants and donations of food and money. In February, the economy worsened and the pantry served 376 orders, 150 more than in January. Overwhelmed, it ran out of food and had to close for three days. Emergency appeals and phone calls went out for more food.

Eventually the situation stabilized as more supplies and parishes came forward. Poverty could strike anywhere, at any time. One day, a Cadillac was seen parked on Moody Street with a man putting food in the trunk. Questioned, the pantry volunteer replied that when someone lost his job, the mortgage still had to be paid and the children fed.

The Food Pantry remained at St. Jean Baptiste until the closing of the parish when it moved to space in the former high school.

*   *   *   *   *   *   *

The committee presented the pastoral proposal to Fr. Arel and his provincial council on November 26, 1991. Pleased and even enthusiastic about the proposal, the provincial council promised to study its contents more thoroughly. On December 11, Fr. Arel delivered to the parish a letter stating that if seven conditions that were set forth in the letter were met, then the Oblates "would be willing to continue staffing the parish."

A reply would be needed before January 14, so that a recommendation to the incoming provincial council could be made. The committee agreed to all the conditions, which were mostly technical, affecting the implementation of the plan.

Throughout January and the beginning of February, the committee worked on the implementation of the parish proposal, planning fundraisers and naming committees in preparation for the celebration of the parish's 125th anniversary in April 1993.

All seemed to be going well until February 23, 1992 when the new provincial, Fr. George Capen, and his provincial council met with the parish council to announce, as stated in a press release issued February 18: "The Missionary Oblates of Mary Immaculate have decided to withdraw from St. Jean Baptiste Parish in Lowell, effective July 1, 1992."

Stunned, the committee chartered a bus and fifteen members traveled unannounced to the archdiocesan Chancery on February 26, to present the parish's case to Bishop Hughes. The archdiocese had not asked the Oblates to leave and, unaware of the parish proposal, which the Oblates had not forwarded to him, Bishop Hughes requested copies and asked for another meeting on March 5 to discuss the proposal and the future staffing of the parish. He also requested that the meeting include Fr. Capen and other members of his council as well as representatives of the various boards and committees of the parish.

After the March 5 meeting, Albert Daigle told the press, "I'm optimistic. At least there's a ray of hope." John Walsh, the official spokesman for the archdiocese stated that a distinction had to be made between the Oblate's decision to leave and the decision of the archdiocese concerning the parish's future, "A decision to close the parish has not been made."

It was decided at the meeting, that Rev. Timothy Shea, a diocesan vicar, and Sister Mary Ann Doyle, of the planning office, would come to Lowell to work with the parish council and the finance council to work out a plan for the continuation of the parish and to study the possibility of sharing a pastor with another parish.

By the end of May, the archdiocese had reached its own decision. On Friday, May 29, the newly appointed Bishop for the Merrimack Region, Bishop John McNamara, met with Fr. Lauzé, Fr. Shea and Sister Doyle. After the meeting, Fr. Lauzé prepared a message to be read at all the Masses on both Saturday and Sunday. After restating that the Oblates were leaving, he announced the archdiocese's decision concerning the future of the parish:

A diocesan priest will be assigned the administration of the parish and will provide pastoral care from July 1, 1992 to June 27, 1993. Although this priest has not, as yet, been named it is anticipated that he will assume this responsibility in addition to his present full time assignment. Moreover, it may not be possible to locate a French-speaking priest for this role. Thus, the planning process will have to consider some adjustments in our services in order to accommodate his schedule and abilities.

The Archdiocese regrets that, due to limitations of personnel and the ongoing need to reevaluate the distribution of personnel in order to serve all in the Archdiocese in a responsible way, it will not be able to assign a priest for full or part time ministry beyond June 27, 1993. While the absence of a priest will bring an end to life in St. Jean Baptiste parish, as we have known it over the past 125 years, this next year will offer the opportunity to celebrate what has been, to give thanks to God for many blessings and to plan creatively for a new way of being Church together.

Fr. Lauzé ended his message with an invocation to the Holy Spirit for the days ahead, asking the parishioners to pray "for a deep sense of gratitude for all that has been in the history of this parish and an openness to whatever God asks of us now."

On July 1, 1992, Fr. Lauzé, the last Oblate pastor of St. Jean Baptiste parish, arrived in Augusta, Maine, for his new assignment as director of the St. Paul Retreat Center.

The Oblates turned the parish over to the archdiocese, but there were still a number of Oblates living at the rectory, most of them elderly. In 1992, the community consisted of Fathers George Rivard, Léo Monette, George Protopapas, Normand Fillion, Paul Ouellette, Robert Paradis and Albert Martineau with Fr. Lauzé as administrator and superior.

With Fr. Lauzé's reassignment and the official withdrawal of the Oblates, Fr. Albert Martineau was named director of the Oblate community, as the province set about finding new residences for its members. Fr. Martineau, the last to leave, would stay until after the closing of the parish in June 1993, when he would return to St. Joseph Shrine where he had served for many years.

Cardinal Bernard Law, the archbishop of Boston, named Fr. Brian Kiely as administrator of the parish. Father Kiely, a diocesan priest, had been serving in the Virgin Islands for a number of years. Arriving in Lowell in September 1992, he took up residence at the rectory of St. Louis de France.

All of these events in quick succession had taken a terrible toll on the parishioners and would have profoundly discouraged them had it not been for the undaunted courage of the preservation team and the understanding character of Fr. Kiely himself. Honest, open-minded, and very kind, he did everything he could to help them and make the situation easier to bear.

He enrolled in French courses so as to be able to speak in French at the Masses, and he met with Prof. Claire Quintal, founding director of the French Institute at Assumption College, one of the most respected Franco-American authorities in the country, in order to learn more about Franco-American culture and to explore possibilities for the future of the church and parish.

From the very start of his discussions with the parishioners, he told them, "I will never lie to you. I will tell you the truth, even when you don't want to hear it." Soon, genuine affection and respect grew between the people and their new administrator, as they labored through those difficult times and sought by every means possible to save their church.

In the midst of all these anxieties, the monthly bills still had to be paid and the recurring expenses met. So, the parish held a Benefit Golf Tournament at the Passaconway Country Club in Litchfield, N.H. on Wednesday, September 23, 1992 – even some who couldn't golf went – and on February 7, 1993, a giant Country Store was held in the parish hall.

The main activity of the committee, however, was to find a way to save the church. They knew that it would take a miracle but they prayed, and worked very hard. One of their plans was to ask the Oblates to deed the church to the parishioners who would in turn form a corporation for the purpose of preserving it by using part of it for a museum and chapel, with the lower church possibly being turned into offices and meeting halls. The Oblates still held the title to the church properties and any plan for a transfer would need their cooperation.

The pledge campaign had raised $170,000 and the committee was certain that more money would come if there were in place a plan to save the church. Already, a letter had been sent to all who had pledged, asking them whether they wanted their money returned, used to pay ongoing expenses, or to pursue "new options to preserve St. Jean Baptiste church." Only two parishioners asked for their money back.

The idea of transforming St. Jean Baptiste church into a cultural center had merit and Fr. Kiely even discussed with Claire Quintal what other Franco-American communities were doing in this area. Unfortunately, the plan was never able to take form and the inevitable outcome now became clear.

For over a year, the committee had been discussing and making plans for the celebration of the parish's 125th anniversary in 1993. However, in the spring of 1992, in the midst of all the uncertainty and turmoil surrounding the parish's future, many parishioners no longer wanted to go forward with the celebration. As they put it, "Why celebrate it? We might not even make it."

In May 1992, the committee called a general meeting of the parish to decide the issue. During the discussions, Albert Daigle rose and said, "If your mother was on her deathbed and she was 92, you'd still celebrate her birthday. Maybe we'll make 125 years." The common sense *"bon sens"* of his argument carried the issue and eventually, the following committee was formed to organize the anniversary: Rev. Brian Kiely, Sister Cécile Poulin scq, Monique Frigon Blanchette, Denise Châteauneuf, Thérèse M. Daigle, Irène R. Desmarais, Theresa B. Doré, Suzanne Fréchette, Jeanne Gagné, Gérard R. Geoffroy, Laura B. Geoffroy, Bob LaFleur, Claire Lemieux, Michelle Lemieux, Denise Marcouillier, George Motard, Bernard B. Péloquin, Marthe Biron Péloquin, Richard Provencher, Roger Racette Sr., Aurore Boissonneault (Zounne), Albert A. Daigle.

The parish`s "birthday party" was set for Saturday afternoon, April 17. 1993, at the four o'clock Mass, to be followed by a grand banquet at the Franciscan Center in Andover.

The mood of the parishioners was expressed well by Estelle LaFleur, when she stated, "I'm very glad we can celebrate the 125th, but I don't want to think about the closing right now. It's very heartbreaking to know that

391

something that has been a very big part of my family for many years isn't going to be around anymore."

Cardinal Law was the principal celebrant of the anniversary Mass with Bishop McNamara, Fr. Kiely and a large number of Oblates as concelebrants. In his opening words, the cardinal chose to stress the positive, "I walk with you and I share the beauty of this moment. I'm conscious of the fact . . . this is a bittersweet moment . . . but we focus on what is sweet."

The church was full as a great many former parishioners had come to celebrate the faith-filled history of the parish. La Chorale Orion sang the Mass beautifully both in French and in English.

The banquet was a lavish affair with an elegant meal accompanied by an appropriate programme. Albert Daigle served as master of ceremonies. Cardinal Law, Bishop McNamara, Tarsy Poulios, the mayor of Lowell, Father Kiely and Fr. Capen, the Oblate provincial, each spoke fitting words of praise for the occasion. Attorney Arthur L. Eno Jr., president of the Société Historique Franco-Américaine, recounted the history of the parish.

Adding to the celebration was a carefully prepared memorabilia room containing engravings, photographs and artifacts from the parish's long history. In addition to this, an illustrated souvenir program was given to each person in attendance.

At the end of the speaking program, Mr. Daigle, on behalf of the parish, presented five special awards to each of the following: Jeanne Hardy, Roger Racette Sr., Roland Marchand, Gérard Tremblay, and Maurice Châteauneuf in recognition of a lifetime of devotion and service to the parish. The awards consisted of large, specially commissioned and framed photographs of the interior and exterior of the church. All in all, it was a very moving and memorable evening for everyone.

That year, Franco-American Week was held from Saturday, June 19, 1993 to Sunday, June 27. As was the custom, the week-long celebrations would end with a Mass on Sunday morning at St. Jean Baptiste. It had long been decided that the parish would be dissolved on June 28, 1993, and that the celebration of the last Mass would coincide with the conclusion of Franco-American Week on Sunday, June 27.

As the parishioners prepared themselves for the bitter event to come, another chapter in the parish's remarkable history also came to an end. The Little Sisters of the Holy Family had been present in the parish since 1900. Blessed Mother Marie Léonie herself had brought the first sisters to the rectory and had worked side by side with them in establishing the community. The sisters still took joy in pointing out where she had washed the laundry in the cellar.

Their humble life of prayer and work in support of the priesthood had never gone unnoticed and was greatly admired by the parishioners. From 1900 to 1968, fifty young women from the parish had joined the congregation. One of them, Marie-Anne Coutu, Mère Sainte-Adèle, would even become Superior General.

In their desire to be faithful to the mission entrusted to them by Mother Léonie, they had decided to remain until the last possible moment. The Little Sisters of the Holy Family left the rectory convent on Saturday June 26, 1993, thus ending nearly a century of commitment to the parish.

That Sunday morning began with a brief ceremony at the Little Canada Monument on Aiken Street. Afterwards, the participants processed to St. Jean Baptiste for the last Mass. Fr. Kiely welcomed the members of the Franco-American Week Committee and the very large congregation, which filled the church, in an eloquent address given in both French and English. Bishop McNamara was the principal celebrant with Fr. Capen, the Oblate provincial, and a number of Oblates and diocesan priests concelebrating. Bishop Hughes presided and gave the homily. Once again, La Chorale Orion sang the Mass in French and English.

Throughout the service, the parishioners as well as many who had come to attend the Mass were in tears, some sobbing openly. The mood was one of mourning. As one of the parishioners stated, "It's as bad as having a death in the family." Another added, "This church is my life. We don't want to leave." Quite a few women wore black dresses as a sign of mourning and the men, black armbands.

There was also quite a bit of anger. At the offertory collection, when the baskets were passed, many people threw in pennies painted red signifying, "Never again, not one red cent."

In his closing remarks at the end of the Mass, Bishop McNamara was loudly applauded when he stated that St. Jean Baptiste parish would never die, but would live on forever in the hearts of its parishioners, both here below as well as in heaven.

At the close of the Mass, the Chorale Orion sang the much-loved Marian hymn *"J'irai la voir un jour."* Even after everyone had left the church, they continued prayerfully singing the hymn until the last verse and the last refrain echoed softly in the church:

> *Au ciel, au ciel, au ciel,*
> *J'irai la voir un jour.*
> *Au ciel, au ciel, au ciel,*
> *J'irai la voir un jour.*

(In heaven, in heaven, in heaven,
I will see her there one day.
In heaven, in heaven, in heaven,
I will see her there one day.)

St. Jean Baptiste parish was officially dissolved on Monday, June 28, 1993. The official registers along with the parishioners were transferred to St. Louis de France parish. The statue of St. Jean Baptiste was placed in the sanctuary of St. Louis church.

* * * * * * *

Since the early 1960s, the Spanish-speaking population of Lowell had continued to grow. The Spanish-speaking Oblates had begun ministering to them at first in the lower church, at St. Joseph Shrine, and then at other locations. In 1990, their Catholic population being numerous enough, the archdiocese created the Hispanic parish of Nuestra Señora del Carmen, Our Lady of Mt. Carmel. The parish, however, did not have a church of its own, although it did have a pastoral center in the former St. Jean Baptiste convent.

Soon after the dissolution of St. Jean Baptiste parish, the archdiocese turned the St. Jean Baptiste church, the rectory, and parish hall over to the new Hispanic parish. Once again, St. Jean Baptiste church had become a parish church, and in September 1993, the Spanish-speaking Oblates moved into the rectory.

By a series of providential and unplanned circumstances, the long-awaited centennial history of St. Jean Baptiste parish – whose author had spent twenty-five years in research and preparation – was published in the fall of 1993. The official launching and book signing by the author, Fr. Richard Santerre, now a priest of the Archdiocese of Boston, took place on Sunday, December 5, 1993 at the Mogan Cultural Center of the National Park. The book *La Paroisse Saint Jean-Baptiste et les Franco-Américains de Lowell, Massachusetts, 1868 à 1968* had been the recipient of a public grant from the Lowell Historic Preservation Commission and, within a year, the entire edition had sold out. Among the speakers for the occasion was Fr. Anatole Lessard, pastor from 1964 to 1970, who gave the keynote address. In his presentation, he spoke movingly about his years at St. Jean Baptiste as well as the merits of the book.

The Franco-Americans of Lowell continue to remember. Every year, Franco-American Week celebrates the faith and heritage of the community and, year after year, more and more researchers, some from the National Park Service, bring to light the riches of the city's Franco-American history. They accomplish this in various ways from exhibits to folk festivals, from scholarly articles to lectures and publications.

In 1994, Oblate Fathers Paul Ouellette and Lucien Sawyer published an illustrated history of St. Joseph Cemetery on the occasion of its centenary: *St. Joseph Cemetery. Centennial Celebration 1894-1994.* Fr. Sawyer published an edited English language translation of Fr. Gaston Carrière's biography of Fr. Garin, *L'inoubliable Fondateur* under the title, *The Man Lowell Remembered, André-Marie Garin, OMI, 1822-1895. His Missionary Life. His Legacy to Lowell. A Tribute of gratitude from the Oblates of Lowell.*

Unfortunately, during this period, *Le Journal de Lowell,* founded in 1975, published its last issue in December 1995. The rising cost of paper and postage had made it impossible to continue. The publication would be sorely missed. But, *autre temps, autres moeurs,* life goes on in other ways. In the fall of 2001, Cécile Provencher succeeded in creating an internet site under the heading, "The Franco-Americans in Lowell, Massachusetts," accessible through the University of Massachusetts at Lowell's web site. Albert V. Côté joined her in the effort and today Cécile Provencher provides the web design and is webmaster while the content is compiled by Albert V. Côté.

Bernard Cardinal Law resigned as archbishop of Boston on December 13, 2003. His successor, Bishop Seán O'Malley, OFM cap., was installed as archbishop on July 30. In the fall, the new archbishop announced that at the beginning of 2004, he would be forming committees to start the process of completely reorganizing the distribution of parishes throughout the archdiocese. This "reconfiguration," as it was called would result in the closing or merger of a significant number of parishes.

As he pointed out in an announcement on January 9, this process was already under way in Lowell and Lawrence. On January 9, 2000, St. Joseph Lithuanian parish in Lowell, was suppressed. In 2001, Ste Thérèse parish in Dracut had been merged on August 27 with Our Lady of the Assumption and the resulting new parish was named Ste Marguerite D'Youville. At the end of May 2004, the archdiocese announced its decisions: over sixty parishes in the archdiocese were to be closed or merged.

In Lowell, Notre Dame de Lourdes parish was suppressed and the church and its properties put up for sale. Sacred Heart was merged with Ste Marie in South Lowell and Ste Marie church was renamed Holy Family church, with Sacred Heart church being put up for sale. St. Louis de France was also suppressed, and the church and rectory given to Ste Marguerite D'Youville parish. The school, however, was kept open and also attached to Ste Marguerite. Ste. Jeanne d'Arc too was suppressed, but the school continued to operate by being attached to St. Rita parish. The fate of Ste Jeanne d'Arc parish, however, is not yet final, since the parishioners, like those of many others throughout the archdiocese, appealed the decision to the Vatican.

Nuestra Señora del Carmen parish was dissolved on August 31, 2004. Its parishioners were transferred of St. Patrick's where the Vietnamese and Cambodian Catholics also worship. The Oblates agreed to staff St. Patrick's and moved there with their parishioners, while the former St. Jean Baptiste church and rectory were put up for sale.

All of these events in rapid succession caused an unimaginable amount of pain and suffering. As one person put it, "the hearts of the people of Jeanne d'Arc have been broken." The impending fate of St. Jean Baptiste church immediately caused alarm both within the preservation community and among the population in general.

Too many remembered the demolition of the magnificent granite St. Peter church on Gorham Street in the late 1990s and there was the precedent of demolitions and radical transformations of other historic churches within the archdiocese.

On July 27, 2004, Mayor Armand Mercier, with the support of the community, presented before the Lowell City Council, a motion according to which the boundaries of the Downtown Lowell Historic District would be "modified by extending the district to include St. Jean Baptiste Church now known as Nuestra Señora del Carmen Church and related buildings at 725-741 Merrimack Street." By extending the boundaries, the church, rectory, and the small building near Aiken Street would be protected from destruction or exterior alteration.

The historic nature and value of the buildings was well known. Mayor Mercier, who had grown up in the parish, was a founding member of the Franco-American Day Committee. Within the Park Service, there was the hope that a plan could be devised to turn the church into a museum of religions.

The first motion to extend the boundaries passed. A second reading and public hearing were ordered for August 24, one week before the church and rectory were to go up for sale. The speakers in favor at the hearing represented a wide segment of the population, there were no opposing speakers. After a brief discussion, the motion to extend the boundaries passed unanimously.

*   *   *   *   *   *   *

Today, Lowell is a city of museums, festivals, galleries, and upscale mill apartments. Never have the city's history and culture been so prized. Whatever the future may hold for St. Jean Baptiste parish's historic church and rectory, the memory of its people will be forever alive and, hopefully passersby will say in the words of Mother Theresa of Calcutta, "Something beautiful for God happened here."

Appendices
1. Baptisms in 1868

Born Baptized	Child Parents	Priest
April 13 April 18	Joseph Edmond Buisson Edmond Buisson and Aristine Gill (Baptized in St. Patrick church)	A. M. Garin, O.M. I.
May 1 May 3	Narcisse Ducharme Narcisse Ducharme and Mélina Laflamme	A. M. Garin, O.M. I.
May 1 May 3	Pierre Napoléon Beauregard Pierre Beauregard and Marie Laflamme	A. M. Garin, O.M.I.
May 9 May 10	Pierre Corneille Perrault Pierre Perrault and Phébée Garan	A. M. Garin, O.M.I.
May 12 May 12	Marie Exilda Roy Fabien Roy and VirginieRaymond	A. M. Garin, O.M.I.
May 19 '67 May 17	Hilaire Paradis Hilaire Paradis and Caroline Boucher	A. M. Garin, O.M.I.
May 17 May 17	Marie Eléonore Molleur John Molleur and Victorine Laflamme	A. M. Garin, O.M.I.
May 29 May 30	Rose Raymond Jean-Baptiste Raymond and Rose Godin	A. M. Garin, O.M.I.
May 31 May 31	Marie Anne Boudreau Isaïe Boudreau and Sara McKay	A.M. Garin, O.M.I.
June 7 June 7	Charles Bariteau Antoine Bariteau and Edesse Marcil	A. M. Garin, O.M.I.
June 10 June 12	Eugène Laflamme Eugène Laflamme and Odylle Bourré	A. M. Garin, O.M.I.
June 7 June 14	Marie Rosanna Gaudet Alexandre Gaudet and Nathalie Cyr	A. M. Garin, O.M.I.
Nov. '67 July 5	Alfred Bourque Alfred Bourque and Rose Gaudreau	A. M. Garin, O.M.I.
Feb. 19 July 5	Louis Joseph Lapierre Joseph Lapierre and Eliza Martel	A. M. Garin, O.M.I.

Born Baptized	Child Parents	Priest
July 2 July 5	Pierre Zephirin Girard Pierre Girard and Christine Falville	A. M. Garin, O.M.I.
Dec. 3 '67 July 12	Onésime Fornet Nazaire Fornet and Marie Bolduc	A. M. Garin, O.M.I.
July 13 July 14	Marie Exilda -- Unknown	A. M. Garin, O.M.I.
July 14 July 16	Joseph Baptiste Fontaine Joseph Fontaine and Georgina Desmarais	A. M. Garin, O.M.I.
July 26 July 26	Napoléon Lafontaine Salomon Lafontaine and Célina Roy	A. M. Garin, O.M.I.
July 28 Aug. 2	Alfred Labonne David Labonne and Julie LaCharité	J. Cosson, O.M.I.
April 1 Aug. 5	Georges Edmond Lesieur Narcisse Lesieur and Julienne Gaudreau	A. M. Garin, O.M.I.
July 28 Aug. 10	Joseph Médard Bernier Antoine Bernier and Marie Roy	A. M. Garin, O.M.I.
Aug, 11 Aug. 13	Joseph Ouimet Isaac Ouimet and Zoé Gamache	J. Cosson, O.M.I.
Aug. 18 Aug. 19	Octave Gaudet Cleophas Gaudet and Marie Henriette Chaillor	J. Cosson, O.M.I.
Aug. 22 Aug. 23	Arthur Toussaint Tétreault Adolphe Tétreault and Sophie Lalumière	J. Cosson, O.M.I.
Aug. 15 Aug. 23	Gilbert Rémillard Gilbert Rémillard and Delima Constantineau	A. M. Garin, O.M.I.
July 12 Aug. 30	Louis Gamache William Gamache and Marie Duquet	A. M. Garin, O.M.I.
Aug. 25 Sept. 6	Joseph Arcade Mercier Alarie Mercier and Marie Lemire	A. M. Garin, O.M.I.
Sept. 5 Sept. 13	Francis Delphis Ada Hubert Flavien Hubert and Rosalie Desmarais	A. M. Garin, O.M.I.
Sept. 26 Sept. 27	Marie Félicité Grenier Jean-Baptiste Grenier and Félicité Le Maître	J. Cosson, O.M.I.

Born Baptized	Child Parents	Priest
Sept. 28 Sept. 29	Zoël Fortunat Carpentier Joseph Carpentier and Aurélie Beauregard	J. Cosson, O.M.I.
Oct. 1 Oct. 4	Victorine Tiffault Pierre Tiffault and Marie Anne Hickey	J. Cosson, O.M.I.
Oct. 4 Oct. 4	Virginie Roberge Onésiphore Roberge and Virginie Ducharme	J. Cosson, O.M.I.
Sept. 27 Oct. 10	Clara Emma Lizotte Antoine Lizotte and Émélie Ratelle (Baptized at West Boylston, MA)	A. M. Garin, O.M.I.
July 16 Oct. 10	Emma Jane Brousseau Joseph Brousseau and Marie Jane Beaulieu (Baptized at West Boylston, MA)	A. M. Garin, O.M.I.
March '67 Oct. 12	Mary Couleaf John Couleaf and Marguerite Fox (Baptized at West Boylston, MA)	A. M. Garin, O.M.I.
Oct. 8 Oct. 12	Josephine Couleaf John Couleaf and Marguerite Fox (Baptized at West Boylston, MA)	A.M. Garin, O.M.I.
Oct. 11 Oct. 16	Francis Joseph Coughlin Frank Coughlin and Mary Malloy (Baptized at West Boylston, MA)	A.M. Garin, O.M.I.
Oct. 12 Oct. 13	Adelard Joseph Hubert Louis Hubert and Marguerite Lajoie	L. Lebret, O.M.I.
Sept. 9 Oct. 18	Joseph Henry Miller Joseph Miller and Aurélie Richer	L. Lebret, O.M.I.
Oct. 17 Oct. 18	Emma Tremblay Toussaint Tremblay and Julie Garon	L. Lebret, O.M.I.
Oct. 16 Oct. 18	Émélie Amanda Bissonnette Elisephore Bissonnette and Marceline Benoit	L. Lebret, O.M.I.
Aug. 28 Oct. 18	Marie Adelina Raymond Joseph Raymond and Philomène Lanoue	L. Lebret, O.M.I.
Oct. 18 Oct. 18	Marie Eugénie Melvina Turcotte Isidore Turcotte and Hélène Allard	L. Lebret, O.M.I.

Born Baptized	Child Parents	Priest
Oct. 2 Oct. 20	Jean-Baptiste Alfred Duquette Michel Duquette and Mathilda Langevin	L. Lebret, O.M.I.
Nov. 11 Nov. 15	Émélie Charlotte Georgina Poirier Jean-Baptiste Poirier and Émélie Langlois	A. M. Garin, O.M.I.
Nov. 8 Nov. 16	Marie Léa Dorion Félix Dorion and Angèle Saien	A. M. Garin, O.M.I.
Nov. 5 Nov. 16	Edmond Treflé Bergeron Louis Bergeron and Celina Dufresne	A. M. Garin, O.M.I.
Nov. 19 Nov. 22	Emma Mathilda Prairie Isaïe Prairie and Aurélie Lafaille	A. M. Garin, O.M.I.
Aug. 14 '66 Dec. 11	John Albert Wood Albert Wood and Louisa Stanley	A.M. Garin, O.M.I.

2. Marriages in 1868

Date	Spouses	Priest
April 26	Jules Lavallée and Marie Lacouture (at St. Patrick's church)	A. M. Garin, O.M.I.
April 28	Isaac St. Armand and Henriette Fortin	L. A. Lagier, O.M.I.
May 3	Alexandre Graton and Marie Emilie Denault	L. A. Lagier, O.M.I.
May 16	Damase Raymond and Elmire Lanciaux	A. M. Garin, O.M.I.
May 31	Hiram Brown and Sophie Courchène	A. M. Garin, O.M.I.
June 11	Télesphore Lantagne and Rose Molleur	A. M. Garin, O.M.I.
June 14	William Roy and Tharsile Racicot	A. M. Garin, O.M.I.
July 6	Edouard Dufaut and Melanie Pitre	A. M. Garin, O.M.I.
July 8	Narcisse Desmarais and Marie St. Denis	A. M. Garin, O.M.I.
July 11	Napoléon Gauvreau and Alexandrine Larivière	A. M. Garin, O.M.I.
August 3	Louis Landry and Marie Audet	A. M. Garin, O.M.I.
August 4	Onésime Proulx and Marie Desmarais	A. M. Garin, O.M.I.
August 26	Jean-Baptiste Laflamme and Julia Rynehart	A. M. Garin, O.M.I.
September 7	Moyse Patenaude and Elmire Tétrault	A. M. Garin, O.M.I.
September 17	William Traversy and Annie Boisclair	A. M. Garin, O.M.I.
September 27	Joseph Blais and Julie Charette	G. Cosson, O.M.I.
September 28	Médard Lanciau and Delphine Alexandre	G. Cosson, O.M.I.
October 5	Boniface Lebrun and Octavie Allard	A. M. Garin, O.M.I.
October 6	Moyse St. Denis and Osylle Desmarais	A. M. Garin, O.M.I.
October 14	Pierre Gauthier and Elisabeth Masson	L. Lebret, O.M.I.
October 26	Honoré Lacombe and Marguerite Bastien	L. Lebret, O.M.I.
October 31	Charles Gaudreau and Florence Phaneuf	L. Lebret, O.M.I.
November 1	Joseph Dufaut and Asilda Fontaine	A. M. Garin, O.M.I.
November 8	Gédéon Lemay and Marie Thomas	A. M. Garin, O.M.I.
November 9	Pierre Desmarais and Célina Murray	A. M. Garin, O.M.I.
November 10	Charles Alain and Mary Elkin	A. M. Garin, O.M.I.
November 16	Damase Bellerive and Olympe Hébert	L. Lebret, O.M.I.
November 16	Joseph St. Onge and Joséphine Masson	L. Lebret, O.M.I.
November 17	Magloire Simard and Sophronie Patenaude	L. Lebret, O.M.I.
November 22	Léonard Schervager and Louise Montemont	A. M. Garin,.O.M.I.
November 27	Pierre Ethier and Vitaline Langelier	A. M. Garin, O.M.I.

3. Vocations to the Priesthood

Oblates of Mary Immaculate

	year of ordination		year of ordination
Henri Constantineau	1888	Maurice Savard	1931
Joseph Paillé	1902	Léo Desmarais	1932
Guillaume Ouellette	1903	Eugène Labrie	1932
Omer Plourde	1903	Georges Saint-Jean	1932
Julien Racette	1904	Victor Alexander	1933
Eugène Turcotte	1904	Gérard Chouinard	1933
Hervé Racette	1905	Lauréat Savard	1933
Edouard Carrier	1907	Louis Desruisseaux	1934
Edouard Chaput	1910	Roland Gaulin	1934
Joseph Bolduc	1913	Armand Morissette	1935
Alphonse Archambault	1914	Henri Bolduc	1936
Rosario Jalbert	1914	Charles Dozois	1936
Aurélien Mercil	1917	Joseph Morissette	1938
Lucien Brassard	1921	George Protopapas	1943
Paul Germain	1922	Albert Lirette	1945
Emile Bolduc	1923	Lionel Thériault	1947
Donat Morrissette	1923	Roland Bourgeois	1949
Arthur Saint-Cyr	1923	Maurice Bouvier	1956
Arthur Lemire	1926	Roger-J. Lamoureux	1959
Léon Loranger	1927	Roger-E. Lamoureux	1983
Arthur Salvas	1927		

Franciscans
Armand Fréchette, O.F.M. 1945
Bro. Joseph Albert Décelle, O.F.M.

Marists
Léon Boissonnault, S.M. 1926

Missionaries of LaSalette
Raymond Isabelle, M.S. 1944

Company of Mary
Léandre Lirette, S.S.M. 1920

Jesuits
Georges Marin, S.J. 1926
Bro. Rodolphe Boudreau, S.J.

Missionaries of the Holy Apostles
Raymond Dubuque Cangelosi, M.S.S.A 1967

Diocesan Priests

Victor Choquette	1902
Hector-Edmond Ouimet*	1904
Joseph Blais*	1909
Msgr. William Drapeau	1917
Philippe Germain	1918
Antonio Vigeant	1918
Msgr. Hermann Morin	1920
Félix Tessier	1920
Joseph Leclerc	1925
Alfred Lirette	1930
Marcel Généreux*	1939
Raymond Drapeau	1952

*Former Oblates

4. Vocations to Religious Life: Brothers

Oblate Brothers
Joseph Boisclair
Augustin Côté
Louis Desjadons
Alfred Jutras
Alphonse Marion

Marist Brothers
Family and religious name

Ernest Béland	(Ernest-Gérard)
Paul-A. Benoit	(François-Xavier)
Paul Blanchard	(Paul-Wilfrid)
* Emile-J. Brouillette	(Léo [Légoncianus])
Omer-A. Daigle	(Henri-Omer)
Richard Dégagné	(Philippe-Richard)
Roland Dubois	(Roland-Paul)
* Omer-A. Duprez	(Louis-Omer)
Henry Généreux	(Henri-Firmin)
Joseph-Edgar Lavigne	(Edouard-Michel)
Pierre Lirette	(Pierre-Antoine)
Henry Morneau	(Henri-Lucien)
Albert-E. Racicot	(Paul-Félix)
Aimé-O. Rainville	(Victor-Aimé)
Roger Renaud	(Pierre-Maurice)

* Former Provincial

Claretian Brother
Richard Paquette, C.M.F.

5. Vocations to Religious Life: Sisters
Grey Nuns of the Cross of Ottawa (Sisters of Charity of Ottawa)

1885	Marie Fréchette	(St-Barnabé)
1886	Olivine Pelland	(St-Lazare)
1887	Marcelline Ouellette	(St-Hippolyte)
1889	Marguerite Langlois	(Ste-Priscille)
	Victoria Hamilton	(St-Vital)
1890	Gratia Lavergne	(St-Ulric)
1892	Emma Allard	(Ste-Pulchérie)
1893	M.-Victorine Després	(St-Wilfrid)
	Clara Gagner	(Ste-Marthe)
	M.-Louise Lamoureux	(St-Pascal)
1894	Ernestine Michaud	(Ste-Aglaé)
1895	M.-Anne Milot	(Ste-Julie)
	Régina Dupuis	(St-Arthur)
	Marie-Emma Lavergne	(St-Jules)
	Elisabeth Dumas	(St-Aimé)
1896	Rébecca Marcotte	(St-Philibert)
	Esther Montminy	(Ste-Esther)
	Alexina Pépin	(Ste-Evéline)
	M.-Louise Plourde	(St-Hubert)
	A. Bordeleau	(St-Polycarpe)
1897	Rose-Anna Gagnon	(St-David)
	Hélène Gagné	(Ste-Marcelline)
	Olive Dubois	(Ste-Olive)
	Emma Bertrand	(Ste-Emma)
	Antoinette Veillette	(Ste-Euphrosine)
1898	Marie-Jeanne Carrier	(Marie-Jeanne)
	Corinne-Albia Jutras	(Ste-Alphonsine)
	Elizabeth Boisvert	(Ste-Stéphanie)
1899	Marie-Anne Lantagne	(Ste-Angèle)
	Marie-Eléonore Goupil	(Marie-Edouard)
	Florida Létourneau	(St-Blaise)
	Marie-Anne Joly	(St-David)
	Marie-Anne Lincourt	(Marie-Eugénie)
	Marie-Clara Germain	(St-Benoît-Labre)
1900	Marie-Elise Carrier	(St-Viateur)
	Marie-Flore Dubois	(Ste-Prudentienne)
	Elisabeth Gagné	(St-Adalbert)

1901	Clara Dubois	(Ste-Marie)
	Émélie Dubois	(Marie-Claire)
	Alphonsine Guilbeault	(Ste-Albina)
1902	Marie-Louise Guay	(Paul-Emile)
	Louise-Elvina Dubois	(St-Jérôme-Émilien)
	M.-Eugénie Roux	(St-Aldéric)
1903	Valérie Berthiaume	(St-Flavien)
	Évangéline Turcotte	(Louis-Paul)
	M.-Agnès Cinq-Mars	(St-Conrad)
	Eugénie Dubois	(St-Hilarion)
1905	Anne-Ombéline Mayer	(St-Jean d'Avila)
1907	* Aurore Drapeau	(Mother St-André Corsini)
	M.-Emma Lamoureux	(Ste-Théodorine)
1908	Angélina Genest	(St-Rodrigue)
	Eva Paquin	(St-Majoric)
	Bernadette Brouillette	(Marie-Élie)
	Alexandra Archambault	(St-Christophe)
	Aurore Bertrand	(St-Achille)
	M.-Anne Tessier	(St-Luc)
	Rosa Jodoin	(Ste-Clémence)
1909	Eva Blais	(Ste-Ermélinde)
	Augustine Dancosse	(Ste-Léopoldine)
	M.-Alida Lemire	(St-Joseph)
	Florence St. Martin	(St-Jacob)
1910	Léonide Chaput	(St-Valère)
	Rose-Alba Masse	(Marie-Irmine)
	Poméla Dubois	(Ste-Praxède)
	Corinne Landry	(Ste-Félicité)
1911	Aldéa Héroux	(Ste-Cécile)
	Laura Paquin	(Ste-Fabiola)
	Virginie Gilbert	(St-Diomède)
	Aurore Lapointe	(Ste-Clarisse)
	Philomène Martin	(St-Priscillien)
1912	Rose Labrecque	(Marie-Henri)
	M.-Rose Bertrand	(St-Jovite)
	Herménie Dubois	(Marie-Dolorès)
	Berthe Germain	(St-Germain)
1913	Eva Latendresse	(St-Alcide)
	Laura Beaumier	(St-Aquilas)
	Bernadette Mathon	(Marie-Fabiola)
	Corinne Vallerand	(St-Thomas-de-Jésus)
1915	Antoinette Crépeau	(Ste-Marcionille)

	Delphine Régnier	(Marie-Delphine)
	Théodorat Tremblay	(St-Uldéric)
	Blanche Côté	(Ste-Hilarie)
	Léonie Poisson	(Ste-Françoise-Thérèse)
1916	Béatrice Genest	(Ste-Gertrude)
	Bernadette Albert	(Marie-Albert)
1917	Irène Mailhot	(Charles-Edouard)
	Marie-Louise Ouellette	(Louis-Auguste)
	Léontine Parent	(Ste-Rose-de-Viterbe)
	Yvonne Lafontaine	(Marie-Alexandre)
1918	Cécile Garon	(St-André)
	Anne-Marie Dussault	(Ste-Clorinthe)
	Léona Parent	(Marie-Donalda)
1919	Alice Décelles	(Ste-Félicie)
	Évéline Genest	(Ste-Lucie)
1920	Alma Laurin	(Marie-Arthur)
	Antonia Geoffroy	(Ste-Elise)
	Léa Régnier	(Madeleine-du-Sauveur)
1921	Louise-Eva Germain	(Yves-de-Marie)
1922	Marie Rousseau	(Louise-de-Jésus)
	Hedwidge Décelles	(Marie-Hedwidge)
1923	M.-Alice Bibeau	(Louis-Gabriel)
	Blanche Côté	(Ste-Colette)
1924	Évéline Bibeault	(St-Raphaël)
	Alice Boulé	(Marie-Alice)
	Alma-Liliane Jutras	(Marie-Léon)
	Yvonne Généreux	(Ste-Louise)
1925	Régina-A. Savard	(Louis-Maurice)
1926	Albina Prud'homme	(St-Edouard)
	Denise Genest	(St-Ludger)
1927	Lydia Jacques	(Irène-de-Marie)
1928	Jeanne-Alice Tellier	(Marie-Augustin)
	Juliette Bergeron	(Rose-Albert)
1929	Gabrielle Généreux	(Thérèse-du-Sauveur)
	M.-Anne Boulé	(Marie-Eustelle)
	Eva Matte	(Thomas-Marie)
	Simonne Tardiff	(Marie-de-Grâce)
1931	Dalila Ouellette	(Anne-de-Jésus)
	Laurette Montminy	(Ste-Alice)
	Cécile Décelles	(Rose-Cécile)
1933	Germaine Héroux	(Louis-Robert)
	Thérèse-J. Labrecque	(Ste-Myriam)

1940	Agnès Dubois	(Ste-Flore)
1942	Lily Beauchesne	(Paul-Armand)
	Gabrielle Jean	(Jean-de-Milan)
	Yvette Boisvert	(St-François-d'Assise)
1943	Anita Boucher	(Raymond-d'Espagne)
1944	Lilliane Lamoureux	(Louis-du-Sacré-Cœur)
1945	Claire Cayer	(Louis-Richard)
1949	Lorraine Marchand	(Elizabeth-du-St-Esprit)
1950	Cécile Cloutier	(Cécile-Albert)
1954	Angèle Ledoux	(Louis-Raymond)
1957	Doris Lareau	(Pierre-Michel)
	Yvette Lessard	(Joseph-Laurent)
1961	Priscille Malo	(Jeanne-Arthur)
1962	Cécile Provencher	(Cécile-Robert)

*Former Mother General

Little Sisters of the Holy Family

	Rose-Anna Arsenault	(Ste-Zénaïde)
	R.-A. Beaumont	(Ste-Catherine de Bologne)
	Séverine Campbell	(St-Pierre-de-Rome)
	Rosalie Champagne	(St-Joseph-de-Nazareth)
	Aurore Clément	(Ste-Augustine-Marie)
	Rébecca Courtois	(Marie-de-Jérusalem)
	Lucina Coutu	(Marie-Rosario)
*	Marie-Anne Coutu	(Mother Ste-Adèle)
	Marie Coutu	(Marie-de-Jésus)
	Oliva Deschaines	(Ste-Mechtilde-de-Jésus)
	Eugénie Doucet	(Ste-Aimée-de-Jésus)
	Exilia Ducharme	(St-Ephrem)
	Alice Ferland	(Marie-du-Divin-Cœur)
	Antoinette Gagné	(Ste-Augustina)
	Virginie Gagnon	(Marie-de-Béthanie)
	Joséphine Gauthier	(St-Rodriguez)
	Antoinette Geoffroy	(Ste-Théodosie)
	Régina Geoffroy	(St-Grégoire-de-Nazianze)
	Florida Hamel	(Marie-de-l'Annonciation)
	Elisa Hénault	(St-Elie-du-Carmel)
	Emma Hénault	(Ste-Olympe)
	Rita Héroux	(St-Adolphe)
	Malvina Joly	(Marie-Auxiliatrice)
	Marie Joly	(Marie-Dolorosa)

Philomène Jutras	(St-Damien)
Alphonsine Lavoie	(Ste-Catherine-de-Sienne)
Hélène L'Heureux	(Ste-Lutgarde)
Eugénie Lucier	(Ste-Lucina)
Marie Marchand	(St-Pierre-Gonzalès)
Marie-Elise Ménard	(Marie-Alma)
Florence Michaud	(Florence Michaud)
Séraphine Morel	(Ste-Jeanne-de-Chantal)
Anna Nault	(Ste-Mechtilde-de-Jésus)
Hélène Nault	(Ste-Georgie)
Albertine Périgny	(Ste-Emérentienne)
Bella Périgny	(Marie-Edesse)
Hélène Périgny	(Marie-de-la-Charité)
Olivine Périgny	(Ste-Emérentienne)
Noëlla Perron	(Ste-Cécilia-de-Rome)
Alberta Poirier	(St-Donatien)
Blanche Poirier	(Ste-Alda)
Eugénie Poirier	(St-Georges-Augustin)
Régina Poirier	(Ste-Madeleine-du-Crucifix)
Anna Rivet	(Ste-Catherine-de-Recci)
Diana Rondeau	(St-Jovite)
Rose-Anna Rousse	(Marie-de-la-Charité)
Victoria Sawyer	(Ste-Cécilia)
M.-M. Tessier	(Ste-Marguerite-Marie)
Marie-Anne Tessier	(St-Félix)
Emma Tremblay	(Ste-Valentine)

*Former Mother General

Sisters of Charity of Québec

Dora Boisvert	(St-Joseph d'Arimathie)
Irène Bordeleau	(Marie-de-la-Purification)
Albertine Cayer	(Ste-Christiane)
Béatrice Dégagné	(Ste-Béatrix d'Assise)
Thérèse Lebel	(Ste-Mélanie)
Florida Lemire	(Ste-Rose-du-Carmel)
Rose Lemire	(Ste-Rose)
Eva Marquis	(Ste-Raphaëlla)
Cécile Rondeau	(Marie-Thérèse)
Rita Santerre	(St-Justinien)
Anna Tardiff	(St-Salomon)

Grey Nuns of Montréal (Sisters of Charity of Montréal)

Sister Léna Breton
Sister Aldéa Gagnon
Sister Lorraine Lavoie
Sister Juliette Gauthier

Sisters of the Assumption of the Blessed Virgin

E. Choquette	(Aimée-de-l'Assomption)
Jeanne Couture	(Jeanne-du-Sauveur)
Laurette Cloutier	(Gabriel-Archange)
Cécile Morin	(Ste-Anne)
Bertha St-Jean	(Ste-Bertha)
Rolande St-Jean	(Eustelle-de-l'Eucharistie)
Gertrude Sawyer	(Gertrude-du-S.-Sacrement)

Sisters of Saint Joseph, La Grange Park, IL

Claudia Bergeron	(Marie-Cécile)
Éveline Blanchette	(Marie-Alberte)
Eva Blanchette	(Marie-Gilberte)
Alma Caron	(Marie-Cyrille)
Azilda Delude	(Marie-Gertrude)
Emma Delude	(Marie-Hélène)
Antoinette Ferron	(Marie-François de Sales)
Régina Ferron	(Marie-Stella)
Alma Hébert	(François Borgia)
Claura Hébert	(Marie-Régis)
Anna Hébert	(St-Benoît)
Méralda Lavoie	(Marie-Anastasie)
Robéa Lavoie	(Marie-Bertha)
Marie O'Beirne	(Marie-Béatrice)

409

Sisters of Saint Joseph, Orange, California

Marie Bélanger	(Marie-Célestine)
Laurence Charette	(Marie-Fidélis)
Flore Ducharme	(Marie-André)
Eva Lirette	(Marie-Charles)
Eva Lirette	(Marie-Imelda)
* Marie Lirette	(Mother François d'Assise)
Rose-Anna Lirette	(Marie-Elizabeth)
Irène Veillette	(Ste-Emilienne)

*Former Mother General

Little Daughters of Saint Joseph

Agnès Desruisseaux	(Ste-Marie-Cécile)
* Christiane Michaud	(Mother Marie-Pauline)

*Former Mother General

Sisters of the Holy Names of Jesus and Mary

Louise Caisse	(Marie-Cécilius)
Hedwidge Constantineau	(M.-Pierre Canisius)
Germaine Daunais	(Laura-Maria)
Cécile Desruisseaux	(Marie-Joseph-du-Divin-Coeur)
Eva Jean	(Jean-de-l'Eucharistie)
Eva Leclerc	(Thérèse-du-Crucifix)
Denise Pépin	(Marie-Natalie)
Gabrielle Turcotte	(Marie-Marcellina)

Ladies of Jesus-Mary

* Rolande Robillard	(Mother St-Jean-du-Cénacle)

*Former Mother General

Daughters of Wisdom

Jeanne Moisan	(Eustelle-Marie)
Florence O'Beirne	(St-Jean-de-l'Assomption)
Irène O'Beirne	(Irène-de-l'Assomption)
Alice Paquin	(Alice-du-Rosaire)

Little Franciscans of Mary

Irène-Emma Bergeron   (Marie-Dolorès)
Agnès Côté   (Marie-Agnès-du-S.-Cœur)
Yvonne Lussier   (Marie-Arsène)

Sisters of Providence

Antoinette Grenier   (Louise-Rita)
Marie-Alice Lemay   (Marie-Urbana)
Emma Milot   (Hugues)

Congregation of Notre Dame

Balda Marin   (Marie Marin)

Sisters of Notre Dame de Namur

Berthe Bourgeois   (Claire-Marguerite)
Louise Rheault   (Louise-Aimé)

Sisters of Notre Dame of Africa

Mélina Caron   (St-Hyacinthe)
Jeannette Dastous   (Rosilda)

Carmelites

Alice Marin   (Alice-Aimée-de-l'Enfant-Jésus)

Servants of Mary. Queen of the Clergy

Sister Thérèse Décelles

6. Curates at Saint Jean Baptiste Parish

+ Indicates date of death

Adolphe Tortel	January 1870 – April 1873
	July 1883 – October 1887
Christophe Phaneuf	May 1871 – August 1871
	Early April to April 16, 1872+
Jean-Marie Royer	August 1871 – December 1871
Basil Dédebant	August 1873 – October 1874
Joseph Fournier	October 1874 – August 1875
	February 1876 – October 1882
	April 1884 – September 1888
	April 1896 – February 16, 1904+
Aloïs Gladu	August 1875 – February 1876
	January 1882 – March 1885
	October 1887 – January 1888
	September 1899 – October 1899
Louis Victor Petit	End of 1879 – August 1883
	May 1896 – September 1896
Georges Marion	October 1882 – April 1885
	September 1897 – December 1898
Charles Bournigalle	December 1882 – June 1883
	January 1886 – August 1887
	February 1888 – August 1888
Candidus Lagier	March 1883 – June 1890
Joseph-Napoléon Pelletier	August 1883 – August 1891
Joseph Lavoie	April 1885 – August 1885
	January 1890 – February 1892
	January 1896 – April 1896
Phidime Lecomte	April 1885 – May 1885
François Thérien	September 1885 – June 1886
Athanase Marion	July 1886 – July 1903
	September 1917 – August 1933
Zotique Vaillancourt	July 1886 – August 1886
B. Gény	September 1887 – September 1890
	March 1892 – July 1892
Stanislas Lancelon	October 1887 – September 1891
Antoine-Avite Amyot	October 1888 – June 1893
	June 1898 – May 24, 1927+
Alphonse Dazé	August 1890 – February 1893
Pierre Féat	September 1890 – July 1895

Dioscoride Forget	August 1891 – November 1896
Joseph-Hercule Emard	August 1891 – July 1894
	December 1896 – February 1898
Léon Lamothe	June 1892 – April 1896
	April 1897 – December 1909
Joseph Campeau	February 1893 – July 1894
	August 1901 – August 1907
Joïada Forget-Despatis	July 1893 – October 1893
	August 1895 – April 1900
Charles Paquette	August 1894 – September 1896
	September 1899 – September 1901
	May 1911 – March 1917
Louis-Alphonse Nolin	September 1894 – April 1904
	September 1912 – September 16, 1936+
Joseph Edouard Emery	November 1894 – March 1895
	August 1909 – January 1910
	April 1923 – December 1928
Joseph Sirois	June 1895 – September 1895
	August 1897 – August 1899
Jean-Baptiste Frigon	November 1895 – March 1897
Pierre Charles Gagnon	October 1896 – June 1898
	October 1898 – August 12, 1901+
Wilbrod Perron	December 1896 – April 1903
Charles Daveluy	July 1897 – September 1897
	June 1898 – March 1899
Benjamin Desroches	November 1898 – August 1901
	November 1904 – August 1907
Charles Boissonnault	October 1899 – July 1901
Jerôme Diss	August 1900 – October 1905
	August 1912 – June 1913
Louis Lewis	July 1901 – February 1905
Michel Dubreuil	September 1901 – September 1908
Pierre Brullard	June 1903 – January 25, 1912+
Charles Audibert	August 1903 – December 1907
	October 1911 – September 1913
Joseph Augustin Graton	August 1903 – February 1913
	August 1913 – July 13, 1928+
Victor Viaud	September 1903 – September 1908
Armand Baron	October 1905 – July 6, 1936+
Joseph Lefebvre	August 1907 – Marh 4, 1914+

Guillaume Ouellette	August 1907 – August 1913
	December 1918 – Ocotber 1924
Jean Bte. Antoine Barette	May 1908 – January 1910
Joseph Ehrard	September 1908 – August 1909
Joseph Magnan	July 1909 – December 1909
Arthur Bernèche	August 1909 – August 1911
	September 1913 – August 1915
Gustave Bernèche	January 1910 – May 1911
	October 1929 – November 1931
Julien Racette	January 1910 – July 1912
	October 1914 – December 1918
Charles Dénizot	August 1910 – January 1923
Joseph Blais	August 1911 – June 1913
Edouard Chaput	August 1913 – September 1914
Joseph Denis	September 1913 – October 1916
Joseph Bolduc	October 1914 – September 1922
Louis Bachand	October 1916 – January 1928
	August 1949 – August 1954
Joseph Eugène Turcotte	January 1917 – August 1917
Rosario Jalbert	August 1917 – January 1921
	May 1933 – May 27, 1938+
Aurélien Mercil	October 1918 – January 1923
Lucien Brassard	June 1921 – April 1922
	April 1928 – July 1943
Alphonse Archambault	March 1923
Emile Bolduc	June 1923 – June 1933
Arthur Pratt	September 1923 – April 1924
Félix Vachon	September 1924 – May 1, 1928+
Arthur Lemire	April 1927 – August 1933
Narcisse Cotnoir	September 1928 – August 1938
Alphonse Breault	August 1932 – August 1935
Albert Chevalier	September 1932 – February 1933
Arthur Parent	August 1933 – August 1936
Alphonse Houle	August 1933 – July 1938
Edouard Ducharme	June 1934 – September 1935
	April 1936 – August 1936
Esdras Gariépy	August 1934 – November 1935
Amédée Fredette	September 1935 – August 1936
Léon Loranger	June 1936 – September 1948
Eugène Fournier	September 1936 – August 1948

André Payette	August 1936 – June 1937
Fernand Rivard	August 1937 – December 1942
Eméry Lyonnais	August 1937 – August 1950
Armand Morissette	August 1938 – October 1947
Ulric Turcotte	August 1938 – August 1939
Robert Paradis	August 1938 – August 1941
Jean Vallières	September 1940 – September 1946
Albert Beausoleil	August 1941 – September 1944
Arthur Tardiff	May 1939 – June 1943
Roland Lavallée	September 1943 – August 1951
Paul Marquis	July 1943 – September 1950
Gérard Trahan	November 1943 – August 1950
Aldor Boisvert	August 1945 – August 1950
Charles Moreau	August 1946 – August 1950
Alphonse Fournier	September 1947 – February 1948
Gérard Chouinard	August 1948 – August 1949
Henri Bolduc	September 1948 – October 1949
Marcel Généreux	January 1950 – August 1952
	August 1953 – October 1955
Joseph Juaire	September 1950 – August 1951
Roland Bourgeois	September 1950 – August 1960
Jules Guy	August 1950 – July 1954
Marcel Péloquin	September 1950 – September 1951
Normand Fillion	August 1951 – June 1961
Olivier Renaud	September 1952 – September 1953
Donat Morrissette	August 1954 – August 1958
Roméo Murphy	July 1954 – August 1956
	August 1965 – August 1966
Robert Fortier	July 1954 – August 1955
Emile Rossignol	August 1954 – August 1964
Roméo Ferland	August 1955 – September 1957
Joseph Bouchard	September 1956 – August 1964
Nelson Boucher	August 1958 – August 1966
Roland Gaulin	August 1958 – August 1963
Lionel Labrie	August 1963 – September 1965
George Lessard	August 1963 – August 1970
Paul Beauregard	August 1963 – August 1967
Robert Lévesque	August 1966 – March 1970
Paul Lévesque	September 1966 – September 1968
George Dupont	June 1967 – August 1971

Index of Names

A

Abbott, Josiah: page 1
Achin, Henri: page 180, 188, 201, 205
Alain, Charles: page 401
Albert, Bernadette: page 406
Albert, Félix: page 56, 80
Albert, Joseph: 108
Alexander, Mrs.: page 70
Alexander, Alma: page 92
Alexander, Ernestine: page 166
Alexander, Victor: page 320, 321, 402
Alexander, W.: page 109
Alexander, Walter J.: page 196
Alexandre, Delphine: page 401
Alexandre, A.: page 121
Alexandroff, Vladimir: page 235
Alix, Armand: page 191
Allard, Emma: page 404
Allard, Hélène: page 399
Allard, Jean Baptiste: page 8
Allard, Octavie: page 401
Allard, Origène: page 248
Ames, Butler: page 226
Amette, Cardinal: page 186
Amyot, Antoine: page 118
Amyot, Antoine Avite: page 102, 104,
    107, 113, 118, 119, 122, 124, 126,
    127, 143, 147, 154, 193, 210, 213,
    241, 412
Anderson, William: page 81
Antoine, Joseph: page 60, 88, 89
Appleton, N.: page 3
Arcand, Donald: page 351
Archambault, Alexandra: page 405
Archambault, Alphonse: page 402, 414
Archambault, Amédée: page 108, 230
Archambault, Dewey: page 264, 265, 266,
    283
Archambeault, Mrs. Dewey G.: page 222
Arel, Donald: page 384, 388
Arrosa, Miss: page 264
Arsenault, Rose-Anna: page 407
Aubé, Emile: page 248
Audet, Marie: page 401

Audibert, Charles: page 134, 165, 413
Augier, Célestin: page 82, 88
Ayer, Frederick: page 150
Ayotte, George: page 364
Ayotte, Victor: page 36, 45

B

Bachand, Joseph Jérémie: page 216
Bachand, Louis G.: page 193, 216, 217,
    219, 221, 227, 228, 229, 230, 231,
    234, 240, 247, 266, 281, 282, 284,
    285, 288, 299, 300, 301, 302, 354,
    414
Baillargeon, Rosario: page 222
Barette, Jean Baptiste Antoine: page 154,
    193, 414
Baril, Ovide: page 8
Bariteau, Antoine: page 397
Bariteau, Charles: page 397
Barnabo, Cardinal: page 12
Baron, Father Armand: page 119, 146,
    154, 160, 172, 186, 193, 207, 208,
    210, 223, 224, 228, 237, 238, 241,
    246, 249, 260, 261, 262, 263, 327,
    413
Barrette, Raymond: page 366
Basile, Brother: page 14
Bastien, Marguerite: page 401
Baudrand, Father: page 14
Beaucage, Arthur: page 210
Beaucage, René: page 248
Beauchesne, Albertine: page 235
Beauchesne, Lily: page 407
Beaudoin, Égide: page 268, 278, 310
Beaudoin, Lisa: page 374
Beaudoin, Louis: page 374
Beaudoin, Wilfred: page 374
Beaudreau, Joseph: page 8
Beaulieu, Anna: page 263
Beaulieu, Arthur: page 263
Beaulieu, John H.: page 134
Beaulieu, Marie Jane: page 399
Beaumier, Laura: page 405
Beaumont, R.-A.: page 407

Beaupré, Louise: page 176
Beauregard, Aurélie: page 399
Beauregard, Paul: page 415
Beauregard, Pierre: page 397
Beauregard, Pierre Napoléon: page 397
Beausoleil, Albert: page 274, 415
Bedell, Brother Alexandre: page 154, 193, 210, 262, 302, 330
Bedlow, George W.: page 56
Bégin, Cardinal: page 182
Béland, Ernest: page 403
Bélanger, Charles: page 8, 36, 105
Bélanger, Charles: page 291, 295, 305, 316
Bélanger, Marie: page 410
Bélanger, W.: page 276
Béliveau, Robert: page 301, 310, 327
Béliveau, Laurent: page 371
Belle, Father: page 204
Bellegarde, Dantès: page 282, 283
Bellerive, Damase: page 401
Belley, Bernard: page 343, 370
Belley, Richard: Page 343
Belley, Ursula: page 314, 343
Benedict XV, Pope: page 183, 189
Benoit, Josaphat: page 264
Benoit, Marceline: page 399
Benoit, Paul-A.: page 403
Benouville, Guillain de: page 294
Bergeron, Albert: page 159, 251
Bergeron, Célina Dufresne: page 27, 29, 400
Bergeron, Claudia: page 409
Bergeron, Edmond Treflé: page 400
Bergeron, Irène-Emma: page 411
Bergeron, Juliette: page 406
Bergeron, Louis: page 8, 26, 27, 29, 36, 45, 77, 359, 400
Bergeron, Louis: page 359
Bergeron, Mr.: page 26, 27, 29, 45, 77
Bernanos, Georges: page 316
Bernèche, Arthur: page 175, 414
Bernèche, Gustave: page 414
Bernier, Antoine: page 398
Bernier, Joseph Médard: page 398

Berthiaume, Valérie: page 405
Bertrand, Aurore: page 405
Bertrand, Emma: page 404
Bertrand, J.: page 276
Bertrand, M.-Rose: page 405
Bibeault, Alfred: page 187
Bibeault, Éveline: page 406
Bibeau, M.-Alice: page 406
Bigonesse, Charles: page 77
Bilodeau, Miss Exilda: page 213, 230
Bilodeau, Lucienne: page 327
Biron, Mrs. Louis: page 266
Bissonnette, Elisephore: page 399
Bissonnette, Émélie Amanda : page 399
Blais, Eva: page 405
Blais, Joseph: page 401, 402, 414
Blanchard, Paul: page 403
Blanchette, Eva: page 409
Blanchette, Éveline: page 409
Blanchette, Monique Frigon: page 385, 391
Blanchette, Paul: page 359, 379
Blanchette, Tancrède: page 319
Blazon, Irène: page 219
Boisclair, Annie: page 401
Boisclair, Joseph: page 403
Boissonnault, Charles: page 413
Boissonnault, Charles A.: page 10
Boissonnault, Léon: page 402
Boissonneault, Aurore: page 385, 391
Boisvert, Aldor: page 415
Boisvert, Charles H.: page 114, 134
Boisvert, Dora: page 408
Boisvert, Elizabeth: page 404
Boisvert, Elizabeth: page 262
Boisvert, Moïse: page 114
Boisvert, Jacques: page 134, 135
Boisvert, Yvette: page 407
Bolduc, Emile: page 210, 228, 240, 241, 242, 243, 244, 245, 246, 247, 250, 251, 252, 253, 256, 261, 266, 267, 268, 269, 271, 275, 277, 278, 290, 291, 308, 309, 311, 312, 314, 318, 320, 324,262, 328, 329, 330, 331, 332, 340, 359, 360, 362, 379, 380, 402, 414

Bolduc, Henri: page 306, 307, 308, 310, 311, 312, 314, 315, 316, 317, 318, 320, 322, 324, 328, 329, 330, 331, 332, 379, 402, 415
Bolduc, Israël: page 306
Bolduc, Joseph: page 193, 241, 402, 414
Bolduc, Marie: page 398
Bolduc, Marie-Ange: page 331
Bolduc, Zéphirin: page 241
Bonhomme, Bishop Joseph: page 233, 234
Bonnet: page 207
Bonnet, Henri: page 293
Bonney, A.P.: page 81
Boott, J. W.: page 3
Boott, Kirk: page 3, 6, 225
Bordeleau, Irène: page 408
Botrel, Théodore: page 207
Bouchard, Joseph: page 329, 334, 415
Boucher, Anita: page 407
Boucher, Caroline: page 397
Boucher, Father: page 60, 121
Boucher, Nelson: page 334, 345, 354, 415
Boucher, Gertrude: page 218, 219
Boucher, Lilliane: page 219
Boudreau, Rodolphe: page 402
Boudreau, Isaïe: page 397
Boudreau, Marie Anne: page 397
Boulanger, Achille: page 362
Boulé, Alice: page 406
Boulé, M.-Anne: page 406
Bourassa, Henri: page 132, 189
Bourassa, Mrs. Marcel: page 335
Bourassa, Napoléon: page 174
Bourassa, Yvon: page 371
Bourbeau, David: page 8
Bourbonnière, Avila: page 99, 122
Bourgeois, Berthe: page 411
Bourgeois, Homer W.: page 341, 362, 368, 371
Bourgeois, Marguerite: page 222
Bourgeois, Roland: page 248, 310, 402, 415, 304
Bourget, Bishop Ignace: page 10, 14, 23
Bournigalle, Charles: page 44, 88, 412
Bourque, Alfred: page 397
Bourré, Odylle: page 397
Bouvier, Maurice: page 402

Bradley, Bishop: page 116
Bradt, Gerrit: page 26
Brady, Bishop: page 109
Brassard, Lucien: page 213, 224, 228, 249, 262, 284, 320, 322, 347, 402, 414
Breault, Alphonse: page 256, 264, 414
Breault, Officer: page 108
Brenton, Sister Léna: page 409
Brissette, Normand: page 382
Brouillette, Bernadette: page 405
Brouillette, Emile-J.: page 200, 205, 403
Brouillette, Alice: page 121
Brousseau, Emma Jane: page 399
Brousseau, Joseph: page 399
Brown, Hiram: page 401
Brullard, Pierre: page 134, 154, 413
Brunelle, Alice: page 385
Brunelle, Gérard: page 362
Brunelle, Michael: page 385
Brunelle, Oliva: page 196
Brun, Herménégilde: page 142
Bruyère, Mother: page 68, 228, 329
Buisson, Edmond: page 27, 397
Buisson, Joseph Edmond: page 27, 397
Bunoz, Bishop: page 210
Burke, James: page 291
Byrne, Patrick: page 6

C

Cabanel, Canon: page 187
Cabrol, Louis De: page 294
Cadieux, Marcel: page 365
Cadorette, Albert: page 134
Cagney, James: page 251
Caisse, Doctor: page 153
Caisse, Camille: page 122
Caisse, Louise: page 410
Caisse, Wilfred: page 100
Callahan, John: page 91
Campbell, Hugh: page 56
Campbell, Séverine: page 407
Campeau, Basile: page 149
Campeau, Joseph: page 121, 131, 132, 142, 146, 147, 149, 150, 151, 152, 153, 154, 155, 165, 171, 210, 413

Cangelosi, Raymond Dubuque: page 402
Capen, George: page 388, 389, 392, 393
Cardijn, Canon Joseph: page 252, 300
Cardinal, Laurent: page 381
Carney, James: page 28
Carolin, William: page 106, 116
Caron, Alma: page 409
Caron, Mélina: page 411
Caron, Thomas: page 165
Carpentier, Joseph: page 399
Carpentier, Zoël Fortunat: page 399
Carrier, Edouard: page 195, 255, 267, 275, 276, 291, 310
Carrier, Marie-Elise: page 404
Carrier, Marie-Jeanne: page 404
Carrière, Gaston: page 360
Carter, Jimmy: page 374
Cartier, Georges-Étienne: page 36
Carufel, L. E.: page 65
Casaubon, Mr.: page 60
Cayer, Albertine: page 329, 408
Cayer, Claire: page 407
Cécile de la Croix, Sister: page 304
Chabot, Raoul: page 310
Chaillor, Marie Henriette: page 398
Chalifoux, Joseph L.: page 9, 108, 116
Chalifoux, Philippe: page 191
Chamberlain, Mr.: page 201
Chambon, Albert: page 294, 306
Chambré, A. St. John: page 103, 106, 116
Champagnat, Marcellin: page 183, 271
Champagne, Jeanne: page 252
Champagne, Joseph: page 134
Champagne, Rosalie: page 407
Champlain, Samuel de: page 1
Chaput, Edouard: page 402, 414
Chaput, Léonide: page 405
Charette, General Baron de: page 77
Charette, Julie: page 401
Charette, Laurence: page 410
Charlebois, Bishop Ovide: page 209, 210
Charles, Prince of Wales: page 367
Charles-Roux, François: page 318
Châteauneuf, Denise: page 385, 391
Châteauneuf, Hervé: page 248
Châteauneuf, Maurice: page 392

Chevalier, Father: page 121
Chevalier, Albert: page 414
Chevalier, Michel: page 4, 6
Chevrot, Georges: page 294
Chiniquy, Charles: page 22, 76, 154
Choquette, E.: page 409
Choquette, Elzéar H.: page 49, 77, 153
Choquette, Victor: page 402
Chouinard, Gérard: page 256, 276, 302, 303, 304, 305, 306, 402, 415
Chouinard, Gustave: page 303
Chrétien, Joseph A. N.: page 205, 297
Chryseuil, Brother: page 94, 95, 147, 184
Church, Mr.: page 115
Cinq-Mars, M.-Agnès: page 405
Clancy, Father: page 278
Claudel, Paul: page 353
Clément, Antoine: page 293, 306, 360
Clément, Aurore: page 407
Clermont, Jacqueline: page 334
Clermont, Mrs. Hector: page 335
Clouâtre, William: page 191
Cloutier, Cécile: page 407
Cloutier, Laurette: page 409
Clut, Bishop Isidore: page 88
Coburn, Franklin: page 28
Coderre, Aldéric: page 222
Cognac, Henri: page 191
Collignon, Bishop Louis: page 280, 281, 282, 325, 351
Colombe-du-Précieux-Sang, Sister: page 70, 71
Comeau, Lumina: page 216
Conrad, Brother: page 321, 322
Constantin, Brother: page 251
Constantine, Mrs.: page 70
Constantineau, Cyrille: page 49
Constantineau, Delima: page 398
Constantineau, Henri: page 49, 86, 87, 99, 138, 140, 402
Constantineau, Hedwidge: page 410
Constantineau, Honoré: page 36, 86
Coolidge, Governor: page 191
Cooray, Thomas Cardinal: page 363
Corcoran, Patrick: page 55
Cormier, Edouard: page 8

Cornellier, Délia: page 100
Corriveau, Mr.: page 233
Corriveau, Mrs.: page 233
Corriveau, Candide: page 233
Cossette, Paul: page 187
Cosson, J.: page 40, 41, 42, 398, 399
Côté, Agnès: page 411
Côté, Albert V: page viii, 366, 395
Côté, Augustin: page 403
Côté, Barbara: page viii, 366
Côté, Blanche: page 406
Côté, Richard: page 374
Côté, Elzéar: page 222
Côté, Jean S.: page 49
Côté, Joseph: page 362
Côté, Léon-M.: page 222
Coté, Mrs. C.: page 222
Côté, Mrs. Joseph: page 362
Cotnoir, Narcisse: page 253, 262, 414
Coughlin, Francis Joseph: page 399
Coughlin, Frank: page 399
Couillard, Robert: page 374
Couleaf, John: page 399
Couleaf, Josephine: page 399
Couleaf, Mary: page 399
Courchêne, Alfred: page 36
Courchêne, Edouard: page 8
Courchêne, Joseph: page 10
Courchène, Sophie: page 401
Courchesne, Edouard: page 36, 109
Courtney, William F.: page 109, 121
Courtois, Rébecca: page 407
Coutu, Lucina: page 407
Coutu, Marie-Anne: page 393, 407
Couture, Jeanne: page 409
Crépeau, Antoinette: page 405
Crépeau, Emma: page 143
Cushing, Richard Cardinal: page 281, 296,
    311, 312, 324, 325, 329, 330, 337,
    345, 354, 359, 363
Cushing, Sheriff: page 116
Cyr, Louis: page 104
Cyr, Myles: page 368, 369, 370
Cyr, Nathalie: page 397
Cyr, Roger: page 369, 370

D

Dacey, Father: page 110
Daigle, Albert A.: page viii, 359, 369, 385,
    389, 391, 391, 392
Daigle, Albert A., Jr.: page 385
Daigle, Dianne B.: page 385
Daigle, Nicole I.: page 385
Daigle, Omer-A.: page 403
Daigle, Thérèse M.: page viii, 385, 391
Daignault, Elphège: page 203
Dalphond, Alphonse: page 134
Dancosse, Augustine: page 405
Daniel, Kathleen: page 385
Daoust, Charles R.: page 101, 196
d'Arcy, Bishop John: page 387
Dastous, Jeannette: page 411
Dastous, Robert: page 346
Daunais, Germaine: page 410
Daveluy, Charles: page 126, 413
David, Mrs.: page 70
David, Philias: page 59, 102
Davis, Betty: page 346
Dawson, Robert: page 56
Day, Hélène: page 381
Dazé, Alphonse: page 88, 97, 412
Debergh, Joseph: page 310, 313, 314, 365,
    369, 371, 372, 375, 376, 383
De Blois, Rosalie: page 319
Décelle, Joseph Albert: page 402
Décelles, Alice: page 406
Décelles, Cécile: page 406
Décelles, Hedwidge: page 406
Décelles, Thérèse: page 411
Dédebant, Basile: page 15, 16, 44, 46, 78,
    412
Dégagné, Béatrice: page 329, 408
Dégagné, Richard: page 403
de Gaulle, Charles: page 293
Délisle, Elie: page 166
Délisle, Xavier: page 205
Delude, Azilda: page 409
Delude, Emma: page 409
Demers, Brother: page 142
Denault, Marie Emilie: page 401
Denis, Joseph: page 193, 414

420

Dénizot, Charles: page 51, 163, 186, 189, 190, 193, 197, 241, 261, 262, 310, 326, 414

Desaulniers, H. L.: page 44

Deschaines, Oliva: page 407

Deschâtelets, Léo: page iv, vi, 328, 363

Descheneaux, Omer: page 221

Descheneaux, Rodrigue: page 196

Deschênes, Miss: page 233

Descôteaux, Mrs. Robert: page 335, 359

Descôteaux, Pierre: page 362

Desilets, Mrs.: page 66

Désiré, Brother Henri: page 185

Desjadons, Louis: page 210, 262, 310, 326, 327, 403

Desjardins, Alphonse: page 165

Desmarais, Berthe: page 235

Desmarais, Georgina: page 398

Desmarais, Irène R.: page 345, 346, 385, 391

Desmarais, Léo: page 402

Desmarais, Marie: page 401

Desmarais, Narcisse: page 401

Desmarais, Osylle: page 401

Desmarais, Pierre: page 401

Desmarais, Rosalie: page 398

Desnoyers, Anthime: page 241, 271, 301

Desormeau, Alphonse: page 105

Després, M.-Victorine: page 404

Desrochers, Albini: page 222

Desroches, Benjamin: page 413

Desrosiers, Edouard: page 222

Desruisseaux, Agnès: page 410

Desruisseaux, Cécile: page 410

Desruisseaux, Louis: page 402

Desruisseaux, Pauline: page 345

Dilts, Hyacinth: page 154

Dion, Aurore: page 327

Dion, Georges: page 268, 278, 291

Dion-Lévesque, Rosaire: page 264

Diss, Jerôme: page 413

Dobelle, Sergeant: page 187

Donovan, Mayor: page 73

Dontenwill, Bishop Augustin: page 155, 194, 213

Doré, Theresa B.: page 391

Dorion, Félix: page 400

Dorion, Marie Léa: page 400

Doucet, Eugénie: page 407

Dougherty, Cardinal: page 198

Doyle, Mary Ann: page 389

Dozois: page 77

Dozois, Calixte: page 8

Dozois, Charles H. : page 379, 402

Dozois, Father: page 128

Dozois, Hilaire: page 8, 10, 102, 114

Drapeau, Aurore: page 298, 405

Drapeau, William: page 174

Drapeau, Msgr. William: page 402

Drapeau, Raymond: page 402

Drouet, Father: page 92

Dubé, Mrs. Francis: page 345

Dubé, Gilbert: page 358

Du Bief, Jacqueline: page 305

Dubois, Agnès: page 407

Dubois, Clara: page 405

Dubois, Émélie: page 405

Dubois, Eugénie: page 405

Dubois, Herménie: page 405

Dubois, Jacqueline: page 253

Dubois, Louise-Elvina: page 405

Dubois, Marie-Flore: page 404

Dubois, Olive: page 404

Dubois, Poméla: page 405

Dubois, Roland: page 403

Dubreuil, Michel: page 153, 154, 413

Dubuque, Hugo: page 92

Ducatillon, Joseph: page 271

Ducharme, Albéric: page 165

Ducharme, Edouard: page 209, 414

Ducharme, Exilia: page 407

Ducharme, Flore: page 410

Ducharme, François: page 36

Ducharme, Narcisse: page 397

Ducharme, Thaddée: page 134

Ducharme, Virginie: page 399

Duchaussois, Bishop: page 231

Dufaut, Edouard: page 401

Dufaut, Joseph: page 401

Duff, Stanislas: page 45

Dufresne, Celina: page 400

Dufresne, Joseph: page 8

Dufresne, Rose: page 147
Duhamel, Bishop: page 60, 116, 124, 149
Duhamel, Edouard: page 193
Duhamel, Mother: page 167
Dumais, Father: page 287
Dumais, Madeleine: page 334
Dumas, Elisabeth: page 404
Dumas, Father: page 316
Dumont, Annette: page 219, 235
Dumont, Jeanne: page 311
Dumont, Sévère: page 142
Dunne, Dennis: page 377
Duplessis, Georges: page 320, 322
Dupont, George: page 385, 415
Dupré: page 207
Duprez, E. H.: page 80
Duprez, Mrs.: page 70
Duprez, Omer-A.: page 377, 403
Dupuis, Régina: page 404
Duquet, Marie: page 398
Duquette, Cécile: page 304
Duquette, Jean-Baptiste Alfred: page 400
Duquette, Michel: page 400
Durocher, Father: page 23
Dussault, Anne-Marie: page 406
Duthoit, Captain: page 187
Duval, A. N.: page 109
Duvalier, François: page 351
d'Youville, Mother: page 329, 330, 337, 338

E

Ehrhard, Jos.-Charles: page 154, 193, 414
Élie, Georgette: page 359, 362
Elkin, Mary: page 401
Emard, Bishop: page 102
Emard, Joseph-Hercule: page 97, 102, 121, 413
Emery, Joseph Edouard: page 133, 210, 413
Eno, Arthur L.: page 204, 205, 210, 227, 236, 251, 266, 293
Eno, Arthur L., Jr. (Louis): page vii, 392, 377
Eno, Mrs. Arthur: page 346
Eno, Madeleine: page vii

Ethier, Pierre: page 401
Exilda, Marie: page 398

F

Fabre, Bishop: page 60
Fabre, Father: page 16
Fallaize, Bishop Pierre: page 256
Fallon, Michael: page 141, 142, 154, 156, 157
Falville, Christine: page 398
Farley, Leo: page 371
Farley, Philip: page 110, 114, 118
Faucher, Joseph: page 275, 299
Fauconnier: page 82
Féat, Pierre: page 113, 412
Fecteau, E.: page 36
Fenwick, Bishop Benedict: page 6
Ferland, Alice: page 407
Ferland, Roméo: page 310, 415
Ferron, Antoinette: page 409
Ferron, Régina: page 409
Filiatreault, Frank: page 222
Filion, J. A.: page 134
Fillion, Normand: page 310, 327, 334, 343, 390, 415
Finn, Lizzie: page 35, 60, 71
Flanagan, Father: page 273
Florentius, Brother: page 200, 205
Foisy, J. A.: page 134
Fontaine, Asilda: page 401
Fontaine, J.: page 111
Fontaine, Joseph: page 398
Fontaine, Joseph Baptiste: page 398
Forbes, Bishop John: page 209
Forbes, Archbishop William: page 225
Ford, Patrick: page 84
Forget-Despatis, Joïada: page 118, 126, 124, 413
Forget, Dioscoride: page 97, 112, 113, 114, 115, 118, 413
Forget, Jean-Marie: page 113
Fornet, Nazaire: page 398
Fornet, Onésime: page 398
Fortier, Adolphe: page 210, 262
Fortier, Ovila: page 267
Fortier, Robert: page 415

Fortin, Henriette: page 401
Fortin, Léonce: page 164
Foucault, Victorine: page 270
Fournier, Alexandre: page 46, 137
Fournier, Alphonse: page 415
Fournier, Eugène: page 262, 299, 326, 414
Fournier, Henri: page 221
Fournier, Joseph-Alexandre: page 44, 45, 46, 47, 48, 49, 51, 61, 75, 78, 82, 83, 86, 89, 110, 126, 128, 130, 136, 137, 138, 412
Fournier, Joseph-Emmanuel: page 136, 137
Fournier, Pierre: page 49
Fox, Marguerite: page 399
Francis, Brother: page 205, 219, 220
Fréchette, Armand: page 402
Fréchette, Louis: page 146
Fréchette, Marie: page 404
Fréchette, Suzanne: page 385, 391
Fredette, Amédée: page 414
Frère, André: page 293
Frigon, Jean-Baptiste: page 413
Froc, Michel: page 44

G

Gage, Daniel: page 93
Gagné, Antoinette: page 407
Gagné, Claire: page 293
Gagné, Elisabeth: page 404
Gagné, Hélène: page 404
Gagné, Jeanne: page 385, 391
Gagner, Clara: page 404
Gagnon, Sister Aldéa: page 409
Gagnon, Ferdinand: page 79
Gagnon, Mrs. Joseph: page 235
Gagnon, Lysiane: page 360, 361
Gagnon, Pierre Charles: page 110, 124, 126, 131, 149, 413
Gagnon, Raymond: page 248
Gagnon, Rose-Anna: page 235
Gagnon, Rose-Anna: page 404
Gagnon, Virginie: page 407
Gamache, Louis: page 398
Gamache, William: page 398
Gamache, Zoé: page 398

Garabedian, Donna: page 376, 385
Garand, Bishop P.: page 199
Garan, Phébée: page 397
Gariépy, Esdras: page 414
Garin, André-Marie: page 15, 16, 20, 22, 23, 24, 25, 26, 27, 28, 29, 31, 33, 34, 35, 36, 37, 38, 40, 41, 42, 43, 44, 45, 46, 50, 53, 54, 55, 56, 61, 62, 65, 66, 67, 70, 72, 73, 75, 77, 78, 79, 80, 81, 82, 83, 84, 85, 87, 89, 90, 91, 92, 93, 96, 97, 98, 99, 100, 102, 103, 104, 105, 106, 107, 109, 110, 111, 113, 114, 115, 116, 117, 118, 119, 122, 123, 125, 133, 136, 139, 141, 150, 152, 155, 174, 221, 231, 245, 247, 327, 357, 359, 360, 362, 623, 370, 371, 376, 379, 383, 395, 397, 398, 399, 400, 401
Garon, Cécile: page 406
Garon, Julie: page 399
Gaudet, Alexandre: page 397
Gaudet, Cleophas: page 398
Gaudet, Marie Rosanna: page 397
Gaudet, Pierre: page 45
Gaudet, Octave: page 398
Gaudreau, Charles: page 401
Gaudreau, Julienne: page 398
Gaudreau, Rose: page 397
Gaulin, Achille: page 222
Gaulin, Gilberte: page 219
Gaulin, Roland: page 402, 415
Gauthier: page 77
Gauthier, Joséphine: page 407
Gauthier, Pierre: page 401
Gauthier, Sister Juliette: page 409
Gauvreau, Napoléon: page 401
Gélinas, L. C.: page 196
Généreux, Gabrielle: page 406
Généreux, Hélène: page 235
Généreux, Henry: page 403
Généreux, Marcel: page 310, 402, 415, 313
Généreux, Simonne: page 300
Généreux, Victor D.: page 371
Généreux, Yvonne: page 406
Genest, Angélina: page 405

Genest, Béatrice: page 406
Genest, Denise: page 406
Genest, Évéline: page 406
Gény, B.: page 82, 84, 146, 412
Geoffroy, Antoinette: page 407
Geoffroy, Antonia: page 406
Geoffroy, Gérard R.: page 385, 391
Geoffroy, Joseph: page 263
Geoffroy, Laura B.: page 385, 391
Geoffroy, Marguerite: page 263
Geoffroy, Régina: page 407
Germain, Arthur: page 222
Germain, Berthe: page 405
Germain, Louise-Eva: page 406
Germain, Marie-Clara: page 404
Germain, Paul: page 402
Germain, Philippe: page 402
Gervais, Alfred: page 151
Gilbert, Assunta M.: page 371
Gilbert, Edward M.: page 371
Gilbert, Virginie: page 405
Gill, Aristine: page 27, 397
Gill, Catherine: page 66
Gilly, Commander: page 293
Gionet, Aimée: page 165
Girard, Prime: page 276
Girard, Pierre: page 398
Girard, Pierre Zephirin: page 398
Girouard, Camille: page 283
Giroux, Thomas C.: page 8
Gladu, Aloïs: page 44, 61, 64, 75, 78, 82,
    89, 412
Gobeil, M.: page 8
Godin, Rose: page 397
Goësbriand, Bishop Louis de: page 11, 16,
    45, 67
Gonzalvus, Brother: page 185
Goodwin, Mr.: page 172
Goupil, Marie-Eléonore: page 404
Goyette, Gaston: page 279
Goyette, Napoléon: page 142
Grandin, Bishop Vital: page 91
Graton, Alexandre: page 401
Graton, Joseph Augustin: page 142, 154,
    159, 163, 170, 178, 193, 208, 210,
    225, 241, 242, 413

Grégoire, Edouard: page 222
Grégoire, Mrs. G.: page 222
Grégoire, Laurier: page 253, 273
Grenier, Antoinette: page 411
Grenier, Jean-Baptiste: page 398
Grenier, Marie Félicité: page 398
Grenier, Marie Louise: page 362
Grew, Mrs. Wilbert: page 327
Grouard, Bishop: page 128, 231, 232
Groulx, Abbé Lionel: page 202
Guay, Marie-Louise: page 298, 405
Guérin, Monsignor Joseph: page 294
Guertin, Bishop: page 383
Guigues, Bishop: page 46
Guilbault, Louis Napoléon: page 178, 207
Guilbeault, Alphonsine: page 405
Guillard, Joseph: page 41, 42, 108, 109,
    115, 121, 124
Guillemette, Léo: page 358
Guillet, Joseph Henri: page 62, 63, 66, 76,
    77, 87, 92, 102, 103, 114, 115, 153,
    164, 188, 210, 225
Guilmette, Gédéon: page 263
Guy, Bishop Joseph: page 232, 235, 289
Guy, Jules: page 306, 415

H

Hadley, Judge S. P.: page 116
Hall, Thalles P.: page 93
Hamel, Florida: page 407
Hamelin, Xavier: page 49
Hamilton, Victoria: page 404
Hamon, E.: page 39
Hardman, Mrs. Robert: page 335
Hardy, Jeanne: page 385, 392
Hardy, Mrs. Hervé: page 335, 359
Harnois, Pascal: page 55
Harris, Principal: page 220
Harsus, Doctor: page 264
Harvey, Clifford: page 248
Harvey, Joseph: page 196
Hébert, Alma: page 409
Hébert, Anna: page 409
Hébert, Claura: page 409
Hébert, Louis Philippe: page 115, 117
Hébert, Olympe: page 401

Hébert, Osa: page 362
Hélène de la Croix, Sister: page 321
Hémond, Phydime: page 203
Hénault, Elisa: page 407
Hénault, Emma: page 407
Henri-Désiré, Brother: page 185
Héroux, Aldéa: page 405
Héroux, Clorilda: page 171
Héroux, Germaine: page 218, 219, 406
Héroux, Jeanne: page 267, 269
Héroux, Rita: page 407
Hibbard, Joseph H.: page 201
Hickey, Augustin: page 181, 183, 203
Hickey, Marie Anne: page 399
Hickey, Bishop William: page 202
Hildreth, Fisher: page 56
Hitler: page 254
Honorat, Father: page 14
Hood, Mr.: page 115
Hotin, Arthémise: page 222
Houde, Clara: page 241
Houde, François X.: page 364
Houle, Alphonse: page 262, 414
Houle, André: page 376
Hubert, Adelard Joseph: page 399
Hubert, Flavien: page 398
Hubert, Francis Delphis Ada: page 398
Hubert, Louis: page 399
Hughes, Bishop Alfred: page 384, 385,
    389, 393
Huot, Marie-Jeanne: page 285, 360
Hyacinth, Father: page 76

I

Isabelle, Raymond: page 402

J

Jackson, P.T.: page 3
Jackson, Mr.: page 201
Jacques, J. N.: page 135, 153
Jacques, Lydia: page 406
Jacques, Wilfrid: page 222
Jadaa, John: page 346
Jalbert, Eugène: page 202
Jalbert, Rosario: page 193, 262, 402, 414
Jay, Pierre: page 163

Jean: page 77
Jean, Albert: page 164
Jean, Auguste: page 62
Jean, Corinne: page 252
Jean, Eva: page 410
Jean, Gabrielle: page 407
Jean-Honoré, Brother: page 94
Jean-Marie, Sister: page 338
Jodoin, Rosa: page 405
John Paul II, Pope: page 372
Jolicoeur, Rose: page 185
Joly, Mrs. Hervé: page 345
Joly, Malvina: page 407
Joly, Marie: page 407
Joly, Marie-Anne: page 404
Joseph-Athanasius, Brother: page 94
Joséphat, Sister: page 227
Joyal, Brother Donat: page 310
Joyce, Father: page 102, 115
Juaire, Joseph: page 415
Jules-Bois, H. A.: page 263, 264
Julien-Emile, Brother: page 185
Jutras, Alfred: page 403
Jutras, Alma-Liliane: page 406
Jutras, Brother A.: page 193
Jutras, Corinne-Albia: page 404
Jutras, Philomène: page 408

K

Keane, Monsignor: page 87
Keely, P.C.: page 54, 55 , 56, 84
Kelley, Bridget: page 56
Kelley, Michael: page 56
Kelley, Sabina: page 56
Kennedy, John: page 105
Keough, Bishop: page 281
Kerouac, Jean "Jack": page 364, 381
Kiely, Father: page 392
Kiely, Fr. Brian: page 390, 391, 392, 393
King, John: page 363
King, Léo: page 371
Kinkelin, Artist: page 177
Knapp, Charles L.: page 114, 115

L

Labonne, Alfred: page 398

Labonne, David: page 398

Labossière, J. B.: page 178, 197, 426

Labouré, Théodore: page 267

La Boulaye, André-Marie Lefebvre de:
    page 235, 238, 240

Labrecque, Arthur: page 172

Labrecque, Rose: page 405

Labrecque, Thérèse-J.: page 406

Labrie, Cécile: page 222

Labrie, Eugène: page 284, 320, 322, 324,
    402

Labrie, Lionel: page 415

Labrie, Lucille: page 346

Lachance, Gabrielle: page 311

Lachance, Jean: page 8

Lachance, Olivette: page 219

Lachance, Thomas: page 8

LaCharité, Julie: page 398

Lacombe, Honoré: page 401

Lacourse, Marcel: page 248

Lacouture, Marie: page 27, 401

Lacroix, Gérard: page 346

Lacroix, Bishop Marc: page 284

Lafaille, Aurélie: page 400

Lafaille, Moïse: page 36

Laflamme, Charles: page 100, 108

Laflamme, Eugènc: pagc 397

Laflamme, Jean Baptiste: page 8

Laflamme, Jean-Baptiste: page 401

Laflamme, Marie: page 397

Laflamme, Mélina: page 397

Laflamme, Victorine: page 397

Laflèche, Bishop Louis: page 61, 91

Lafleur, Estelle: page 385

Lafleur, Robert: page 385, 391

Lafontaine, Napoléon: page 398

Lafontaine, Salomon: page 398

Lafontaine, Yvonne: page 406

Lafortune, Albert: page 263

Lagassé, Yvonne: page 362

Lagassé, Siméon: page 134

Lagier, Candidus: page 71, 72, 78, 82, 412

Lagier, Jean-Marie: page 20

Lagier, Lucien: page 14, 20, 21, 22, 23,
    24, 27, 28, 31, 40, 45, 71, 78, 363,
    401

Lajoie, Marguerite: page 399

Lalande, H.: page 253

Lalande, Louis: page 146

Lally, Matthew: page 188

Lalumière, Scholastique: page 45

Lalumière, Sophie: page 398

Lambert, Alfred: page 146

Lambert, Jeannette: page 311

Lambert, Joseph E.: page 161, 164, 196

Lamontagne, Georges A.: page 8

Lamontagne, Henri A.: page 8

Lamontagne, Jean A.: page 8

Lamontagne, Pierre E.: page 8

Lamothe, Anna de: page 191

Lamothe, Léon: page 99, 113, 126, 136,
    141, 146, 153, 154, 193, 197, 262,
    413

Lamoureux, Joseph: page 256

Lamoureux, Dr. Joseph: page 172, 228,
    238

Lamoureux, Léon: page 359

Lamoureux, Léontine: page 187

Lamoureux, Lilliane: page 407

Lamoureux, M.-Emma: page 405

Lamoureux, M.-Louise: page 404

Lamoureux, Roger-E.: page 402

Lamoureux, Roger J.: page 338, 402

Lancelon, Stanislas: page 82, 412

Lanciau, Médard: page 401

Lanciaux, Elmire: page 401

Lanctôt, Médéric: page 36

Landry, Corinne: page 405

Landry, Estelle: page 235

Landry, Godfroy: page 36

Landry, Louis: page 401

Landry, Suzanne: page 334

Langelier, Côme C.: page 36

Langelier, Vitaline: page 401

Langevin, Mathilda: page 400

Langières, Georges E.: page 134

Langis, Dentist: page 153

Langlais, Abraham: page 187

Langlais, Henri: page 276

Langlois, Amanda: page 303

Langlois, Émélie: page 400

Langlois, Jeannette: page 385

Langlois, Marguerite: page 404

Lanoue, Philomène: page 399
Lantagne, Marie-Anne: page 404
Lantagne, Télesphore: page 401
Lapierre, Consul: page 306
Lapierre, Joseph: page 397
Lapierre, Joseph-S.: page 8, 36, 45, 126
Lapierre, Louis Joseph: page 397
Lapointe, Aurore: page 405
Laquerre, Father: page 278
Lareau, Doris: page 407
Larivière, Alexandrine: page 401
Larmand, Blanche: page 362
Laroche, Armand: page 221, 346
Larochelle, Girardine: page 100
Larrivée, Alberta: page 349
Larue, Urcisse: page 196
Lashua, Ralph: page 191
Latendresse, Eva: page 405
Latulippe, Bishop: page 183
Laurent, Alfred: page 307
Laurin, Alma: page 235
Laurin, Alma: page 406
Laurin, Camille: page 36
Lauzé, Michael: page 374, 383, 384, 385, 386, 389, 390
Lauzon, Father: page 121
Lauzon, Tharsile: page 306
Lavallée, Jules: page 27, 401
Lavallée, Léon: page 371
Lavallée, Roland: page 299, 415
Lavergne, Gratia: page 404
Lavergne, Marie-Emma: page 404
Laverlochère, Father: page 23
Lavigne, Alex.: page 36
Lavigne, Joseph-Edgar: page 403
Lavigueur, Célestin: page 77, 78
Lavoie, Alphonsine: page 408
Lavoie, Jean: page 362
Lavoie, Mrs. Jean: page 362
Lavoie, Joseph: page 88, 412
Lavoie, Sister Lorraine: page 409
Lavoie, Méralda: page 409
Lavoie, Robéa: page 409
Law, Cardinal Bernard: page 390, 392, 395
Leavitt, Mr.: page 40

Leavitt, Mrs.: page 40
Lebel, Thérèse: page 408
Leblanc, Alfred: page 196
Leblanc, Gérald: page 221
Leblanc, Mrs. Olivier: page 48
Lebret, L.: page 41, 42, 399, 400, 401
Lebrun, Amédée: page 187
Lebrun, Boniface: page 401
Lebrun, Mr.: page 231
Leclair, Louis: page 8
Leclerc, Eva: page 410
Leclerc, J.-B.: page 15
Leclerc, Joseph: page 209, 402
Lecomte, Moïse: page 99
Lecomte, Phidime: page 412
Ledoux, Angèle: page 407
Ledoux, Ovide: page 165
Lafebvre, Alice: page 345
Lefebvre, Camille: page 129
Lefebvre, Joseph: page 109, 111, 116, 118, 124, 126, 127, 129, 135, 140, 141, 142, 147, 148, 151, 153, 154, 172, 413
Lefebvre, Joseph Médard: page 140
Légaré, Father: page 75
Légaré, Joseph A.: page 226, 227, 228
Légaré, Virginie: page 276
Legrain, Dom: page 328
Lelièvre, Victor: page 158, 161
LeMaître, Félicité: page 398
LeMay, Armand: page 364, 365
Lemay, Gédéon: page 401
Lemay, Jacqueline: page 338
Lemay, Joseph: page 8
Lemay, Marie-Alice: page 411
Lemieux, Claire: page 385, 391
Lemieux, Michelle: page 385, 391
Lemire, Anselme: page 8
Lemire, Arthur: page 209, 223, 402, 414
Lemire, Florida: page 408
Lemire, Germaine: page 188, 374
Lemire, Jean: page 8
Lemire, M.-Alida: page 405
Lemire, Marie: page 398
Lemire, Paul: page 248
Lemire, Rose: page 408

Lemius, Joseph: page 161
Léo, Brother: page 200, 205, 403
Leo XII, Pope: page 12
LePailleur, Canon: page 152
Lescot, Elie: page 271, 280, 281
Lesieur, Georges Edmond: page 398
Lesieur, Narcisse: page 398
Lesieur, Paul: page 8
Lessard, Anatole: page iii, iv, vi, viii, 349,
    350, 352, 355, 357, 359, 362, 368,
    394
Lessard, George: page 359, 415
Lessard, Odina: page 349
Lessard, Simone: page 311
Lessard, Yvette: page 407
Letendre, Mrs. Joseph: page 345
Letendre, Paul-Emile: page 317
Létourneau, Florida: page 404
Létourneau, Roland: page 248
Levasseur, Brother Ovide: page 154, 193,
    210, 262, 301
Lévesque, Paul: page 415
Lévesque, Robert: page 415
Lewis, Louis: page 132, 208, 413
L'Hermitte, Achille: page 310, 313, 314,
    376
L'Heureux, Hélène: page 408
Lincourt, Marie-Anne: page 404
Lippé, Spiridon: page 196
Lirette, Albert: page 402
Lirette, Alfred: page 402
Lirette, Eva: page 410
Lirette, Léandre: page 402
Lirette, Marie: page 410
Lirette, Pierre: page 403
Lirette, Rose-Anna: page 410
Lizotte, Antoine: page 399
Lizotte, Clara Emma: page 399
Loiselle, J. L.: page 36
Loranger, Léon: page 261, 265, 266, 284,
    292, 293, 402, 414
Lord, Raymond: page 365
Lorrain, Mr.: page 141
Louis-Robert, Sister: page 321, 354, 360
Louis Viateur, Brother: page 318, 319,
    321, 322
Lowell, Francis Cabot: page 2, 3

Loyson, Charles: page 76
Lozeau, N. M.: page 165
Lucier, Eugénie: page 408
Lussier, Yvonne: page 411
Lyonnais, Eméry: page 254, 255, 256,
    262, 273, 275, 297, 310, 415
Lyons, Marguerite: page 359

M

Mabathoana, Bishop: page 310
MacMillan, Sister: page 167
Magee, Brother Patrick: page 355
Magloire, Paul: page 310
Magnan, Joseph: page 414
Maguire, Robert: page 362
Mahoney, John: page 6
Mailhot, Irène: page 406
Maillé, J. A.: page 134
Maillet, Fernand: page 317
Mailloux, Florida: page 362
Major, Julienne: page 46
Mallet, Mother: page 330
Malloy, Mary: page 399
Malo, Arthur: page 346, 359
Malo, Priscille: page 407
Mangin, Joseph: page 43, 72, 124, 125, 126,
    127, 129, 133, 134, 135, 136, 151
Mangin, Charles: page 126
Marchand, Lorraine: page 407
Marchand, Marie: page 408
Marchand, Yvonne: page 183
Marchand, Roland: page 392
Marcil, Edesse: page 397
Marcotte, Albert: page 248
Marcotte, Rébecca: page 404
Marcouillier, Denise: page 385, 391
Marie-Arthur, Sister: page 161
Marie de l'Incarnation, Sister: page 152
Marie-du-Bon-Conseil, Sister: page 153,
    329
Marie-du-Calvaire, Sister: page 233, 234
Marie-du-St-Sacrement, Sister: page 69,
    70, 71, 129
Marie-Eustelle, Sister: page 329
Marie-Léonie, Blessed Mother: page 129,
    130, 392, 393

Marie, Sister: page 17
Marin, Alice: page 209, 411
Marin, Balda: page 411
Marin, Georges: page 209, 402
Marin, Joseph: page 154, 171, 211
Marin, Joséphine: page 211
Marin, Samuel P.: page 8, 9, 36, 45, 63, 80
Marion, Brother Alphonse: page 193
Marion, Athanase: page 82, 113, 126, 193, 210, 241, 262, 412
Marion, Georges: page 44, 72, 73, 78, 126, 412
Marion, Isaïe: page 193
Markham, Bishop: page 306
Marquis, Eva: page 408
Marquis, Paul: page 415
Martel, Eliza: page 397
Martineau, Albert: page 370, 390
Martin, Paul: page 320, 322
Martin, John: page 248
Martin, Philomène: page 405
Masse, Rose-Alba: page 405
Masson, Elisabeth: page 401
Masson, Joséphine: page 401
Masson, Paula: page 385
Mathon, Bernadette: page 405
Matte, Eva: page 406
Mayer, Anne-Ombéline: page 405
Mazenod, St. Bishop Eugene de: page 12, 14, 20, 21, 22, 42, 80, 128, 231, 370, 371, 372
McAlvin, John: page 56
McDermott, Father: page 7, 17
McDonald, Sister Marie: page 388
McEvoy, John: page 148
McGrath, James: page 60, 62, 64, 65, 72, 81, 82, 86, 99, 100, 102, 104, 116
McKay, Sara: page 397
McNamara, Bishop John: page 389, 392, 393
Medeiros, Cardinal Humberto: page 371
Melançon, Bishop: page 349
Ménard, Marie-Elise: page 408
Mercier, Alarie: page 8, 36, 398
Mercier, Armand: page 396
Mercier, Cardinal: page 190

Mercier, Joseph Arcade: page 398
Mercier, Joseph: page 191
Mercil, Aurélien: page 191, 193, 197, 262, 402, 414
Messières, René de: page 293
Messier, Irène: page 235
Michaud, Christiane: page 410
Michaud, Ernestine: page 404
Michaud, Florence: page 408
Mignault, Dr. Déodat: page 8
Mignault, Father: page 8
Miller, Aurélie Ritchie: page 27, 29, 399
Miller, Emma: page 66
Miller, Jean Baptiste: page 49
Miller, Joseph: page 8, 26, 27, 31, 66, 399
Miller, Joseph Henry: page 399
Millette, Father: page 60
Milliner, Désiré: page 293
Milot, Arthur: page 261
Milot, Louis Napoléon: page 165, 196
Milot, M.-Anne: page 404
Milot, Sister Emma: page 373, 411
Mirault, A.: page 82
Mogan, Patrick: page 367
Moisan, Jeanne: page 410
Moisan, Lilliane: page 327
Moisan, Marie Anne: page 252
Molleur, John: page 397
Molleur, Marie Eléonore: page 397
Molleur, Rose: page 401
Monette, Léo: page 390
Mongeau, Archbishop Gérard: page 379
Mongeau, Georges E.: page 187
Monpellier-Beaulieu, Adéline: page 149
Montemont, Louise: page 401
Montferrand, L. T.: page 36
Montfort, Sister St. Louis de: page 212
Montminy, Esther: page 404
Montminy, Joseph F.: page 196
Montminy, Laurette: page 406
Moody, Paul: page 2, 3
Moreau, Albina: page 174
Moreau, Charles: page 415
Morel, Séraphine: page 408
Morier, Clarina: page 228, 234, 300
Morin, Father: page 122

Morin, Msgr. Hermann: page 402
Morin, Alphée: page 254
Morin, Cécile: page 409
Morin, Diane: page 264
Morin-Dubé, Diane: page 291, 295
Morin, J. B.: page 166, 169, 171
Morin, Joseph: page 187
Morin, Rose: page 371
Morissette, Armand: page 82, 161, 255,
    261, 267, 292, 264, 306, 328, 364,
    380, 381, 402, 415
Morissette, Joseph: page 261, 402
Morize, André: page 264, 293
Morneau, Henry: page 403
Morrissette, Donat: page 308, 309, 310,
    324, 332, 333, 334, 336, 337, 341,
    342, 350, 352, 402, 415
Morrissette, Gédéon: page 332
Morse, Bradford: page 362
Motard, George: page 385, 391
Mullen, Father: page 180
Murphy, Roméo: page 310, 351, 415
Murray, Célina: page 401

N

Nadon, Tarsile: page 113
Nault, Anna: page 408
Nault, Hélène: page 408
Nicol, Philippe: page 147
Ninteau, Angéline: page 235
Nolin, Louis-Alphonse: page 107, 113,
    126, 128, 132, 173, 183, 193, 210,
    238, 241, 261, 262, 413
Norman, Sister: page 227, 228
Normandin, Germain: page 222
Noue, Count Jéhan de: page 293
Noury, Eugène: page 324, 325, 326, 343
Noval, Minnie: page 263
Novello, Russell: page 346

O

O'Beirne, Florence: page 410
O'Beirne, Irène: page 410
O'Beirne, Marie: page 409
O'Beirne, Jean: page 268

Obin, Arthur: page 376, 377, 378, 379,
    383, 384, 387
O'Brien, John: page 7, 17, 18, 24, 27, 40,
    46
O'Connell, Cardinal William: page 150,
    151, 155, 165, 177, 178, 181, 196,
    203, 217, 234, 235, 239, 240, 296
Odélia, Sister: page 227
O'Malley, Bishop Seán: page 395
O'Riordan, Father: page 109
Ostiguy, Henri: page 248
Ouellette, André: page 346, 359, 362
Ouellette, Mrs. André: page 345
Ouellette, Dalila: page 406
Ouellette, David: page 385
Ouellette, Guillaume: page 154, 172, 193,
    262, 402, 414
Ouellette, Guy: page 385
Ouellette, Joseph: page 307
Ouellette, Marcelline: page 404
Ouellette, Marie-Louise: page 406
Ouellette, Paul: page 390, 395
Ouimet, Hector-Edmond: page 402
Ouimet, Isaac: page 398
Ouimet, Joseph: page 398

P

Pagé, Evariste: page 107
Pagé, Olivier: page 222
Paignon, H.: page 36
Paillé, Joseph: page 402
Palmer, Mayor: page 116
Pampelonne, Baron Charles de: page 337
Paquette, Arsène: page 49
Paquette, Aurélie: page 147, 150
Paquette, Charles A.: page 108, 113, 193,
    413
Paquette, Marie: page 82
Paquette, Richard: page 403
Paquette, Roland: page 359
Paquin, Alice: page 410
Paquin, Arthur: page 222, 359, 361, 362,
    374
Paquin, Mrs. Arthur: page 362
Paquin, Eugène: page 385
Paquin, Eva: page 405

Paquin, Hervé: page 385
Paquin, Laura: page 405
Paquin, Léa: page 362, 346
Paquin, Raymond: page 362
Paquin, Roland: page 362
Paquin, Stanislas O.: page 222, 362
Paradis, Gracia: page 218
Paradis, Hilaire: page 397
Paradis, Miss: page 219
Paradis, Robert: page 326, 390, 415
Paradis, Rose Anna: page 209
Parent, Arthur: page 257, 414
Parent, Georges: page 221
Parent, Léona: page 406
Parent, Léontine: page 406
Parent, Louis-Marie: page 310, 311, 338
Parent, Mrs. page 70
Parthenais, Mr.: page 77, 141
Pascal, Bishop: page 121
Passaconaway, Chief: page 2
Patenaude, Joseph: page 36
Patenaude, Moyse: page 401
Patenaude, Sophronie: page 401
Patenaude, Xiste: page 49
Patrice, Brother: page 94
Paul-Ambroise, Brother: page 251
Paul-Emile, Sister: page 298
Paul-Marie, Brother: page 94
Paul VI, Pope: page 370
Payette, Doctor: page 153
Payette, André: page 415
Payette, Joseph: page 196
Pelland, Olivine: page 404
Pellerin, Thomas M.: page 371
Pelletier, Ephrem: page 164, 187
Pelletier, Joseph-Napoléon: page 55, 72, 75, 82, 83, 262, 412
Pelletier, Lucien: page 222
Pelletier, Napoléon: page 371
Pelneault, J. B.: page 171
Péloquin, Bernard B.: page 385, 391
Péloquin, Marcel: page 415
Péloquin, Marie: page 345
Péloquin, Marthe Biron: page vii, 385, 391
Péloquin, Mrs. Lionel: page 359

Pépin, Alexina: page 404
Pépin, Denise: page 410
Pépin, Maurice: page 305, 316
Pépin, Rodolphe: page 207, 222, 265, 266, 272, 281, 295, 305
Périgny, Albertine: page 408
Périgny, Bella: page 408
Périgny, Hélène: page 408
Périgny, Olivine: page 408
Perrault, Pierre: page 397
Perrault, Pierre Corneille: page 397
Perreault, Raymond: page 346
Perreault, Robert: page 359
Perron, Angéline: page 235
Perron, Noëlla: page 408
Perron, Wilbrod: page 126, 131, 413
Petit, Louis Victor: page 44, 61, 78, 412
Phaneuf, Christophe: page 42, 43, 44, 128, 412
Phaneuf, Florence: page 401
Phelan, Mother: page 70
Pichette, Mrs. N.-J.: page 222
Pickman, Mayor: page 116
Pierre-Vincent, Brother: page 94
Pinault, E. J.: page 121
Pintal, Léo: page 222
Pinto, Bishop Edwin: page 351
Pitre, Melanie: page 401
Pius IX, Pope: page 12
Pius X, Saint: page 161
Pius XI, Pope: page 224, 252
Pius XII, Pope: page 281, 305, 312, 315, 324
Plamondon, Gérard: page 359
Plamondon, Olivier: page 8
Plante, Sister: page 69, 70
Plourde, M.-Louise: page 404
Plourde, Omer: page 402
Plumey, Bishop: page 310
Plunkett, Patrick: page 337
Poirier, Alberta: page 408
Poirier, André: page 248
Poirier, Blanche: page 408
Poirier, Émélie Charlotte Georgina: page 400
Poirier, Eugénie: page 408

Poirier, Jean-Baptiste: page 400
Poirier, Régina: page 408
Poisson, Doris: page 314
Poisson, Léonie: page 406
Poitiron, Mr.: page 207
Poitras, Edwin: page 293
Pollard, Mr.: page 115
Poor, Sister Jeanne: page 387
Potvin, Irène: page 218
Poulin, Sister Cécile: page 385, 391
Poulios, Tarsy: page 392
Powers, Thomas: page 387
Prairie, Emma Mathilda: page 400
Prairie, Isaïe: page 400
Pratt, Mr.: page 115
Pratt, Arthur: page 414
Primeau, Bishop Ernest: page 351
Primien, Brother: page 94
Priscillianus, Brother: page 94
Protopapas, George: page 390, 402
Proulx, Onésime: page 401
Proulx, Mrs. Elphège: page 345
Provencher, Arthur: page 263
Provencher, Mrs. Arthur: page 345
Provencher, Officer: page 108
Provencher, Cécile: page 395, 407
Provencher, Félix: page 8
Provencher, Richard: page 385, 391
Prud'homme, Albina: page 406

Q

Quintal, Prof. Claire: page viii, 390, 391

R

Racette, Hervé: page 176, 177, 181, 184, 402
Racette, Jules: page 176
Racette, Julien: page 176, 193, 262, 402, 414
Racette, Roger: page 222, 385, 391, 392
Racette, Rose: page 345
Racicot, Albert-E.: page 403
Racicot, Arthur: page 49
Racicot, H. A.: page 71, 82
Racicot, Maurice: page 36
Racicot, Miss: page 187

Racicot, Mr.: page 141
Racicot, Tharsile: page 401
Rainville, Aimé-O.: page 403
Rapin, Laurent: page 381
Ratel, Marie: page 118
Ratelle, Émélie: page 399
Raymond, Damase: page 401
Raymond, Jean-Baptiste: page 10, 397
Raymond, Joseph: page 36, 399
Raymond, Marie Adelina: page 399
Raymond, Rose: page 397
Raymond, Virginie: page 397
Régnier, Delphine: page 406
Régnier, Léa: page 406
Reilly, John F.: page 371
Rémillard, Gilbert: page 398
Rémy, Narcisse: page 8
Renaud, Mr.: page 141
Renaud, Olivier: page 415
Renaud, Paul D.: page 295
Renaud, Roger: page 403
Rheault, Mrs. Adélard: page 345
Rheault, Louise: page 411
Rhéaume, Bishop Louis: page 209
Richard, Ferdinand: page 310
Ricard, Frank: page 209, 210, 231
Richard, John B.: page 187
Richard, Léo: page 248
Richardson, Elliott: page 362
Richardson, Alden: page 53, 54
Richer, Aurélie: page 399
Richer, Captain: page 305
Richer, Rodolphe: page 222
Rivard, Fernand: page 262, 267, 415
Rivard, George: page 390
Rivet, Adélard: page 196
Rivet, Anna: page 408
Rivet, Marie Ange: page 235
Roberge, Lorraine: page 218
Roberge, Onésiphore: page 399
Roberge, Virginie: page 399
Roberge, Yvette: page 311
Robert, Delphis: page 196
Robillard, Rolande: page 410
Rochette, Elisée: page 196
Rochette, Gédéon: page 187
Rocheville, Frédéric: page 187

Rodrigue, Mr: page 206

Rodriguez, Sister St. Alphonse: page 227, 228

Rogers, John Jacob: page 188, 191, 266

Rondeau, Cécile: page 408

Rondeau, Diana: page 408

Rondeau, Gertude: page 304

Rondel, Roland: page 294

Rossignol, Emile: page 310, 334, 339, 415

Rougier, Louis: page 293

Rousseau, Ferdinand: page 359

Rousseau, Joseph: page 187

Rousseau, Marie: page 406

Roussel, Marcel: page 49

Rousse, Rose-Anna: page 408

Roussin, Camille: page 187

Routhier, Bishop Henri: page 347

Routhier, Joseph: page 165

Roux, Brother Louis: page 14

Roux, M.-Eugénie: page 405

Roy, Arthur: page 49

Roy, Célina: page 398

Roy, Dr. J.-H.: page 107

Roy, Joseph: page 144

Roy, Emilie: page 86

Roy, Fabien: page 36, 397

Roy, Marie: page 398

Roy, Marie Exilda: page 397

Roy, Monsignor Camille: page 265

Roy, Mrs. Basilide: page 48

Roy, Robert: page 248

Roy, Vitaline: page 332

Roy, William: page 401

Roye, Camille: page 156

Royer, Jean-Marie: page 44, 412

Ruocco, Bishop Joseph: page 371

Ryan, Sister: page 70, 71

Rynehart, Julia: page 401

S

Saien, Angèle: page 400

St. Alain, Sister: page 152, 304

St. Albert, Mother: page 198, 199

St. Aldémar, Sister: page 212

St. Alphine, Sister: page 153

St. André, Sister: page 70

St. André Corsini, Mother: page 298, 312

St. Armand, Isaac: page 401

St. Armaud, Henri: page 248

St. Benoît Labre, Sister: page 234

St. Bruno, Mother: page 227, 235, 236

St. Célien, Sister: page 212

St. Cyr, Dr.: page 43

St. Cyr, Arthur: page 276, 281, 282, 283, 284, 270, 402

St. Cyr, Charles: page 270

St. Denis, Marie: page 401

St. Denis, Moyse: page 401

St. Denis, Sister: page 129

St. Dosithée, Sister: page 70, 71

St. Féllix, Sister: page 70, 71

St. Hilaire, Arthur: page 196

St. Hilaire, Iréne: page 218

St. Hilaire, James: page 196

St. Hilaire, Robert: page 248

St.-Jean, Bertha: page 409

St. Jean, Georges: page 233, 402

St.-Jean, Rolande: page 409

St. Léandre, Sister: page 321

St. Luc, Sister: page 152

St. Margaret Mary: page 82, 157

St. Nazaire, Morther: page 330

St. Nil, Sister: page 212

St. Onge, Joseph: page 401

St. Patrice, Sister: page 129

St. Pierre, Annette: page 362

St. Pierre, Sister: page 70, 71

St. Sébastien, Sister: page 129

St. Théodore, Sister: page 150

St. Yves, Sister: page 227

St. Zoël, Sister: page 153

Ste. Adéle, Mother: page 393

Ste. Agnès d'Assise, Sister: page 212

Ste. Béatrix d'Assise, Sister: page 329

Ste. Bernadette, Sisters: page 129

Ste. Célestine, Sister: page 321

Ste. Christiane, Sister: page 329

Ste. Christine, Sister: page 150

Ste. Clothilde, Sister: page 70, 71

Ste. Estelle, Sister: page 321

Ste. Françoise: page 227

Ste. Léontine, Sister: page 130, 198, 220

Ste. Solange, Siter: page 166

Ste. Théodorine, Sister: page 256
Ste. Ursule, Sister: page 152
Ste. Zoé, Sister: page 153, 329
Saltonstall, Governor: page 266
Salvas, Arthur: page 402
Sans-Cartier, Laurier: page 264
Sanscartier, Lucien: page 222
Santerre, Richard: page viii, 359, 362, 394
Santerre, Rita: page 408
Sauvageau, Gislaine: page 362
Sauvageau, Roger: page 362
Sauvageau, Mrs. Roger: page 362
Savard, Lauréat: page 235, 402
Savard, Maurice: page vii, 402
Savard, Régina-A.: page 406
Sawyer, Anisie: page 166
Sawyer, Avila: page 197
Sawyer, Gertrude: page 409
Sawyer, Josephat: page 196
Sawyer, Lucien: page viii, 395
Sawyer, Luther: page 65
Sawyer, Victoria: page 408
Schervager, Léonard: page 401
Scott, Sir Walter: page 125
Seitz, Bishop Paul: page 351
Seznec, Jean: page 293
Sharkey, Don: page 313
Shaw, Agent: page 84
Shea, Timothy: page 389
Sicard, Louis: page 221
Simard, Magloire: page 401
Simard, Marie-Louise: page 331
Sirois, Joseph: page 113, 126, 413
Skalkeas, Albina: page 234
Slocombe, Sister: page 17
Smit, Rodolphe: page 288
Smith, Wade: page 178
Soulard, Eugénie: page 222, 235
Soullier, Louis: page 105
Spencer, Lillie M.: page 131
Stanley, Louisa: page 400
Staves, Léo: page 310
Stéphane, Brother: page 318
Stott, Mayor: page 116
Stratonique, Brother: page 93, 147
Sullivan, Lillian M.: page 371

T

Tague, Raymond: page 362
Taillon, L. O.: page 116, 118
Tardiff, Anna: page 408
Tardiff, Arthur: page 273, 415
Tardiff, Jeannine: page vii
Tardiff, Simonne: page 406
Tarte, Israël: page 132
Tati, Jacques: page 359
Tekakwitha, Kateri: page 267
Tellier, Jeanne-Alice: page 406
Tellier, Sister Alice: page 376
Telmon, Father: page 14
Tessier, Félix: page 402
Tessier, Marie-Anne: page 408
Tessier, M.-Anne: page 405
Tessier, M.-M.: page 408
Tétrault, Elmire: page 401
Tétreault, Adolphe: page 8, 398
Tétreault, Arthur Toussaint: page 398
Tétreault, Jérémie: page 8
Thellen, Délia: page 252, 327, 359
Théophane, Brother: page 93, 94, 96
Theresa of Calcutta, Mother: page 396
Thérèse-de-Jésus, Sister: page 72
Thériault, Frédéric: page 196
Thériault, Lionel: page 248, 402
Thérien, François: page 412
Thibault, Joseph: page 327
Thomas, Marie: page 401
Thompson, Mayor: page 191
Tiffault, Pierre: page 399
Tiffault, Victorine: page 399
Tortel, Adolphe: page 33, 34, 37, 41, 42,
    43, 44, 45, 78, 99, 107, 412
Touchette, Mr.: page 75
Toupin, William: page 385
Tourangeau, Rosaire: page 196
Tousignant, Armand: page 359, 385
Tousignant, Dolor: page 248
Tousignant, Jeannine: page 346
Trahan, Gérard: page 415
Traversy, William: page 401
Tremblay, Emma: page 399, 408
Tremblay, Georges: page 273
Tremblay, Gérard: page 359, 385, 392

Tremblay, Marie: page 140
Tremblay, Paulette: page 330
Tremblay, Pierre: page 105, 262
Tremblay, Théodorat: page 406
Tremblay, Toussaint: page 399
Tremours, Raymond Massiet de: page 294
Trudel, Eugène: page 250
Truman, President Harry: page 305
Turcot, E. L.: page 186
Turcotte, Edmond: page 205
Turcotte, Joseph Eugène: page 185, 186,
    188, 192, 193, 195, 197, 198, 199,
    202, 203, 204, 205, 210, 211, 213,
    215, 221, 227, 230, 240, 241, 310,
    313, 402, 414
Turcotte, Évangéline: page 405
Turcotte, Gabrielle: page 410
Turcotte, Isidore: page 399
Turcotte, Louis P.: page 124
Turcotte, Marie Eugénie Melvina: page
    399
Turcotte, Nazaire: page 185
Turcotte, Ulric: page 415
Turquetil, Bishop Arsène: page 256

V

Vachon, Félix: page 210, 225, 414
Vaillancourt, Zotique: page 412
Valeur, Robert: page 337
Vallerand, Corinne: page 405
Vallières, Jean: page 415
Vallières, Yvette: page 222
Vandenberghe, Florient: page 15, 16, 18,
    19, 38
Vandry, Monsignor Fernand: page 306
Veillette, Aldéric: page 191
Veillette, Antoinette: page 404
Veillette, Irène: page 410
Verdier, Cardinal: page 224
Vétérin, Brother: page 220
Viau, Frank: page 36
Viau, Luc: page 8, 36, 45
Viau, Pierre: page 8
Viaud, Victor: page 134, 154, 163, 193,
    208, 262, 413
Vigeant, Antonio: page 402

Vigeant, Paul: page 153
Villeneuve, Cardinal Rodrigue: page 235,
    238, 231, 236, 268, 280, 281
Vincelette, Dr. Arthur: page 82
Vincelette, Mrs. Dr.: page 70
Vincelette, Edouard: page 99, 109
Vincent, Cécile: page 222, 235
Violette, F.: page 262
Violette, Richard: page 346, 359
Violette, Mrs. Richard: page 346
Voisin, Albert: page 343

W

Wagner, Pauline: page 385
Walsh, Louis: page 127, 146, 147
Walsh, John: page 389
Wannalancit, Chief: page 2
Watelle, Adolphe, Sr.: page 156
Watelle, Adolphe, Jr.: page 157
Watelle, Henri Camille: page 156, 157,
    158, 159, 160, 161, 164, 165, 167,
    170, 171, 174, 175, 176, 177, 189,
    255
Watson, Arthur: page 385
Watson, Isabelle Y.: page 385
Weaver, Benjamin: page 53
Wheelock, Andrew: page 142
Whitcomb, Mr.: page 131
Wiggin, William: page 142
Williams, Bishop John: page 10, 12, 15,
    16, 17, 18, 19, 28, 31, 37, 45, 87,
    91, 109, 121, 122, 128, 135, 141,
    144, 146, 150
Williams, Charles M.: page 153
Wood, Albert: page 400
Wood, General Leonard: page 201
Wood, John Albert: page 400
Wright, Colonel Carroll D.: page 63, 64

Z

Zettek, Charles: page 341